Advance Praise for
Celtic Queen Maeve and Addiction

In the popular imagination, the great drinkers are always Celts. It seems singularly appropriate, then, that a Jungian analyst should come up with a Celtic myth that embraces the ecstasy, the addiction, and the healing that belong to the archetypal behavior we know as "alcoholism." But when that Jungian analyst is Sylvia Perera, we know that, as well, we are going to encounter the dark feminine background of the syndrome, which has so often been analyzed in terms of masculine structures of power and their dissolution. This is a text that opens a new path of understanding of what alcoholic men and woman are seeking to integrate from the beginning of their dance in the Moon with Queen Mab. What the reader who takes up this book is likely to experience is the pleasure of moving with ideas that celebrate the inconstancy of affect and respect the integrity of emotional process that inheres in even the darkest nights of all our souls.

—John Beebe, President,
The C. G. Jung Institute of San Francisco

Sylvia Perera's reclamation of Maeve, the ancient Celtic Goddess, answers contemporary women's yearning for a robustly evocative, multi-dimensional image of feminine wholeness. Perera luminously portrays Maeve's vivid passion, shamanic ardor, and permeable, shapeshifting, fluidity to give us an ageless, full-bodied, yet transcendent archetypal image of the feminine self that does much to restore the Celtic mythopoeic imagination to its rightful place in our psyches. Perera masterfully weaves mythology, clinical work, and psychotherapy into a resonant and deeply layered book while intertwining a specific lesson on the ways deep healing can be found underneath seemingly blind compulsions.

—Claire Douglas, editor of
C. G. Jung's *The Visions Seminar*
author of *Translate This Darkness*

Perera's *Maeve* introduces us to a spiritual attitude that helps us embody our psyches through the discovery and possession of our body's passionate loves and hates, a process that can culminate in profound reverence for those passions as well. . . . [Perera] provides us with a mythic container from a Celtic past that has continued to inform many strands of our diverse American culture. Her vessel can hold the feminine principle in a highly differentiated form as it is relevant to the psychologies of both men and women. In bringing to bear a psychological attitude, Perera thus makes old Celtic myths available to our contemporary consciousness and regains for us the wisdom of embodied appetite that has largely been lost.

—Mark Sullivan, analyst,
from "Divine Appetite," in
The San Francisco Jung Institute Library Journal

Celtic Queen Maeve and Addiction

An Archetypal Perspective

Sylvia Brinton Perera

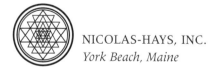

NICOLAS-HAYS, INC.
York Beach, Maine

First published in 2001 by
NICOLAS-HAYS, INC.
Box 2039
York Beach, ME 03910

Distributed to the trade by
RED WHEEL/WEISER
Box 612
York Beach, ME 03910

Library of Congress Cataloging-in-Publication Data
Perera, Sylvia Brinton.
   [Queen Maeve and her lovers]
   Celtic Queen Maeve and addiction. Sylvia Brinton Perera.
         p. cm. (Jung on the Hudson book series)
   Originally published: Queen Maeve and her lovers. New York:
     Carrowmore Books, ©1999.
   Includes bibliographical references and index.
   ISBN 0-89254-057-5 (pbk. : alk. paper)
     1. Mythology, Celtic—Psychological aspects. 2. Archetype
(Psychology) 3. Jungian psychology. I. Title: Celtic Queen Maeve and
addiction. II. Title.
   BF175.5.M95 P47 2001
   150.19'54—dc21   2001030701

TCP
Cover design by Kathryn Sky-Peck
Cover illustration is the Maeve panel from the Gundestrup cauldron in
the National Museum, Copenhagen.
Typeset in 9.5/13.5 Meridien

PRINTED IN CANADA

08 07 06 05 04 03 02 01
8 7 6 5 4 3 2 1

*The paper used in this publication meets the minimum requirements of the
American National Standard for Information Sciences—Permanence of Paper for
Printed Library Materials Z39.48-1992 (R1997).*

Credits

The author would like to thank the following authors, translators, editors, and publishers for permission to reprint material copyrighted or controlled by them.

Thomas Kinsella for permission to quote from *The Tain (Tain Bo Cuailnge),* edited and translated by Thomas Kinsella. Copyright © 1970 by Thomas Kinsella. Published by Oxford University Press, London.

Desmond O'Grady for permission to quote poems XV and LT from *The Gododdin: A version by Desmond O'Grady, Ink paintings by Louis Le Brocquy.* Text copyright © 1977 by Desmond O'Grady. Published by Dolmen Editions, Dublin.

Viking Penguin, a division of Penguin Books USA, for permission to quote the poem "First Lesson" from Philip Booth's *Relations: New and Selected Poems 1950–1985.* Copyright © 1957 by Philip Booth. Published by Viking Penguin, New York.

Constable Publishers for permission to quote from "The Isles of the Happy" from *Selections from Ancient Irish Poetry* by Kuno Meyer. Copyright © 1959 by Constable & Company, Ltd., London.

Simon & Schuster for permission to quote from "The Countess Cathleen" in *The Collected Plays of W. B. Yeats,* revised edition. Copyright © 1934 by Macmillan Publishing Co.; copyrights renewed © 1962 by Bertha Georgia Yeats, and 1980 by Anne Yeats.

Scribner, a division of Simon & Schuster, for permission to quote "The Hosting of the Sidhe" from *The Collected Works of W.B Yeats, Volume I: The Poems,* revised and edited by Richard J. Finneran. Copyright © 1997 by Scribner, a Division of Simon & Schuster, New York.

Henry Holt and Company for permission to quote material from *Ancient Irish Tales* by Tom Peete Cross and Clark Harris Slover. Copyright 1936, © 1964 by Henry Holt and Company, Inc. Reprinted by permission of Henry Holt and Company, Inc., New York.

University of California Press for permission to quote from *The Mabinogi and Other Welsh Tales* by Patrick Ford. Copyright © 1977 by the Regents of the University of California.

Inner Traditions International for permission to reprint lines from a poem in *Merlin: Priest of Nature* by Jean Markale, published by Inner Traditions, Rochester, VT. English translation copyright © 1995 by Inner Traditions International.

Little, Brown, and Company for permission to reprint Emily Dickinson's poem "I can wade grief" from *Final Harvest: Emily Dickinson's Poems.* Selected by Thomas H. Johnson. Copyright © 1961. Published by Little, Brown and Company, Boston.

New Directions Publishing Corporation for permission to quote from "The Force That Through the Green Fuse Drives the Flower" by Dylan Thomas, from *The Poems of Dylan Thomas.* Copyright © 1939 by New Directions Publishing Corp. Reprinted by permission of New Directions Publishing Corp.

Alcoholics Anonymous World Services, Inc. New York, NY, for permission to reprint the Twelve Steps of Alcoholics Anonymous.

The National Museum in Copenhagen for permission to reproduce a panel from the Gundestrup Cauldron. Reproduction rights Copyright © by The National Museum.

Dùchas, The Heritage Service, Dublin, for permission to reproduce the Trispiral from Newgrange.

In memory
of my grandmother
Retta Williams Hoopes Brinton,
who kept alive the ways of the ancestors.
And of my aunt Fan Hemeon,
driven from her home during the Time of Troubles
like Fionnghuala daughter of Lir.
Their stories nourished my childhood.

For
all those who know the pain of exile
and must set forth to find
the home that lies ahead.

Contents

Illustrations

Acknowledgments

I have received help from many sources in writing this book and want to acknowledge my appreciation to all of them. First I want to express gratitude to the poets, translators, and scholars of the Irish and Welsh material in which I have happily steeped myself. Because my knowledge of ancient and modern Gaelic is less than rudimentary, I have used their books as sources. I trust that they will be glad to see how the old texts are so deeply relevant to the modern psyche, and I hope that other readers will become aware of the treasures in Celtic lore that are still too little appreciated. In order to explore Celtic mythology more fully, I urge you to read the literature. Much has been translated, and references to some of this rich trove are stored in the bibliography.

I also want to give thanks to my mentors in the discipline of psychology. From Jung and his followers I have learned to honor the individual psyche and its connections to the archetypal energy patterns that structure our experiences throughout life. From them I have learned to work with the psyche's need for intimate relationships to inner depths and to outer others, its potential for creatively embracing the imaginal dimension, and its quest to live the symbolic life as each of us struggles towards the unfolding of what we are meant to be. From many practitioners working with the fertile post-Freudian, Object Relations, Self Psychology, and

Intersubjectivity theories, I have learned to strengthen my own clinical skills and understanding. Some of these clinicians are apparently rediscovering seminal insights that Jung put forth even though they are not acknowledging him directly. His message is in the air, effecting our notions of the Self, dream interpretation, the plurality of the psyche, transference and countertransference dynamics, mind-body integration, and the individual's relationship to transpersonal factors, among others. By conveying these rediscoveries in currently acceptable psychoanalytic terminology, many contemporary writers are fostering the assimilation of his ideas into revisions of post-Freudian thinking. From the other side those trained in Jungian institutes today have moved beyond the confines of classical Jungian symbol amplification to ground Jung's work more adequately in developmental and clinical processes and practice with greater awareness of the interpersonal aspects of transferential and counter-transferential dynamics, dynamics that Jung himself first elucidated but did not fully explore on the personal level. These post-Jungians have helped to integrate Jung's insights with the theories of other psychological schools. To individually name all of the writers who have fertilized my thoughts would take many pages. I am, nevertheless, grateful to all of them, for they are participating in the creation of important linkages in psychoanalytic writing and practice that maintain the healthy development of the field.

One group in particular deserves special mention. These are the clinicians and researchers who have begun to uncover and explore the archetypal, spiritual, and social material that deals with women and the feminine principle. This vast store was long hidden or marginalized in most of the world's cultures. From Jane Harrison, Esther Harding, and Erich Neumann to Marija Gimbutas and on, writers in the West who are no longer even called "feminist" have helped all of us in many disciplines begin to reclaim our fuller heritage.

Further, I wish especially to name several friends. Suzi Naiburg, my editor at Carrowmore Books, patiently helped me unfold my thoughts for the hardcover edition. After each encounter with her incisive mind, my own impressions of the material have been enriched. Roberta Goodman, a talented artist and art therapist, accepted my invitation to create the illustrations that enliven the book. In her drawings she has caught and conveyed the power of the original objects. Gertrude Ujhely has offered her colleagal support since we were students together at the C. G. Jung Institute of New York. She read various stages of the manuscript with inimitable care and thoughtfulness. Her astute comments have helped me refine and deepen my own. Laura Nault Massell has reached across from her own scientific discipline to offer the kind of attentive and critical reading that any writer would treasure. I thank Irish singer Cathy Ryan and medievalist Michael Paull for their kinship, intellectual and emotional affirmation, and the wonderful trips we lead together in Ireland. Poet Morgan Farley encouraged me with her perceptive and sustaining interest. Betty Lundsted, publisher of Nicolas-Hays, birthed this volume into its present form in the final weeks of her life. Her intelligent, warmly wry, always honest voice echoes vividly in my memory.

Others I particularly want to thank for their invaluable support and encouragement are my children, Deborah Massell and David Massell; friends and colleagues from the Jungian Women's Gathering; and a pen pal with whom I share a joy in the lore of holywells and things Celtic in America, writer Susan Shaughnessy. Joan Carson, former editor of *Quadrant*, gave me my first introduction to Celtic literature with copy from *The Welsh Triads*. Other friendships have nurtured and sustained me, and I treasure them even though I do not name all of them here. Most importantly, throughout the many stages of this work, E. Christopher

Whitmont was my companion, generous with his stimulating critique and encouragement. Sharing life and ideas with him always enlivened my own creative process.

I want also to express appreciation to the analysts-in-training who began to explore Celtic symbolism in clinical practice with me at the C. G. Jung Institute of New York, to the participants at Jungian workshops in San Francisco, Washington, DC, Denver, Santa Fe, and to those who even traveled to Ireland to hear parts of the work during the process of making this book. Several among them who are substance abuse counselors or students of the Celts have made astute linkings within the material.

Finally, I want to acknowledge my immense gratitude to friends, family, colleagues, and former clients who have given me permission to use their personal material. I have, of course, changed details to hide their identities. Their insights and generosity sustained my process throughout the long pilgrimage to Knocknarea.

Introduction

This book rises out of my love of Celtic mythology and culture, my work with individual clients in psychotherapy, and my interest in a wide range of psychological writings and their application to problems of ecstatic consciousness and addiction in modern life. Each source is personally important to me, and each flows from deep levels in the "objective psyche," what C. G. Jung has also called "the collective unconscious." The three sources are as closely interconnected as the ancient triple spiral design that forms one theme throughout these pages.

In exploring my love of mythology and in particular my fascination with Celtic myth, I have come to realize the relevance of its motifs and images to pre-ego states and to mystic consciousness. The myths have helped me to make sense of material encountered in my work as a psychoanalyst. Analytic material from the consulting room has also illuminated some of the meanings of the myths. My understanding of mythic and psychological dimensions has in turn been enriched by my study of the relatively recent art of psychotherapeutics, especially the profound and prolific works of C. G. Jung. For many years I thought reading psychology was a miserable alternative to soaking up art, novels, and poetry and pondering new theories in science. Now these three streams of mythology, clinical work, and the art of psychotherapy have come together to inform my approach to problems I have known in myself and in many of the psychoanalytic clients with whom I work. Insights gained from mythic structures and clinical work also contribute to understanding contemporary social and ethical issues because culture can be seen as a complex expression of the multileveled and multivalent collective psyche. I hope that exploring these interweavings in what follows will deepen and widen rather than confuse my discussion. The descriptions of ecstasy, addiction, and healing as they manifest in the psychoanalytic field are indeed watery and interwoven, as are the pathways through Celtic myth.

My interest in Celtic mythology did not begin with reading Yeats and Synge. Naively I took their works for modern—until I saw the extraordinary revivals of Yeats' "Full Moon in March" and "The Only Jealousy of Emer" that Jean Erdman directed in New York, no doubt influenced by the work of her husband, Joseph Campbell. The dramatic material resonated in the deepest layers of my psyche—at such archaic levels that I was shaken. I wondered about the people for whom the swineherd's severed head sang of love and truth to the queen and for whom the brutal warrior submitted to watery otherworldly women. When in 1978, I researched the Gawain tales for a class in symbolism and clinical practice and found titles referring to the Celtic sources of Arthurian legends, my growing curiosity turned to fascination and discomfort. "The material feels nearly crazed and too fluid, full of inconsistencies and restless mysteries," I confided in my journal. "It is surely the most difficult of all mythologies to comprehend."

I was trying to grasp Celtic consciousness with the rational mind of a father's daughter steeped in classical Mediterranean mythology. In spite of my training as an art historian and Jungian analyst, I still had little conscious sense of how to navigate the archaic currents of this material.

Synchronously, I was asked to teach a course on Celtic symbolism to psychoanalytic candidates at the C. G. Jung Institute of New York. In preparation I opened myself to experience the Celtic wildness of imagination, its vivid passions, and its very permeable boundaries between ordinary and supernatural reality. I felt challenged to enter a world that is brimming with riddles and fantastic images, a world I slowly learned to explore by finding shared points of reference and piecing together repeated themes and variations. I came to realize that such exploration is not very different from the ways I explore the communications of a psychoanalytic client whose inner reality I need to understand and companion. I could grasp the Celtic archetypal material and apprehend my own reactions with skills I use to appreciate dreams and monitor my relationships with analysands who are still unconscious of the energy patterns that compel them and open into the field between us.

"The Wooing of Etain"

Let me give an example. One famous tale, sometimes called the most beautiful in Irish mythology, captured me with its passages of sensuous description and curious adventure. But it also forced me, in particularly rigorous ways, to suspend disbelief. Leaping chaotically from one place and time to another, the story of "The Wooing of Etain"[1] feels like an unstrung strand of seemingly disparate beads. It lacks the continuity we are accustomed to finding in literature written in one voice by one relatively coherent individual describing consistent figures. In the tale I read of rival godly and human lovers for Etain, the fairest maiden in Ireland, and the shapeshifting forms she takes over a thousand years. At first Angus wins her for his foster father, the god Midir. To do so Angus gets his own father, the Good God, the Dagda, to accomplish geological miracles for her brideprice. Going home with Midir, Etain is transformed by his jealous wife into a pool of water. The forces of nature then churn this pool creating a worm that becomes a beautiful and magical red fly. As a fragrant and sweetly singing fly, Etain is driven off onto the rocks and waves of the sea by the magic wind roused by Midir's wife. After seven years she comes to the breast of young Angus, who guards her in a beautiful bower for his own satisfaction. Called to visit his foster-father, Angus leaves Etain, who is again driven away by the queen's magic wind. Seven years later she falls into a cup and is swallowed by another queen. Reborn in human form after one thousand and twelve years, she becomes queen of an earthly kingdom, only to be wooed once more by Midir, her supernatural lover. Appearing in disguise, Midir reclaims her by winning a chess game and accomplishing more geological feats for her current royal husband. Finally in Midir's arms, Etain is again shapeshifted, this time into a swan. The two restored lovers fly out of the court together. When her earthly husband protests and tries to destroy the *sidh* mound where the god lives, her earthly husband is given a chance to regain his wife if he can choose Etain from among fifty women who are now magically like her in form and dress. Remembering the task at which his queen excelled, her husband sets them all to the ritual pouring out of drink. Mistakenly, however, he chooses his own daughter instead of his wife. With her the king incestuously conceives another daughter who is born and cast out. When grown, this child herself is chosen as his queen, and she becomes the wife of her own grandfather and father and bears him a royal son.

Without interpreting all the individual elements of this story, we can readily feel that its time- and shape-defying fluidity entrances the reader in the cycles and permutations of a magical, supernatural realm that the ancient Celts felt was very close to ordinary reality. Like a stream of consciousness or a drunken dream, the story's images evoke the sensation of being awash between worlds. We feel our mental structures bent and expanded as we wonder about the deeper meanings of the tale. Are we to learn about different kinds of interpenetrating relations between nature and the supernatural? Are we to understand something of the cultural eras that transformed the physical and metaphysical landscapes? Are we to discover a conflict of dynasties and/or rival religions? Is there an archetypal pattern underlying the story of the old and new wives of Midir that could help us fathom human jealousies? So little can be pinned down for our understanding, yet we are gripped by details that are intensely vivid and focused.

These details may have druidic meanings or spell out an esoteric subtext. For example, I learned that flies are often a sign of prosperous kingship in a cattle-raising tribe and might therefore be desired rather than swatted away. Red is often the color of otherworld figures in Celtic myth, so a beautiful, singing red fly holds special import. I discovered that a Gaelic word for the humming of a fly, *cronan*, also refers to music and may here be a riddling reference to the powers of the ancient bards to heal, soothe, and arouse with the powers of their arcane craft. The druidic musician poets were also renowned for their word magic—an ability to convey several layers of meaning with similar sounding words. Was Etain a patroness of bardic lore across all the generations of early Irish culture? She was said to be a sun goddess, and like another solar divinity Brigid may have also ruled the poetic arts. The specific cycles of the years of her turbulence undoubtedly have mythic and perhaps mythic-historic meanings, as do the motifs of triple incest and the struggles between earthly and supernatural lovers for relationship to the ever-transforming goddess-queen. That she is timeless, reborn in her daughter and granddaughter, and possesses the skill at pouring out the king's mead tells us that Etain has many similarities to Maeve. In one story we are even told that Maeve's mother was part of Etain's retinue, and the sun goddess, on her way westward, dropped her from the sky onto Rathcrogan, the site that became a sacred center of Maeve's people. But today we have lost most of the keys that were readily available to initiates into the spiritual traditions of the ancient Irish. We can peer through the keyholes, but we can no longer unlock all the mysteries. Nor can we easily and rationally focus the tale into any neat linear coherence. It remains polymorphous. The images defy common-sense categories and make us reel as we try to follow the heroine's metamorphoses. Thus the mythopoetic material forces us to experience the mystery of life's changes as the expression of an endlessly creative and regenerative transcendent process.

Exhilarated by such literary experiences that nearly defeat the ego, sometimes afraid of the fluidity, and even initially defensive against the seeming madness of stories such as this one, I nonetheless began to steep myself in ancient Celtic lore in order to teach it. Slowly I found myself steering in its turbulent eddies without fear of drowning. I even become a devotee, dedicated to understanding the symbolism of Celtic rites, visions, and potencies. I came to appreciate the Celtic material as one of the major currents underlying all of Western culture, as vital and important as the Graeco-Roman and Judeo-Christian influences.

The Survival of Celtic Myth

Some scholars call the Celts the "Fathers of Europe."[2] Probing into the archaeological, textual, and folkloric remnants of their culture, however, I discovered that underneath all the patrifocal interpretations a far more ancient current hums. It intones a transcendent reality that is deeply primeval and endlessly fascinating. Listening to it, I discovered that the tales express the compelling patterns of magical and mystical consciousness that cluster around the Great Goddess and her consorts. These patterns began to take form in the earliest human hunting and gathering and later agricultural societies all over the world, and they were recently still vigorously alive in many "Third World" cultures alongside the infiltrations of modernism. Indeed they still live in several esoteric traditions worldwide, and they form the implicate basis of much that has been codified in patrifocal terms. In old Celtic material we can feel the confusing harmonies that resulted when these deepest layers roiled together with later cultural accretions that focus on kingship and warrior prowess. This confluence began the age that has led to our present. Now as we come to the chaotic threshold of another age, we are finding again that these early currents are still potent in our "modern" psyches, finding expression in our dream images, passions, and creative and spiritual impulses.

In studying Welsh and Irish material, I also recognized a personal strand in the interweavings that have gone into this study. One of my grandmothers was a living descendant of those ancient pagans. Although she appeared an ordinary Pennsylvania Quaker housewife, the superstitions that she conveyed to my child self's rapt attention shone with glimmers of authentic and sacred customs of an ancient religion. From listening to her cluttered yet beautiful patchwork of memories and fabrications, I discovered that I already knew about stories that jumped time and forms that changed shape. I already had intimations of the archaic Celtic Mare Goddess. My Grandmother had taught me how to wish on every white horse we saw, holding my breath and silently repeating an old rhyming spell. Alongside my grandmother I had dimly experienced the powers of the Beltane Festival from watching her ritually wash her face—and washing my own—in the May morning dew to gain its special Sabbat magic.[3] With her I attended the Lughnasa Harvest Goddess at a pageant wedding in the suburban neighborhood's vegetable garden. The land's owner wore her wedding dress and a yellow squash "torc" to receive the first fruits of summer that we placed at her feet. From my grandmother I knew the importance of ritual, genealogy, and land to establish her family's multivalanced place in the cosmos. Every afternoon one summer while she took her nap, she had me ceremonially copy the names of my ancestors that some family genealogist had traced through the generations as far back as Adam and Eve. On waking she told me where many of them had lived and the stories about them that she had heard from her own aunts and grandmothers, so I could feel anchored in the vast space-time of human history. She helped me to pronounce the curious names on that list and to unravel the words scrolled into a prized old valentine sent from one ancestor to his betrothed and framed on her guest-room wall. This "true lover's knot" formed an interlacing pattern that I later recognized was a typical medieval Celtic design. It hangs now beside the desk at which I write.

With growing rational and scientific vision, I came to regard my grandmother's rituals as "peculiar." She did them, but she could not explain their meanings or magic. As an adolescent, I left her ways to join my father's culture. But teaching that class on Celtic symbolism led me far back to my Celtic roots. It returned me to the memories of my grandmother and it led further. It gave me the first of a series of conscious encounters with the rich alluvial deposit that lies in the depths of Western European culture—just as it lies in my own psyche and in the deepest layers of all of us. There I was given a glimpse of the archetypal source-ground that flows into all cultures around the globe. Delving into Celtic material to find a way to teach it, I realized I was already at home in a home I and so many in the modern world had abandoned.

In 1981, I also began to discover the relevance of Celtic themes to modern psychoanalytic process. I discovered the tales to be extraordinary mirrors for much of the pre-Oedipal dynamics of clients I work with in the consulting room. Analysands may arouse and channel aggressive drives through rituals enacted in analysis that are often similar to the rites of ancient Ireland that initiated the great warrior Cuchulainn.[4] Patterns in psychotic imagery mirror myths of the Celtic Earth Goddess.[5] Many aspects of dreams—their structure, logic, and context—may be appreciated by analogy to Celtic spirals and interlacing designs.[6] In the consulting room poignant healing ceremonies may emerge to foster the analysand's ego development. They touch the embodied magic levels of consciousness where Celtic myth and contemporary need intersect. These are but a few of the themes that I have found illuminated by interweaving ancient and archetypal Celtic patterns with modern psychotherapeutic practice.

Mythic motifs and images float into my consciousness as I sit with a client. They rise alongside affects and personal memories, reflections about previous sessions and different clients, ideas from reading, and all the other useful flotsam that needs to be sorted for its relevance to the current communication between that individual's psyche and my own to aid in the exploration of the client's issues. The mythologems' order, beauty, and depth sometimes become palpably evident, shining through the many hours spent with individual clients. Although rarely communicated directly to the client,[7] their spirit beckons and gives meaning to the emotional upheavals that distressed and growing humans bring to share in the ritual space of therapy. The archetypal patterns also can illuminate confusions that I feel after sessions when I reflect on client's material and my own psychic and somatic reactions to it. Thus I find my work as a therapist enlivened and enriched by reflecting on the isomorphic structures common to ancient myth and the modern psyche. As an intuitive and feeling type, I also crave the structure of the mythologems around which to weave my thoughts and clinical perceptions. The myths provide images that clarify the muddles and deepen the oversimplifications my thinking can produce, just as they help me to find patterns latent in the personal clinical material. Like a Celtic interlace, these patterns have sometimes revealed their astonishing coherence. I love these interweavings. I find them a source of personal motivation and sustenance as much as the intense intricacies of the transference and countertransference field, which is another layer of the interlace itself.

Although this coherence ever and again slips away into a tangled web, I have learned to trust that its effects persist and even shape the seemingly chaotic psychic and somatic energies between analyst and analysand into patterns of isomorphic resonances that are as wondrous as the computer simulations of the repetitions that vivify chaos theory.[8] Searching to find the threads of meaning and the coherence between deep archetypal structures, personal psychology, the interpersonal relational field, and modern culture requires the intense concentration that has made practicing the art of psychotherapy a form of meditation for me.

The plunder of ancient myth for its use in a modern psychological context is always suspect however. In spite of all our scholarship and intuitions, we cannot know exactly what the ancients meant. We can surmise and try diligently to honor the complexity of the sources. We can use comparative mythological and anthropological methods. But even as we may intuit their deep structures, we cannot know the ancient myths in their original context, and we inevitably bend them to our own. Pagan Celtic material in particular has been filtered through Roman and Christian lenses. Recent archaeological and folkloric studies have helped us to peel away these latest overlays, but we are still dependent upon written records of a sacred oral tradition that were transcribed by those who stood outside that tradition. Although the *drui*, the Celtic shamanic priesthood, was literate and sometimes used the Greek alphabet in commercial dealings, the learned Celts conveyed their complex lore only orally, "from mouth to ear." Thus we know it primarily from the writings of those who ground their own axes as they shaped the older material. The Romans, who wrote of the Celts in Gaul and Britain and sent their children to study the art of oration with druid masters, still thought themselves to be the civilized conquerors of Celtic "barbarians." The early medieval scribes who gave us the manuscript versions of some pagan material still had a strong connection to the old tradition, but they adapted it to their new Christian culture as well.[9]

We also know some Celtic material from living sources like my grandmother and her "peculiar" rituals. Many of these rites have survived in Ireland, the British Isles, Bretony, and even in pockets of exiled Celts in settlements that were once British colonies, from Australia to Pennsylvania, Kentucky, and Cape Breton Island. Folk traditions and storytelling among those who live close to the land and depend on its cycles retain important elements of the ancient themes. Often enough, however, the farmer driving his herds up to the hilltop fair on Lughnasa or between two bonfires on Beltane, the woman washing her face in Mayday dew, or even the parents dressing their children in costumes to visit neighbors for Halloween sweets, have no inkling of the powerful ritual bases of these actions. No more do we usually remember that Candlemas and Lammas and All-Saint's Day and many of the saints themselves are remnants of Celtic traditions deliberately recut into Christian designs. Yet we can readily see from symbolic material brought to our consulting rooms that the archetypal form patterns supporting the myths still resonate in deep and embodied layers of the human psyche and affect our modern responses. This book grew out of some of my explorations of those resonances.

I have included a great deal of mythological lore in the pages that follow in part because I love its passions and intricacies. Also I feel the importance of reclaiming this ancient pagan material for parochial Western culture. Many individuals are seeking to go beyond the mainstream by opening their consciousness towards Eastern and Native American traditions. They may discover, as I have, that there are remarkable parallels between these traditional cultures and that of the ancient Celts. They may see that the shamanic current remains vigorously alive in Irish folklore. Most of the far flung descendants of the Celts of Ireland, the British Isles, and Europe are cut off from their own mythological and psychological roots and not enough in touch with the rich heritage of the archetypal background. Many modern Irish think there is nothing but clan, booze, St. Patrick's Church and parades, the Time of Troubles, and exile to bond them. Especially, individuals prone to addiction, with depressed and hungry souls cut off from their personal and cultural lineage, may find a source of self-esteem and hope as they begin to recognize the mythic patterns their very miseries express. For the archetypal background continues unconsciously to shape "modern" actions and thoughts in sickness and in health. The beserker spirit is still painfully alive as I write these words, in Ireland, as it is in other locations such as Africa, America, Germany, the Middle East, and what was once called Yugoslavia. Now it flourishes under the rationalizations of religion, tribalism, nationalism, fundamentalism, terrorist *jihad,* or ethnic cleansing. Maeve's patterns are also still alive under many names. Her spiritually deep mythology has been distorted into acted-out intoxication. Hence too many now get inebriated on substances and wildly rampant passions rather than on the awesome meanings that reverberate through us in moments of visionary participation in the vast mystery of life and death. Our culture thus also suffers from a lack of collective healing rites to mediate the multiple powers of the archetypal pattern represented by Maeve.

Maeve and Addiction

Working with clients who are recovering addicts, I began to make specific connections between material from the deepest levels of the psyche and the myths and rituals of the great Irish goddess, Maeve. Maeve, written *Meadhbh* or *Medb* in Gaelic, means "the inebriating one," "the one who makes drunk." She represents the profound and archetypal need for experiences of ecstasy and the transformative fullness of emotion and vision such experiences may produce. Initiations involving her drink, the *medb* or mead, were sacred in Celtic society. Unlike the ancient Celts, we do not usually have a sense of sacred and ritualized ecstatic participation in our psychological and spiritual matrix. Because we have unconsciously torn parts of Maeve's rites out of their sacral context, we often find ourselves askew and addicted. If I could rediscover and experience the various aspects of the pattern of Maeve's wholeness, I wondered, would

I be better able to understand what we need for healing our addictive behaviors? I decided to explore.

To find Maeve's archetypal image pattern, I began to examine various Irish sources in which the goddess is mentioned. The material is scattered in many tales. Sometimes only a name or a phrase gave me a clue to her original powers. Sometimes I found amplifying material clustered around a similarly constellated divine figure from a different area of Gaelic-speaking lands. Slowly I put these bits together to create the glimmerings of a picture of this great Celtic goddess. Then I began to examine the ways in which some of the archetypal patterns clustered around the figure of Maeve have been distorted in modern, secularized variants. Specifically I looked at the differences between the uses of inebriation in rituals sacred to the goddess and in the compulsions of modern addictions. I wanted to see if there might be any correlations. Were the patterns in her myths helpful in describing aspects of pathology? More importantly could they point towards healing? If I looked into Maeve's mythology, would I be able to discover how the same structures can underlie both our defenses against the pains of life and relationship as well as our capacities to embrace them and support transformative experiences of deep and cohesive authenticity in relations to ourselves and others?

Maeve and Healing

We know from the study of many kinds of healing practices that our symptoms can often be read as symbolic expressions of our misaligned relations to archetypal structures. Although the symptoms may cause us to experience dis-ease, even as some of them may have once provided means of defending against pain, they also point to underlying energy patterns, or generative archetypal fields, that shape psyche and soma, spirit and matter. We know that distorted or partial forms are inevitable in our personal lives because incarnation imposes

limitations upon archetypal potentials. The stories of our
development and relationships poignantly express the
limitations that all earthly life is heir to. In therapy we
explore these personal experiences through analysis that takes
us back to our roots in order to understand the particularities
of each individual's mold. Inevitably in this process we come
to glimpse the underlying energy patterns around which the
personal experiences and behavior patterns have clustered.
We can become aware of these deeper archetypal patterns
through reflecting on and emotionally grounding the
symbolic and metaphoric images that dreams or visions bring
us. We can also become aware of the archetypal dimension
when intense emotions connected with old relationships
point to it. Thus we can see the archetypes at work
structuring the many forms of relationship that arise in the
transference and countertransference field between client and
therapist. Both therapist and client then can become
participant observers in a humanly shared field of energy and
information that opens into archetypal depths.

In psychotherapy we may learn to witness
empathically the passions and symbolic images of these
archetypal fields as we experience their power. As we become
witnesses, we can begin to seek the healing potential in the
larger symbolic patterns. Over time in the ritually maintained
time and space of therapy, we may be able to step back or
disidentify from the patterns of perceiving, feeling, thinking,
and relating that originally possessed us—from our old and
habitual histories. As we become aware that these diseased
patterns are only partial aspects of a larger archetypal
potential, we may be able to shift from unconscious and
compulsive identity with our personal complexes towards
more conscious appreciation of the underlying patterns they
have partially expressed. As we can assimilate the impact and
meaning of the emotions and symbolic images evoked by and
pointing towards their larger and balanced patterns, the
emotions and images can then function as medicines, and
we may transform our relationship to our symptoms and
our disease.[10]

The intensity of our experience of the affects and symbolic images of the potent archetypal energy field can transform our relationship to it and promote psychic and somatic rebalancing. It can even lead us towards a cognitive and emotional understanding of the meaning of the poison in our particular lives. We may come to accept why we were destined to suffer such intensities, not only causally as a result of genetic and childhood dynamics but also purposefully as a piece of life we have been given to struggle with and grow from. The emotions and images encountered in the therapeutic process can thus act on the witnessing consciousness subtly and deeply to allow us to find self-esteem and what Jung called *amor fati* (love of one's fate) even as they realign psyche and soma with the larger structure and life-giving potentials inherent in the archetypal energy patterns.

Such a mode of treatment is represented in the story of the Biblical Israelites in the desert who railed against God's mandate for them and were bitten by fiery snakes, an image representing the burning resentment they felt as victims of the long journey. Suffering the painful symptoms that made them conscious of their misalignment with their fate, they asked for help. Then the same power that had sent the snakes instructed Moses to create a fiery brass serpent and set it before the sufferers. Each one who gazed on the image symbolizing the poisonous affliction that possessed them found healing and lived.[11] Could Maeve's image serve us as the brazen serpent? Could it be seen as representing ecstasy, addiction, and healing?

Treatments for Addiction

Many kinds of treatments are now available for addiction. Some programs promote abstinence and use medications (such as antabuse, valium, prozac, and methadone) to help patients develop an ability to stop substance abuse, but they may not seek to explore psychological dynamics or look into the archetypal roots of the disease. Others focus only on keeping addicts safe, providing life-survivor skills, but they choose to do nothing about the addiction itself. Still others help drinkers who are able to enforce limits and who need to feel in charge of their habit simply to cut it down to more manageable levels.[12] Twelve-step programs provide valuable structures for the recovering addict that often surprisingly echo aspects of the mythology of Maeve. But they do not go far enough for some individuals. For me depth psychotherapy or psychoanalysis, practiced with a spiritual as well as with interpersonal and embodied perspectives, is also essential. It provides the most complete arena in which individuals may explore the deep personal and archetypal roots of their personalities. Then they may discover and create the relational experiences and rituals that permit the growth potentials that arise when struggling with archetypal levels of personal problems. While I appreciate that such transpersonally oriented psychoanalysis is not the only way to move towards healing, it is the way I have followed and find most valuable in working with clients. Each person in recovery struggling to develop an embodied individual consciousness attuned to conscience and transpersonal intent may thus discover the personal meanings of the disease in her or his life as a connection to archetypal dynamics and the objective psyche. From this vantage it may also be possible to find the ways that each individual client can contribute towards dreaming the myth onwards to support the vast cultural change that is underway. Living in an age that is called an age of addictions necessitates our looking at the connections between the archetypal structure of the mythologem and what is seeking to be healed and born on a collective level as well.

While Alcoholics Anonymous focuses on one addiction, the archetypal approach I describe is not substance specific. I consider that many kinds of addictive dependencies and behaviors are informed by the same underlying pattern. Even though different individuals and even groups have different drugs and/or addictive processes of choice, their pattern of use seems to lie along a single spectrum. At one end of the continuum is the employment of powerful substances and mood-altering behaviors for the enhancement of life or relief from painful states. At the other fully addictive end is bondage in which one cannot give up the use of the drug whenever the individual needs to, because the psychological and/or physiological dependency has become compulsive and led to increasing loss of control over all aspects of life. Part of this extreme bondage is manifest in the great difficulty and inevitable pain of withdrawal.

My experience with addiction comes in part through my clients, but it is inevitably also more personal. Indeed at certain stages of writing this book, I have felt the pull of various compelled dependencies again, and their siren call has kept me humble even as it has helped me to steer my way through some of the material that follows. My primary clinical experience is with adults in recovery, adults already conscious of the suffering inherent in their addictions and struggling towards sobriety. Indeed I rarely work with anyone still actively using drugs or alcohol, since I find that the therapy cannot take. The client cannot adequately bond to the therapy process to observe and feel the underlying fears, passions, and needs that are both expressed and defended against by the addiction. Nor can he or she focus responsibly until the mind-bending and physically based enthrallment of the disease is loosened. Instead a split can form between the intention to work on personal issues in therapy and the countervailing impulse to remove them from consciousness with self-medication. Because loyalty to the diseased pattern is sustained by its biological effects, acupuncture, hospitalization, and other treatments affecting the body to help end active addictive behaviors may initially be necessary. Nonetheless, my own experience and that of colleagues in programs for chronic, inner city, and/or youthful abusers suggests that even those on "crack street" and their therapists and families may find this material helpful in relating to the problems of those they treat and live with. This

book is also for those who are only dimly conscious of the
addictive patterns that seem to support them and that nearly
all of us support. There are many who can be said to be
addicts or who define themselves as addicted—from food,
television, and intensity junkies and rageaholics to members
of Debtors and Shoppers Anonymous. These addictions, too,
numb our fears and longings and focus our emotions but kill
only a portion of our consciousness. For all of us I want to
hold up the image of Maeve in her rich multivalent meanings
as an archetype of ecstasy, addiction, and healing.

Nonetheless these reflections on Maeve are not
intended as another description of addictive behavior,
propensity, and treatments. There is an immense literature on
the subject already, and references to some of these studies
may be found in the bibliography. Nor are Maeve's myths
themselves communications I would relate to my analysands,
for they are not alternatives to working through the issues
individually in the intense intricacies of personal process.
Only rarely might recounting a story help to validate an
experience already deeply felt. I use these reflections and
myths as part of an inner fund of thoughts, images, and
memories that enable me to tune in empathically and
resonate with the client and the interpersonal field between
us. They also sensitize me to larger patterns that can clear my
view and sustain me when the relational work gets snagged.

Interweavings

Although I interweave clinical material into the text, in what
follows I seek primarily to explore one archetypal pattern
behind the age-old and omnipresent necessity for the
expansion of consciousness through ecstatic and visionary
experiences. When misused, such potentials for altering
consciousness may lead to addiction. Specifically in the stories
and rites of the goddess Maeve, I discern four initiatory
patterns that I describe in Part I. These involve states of

consciousness, intensified and solemnized by the sacred mead, that were life enhancing and benefited ancient Irish society. Examining those patterns again from the perspective of their desecrations into blind addiction shows us where and how modern usage has gone astray. Thus the multivalent etiology and diverse symptoms of abuse are also illuminated by looking into Maeve's mythic patterns. Finally, as is true of every archetypal structure, the cluster of myths focused around Maeve also suggests paths to healing. In Part II, I return to Maeve's mythology and retrace the spiral suggested by the descriptions of her initiations. Here I invoke more of Maeve's own stories to discover the multiple approaches necessary in the treatment of the addiction-prone individual. The mythic material itself provides a unique pattern to support the embodied and spiritual integration necessary to begin to heal the causes and effects of compulsive abuse in ourselves and our culture.

The longer I work with this material, the more I realize that the picture of Maeve that emerges conveys to me something, seen through female imagery, of what Jung called the Self. Like a rough sketch, it points to an encompassing pattern of energy that suggests the matrix out of which we develop, the forms that can guide us, and the completeness towards which we can seek to grow. I know, however, that whatever can be said of any archetypal energy pattern is not "it," for language belongs to the ego world. Any symbolic image can be seen and described only partially since it bridges between consciousness and the unknowable. In the myths of this old Celtic goddess, I can only say I found a wonder that speaks to my modern consciousness and that has lured me to contemplation and awe.

Part 1

The unfathomable experience that humanity has symbolically expressed for millenia through myths, fables, rituals and ecstasies, remains one of the hidden centres of our culture, of the way we exist in this world.

—Carlo Ginzburg, *Ecstasies*

The magic philter, the love potion, the poet's elixir, the intoxicant, soma, and nectar poured by [the Feminine] . . . are vehicles of transformation, forms of the water of life, which the Feminine itself is. Through them the [ego] . . . rises to a sublimated, intoxicated, enthusiastic, and spiritualized existence [wherein it experiences] vision, ecstasy, and creativity, and to a state of "out-of-[its]selfness" in which [it] is the instrument of higher powers, whether "good" or "evil.". . . The ambivalent female mana figure may guide . . . or beguile. . . . Side by side with sublimation stands abasement . . . . How close ecstasy is to madness, enthusiasm to death, creativeness to psychosis, is shown by mythology, by the history of religions, and by the lives of innumerable great [individuals] for whom the gift from the depths has spelled doom.

—Erich Neumann, *The Great Mother*

Chapter I

The Goddess Maeve

Interweavings Between Maeve's Myths and the Psyche

The Irish Goddess Maeve is one of the grandest figures in
Celtic lore. Different images have clustered around her name
throughout vastly different times in Irish history. As we
examine some of them, we can see how earlier patterns have
both persisted and been changed by the storytellers of later
generations.[1] We know this same phenomenon of layering
occurs in our own psyches. Early structures both survive and
evolve as we, growing around them in our lives, bring new
experiences and even different kinds of consciousness to bear
on the original archetypal patterns that structure the personal
events of our history. Therapy often begins with work on the
adaptations that have enabled us to survive and shaped our
perceptions, emotions, concepts, and behavior. As we press
through their current encrustations, we can begin to trace our
sufferings to earlier and deeper structurally determining
personal experiences. Moving still deeper, we may come to
appreciate that these are themselves grounded in archetypal
dynamics, forming our individualized versions of symbolic
patterns and "giving" us the gifts and problems that make us
become the persons we are meant to be. Thus we may find
that beneath all the later survivals and distortions that make
up our complexes, we can glimpse the pure springs of
generative archetypal structures. Sometimes we can even dig

out the clutter that has impeded their fertile flow into our lives to reclaim the clarity and energy of the "true self."[2] In an analogous process we can study the layers of mythology built around the figure of Maeve to discover her original pattern of wholeness and the archetypal energies within it that resonate with deep levels of the collective psyche of the Celts and all the world's people.

The Great Goddess Maeve survives in modern folklore as a figure that both reveals and conceals a primordial identity. In some stories the old goddess lives on in folk imagination as one of the elfin "gentry," magical *daoine maithe,* or "good people"[3] whose world surrounds and penetrates the world of mortals. Sometimes her powers are given to other deities,[4] or their ancient meanings became Christianized.[5] Sometimes she is merely diminished to a human virago.[6] Sometimes she is rendered demonic.[7] In "Romeo and Juliet" Shakespeare refers to Maeve as the wild and wonderful Queen Mab who leads the fairy revels. Yeats makes her the symbol of all the sleeping glory of the Irish that he wished to rouse again into modern consciousness. He evokes her as

. . . the Queen of all the invisible host, [who]
. . . sleeps high up on wintry Knocknarea
in an old cairn of stones . . .
[and calls her] water-born women . . .
up on the land [to] dance in the moon.[8]

In an Irish folktale collected in modern times called "The Witches' Excursion,"[9] we find a "gay and frisky," "impudent and imprudent" old housekeeper, Madge. She helps her sister crones to cheering glasses of punch before they fly across the sea to England. Earlier in the story Madge tried to give her master, James, a drugged bedtime posset to keep him from noticing their escapade. But he did not drink it, and so he witnesses what follows. Spying on the gleeful old women, James watches them don red caps, seize their brooms, and fly up the chimney. Just in time he snatches Madge's cap and broom and repeats their magic rhyme. Flying across the sea, then through a keyhole and into a castle wine cellar, he finds himself seated regally on a stallion among the ribald company.

With plenty of lights glimmering round . . . he and his companions, with full tumblers of frothing wine in hand [are] hob-nobbing and drinking healths as jovially and recklessly as if the liquor was honestly come by . . . . The heady liquors soon got into their brains, and a period of unconsciousness succeeded the ecstasy.

The women get away, but poor James does not. He awakens in the custody of the lord of the castle. Accused of draining the wine cellars repeatedly during the previous month, he is found guilty and taken to the gallows. Standing at the top of the steps, he suddenly hears the voice of Madge call out from the back of the assembled crowd to remind him of his red hat. When one of the guards fetches it from the dungeons, James puts the magical cap on his head. Contritely he then addresses the crowd. He ends his speech with the witch's rhyme, and like a rocket launched from the English hangman's grip, he blasts into the air to join Madge and her Irish coven. Thereafter he is called "Red James" and he is her man.

This modern folk tale still contains traces of the ancient goddess. By looking at it the way we might examine material brought into psychoanalysis, we can discern the dominant motifs and archetypal images lying under the story line or manifest content. We notice what is present and what is left out. Immediately we find that not only does the name Madge, like Mab, derive from Maeve,[10] but the housekeeper possesses some of the goddess' supernatural qualities. Like the great Maeve herself, whom we shall soon see in her glorious fullness, Madge maintains her connection to wine and horses—albeit broomstick steeds and James' stallion. She too is associated with the color red that was emblematic of the pagan otherworld. Madge is portrayed as a carousing old witch who brews or steals her mind-altering potions and flies to other lands with spell, cap, and stick. Here Maeve's original, numinous libation has become a drug and her celebratory rites, a drunken debauch. Maeve's own sacred mead must now be stolen from a lordly wine cellar.

To the Irish folk telling this old story on winter
evenings around the turf fire, Madge represents the
ambiguously delightful powers of drink to steal a soul from
ordinary life and its collective standards of morality. There are
hints about national rivalries and the ultimate power of the
Irish crone to save her followers from Ireland's oppressors.
The great goddess is diminished but not demonic as she leads
her devotee to stand outside the secular law. She is still
supernatural and fascinating. Her master Red James is in no
way her master. He cannot not resist her powers nor her
brew. In fact he needs and relies on her powers. Her drink
generates the ease that enables joyful communion, and it
alters human consciousness. The transporting influence of
Maeve's cup of sacred red wine is represented by the magic of
rhyme and red headgear that now permits flight to other
lands. In excess it is also the intoxicant that sends James into
a drunken stupor. Maeve's ancient otherworldy powers and
potentiality for inducing states of altered consciousness are
somewhat disguised. Housekeeper Madge still represents an
order different from the secular lord's court, and she is so
powerful that, like a modern Superwoman, she can cross seas
and solid boundaries and rescue her chosen mortal from
secular judgment and even death.

The potencies underlying ecstasy and alcoholism
have just these qualities to radically transform consciousness.
James' initiation into the much changed rites of Maeve
reveals his devotion and service to the goddess' power. As the
old ways trickled down through the millennia, they became
secularized: rites became revels, gods became "little people,"
and sacred wine became intoxicating booze. A similar fate
happens to the old gods in each of us. Acculturation through
our relationships to early caretakers teaches us to tame the
passionate, archetypal emotions with which we are born. We
learn to shift their archaic powers into the relationally
acceptable forms of expression that our culture supports.
Sometimes we press their primal energies into conventional
molds; sometimes we reduce their influence and allow them
to play at the edges of life as merely charming, diminutive

nuisances that we can indulge during vacations from the serious work of living; sometimes we let their full energies loose at certain ritual times, like New Year's Eve or Mardi Gras. In the best of circumstances we learn within our relationship to parental figures to reformulate, condense, sweeten, and blend these energies fruitfully into daily life. An ongoing dialogue between developing individual consciousness and the archetypal forces in their emotional and imaginal manifestations permits the gradual evolution of libido. Primitive aggression then becomes acceptable competition and the adaptive assertion supporting self-esteem, guardianship, and the skills that enable mastery of life's problems. Divine, primal appetite becomes life-enhancing curiosity, ambition, questing, adult sexuality, and even gourmet cooking.

Inevitably when we feel the severe censure of current collective values that would expunge the powers of the archaic gods, or when we are not aided in mediating their powers when these threaten to overwhelm us in childhood, we cannot transform our relationship to them and allow their development in our lives. Instead we seek to distance ourselves from their energies. Fearing and unable to venerate the archaic potencies, we demonize their powers, separating them farther from ourselves. We deny or dissociate from their grip, or we project them onto other folk whom we then fear, scorn, and dread—all the while requiring their presence near us to embody the feared life forces that we try to evacuate from our own lives.

Divine energies will not, however, go quietly or even lie invisibly asleep. Like Maeve in Yeat's poem, they rise up from the watery unconscious to dance in the moonlight of our creative possessions and our lunacies, our "pathologies."[11] When we can welcome their power and learn to dance with it, we find we are supported in our creative outpourings and can more readily mediate the rising flow fruitfully into daily life. When we fear or resist the dance, we inevitably find ourselves seized in its grip and often overwhelmed. We find

then that the energy erupts into and through us, and we
are endangered and endangering. We find ourselves swept
along like chunks of flotsam in a wild flood, forced to honor
the powers unconsciously through our obsessions and
compulsions and other symptoms of psychological and
physical dis-ease. Perhaps even in these discomforts, if we
look closely, we can again recognize the gods just as we can
discover Maeve underneath her later cultural incarnations
as sprightly Mab, Queen Maeve, Madge, and even the
demonized witch.[12]

Indeed remnants of a pre-Celtic cult figure of
"divine maternity and authority,"[13] a *Magna Mater,* underlie all
the later manifestations of Maeve, Mab, and Madge. Through
the narrative threads of her rites and stories, we catch
glimmers of this ancient pattern of wholeness in feminine
form that she represents. As a "complete deity,"[14] the goddess
embodies an energy that manifests in all realms of existence.
She thus provides us with a unitary image underlying and
encompassing many seemingly separated life patterns.

Just as Mab and Madge are less than satisfactory
because they represent diminishments of Maeve, so the
fragmentation of her powers by distributing attributes
throughout a pantheon of deities is also unsatisfactory. Such
multiplication of figures may be useful at stages of therapy
and life involving more developed ego structures, but the
original construct of Maeve is more meaningful for
orientation in deep psychological work. The unitary image
represents the ground from which our development proceeds.
In the language of psychoanalysis the unitary image
represents the archaic object experienced in our earliest
"relationships of sensory contiguity . . . [that] generate a sense
of a bounded sensory surface on which one's experience
occurs (the *beginnings of a feeling of 'a place where one lives'*)."[15]
That ground enables the trust that allows us to rest, just as it
supports our differentiation, our creative fruitfulness, and our
individual transformation. Finding this matrix of our own
valued subjectivity can help us to repair the basic structural

flaws that underlie our pursuit of addictions and psychotherapy as well as our needs for connection to spirit.[16] Conscious relationship to this matrix may even lessen our fear of death as we can later in life imagine allowing our individual ego identity to let go and meld again into the larger field.[17] Such a primal image parallels the insights of modern biologists who seek a model of unifying life forces underlying the morphology and behavior of organisms.[18] Some modern physicists also hypothesize holographic structures of consciousness and a continuum of electromagnetic energy, the vibratory frequencies of which manifest simultaneously or synchronously through all that exists from dense matter to mental activity and spiritual intuitions.[19]

Although we experience ourselves through our many interpersonal and intrapsychic relationships, we, too, often feel an underlying coherence or unity through time and space that we call our identity. With our many facets and even as we change and differentiate over the years, we can usually experience ourselves as the same person, knowing that the plural aspects of us must function together for shared survival. We may even sometimes look back over our lives and glimpse what seems to be a guided process of development that Jung called individuation. We then see that our many experiences and our many selves have an order in their unfolding and cluster around one centered-in-Self whole. Through life we thus grow to experience ourselves to be paradoxically both plural and singular, and when there is an imbalance or disharmony between our sense of multiplicity and unity, we call it pathology. Then we find our sense of identity and selfhood is fragile and fragmented or overly grandiose, and we cannot experience the underlying ordering presence and processes of the larger Self.[20]

Maeve, as a typically "all-purpose" primordial tribal goddess, represents the qualities of encompassing wholeness and grand diversity that we need to mirror and represent our well-functioning selves. She gives us an image of multiplicity within a whole from a time before divine attributes or functions were split among a pantheon of deities that were then regrouped together under some hierarchical order that likely represented the social structures of the narrator's time, leaving each one dispersed and depotentiated through excessive discrimination.[21] As the conveyor of ecstatic and visionary experiences that allow us to expand consciousness to reattune to the pervasive cosmic spirit, Maeve stands firmly against such fragmentation. Even when her powers over life, lust, and death are purposefully derogated by Christian writers, we find that she is still represented as the confuser of neat discriminations. Thus in one late-medieval tale she is said to rename the seven sons[22] she bore with king Ailill, giving them all the same name to better serve her overarching, timeless interests.[23]

Portraits of Maeve

Just as the mother of infancy is the vast holding and transforming environment of the preverbal child, so the goddess of nature encompasses and sustains her people.[24] For the ancient Irish, Maeve was goddess of the earth itself—the sacred land in which her tribespeople lived and on which their existence depended. She was the force in its rushing waters, wind-swept mountains, and fertile plains.[25] She was the enduring substance and the cosmic energy manifesting through the many forms of material substance. As this aboriginal maternal principle or matrix, Maeve held supreme power and authority in her people's lands.

Maeve's body was the earth, and her body processes were earth creating. In one image from the Ulster cycle of myths, we glimpse the pre-Celtic Maeve as creatrix with the power to form the actual, symbolic, and ritual landscapes in which her people lived. Even in this medieval epic, *The Cattle Raid of Cooley* (*Tain Bo Cuailnge*), the ancient goddess' "gush of blood" "dug three great channels." After withholding her menstrual flow when she fought against her foes, Maeve released it again at the end of the battles, magically creating the source of three rivers so large that "a mill could find room in each dyke."[26] Although the source of these rivers was named Maeve's Foul[27] by the medieval monkish disparagers of female body mysteries and the pagan tradition,[28] such rivers were said to flow from the goddess herself as the sacred well-spring of actual life forms. The image of the three turning mills within the three interconnected great ditches recalls the ancient triple spiral designs we know from carvings in the Neolithic Boyne Valley temple, now called Newgrange, that will be discussed later. At Newgrange the turning mill-wheels of the sky[29] provided alignment for architecture, sculpture, and the yearly ritual calendar. The three mills in the epic's description further amplify the mysterious triple spiral symbol. They suggest the ever-turning cycles of time, which express (and flow from) the cosmic triune goddess to transform all living things through life, death, and regeneration, just as the mill wheels transform living grain into the flour that makes up our daily bread.

Maeve's three rivers also represent her triune nature[30] and her original identification with life's waters. The blood of their creation suggests Maeve's power over blood and body initiations, fertility rites, and the blood sacrifice that was often made to Celtic goddesses where three waters converged.[31] A widespread and still enduring cult of rivers and springs presided over by goddesses (and later Christian saints) attests to the procreative, healing, and wisdom-giving waters in Celtic lands.[32] We know that Maeve, like Nerthus, Hera, Artemis, and many other fertility goddesses of old Europe, was associated with specific water sources. Maeve bathed in a sacred pool on the island of Clothrann (later called Quakers Island) in Lough Ree (*Ryve*). To the pool she retired every morning to renew herself in her own waters of life.[33] On the holy island she was served by priestesses who kept her sacred objects, among them the comb and casket that were lost under the waters of another lake when Maeve's chief priestess Erne was drowned in the

lough that still bears her name.[34] In another tale we are told
that Chief Conchobhar of Ulster, a royal husband whom she
had abandoned, came after her at Tara and violated her
while she bathed in the River Boyne. On Clothrann in
Lough Ree, Maeve was watched at her bath—a motif that
runs through mythic history from Artemis and Susanna to
Rhiannon's priestess, Lady Godiva, and her worshipper,
Peeping Tom.[35]

An eleventh-century manuscript tells us that
during an assembly on the shores of Lough Ree, a youth saw
a beautiful woman bathing and asked who she was. Hearing
that she was Maeve, he was plunged into vengeful passion.
We are told that the lad was Maeve's nephew, named
Furbaidhe ("the cut one"), and in one tale his mother was
Maeve's sister Clothra, who had reigned in Cruachan before
her and whom she herself is said to have slain. In another he
is said to be the child of a sister named Eithne, who drowned.
The name of the boy suggested to the scribes that he was cut
at birth from the side of his dead mother. This apparently
gave a rationale for his action. On hearing that the woman
bathing was his mother's sister, he put the hard lump of
cheese he had been eating into his sling and killed Maeve
with a shot to the forehead. This ironic variation on the story
of David and Goliath shows us, as fervently as does the
petulant and lustful virago portrait of Maeve in *The Tain*, how
the scribes of the new religion sought to undermine the great
goddess' majesty. This story of her death represents what they
hoped, in vain, would be an end to her worship.[36]

In the enduring rites of the holy wells, in myth
and poetry, and in the landscape itself, Maeve lives on. When
the scribes named her as the vulvar source from which three
rivers spring, they followed the Celtic tendency to see the
similarity of human bodily forms and functions and the
geography. Thus certain breast-shaped hills across Ireland are
sacred and still called the paps of the goddess by folk who
climb the peaks to lay a stone on the cairns marking her
nipples.[37] Other places are identified with the swollen belly of

the fertile earth mother or the cave openings into her body. At Cruachan (Rathcrogan, Co. Sligo), ancient barrows, cairns, earthworks, stones, and enclosures sculpted ten square miles of the landscape as the oldest and largest ceremonial area in Ireland. Oriented around sacred caves, hills, rocks, and astronomical alignments, these monuments reveal one of the earliest expressions of worship—reverence for the natural forms and patterns of the goddess of the land and sky. Cruachan, the sacred center of Maeve's rites, is considered the mystical cauldron of the goddess of the setting sun, *Crochen Croderg* (blood-red drinking cup), and Maeve's birthplace.[38] The Irish today identify the huge cairn on Knocknarea (*Cnoc na Righe*, Co. Sligo) as Maeve's grave. In all such images of the deity, the physical and mystical geographies are united— much as these are also conjoined for Native Americans and Aborigines. The connections of such places of pilgrimage with their myths were so important to the Irish that the lore of place names (*Dindschenchas*) makes up an entire category of the ancient oral narratives.

This isomorphism and the myths of place reveal the deep Celtic sense of the interpenetration of the realms of nature and the supernatural. For the ancient Celts the natural and supernatural were aspects of a sacred unitary reality in which all life participated. The realms were not separated into opposing dualities as they are for us. Thus a sense of individuality as we know it could neither emerge from, nor fall out of, the embrace of the eternal, mythic dimension. While this kept the tribespeople within the mental diffusions of magic and mythic consciousness, subject to what we would call pre-ego and/or mystical dynamics, it also gave them an existential security for which many of us hunger. A Celtic war chief boasted that the only fears his people knew were those of total catastrophe: that the earth would open, the sea overrun the land, or the sky fall.[39] We would associate such annihilating terrors to psychotic collapse. The Celts hardly concerned themselves with the lesser anxieties about individual destruction that oppress us. Yet exclusion from the larger whole was a powerful threat in Celtic tribal times.

Just as natural life was fused with supernatural, so was individual identity and well-being merged almost wholly into the tribal community.[40] The worst punishments that could be meted out to a person were exclusion from communal rituals and exile.

A similar embeddedness of each particular in the matrix that is typical of this magical level of consciousness enabled the Celts to feel that any hill, spring, or tree was a manifestation of the sacred energies of the goddess' body lying under the tribal assembly mound or focused within the sacred healing spring or holy tree. Celebratory experience of any particular representation of these energies promoted a *participation mystique*, an at-one-ment with the sacred source-ground of all life. Thus dances around the *Bile Meidbe*, a tree species sacred to Maeve, evoked a participatory sense of the dynamic life force coursing in vegetation and the whole of deified nature.[41] And Maeve, the anthropomorphic goddess-queen, on whose shoulders lived a bird and a squirrel, was identified with her more ancient arboreal form.[42] As the focus of enduring cult worship, such trees remained important foci in Celtic ritual and myth (much as they were on Crete and still are in India and other lands). Even today the descendants of the Celts participate in vestiges of such tree rites when they dance around the Maypole.[43] The arousal of participatory ecstasy in the circling, singing communicants often led to young unmarried couples enjoying sex together in the woods and fields on festival nights. These ceremonies celebrated the divine vitality of nature. The modern Celtic poet Dylan Thomas invokes it for our time as

The force that through the green fuse drives the flower
Drives my green age, that blasts the roots of trees
Is my destroyer. . . .
The force that drives the water through the rocks,
Drives my red blood . . . .[44]

As elemental vitality, this aspect of the goddess appears in all the transformative growing, destructive, and regenerative cycles of natural life.

Maeve wore a bird on her shoulder—a Celtic
mark of divinity and an indication of her very ancient role as
bird goddess.[45] She was also called "queen wolf" because she
was devouring and fierce, an apt symbol for the biological
drives supporting aggression, territoriality, and protective
guarding.[46] She had power over the wild pigs that came out
of the Cave of Cruachan to manifest the rampant devouring
appetite that is an aspect of nature.[47] She was the original
owner of the divine white-horned bull, hence sovereign of
the fertile earth and its crops and herds. She was a mare
goddess and could run faster than the swiftest horses.[48] In
human form as warrior, she was so awesome that the sight of
her in battle was said to deprive her enemies of two-thirds of
their strength.[49] As goddess-queen, she chose and dominated
her male partners, and her sexual capacity was immense. She
required "thirty men every day or go with Fergus once."
Fergus, the god whose name means "virile, choice of men,"
was the giant warrior, wise man, beneficent host, and king
who was one of her consorts.[50]

In Maeve's potent shapeshifting forms of water,
earth, vegetation, bird, animal, and human goddess, she
represents the excitability inherent in all living processes:
"The force that through the green fuse drives the flower [and]
Drives my green age." Coursing through all realms of the
universe, this dynamism propels the processes that create
reactivity in chemistry and physics as well as the development
of organisms as diverse as slime mold algae and human
beings. It underlies the elemental forces of attraction and
attachment as well as their opposites. Our every sense is
fueled by such need for excitation.

As the life energy that underlies and manifests
through a multiplicity of life forms, Maeve is the divinity of
maternity, aggression, orality, sexuality, sovereign power and
authority, and artistic and spiritual inspiration. Indeed as the
divine mare, Maeve symbolizes the libido that carries the
entire life process in this natural world and into the realms
beyond.

While we have no visual depictions in Ireland of her as mare goddess, in Romanized stone sculptures of her Gallic counterpart Epona, the goddess is depicted riding on her steed. This combination of figures is usually taken to express two forms of the goddess, implying psychologically that in the Roman ideal, human consciousness is supported by but also atop and in charge of animal instinctuality. In the more archaic Celtic form, we can wonder if the mare goddess enthroned on the animal may instead suggest the force of Maeve as ecstatic possession and polymorphous erotic passion riding her partner. We know that in some trance cults the possessed devotee of the deity is called the horse.[51] For Maeve the steed on which she rides may sometimes be her primary lover, Fergus MacRoech, god of Irish kingship whose penile megalith still stands as the high king's coronation stone on the hill of Tara. His second name labels him "son of the Great Horse." As in depictions of Kali dancing or sitting on her consort, Shiva, and in accounts of Lilith as the first wife of Adam, who rode Adam in lovemaking and was, legend tells us, expelled from Eden only for refusing to take the subservient position, Maeve is the passion that rides us. Like the Vedic *shakti*, she is the force of ecstasy and possession still associated with the female and regally enthroned for the ancient Celts. We experience this libidinous aspect of her most intensely in all the archetypal emotions that involve our body-Self. Such experiences of life energy are both sensate and spiritual. They seem to erupt into and through us to carry us beyond ourselves.

Maeve as Ecstasy

Ecstasy, from the Greek roots *ek*, meaning "from," and *histanai*, meaning "to make a stand," expresses the state of being beside oneself and entranced by energies and awareness pouring from the larger whole.[52] Such an onrush elates or carries us away. Like a deity, it may ravish consciousness and force us to exult (leap out from ourselves) into the matrix beyond consciousness to participate in its spirit. We are then sundered from familiar associations and stability. In trance, we feel that time does not exist and each moment feels eternal. We may feel out of control and dissociated from ourselves and our usual forms of identity and relationships— with all the potential negative and positive connotations of being beside ourselves. Depending on our relation to the energies of the larger whole that encompass and grip our consciousness, we may feel terror and/or bliss; we may act destructively and/or creatively. While we may know the ecstatic horror of "bad trips" and destructive dissociations and impulsive outbursts, we may also sometimes find our experience joyfully expansive and bless its hold on us. Thus ecstasy is often connected to an experience of awesome wholeness in which our small consciousness feels submerged as if it were a drop in the cosmic ocean. Returning to ordinary self-awareness, we may feel renewed because ecstatic experiences can be intensely regenerative.[53]

We may be enraptured (seized as by an avian raptor and carried off) by any archetypal emotion. Excessive rage or love may be euphoric. Terror, shame, grief, greed, power, or joy may carry us beyond ourselves. So may the orgiastic paroxysms of masochism, merged fusions, or intoxicating sadism. Any unconscious enthusiasm may overcome our controls and force us to submit to its rapture or to struggle weakly within its grip to regain our footing. Neurologists give us a medical explanation for the dynamics of archetypal affect. In their view we are transported out of normal consciousness with the aid of mind-altering hormones that are aroused with the emotions. These hormones short-circuit cognitive areas of the brain and go directly from primary limbic regions into the autonomic nervous system, compelling reactions in body organs and evoking subjective experiences of what neurologists call our vivid, precortical matrix.

Sometimes we actively seek ecstatic experiences through the use of inebriating substances as well as through the stimulation of erotic or aggressive passions. Dance and ritual also provide pulse beats, postures, and viscera-gripping sensations to alter consciousness. We may listen avidly to music to get the "high" that it can induce in us by changing our endorphin levels, our emotions, and our consciousness. We may pursue meditative disciplines and/or seek stimulus deprivation to teach us to open to visionary awareness of the indescribable life-force. All of these activities may move us beyond ourselves to participate in the original fullness of body, energy, emotion, and spirit. Psychologically we can say that in all of them, individual consciousness, swelling beyond its ordinary confines and inflated, is experiencing the larger Self, which includes what is beyond consciousness (hence unconscious). All such experiences have the potential to rupture our sense of ordinary reality. While they may lead to wild, even destructive, behaviors that are profoundly negative for the person and those around, they may also grant expanded mind-body consciousness and authentic ecstatic visions of the continuum between the individual and the whole cosmos. Thus they hold the potential for higher wisdom, psychological transformation, spiritual development, and healing if we can suffer their grip within a safe-enough holding context and learn to align our expanded selves creatively with a source transcending reason.

For the tribes of Ireland this source was represented by the figure of Maeve. Experiences of ecstatic communion with her were central in the rites of Celtic society. Because the goddess was also the principle of sovereignty, as we shall see, we can assume that the level of ecstatic experience that Maeve represents was honored and revered throughout the life cycle. For the Celts—and most peoples until recently in earth's history—the original fullness of body, energy, emotion, and spirit had not yet been split apart. While we, too, know this felt wholeness in early childhood and find it again in moments of passionate intensity and visionary expansion, we live in a culture that has rarely supported individual ecstatic experience. The passionate frenzies aroused by the terrors of damnation and the bliss of communion with the divinity were used to enforce submission to the reigning church. Other roads to ecstasy, such as music, dancing, and sexuality, were long prohibited or confined within the walls of dogma. In Western religious traditions, those who sought intimate experience of the divine were called esoteric and might have been specially initiated.[54] More often, however, they were persecuted by the keepers of the exoteric institutions that enforce their doctrines on the multitudes.

Without social affirmation we are more vulnerable to personal experiences that inhibit our natural capacity for surrendering to ecstasy. In childhood when our nascent sense of identity is easily threatened by overwhelming experiences of passionate intensity and altered consciousness, we are dependent on a safe and trusted parental or societal matrix to hold us. If we have been mocked by observers when we were swept up and our guard was down, we learn to connect expansive surrender with shame, and we may fear it as only an explosion or implosion of unbearable emotions. Inevitably when we have been abandoned in our overpowering emotionality, or even misused and/or scapegoated to contain societal and parental anxieties about it, we learn not the joys of surrender but the necessity of maintaining ever vigilant controls. Prevented from any safely mediated experience of our vivid emotional, somatic, and spiritual matrix, we may even lose access to our natural capacity for ecstatic expansion and the transformation of consciousness it brings. Yet the need to reawaken this potential haunts many of us who feel we cannot fit within the societal frames into which we were born.

Thus such moments of intimate participation in the matrix of flowing and encompassing energy are today increasingly sought and often treasured. Sometimes we seek ecstasy through our devotion to activities and substances that make us "high." Some of these, like drugs and alcohol, may threaten us with addiction. Sometimes we try to regain our connection to the ecstatic through pursuing the exciting secular activities that our culture permits or through imported spiritual disciplines—for example, in "native" or Eastern meditative and trance practices. Increasingly studied, experiences of ecstasy may also occur in a wide range of fully participatory creative activities including sex, sports, religion, and the arts. Many individuals are also seeking access to this matrix consciousness in deep levels of therapeutic work.[55] Our psychosomatic regressions into the overwhelming affects associated with early childhood are part of this work. Drawn by unresolved traumata and skewed personal bonds to re-experience and transform our relationship to these archaic energies, we may come to value their poignant intensities for themselves. Thus when the childhood wounds that brought us into therapy are worked through, the deep levels of experience that such healing demands can support new methods of evoking the vivid, numinous energies and new appreciation of the need for conscious service to their source. Moving beyond contemporary therapies, many who have found some degree of personal healing continue to seek experiences of ecstasy in spiritual and creative practices that connect us reverently to the matrix of individual, communal, and cosmic life.

The powerful fusion of the whole body with spirit both dissolves and expands our felt identity. It offers a taste of transcendence, and it may support creativity if we can endure and find form to express its grip on us. At other times we may feel only ravaged and reduced, perhaps motivated to struggle to learn to survive and manage ourselves before its onrush. We think of this overwhelming and integrative power in our individual lives as a deity and call upon it to make us whole and free by ravishing us.[56] In Jungian terms, experience of this larger Self transforms consciousness even as it seems to shatter or defeat the ego, that smaller focus we call our relatively constant sense of identity, volition, memory, and effectiveness. Sometimes we feel the primal energies as possession, obsession, or passion and can learn to step back from their seizures to sift through and claim what is possible to express creatively into daily life. Sometimes, in psychological terms, we call this force the archaic, grandiose self as we struggle to differentiate our personal consciousness from its utterly pervasive grip.

In the myths of Maeve, embodied life with all its profoundly moving sensations and emotions is also transcendent. It is this primary wholeness that holds and molds our individual destinies. We partially emerge from it as we discover our separate boundaries and make discriminations, but unless we become overly identified with these separate forms and ourselves as completely autonomous, we know we are also joined in its larger web. It is into this wholeness that we return for rest and healing. Jung called this unitary, prepsychological fusion of matter and spirit "psychoidal." Every personal complex or constellation of compelled emotion, behavior, and thought ultimately arises from energic patterns that are archetypally formed and based in what we hypothesize as this psychoidal level. Because personal and transpersonal, material and spiritual are still fused and unconditioned in the psychoidal level, we can reach through the fault layers of our personal complexes to touch again the energy patterns as they exist in their archetypal fullness. Here synchronistic and psychosomatic phenomena occur to affect us powerfully, both to undermine structural misconstellations and to provide access to deeper structures around which we may be able to reorient our lives. In psychotherapy the deepest healing and transformative restructuring of personal complexes happens at these levels through experience of the underlying and transcendent form-patterns coming through the whole intrapsychic, somatic, intersubjective, and environmental field. Since these patterns or archetypes of identity and relationship are inevitably misconstellated or only partially experienced in personal life, we can reexperience and come to terms with their deficits through exploring the ways these manifest in spiritually oriented psychotherapy. As the habitual, partial, and detrimental forms are made conscious and release their hold, we can then gain access to the previously unapprehended aspects of the archetypal energy patterns that underlie them. These ever larger and balanced potentials are held up for reflection in the symbolic images dreams bring us. They also constellate experientially in the intersubjective field between client and therapist through transference and counter-transference reactions and through the spontaneous and multileveled (conscious and unconscious) interchange. These moments evoke a shared sense of the deep archetypal structures underlying human relationships. Whether painful and/or wondrous, they can feel as numinous as those Jesus spoke of when he said "where two or three are gathered together in my name, there am I in the midst of them."[57]

The Celts related to the archetypal energy fields as aspects of their tribal deity. They used ritual means to enter into fervent participation with these suprapersonal potentials and to exit from the expanded states of divine possession.[58] We shall see that the rituals opening the doors to ecstatic communion with Maeve also involved the use of a mind-altering substance identified with the goddess.

Maeve as the Celtic Principle of Sovereignty

In Irish myth rulership was subject to a sacred pattern that remained alive among the Celts from the Stone Age. Since Maeve represented supreme power and authority in her people's lands, the Celtic goddess and the queens who represented her in the clan married the men chosen to be chiefs and/or were the mothers of such kings and the ancestress of the royal line.[59] This marriage empowered the rulers "in order that [they] will serve the interests of the queen and through her of the kingdom."[60] Thus the ancient nature goddess evolved into the principle and titular deity of sovereignty.[61] Long after these traditions of sacred kingship had changed in most of the rest of the Western World, the matrifocal Celtic tribes continued to venerate a sovereign and dominant goddess.

Irish chiefs married the eternal goddess of the land in a ritual communion and had sexual intercourse with her symbolic embodiment in her sacred animal or the actual queen. Claiming the goddess queen's liquor and body was the leader's coronation. It granted legal and spiritual dominion over the land. Without such a marriage he could not assess

tributes and taxes, for the men of Ireland would not convene
the Festival of Tara (at which such homages were paid) for "a
king with no queen."[62] Marriage to the goddess also magically
ensured the land's fertility and security, and the state of the
land gave evidence that the king was abiding in his
relationship to the goddess. Thus favored by the divine order
with which he was congruent, he ruled prosperously. "His
reign is good," said the poets who lavished praise on him.

*It was well with Ireland in the time of that king. It was not possible
to drink the waters of her rivers on account of the spawn of her fish;
it was not possible to travel her forests easily on account of the
amount of their fruit; it was not easy to travel her plains on account
of the amount of her honey, all of which had been granted him from
[now Christianized] heaven through the truth of his princedom.*[63]

Another description says,

*There was great bounty then . . . seven ships being brought to Indber
Colptha in June of every year, acorns up to the knee every autumn
. . . [imbas, great wisdom] over the Buas and the Boand [rivers]
each June, and an abundance of peace, so that no one slew his
neighbor anywhere in Eriu—rather that neighbor's voice seemed as
sweet as the strings of harps. From the middle of spring to the middle
of autum, no gust of wind stirred any cow's tail; there was no
thunder, no stormy weather in [the] . . . reign.*[64]

In Irish mythological history the goddess-queen
Maeve set out the conditions of kingship, chose and tested
her partners, and temporarily married those who passed the
kingship tests.[65] She delighted in making her partners vie
with each other to assess their qualities.[66] And like all Celtic
heroines she would "never tolerate self-abasement or self-
contempt. . . . She want[ed] a man conscious of his
responsibilities, and worthy of her esteem and love"[67] even if
at times her consort had to endure the goddess' sexual
attentions to rivals and ultimately his own replacement and
death.[68] As Maeve made clear to one of her husbands, whom
she commended for being "the kind of man [she] wanted,"
not "greedy or jealous or sluggish,"

*I asked a harder wedding gift than any woman ever asked before
from a man in Ireland—the absence of meanness and jealousy and
fear. If I married a mean man our union would be wrong, because*

*I'm so full of grace and giving. It would be an insult if I were more
generous than my husband, but not if the two of us were equal in
this. If my husband was a timid man our union would be wrong
because I thrive, myself, on all kinds of trouble. It is an insult for a
wife to be more spirited than her husband, but not if the two are
equally spirited. If I married a jealous man that would be wrong,
too: I never had one man without another waiting in his shadow.[69]*

Maeve presided over various counties where she
was deity of the land and also over the whole country from
the seat of the high kings at Tara. Her most ancient sacred
seat was at Cruachan in the western province of Connacht.[70]
Here at Carnfree the kings ritually married the goddess in the
ceremony of *Banfhis Rigi*. Maeve was also queen of King
Conchober of Ulster until she left him "through pride of
mind" and against his will, and he subsequently became
leader of the forces against her and her new consort in the
famous epic of *The Tain* or *The Cattle Raid of Cooley*. After
Conchober she again mated with men of Connacht, each of
whom became king "with the consent of Maeve if he became
her husband."[71] And she had many other suitors, for as she
herself put it in one tale, "I have never been without having
one man after another with me."[72] As the principle of
sovereignty, Maeve chose and refused whom she would.
Maeve Lethderg (Half-red, another of her names) thus
refused to let Cormac rule in Tara after his father's death.[73]
It was said of Maeve in Leinster, "great was the power of
M[aeve] over the men of Ireland, for she it was who would
not allow a king in Tara without his having herself as wife."[74]
Probably, as divine ancestress, she mated with the sons of her
partners too for the ritual period of nine generations in
succession.[75]

As the principle of authority, Queen Maeve
dominated the armies in *The Tain*, provided regal judgment in
"Bricriu's Feast," and instigated the sacred marriage *feis* of
many kings. "A shrewd and wise woman, being fierce and
merciless,"[76] it was she who came to symbolize the spirit of
sovereignty itself and the destiny of each particular chief on
whom she bestowed or from whom she withheld her favors.
As the warrior Ferdia told her in the medieval epic expressing

the struggle between the ancient matrifocal pattern and that of later patrifocal institutions,

You've a strong tongue, Medb, your kind husband's no curb. There's no doubt you are master on the [palace] mounds of Cruachan.[77]

Since the goddess' blessing was verified by tribal well-being and prosperity, the length of the king's reign depended on evidence of divine support. He was only king among the Celts insofar as he maintained order in nature and society by giving truthful judgments, defending the land, and living in accordance with his personal taboos (*gessa*). When tribal security and prosperity ended, their loss was deemed to be the king's responsibility. Since he was no longer congruent with the unfolding of good fate, he was removed from power. Often this removal was marked in myth by a sacrificial death ceremony. Since the land and the archetypal principle of sovereignty can support many changes of ruler, the goddess could marry and bear many kings. Nonetheless, the same king could not have two queens and still benefit the land and its people.

The king may have one time of lying with her. When his hour is over, his reign is irretrievably ended. No substitutes will do.[78]

The theme of the king's failing to prosper with a second wife or daughter recurs through the old tales as the new chiefs sought to consolidate personal and patrifocal rule in the face of older custom.

The mythic goddess-queen herself was immortal as the personification of the principle of sovereignty. The motif of self-renewal, even reincarnation, in the old tales symbolized her immortality. She was "her own mother and her own daughter from infinity to infinity."[79] Sometimes the myths tell of her aging and renewal with each of her many consorts. Sometimes she appears as her own daughter, identical with herself. Sometimes she appears as several princesses in the same story under different names that have the same

meaning. The symbolic fact of the immortality of the principle
of queenship was expressed historically by the matrilinear
Picts of Scotland. They held that the queen was the goddess
incarnate. Her daughter was her successor. If the king died
first, the queen might marry again; if she died, her widower
lost his kingship, which now belonged to the queen's
daughter's husband. The primacy of the goddess-queen was
also expressed in Irish custom. As late as A.D. 838, the king of
Munster raided Tara and abducted King Niall's queen as token
of the fact that, having subdued Niall, he was claiming
sovereignty through concrete possession of the queen's
person. Into the twentieth century, poets still pictured the
land of Ireland as a woman with "the walk of a queen"[80] or as
a queen languishing for her lost spouse, the rightful ruler
who gained his kingdom only through marriage to herself.

Maeve as Divine Appetite

Of Maeve it is written: "great was the power and the honour
and the dignity of M[aeve], and great was her desire about
everything."[81] The goddess of divine energy is also the
goddess of desire. She represents and expresses the pre-
patriarchal flow of ecstatic sexuality and the polymorphous,
passionate libido that fuels all our appetites. The Celts held
these sacred and honored them as a powerful, numinous
force that inevitably commanded obedience and could
sometimes be contained in ritual. As a modern scholar
explains, the Celtic goddesses were

*direct and dangerous and devastating like a storm . . . . [T]he loves
of the [goddesses and] heroines of the old sagas are like swift and
terrible visitations, speaking in sudden cries and violent actions.[82]*

In the old stories Queen Maeve, like other Celtic
goddesses and heroines, is overtly lustful. She offers her
chosen partners "the friendship of her thighs" when it suits
her seemingly arbitrary passion or need. In Medieval
Christian literature her magnetic energy is divorced from its

original rituals and the sacred purposes of the sovereignty *feis*, which drew their motivating power from the embodied ecstasies of the goddess. Thus in *The Tain* she is reduced to a lustful virago who uses the erotic passion aroused by herself and her daughter to motivate one warrior after another to fight to his death for her.[83] Other Celtic goddesses drew their chosen partners away from the society governed by outworn ruling principles symbolized by old kings who would not step down for the younger generation. Dierdre seized her young lover by the ears (or testicles as one modern commentator suggests) and demanded he go away with her; Grainne laid a compelling command (*geis*) on Diarmuid that he could not refuse without losing his honor and, hence, his life in the tribe. Such passions compelled the individual wanderings of these heroes away from their duties to the community chieftain and initiated them into the goddess' service. Similarly Tristan and even Cuchullain were led by their loins to follow their goddess-fated paths.[84]

As is true in India, in Celtic lands the ecstasies of sex were probably one of the deepest sources of religious experience until the church damned them and expurgated the myths.[85] In the story of Meilyr (see page 104), for example, we are told that he gained his visionary sight during lovemaking. Orgiastic rites, such as the folk dancing and lovemaking around the hilltop bonfires on Beltane, St. John's night, and Lughnasa as well as the sexual play at weddings and funerals, undoubtedly brought more erotic energy and ecstatic meaning to earthly endeavors than we can read through the screen of dour monastic censorship in the texts. All of these folk rites persisted in some form into the twentieth century in spite of the bishops' specific rantings against them.[86]

The force of desire that Maeve represents binds her lovers to her service. We know it may still fuel our search for experience of her powers as well as our passion for direct relationship to the transcendent—to Maeve herself. However, Roman-Christian, Medieval, Victorian, and even modern arbiters of established culture warned against such compelling zeal when they railed against sexuality. They wanted the goddess of desire married to the old king rather than motivating individuals to leave the established ways he came to represent. They feared the compelling voraciousness of divine appetite as the enemy of social stability. Thus the Catholic priest says in the film *Ryan's Daughter*, "Don't nurse your wishes. You can't help having them; but don't nurse your wishes, or sure to god, you'll end up by having them." He implies Ryan's daughter will make as terrible a mess of things in relation to the established order that forbids such behavior as did Tristan in his passion for Iseult or Diarmuid for Grainne. Too often we have been taught through shaming and instilled fear to hold back or to press all our passion into the vessels sanctioned by the collective.[87] Then as the righteous folk who scapegoat passionate Rosie Ryan in the film, we will have the security of our neighbors' approval, but we may remain untouched and untransformed by the forces calling us to the individual enthusiasms and conflicts through which our destiny unfolds.

To the extent that Western religions have co-opted archetypal appetite into preestablished forms and punished as sinners or heretics those following the passionate paths that may lead beyond those forms, those religions have attempted to control and curtail the possible wide individual variations motivated by desire. The inhibiting dogma had the benefit of helping to raise consciousness and even to discipline the indulgence in eruptive passions that can disrupt society. On the other hand, Western ascetic religions, in denying archetypal desire as a source of life and a primary pathway to access an individual's experience of transcendence have contributed to the splitting off of a primary source of vitality. Such repressive curtailment may force the passion Maeve represents to remain below the surface, unconscious. And when desirousness is unconscious and unmediated, it tends to come forth through the shadow mixed with power and aggression as coarseness, pathology, perversion, and addiction, or through sublimated forms that may lack its fully embodied visionary potential. Then it loses its place and balancing power within the whole pattern of archetypal drives. One of Freud's great contributions to the modern Eurocentric world was his emphasis on the pathologies that result from attempts to bury desire.

In Celtic stories exploring the primal levels of desirousness, the goddesses enraptured their lovers in the talons of raw passion and carried them off. Some stories tell us the hero was compelled by the goddess' ineluctable call and command—sometimes he was literally pulled to her by a golden apple that stuck to his hand. Some heroes heard the call and pined away until they could accept it. Others followed even when they had to suffer the tension between such divine passion and their affection and duty to their tribespeople, even when they had to flee from or battle the forces of the pursuing king to whom they had pledged their service. In all these ways we also may be unconsciously compelled to act out the desires that grip us and demand obedience. But in some myths the goddess also provided an important initiatory rite to test and reward those gripped by their fated hungers. As the source of appetite, Maeve also required a strong human awareness to confront and symbolically and verbally express the compelling desires. She required that her heroes know what they wanted and be able to speak it exactly and on the spot. For example when the warrior Cuchullain confronted the warrior goddess Scathach, she promised

any three things, the three highest desires of your heart . . . if you can ask them in one breath.

Thereupon the hero conveyed his desire for "thoroughness in his training, a dowry for his marriage, and tidings of his future," and these were granted.[88] We see here that the goddess required that her partners honor and also fervently hold, focus, and transmute raw libidinous need into individually willed symbolic discourse. Honed thus into a tripartite magical incantation, such wishes represented the

marriage of transpersonal desirousness with disciplined
individual intent. Inevitably wishes expressed in this ritual
were granted by the challenging goddess, and their fulfillment
provided the next destined step on the protagonist's path.

In this ancient rite the goddess of desirousness,
like the Jungian Self, does not seek repression of passionate
hungers but rewards the partner who can appropriately
respond to her demands and transform raw need into desires
specifically related to time, place, and person. As partner, the
goddess of life energy seeks one who is sovereign, who knows
and can succinctly express a specific spectrum of desires. To be
able to name three wants suddenly on demand and in
expectation of their fulfillment requires freely flowing,
spontaneous access to passion and a clear, articulated sense of
entitlement. Such thrice-focused desire is remarkably difficult
for modern rational consciousness, which is often too far
removed from its repressed libidinous sources or in distorted
relation to them through learned fear and addictive patterns.
How far removed is easy to see. All we have to do at any
moment is to ask ourselves the goddess' question: what three
things do I most want now and here? When there is a limp
sense of entitlement, asking oneself and seeking to answer
the question exercises a necessary psychological muscle.

Maeve and the Displayed Woman

Many relief sculptures on medieval French and British
churches and Irish castles and church buildings portray a
female with legs spread.[89] Worldwide from the Paleolithic
period on, the birth-giving mother has been depicted as a
powerful "displayed woman" with upraised hands, prominent
navel, and with her open legs revealing her huge genitals.[90]
Called by their Irish name, Sheela-na-gig,[91] these stone
figures are recognized as portraits of the earth goddess and
were probably only imported into Ireland in this form in
Norman times. Yet in these blatant renditions focusing on the
vulva as font and tomb of life, we can visually experience

some of the powers represented by the ancient earth goddess, powers that infused the far older erotic rituals, dances, myths, and even sacred architecture of the Neolithic age in many areas of the world.

The Sheelas, like Maeve herself, reveal the mystery of the earth goddess and the female body as the ever flowing source of life itself. In ancient lore the earth goddess' vulva was felt to be the source of the sun's rebirth in winter. Already in the fourth millennium B.C., the passages into the womb-centers of the Irish mound temples were positioned to be penetrated yearly by the sun's rays.[92] The sun-box passage that allows penetration by the winter solstice sunrise into the Newgrange mound represents the open vulva of the cosmic goddess revered in sacred architecture in Ireland before the pyramids were built. At Newgrange the sun's rays enter the dark vaginal passage of the earth mound to signal the start of a new solar year. At nearby Knowth and Dowth the equinoctial sunrises and sunsets reach the inner chambers. This ancient sense of the earth as mother of the sun persisted into the Christian era. A twelfth-century A.D. English Christian invocation is still addressed to "Earth [as] Divine Goddess, Mother Nature," and calls upon her because she "generates all things, and brings forth anew the sun which you have given to the peoples."[93] Across the globe in Micronesia, sculptures of displayed women sit above the village men's houses, facing the sun. In actuality, Samoan girls sat with spread legs facing the sun in a traditional cosmic fertility ritual.[94] We can wonder whether the vulva opens to receive the fertilization of the sun's penetration or whether the vulva thus displayed brings forth the sun. In the paradoxes of magic-level consciousness, both possibilities coexist.

Until recently it was the custom for brides on the way to their weddings to have to view or touch the Sheela-na-gigs on church walls to arouse sexual desire and magically to ensure fertility.[95] Sometimes the Sheelas were also touched to facilitate easy childbirth. On some of the figures we can see the marks where generations of worshippers have rubbed smooth the stone of the bellies or vulvas. Sometimes the

figures are scarred where they have been rubbed with pebbles
to scrape off some of the stone dust that was believed to have
magical powers.[96]

Like the Sheelas, the goddess Maeve was said
to have had huge genitalia, symbolizing abundant fertility.
In Maeve's myths her vulva was the source of fertilizing
waters just as it was her original vessel of sovereignty. Her
libation cup of red liquor was identified with the rhythmically
flowing, sacred vulvae of the queens representing her in the
sacred marriage rites. The vulva then represents to the
ancient Celts the source and grail of life just as it does in
India.[97] It suggests the instinctive power of the spiritual
feminine and the sacred body mysteries of monthly
bloodshed, mating, pregnancy, birth, and death that underlie
the cycle of life. In these rites, like those involving the
Sheelas, the mysteries of the body can be seen and
worshipped as an analog of the endless process of transformation that incorporates what comes in, assimilating and
destroying its old forms to engender new ones. This process
ensures the regeneration that follows destruction in the
seasonal cycles of the religions of nature.

Over church windows and on graveyards where
they join the taking of life to the giving of life, the huge
genitalia of the displayed woman open to reveal the power of
the vulva as an entrance to tomb and womb.[98] Thus the figures
force the worshipper to consider the mystery of death and
renewal both in this world and projected onto the next. As a
divine mystery, the sacred body of the goddess then represents
the source from which we emerge and in which we find our
rest—the source that creates, motivates, sustains, regenerates,
and receives back all life. Focus on the dark vulva makes the
figure a monstrance of the origin and goal of transformation.

As Norman overlords invaded the British Isles
and claimed power in Ireland, they secularized the motif of
the Sheela-na-gig and used it to affirm their right to rule.
Then the displayed female became an apotropaic guardian

and an emblem of the principle of sovereignty by which the Normans claimed their power. In Ireland its appearance heraldically carved onto castle walls may have signified that the non-native owner of the keep was asserting his rights over the area, proclaiming with the image that his seizure of territory was blessed and defended by the old goddess of the land.[99]

Over time the Roman Church also changed the Old Religion's reverence for the displayed female. Sometimes its importance was redrawn to fit dogma. Thus we can find the age-old goddess with vegetation springing from her genitals on an English church baptismal font where souls were ritually birthed into the Church. More often the great and holy vulva as cup of sovereignty and life disappeared, and the original Celtic grail was replaced by the chalice holding Christ's blood. This cup came to signify mystical communion with the sacrificed son of the father and obedience to the Roman Church's rule in Europe. Rural folk, however, still dimly remember the vulva of the fertile goddess in the ritual placement of a horseshoe over a door to pour forth luck. The esoteric rituals of the witches of the Old Religion and the Tantric-based rites of the Western occult traditions still revere the sacred female body as the representation of the goddess' forms and energies. But in secular life the value given to the expansive ecstasies of orgasm and birth shrank as the importance of the less permeable rational ego consciousness grew. Freud himself called orgasm "a little death of the ego."

In church art the once sacred vulva of the goddess also became an entrance to Hell. No longer seen as a portal into visionary, pleromatic consciousness, it became an emblem of dangerous ecstasy that circumvented church dogma to grant individual experience of the transpersonal spirit. No longer seen as the symbol of life, death, and regeneration, it became the passage through which deadly sinners entered their eternal torture. Still feared as the portal of pleasure and orgiastic lovemaking, the vulva was made dangerously devouring and said to be analogous to the head of the Medusa. This demonized genital became an image that terrorizes the Western, rational psyche. Made into a toothed maw, it expresses the fact that our passions, once they are crippled and shamed, become dangerously devouring and eruptive. Rather than leading us to claim the substance and spirit of life, they compel and frighten us. As stoppered energies clamoring to express themselves, they become the fuel of our greed and addictions. Their eruptive power underlies our anxious need for soothing, and their crushing underlies our depressive need for enlivenment. Such embodied passions, when denied their sacrality, do not mirror and mediate ecstatic transcendence. In their distorted demonic forms, they possess us and rouse the terrors that alienate us from the well-springs of life.

The darkly dangerous aspect of Maeve is also depicted in some of the medieval Sheela-na-gig reliefs. Then the goddess appears as a starved and shriveled hag, and the yawning mouth of her womb suggests that she represents insatiable appetite. From the perspective of fearful and resistant consciousness, she is the demanding, sacred tyrant who takes one man after another and has her way with all the consorts she claims. In these sculptures divine appetite appears like a voracious terror, a giant "Gimme" or "hungry cunt" clamoring to be filled and threatening to devour whatever enters it. We meet this appetite with horror when we cannot abide the ruthless power of the life process to enforce its demands on us. We meet it also in the compulsive force behind addictions.

Then the open mouth of the womb suggests a greed that devours life itself. The death crone's bony ribs and haggard face remind us of the loathsome goddess who withheld the regenerating waters of life until she was kissed. Only the brave can endure such an embrace, the ancient Irish said, because it holds the fear of encountering death herself. This hag invites us to find the courage to penetrate the tomb of all our hopes and our safe, accustomed life. Her terrible seduction may mean regeneration and transformation for the destined and prepared initiate. But without the reverence, humility, and strength to accept suffering and the many deaths that the ever changing life process requires us to experience, she is the maw that draws us into our numbing addictions, our frenzied passions, and the living deaths to which they bind us.

We also know this starved death hag as the possessed cravings in us that have no empathy for self or other and no care for life. In her we see mirrored our own devouring appetite that, even if it kills us or another, makes us clutch abjectly for what we think and hope will stop the hunger. Such starved and destructive ravenousness beggars us and fuels our addictions because we feel only its painful emptiness and cannot sustain in memory the quieter moments of fulfillment. This devouring appetite is analogous to what some psychologists assume are the infant's fantasies of destroying the breast with its own voracious need. While we can project such thoughts onto infancy, we inevitably do uncover this fantasy during the therapy of adult addicts in recovery (and also in work with others with early structural wounds to their sense of identity that underlie their psychopathology). They fear that when their need is unstoppered and sober, its unleashed craving mixed with old but still active rage and despair will destroy the nourishing therapist and themselves. Feelings of such freshly opened passion and fears of more deprivation may lure them into another binge to try to close the gape. Orally or sexually, but always aggressively, such need is desperate to fill itself and/or to be filled. Like Maeve, who wanted a bull in one story and was willing to ravage Ireland to get it, such raw demandingness is analogous to the greed and primeval envy that destroys human connections to bounty because it both fears that it can never get enough and must vengefully destroy the potentials of receiving because it *has* never had enough. Here Maeve is also an image of the devouring and compulsive hold of addiction itself—the death hag who binds us, overwhelms our irreverent attempts to rule our lives, and takes our arrogant omnipotence back into her fragmenting and fatal embrace.

Maeve as Inebriation

As if all this were not enough, the word, maeve (written *meadhbh* or *medb* in Gaelic) tells us more. It is a title that means "the inebriating one," "the one who makes drunk," or "she who is of the nature of mead."[100] Mead is a special drink that was used in Celtic ritual. It is made from honey, which was one gift of the fertile earth goddess.[101] Maeve personifies the honey-based power that inebriates, inflames, expands, dissolves, and radically transforms consciousness. This power was a divinity for our Celtic ancestors, as it was in many ancient cultures. The ecstatic states roused by mead were considered sacred and used ritually and communally for the tribe's benefit—by all levels of Celtic society.

In the Indo-Aryan tradition, which runs into both Celtic and Vedic lore, the goddess of "sovereignty is a bride, the server of a powerful drink, and the drink itself."[102] As we shall see, the queen goddess Maeve gave herself as *medb* in the cup. The term *derg flaith* means both "red ale" and "red sovereignty." It intimates, by the Gaelic homophonic equivalences used by the druids in their poetry, the actual confluence of inebriation and rule. The figure of Maeve was associated with the otherworld color red. In the time of the Celtic chieftains, she was goddess of battle and the red of battle blood often spilled in the passionate conflicts surrounding kingship consolidations. Maeve of Cuala was *Lethderg*, Half-Red, or Red-Sided. Maeve of Connacht was described as having red skin. She was the battle goddess in *The Tain* and the creatrix source of the powerful, three-river creating "gush of blood."[103]

The cup of *medb* was filled with red claret or ale in Christian times.[104] It represents the divine principle of sovereignty and the wisdom and the fertile power needed to

rule over tribal lands. Maeve Lethderg would let no king rule,
an old poem tells us, unless "the ale of Cuala comes to
him."[105] Originally, the cup may have contained blood
representing the source of life. Some scholars feel the drink in
the sovereignty ritual's most archaic form was powerful,
sacred, and dreaded menstrual blood,[106] the creative life-
essence that flows in harmony with lunar cycles and not from
wounding. Menstrual blood was once thought to coagulate
within the womb to make and nourish a child and then to be
released again with childbirth.[107] Such blood was also
considered to be the source of inner power, wisdom, healing,
and eternal life.[108] Through drinking Maeve's mead, the Celtic
king magically became—via oral assimilation—potent, wise,
whole, and reborn from the goddess of the land.[109] Thus he
could be Maeve's consort and phallically penetrate the
awesome representative of the goddess and attain the stature
necessary for ruling the tribe.

There is archaeological evidence that long before
800 B.C. when the Celtic tribes arose in the mountains around
Hallstadt (in modern Austria), the Beaker People, who began
to migrate into England from North Europe ca. 3000 B.C.,
were already hard drinking.[110] They probably brought some
form of mead making with them. Two thousand years after
the Beaker People reached Britain in the first millennium B.C.,
Gallic Celts imported wine and wine vessels from the south,
and their traders were intent upon maintaining access to
Mediterranean wine-producing areas.[111] As the Roman writer
Atheneus tells us, "The rich men [of northern Gaul] drink
wine from Italy or Marseilles, and they drink it neat."[112] The
renowned Celtic scholar Anne Ross writes that in Ireland,
"Whereas ale was the favorite drink at the raucous, random
feasts of the boastful chariot warriors and their lords, mead
was the ritual drink at the great calendar festivals . . . . The
official name of the Assembly Hall at Tara was *Tech
Midchuarta*, 'The House of Mead-Circling.' "[113] Into the
nineteenth century, Celtic rulers were judged by the
generosity of their mead feasts. Clan chiefs on the Isle of Man
were expected to provide a certain amount of wine every

year for this purpose. Even today a modern Englishwoman describes her people as "usually two drinks under par,"[114] expressing their habituated need for the life enhancing effects of alcohol.

While the alcoholism among many descendants of these early Celts manifests the debilitating effects of the Celtic love of drink, it is, however, an ancient love with sources in archetypal and spiritual as well as physiological terms. Humans the world over have used grains, grapes, mescaline, peyote, coca, tobacco, palm, and other plants (as well as certain animal secretions) to prepare "divine" intoxicants. There is evidence that other substances besides alcohol itself were also used in ancient Ireland. The opium poppy is known to have been widely grown there in prehistoric times and may have had ritual uses we have not yet rediscovered.[115] Some modern scholars suggest there may also have been early shamanic cult use of the Amanita mushroom. Although not presently native in Ireland, the potent hallucinogen may once have grown under the birch trees and evergreens of ancient forests or been brought as an item of trade.[116]

Indeed the methods and rituals of inebriation lie in the behaviors of our animal kin, and many species insistently seek inebriating substances in laboratory trials. There is also abundant evidence that animals and birds in the wild intentionally partake of intoxicating substances, which are available to them seasonally in the form of fermented fruits and plants.[117]

Since debilitating and "excessive love of wine" among Gallic soldiery was noted by Roman writers, we cannot assume that the Celts lived in some golden age where alcoholism was never a problem. Diodorus Sicilus described Celtic warriors who "drink so greedily . . . that when drunk they fall into a deep sleep or into fits of temper."[118] Livy blames their penchant for alcohol for the ease with which an exiled Roman dictator and his small army "cut the throats of the sodden Gauls as if they were sheep."[119] We also know from the Welsh bard Aneurin's poems that drunkenness contributed to a grim military debacle. He writes of all the hosts who went down to battle at Catraeth:

Though we drank all night by candlelight
and the taste came sweet to the tongue,
the bitterness left in our mouths
will stay long. [120]

Nonetheless, the extraordinary stories and rites of Maeve offer us a glimpse into the ancient, social and sacred uses of inebriation. They point to what is missing in contemporary patterns of intoxication that fail to initiate the modern drinker into a conscious and "ad-dicted" or devoted relationship with the divine.[121] To experience the drink, *medb*, as a sacred substance and its inebriating powers as the goddess Maeve can produce initiatory ecstasy and transformation.[122] The experience of ingesting preparations of such substances is mind altering. It loosens and dissolves habitual boundaries of consciousness and habitual structures of perception and cognition. Used ritually, it allows the communicant to reconnect, *re-ligio*, to unconscious affects and lost or buried perceptual and behavioral capacities. In psychological terms the *medb* and similar substances and mind-altering behaviors facilitate the participant's opening towards the matrix of consciousness and the Self where as yet unmediated progressive as well as regressive qualities await our appreciation.

The infusion of these qualities into everyday, more rational consciousness can either initiate the ritually prepared drinker into an altered state and new identity or make the unprepared drinker toxic. This double potentiality exists in the images of Maeve herself. Like the displayed female sculptures, she may pour forth abundance as the birth-giving mother, a source of transformation, or she may devour and destroy as the starved death hag. She appears in mythic tales as both the beauty, who symbolizes and bestows the new consciousness that enables initiation and sovereignty, and as the leper, who binds and kills those who would derogate and misuse her powers. The same intrinsic polarity is imaged in an Irish tale as the contents of two cups held by sisters of the hero's initiating goddess. The youth is warned that one will fill his need and the other will poison him. When choosing, he must follow the goddess' guidance, submitting his will to the transcendent wisdom of his destiny and the goddess' power over death and life.[123]

Maeve as Death Goddess

Like many deities Maeve is associated with death as well as fertility, inebriation, and initiations. In myth she destroys kings who spurn her and sends warriors to their doom. From the cave called *Oweynagat* (the Cave of the Cats) in her sacred cult center at Cruachan, spirit hosts are said to emerge into the world of mortals every *Samhain* (our Halloween). Monstrous animals and red birds surge from its mouth to ravage the land or threaten mighty heroes, and the dread Morrigan, triple goddess of life, death, and war comes forth at the beginning of the great battles immortalized in the epic *Tain Bo Cuailnge*.[124] Referred to in myth as the most important entrance to the otherworld, *Oweynagat* was also called *Sidh Sinche*, the nipple of Cruachan.[125] The hero Fraech was carried into it by a host from the otherworld for miraculous healing. From it came the cats that carried the sun disk to its midsummer setting. Within its vaults, druid ceremonies took place. The names and stories clustered around this sacred opening into the earth juxtapose death, nourishment, initiation, and healing to remind us that our ancestors readily felt the ancient goddess' powers over the whole cycle. We meet the same motif in the shrine at Catal Huyuk (Anatolia) where the sculpted nipples of the goddess contain vulture beaks.[126]

To peoples embedded in the Great Round of nature and its inconstant cycles, death was equated with "sleeping with the Mother."[127] It was a transformation presaging rebirth analogous to sunset and the burial of seed in the womb-tomb of the mother and to the initiatory incubations within the caves and mounds that changed consciousness. Thus the ancient Celts seemed to their Roman observers unafraid of the passage between life and death. Indeed their warriors were intimate companions of the death goddess, engaging in struggles with her and knowing "the way of the black ravens" that feast on their corpses. The heads of the slain on her battlefield "gardens" were called the mast or seed food of Macha, the Ulster war and mare goddess. In one tale the wolf devouring his slain comrades is called merely "an ant of the ancient earth" by a dying hero. In the tales of the Bronze- and Iron-age tribes, these figures represent the cosmic neolithic goddess as the devourer who eats the dead, thus taking them back into the source from which all life emerges.

Images of an accessible otherworld under the earth or in the happy Isles of the Blest made the Irish feel that their deceased ancestors dwelt nearby and were able to be roused to answer human needs. The spirits of the dead revisited the homes of the living after dark and on the festivals marking the open cracks in the agricultural year, especially at *Samain* and *Beltane* when the new winter and summer cycles began. Mortals and denizens of the supernatural worlds had frequent concourse at caves, mounds, trees, and water places where the veil between this world and the next was felt to be easily permeable. Humans were called to participate in the wars and festivities of the *sidh* people as often as the spirits came forth to mingle and meddle in human affairs.

Yet we, who treasure the value of individual life emerging from the background of all we find unconscious, have a more final sense of mortality. Already so separated from the matrix of nature, we feel that death is a less readily bridged separation. Unlike the Ulster heroes who boasted of their bravado during bloody carousals where the drinkers cut each other down or thought to repay debts in the otherworld, we are closer to Dierdre when she laments the tragic betrayal and death of her beloved. Unlike the Celtic heroes, who were also confident they would live forever for their tribes in bardic praise poems, we are less certain of rebirth in the eternal cycle of life, death, and regeneration.

For us Maeve may be the dangerous death mother and adversary. While her inebriation can cause the loss of ordinary, limited consciousness, the psychic death of personal identity, and the mystical expansion of consciousness, it can also provide a means of evading life,[128] unleashing destructiveness, and leading to suicide and actual death. We acknowledge with conscious pain that intoxication can result in the obliteration of consciousness, enslavement to addictions, and the same drunken stupors that enabled Roman soldiery to overrun their Gallic counterparts. Maeve is thus the symbol of the irrational force underlying self-obliteration and the extinction of individual life, life that is felt more precious because it is so fragile and hard won.

To withstand her as death dealer requires repeated and valiant efforts. The heroic ego, personified in the young solar deity Cuchullain in *The Tain*, symbolizes the qualities of ardor, trained strength, intelligence, indomitable will, and honor required by those who have stepped outside the ancient round of nature. Cuchullain stands alone against Maeve and all her forces. He is the warrior whose name is remembered as the quintessential opposer of the death goddess, the defender of his people, land, and herds against her incursions. Yet even he does not slay his adversary when at the end of the battles he has the opportunity. Maeve leaves the war and reverts to her ancient powers of earth creating, letting loose three rivers with her menstrual flow. The greatest warrior does not slay her because he still needs the goddess of threatening death to be the adversary and passion that motivate his short, praiseworthy, and heroic life. He needs her, too, as the source of renewal and blesses her in another form for succoring him with milk from her cow.[129] He stands within a culture that still knew and revered the fact that she could not be slain.

Chapter 2

Inebriation as Initiation

In Celtic usage the powers of Maeve's inebriant were sacred
and often managed by careful preparation and ritual
communion as they are in many religions. The preparation
established readiness for the onset of the ritual's altered and
fluid consciousness, and it also structured alternative channels
into which the freed energy and vision might flow. The rituals
themselves were containers supporting the participants'
loosened consciousness. They mediated the drink's powerful,
mind-altering effects. They focused intensified awareness
into forms that were accessible and meaningful to the
communicants. Thus collective preparation and sacred ritual
forms enabled the participants' relatively de-structured
awareness to move under the influence of the *medb* into
culturally desirable new patterns.

Celtic society was differentiated roughly according
to functional roles—warriors, farmers and herders, druids and
poets, and rulers.[1] These different segments of Celtic society
had their own particular ceremonies and purposes for using
the *medb*. Each partook of the sacred drink to overcome
inhibiting constrictions, to expand and support new structures
of consciousness, and thus, to enhance specific capacities to
serve the tribe. Because the four tribal functions are analogous
to functions required today of a single individual to live an
adequately balanced and fulfilled life, looking at them can
provide us with templates through which we can also explore

some contemporary uses of drugs and alcohol. We still use alcohol and other inebriating substances to court expanded consciousness, a wider and more intense or more secure sense of self, and enhanced functioning. Through inebriation, we try ultimately to satisfy what Jung called "the spiritual thirst of our being for wholeness, expressed in medieval language [as] the union with god."[2] Understanding how the rituals of Maeve were structured as containers for expanded consciousness within the Celtic cultural matrix can help us to see ourselves. In chapter 5 we will look at some parallels between tribal uses and contemporary misuses to discover what is missing in today's fragmented and dissociated rituals of the *medb*. We can then see the ways that modern addictions represent debased forms of the ancient rituals. First, however, we must understand the *medb* rites in ancient Irish culture.

Warrior Initiation

For Celtic warriors the long period of preparation for battle, which included hospitality and training at the camp of their war-chief, was described as a "mead-feast" or a "wine-feast." We have archaeological reminders of its import and scope. The forty-year-old Celtic warrior chieftain buried at Hochdorf (now in Germany) took his mead feast with him to the otherworld. In his grave stood a bronze cauldron holding the sediment of 400 liters of fermented honey or mead.[3] Nearby hung the ornamented drinking horns of eight choice companions and the larger one of the chieftain himself, which could hold a draught of five liters.[4] In myth we are told that "At any time in [the Ulster chief] Conchobor's room there were thirty noble heroes drinking out of Gerg's vat, which was always kept full."[5] "It could hold a hundred measures of coal-black drink, enough to fill the men of Ulster for the whole evening."[6]

Participation in the communal *medb* ritual by living Celtic warriors

bound the[m] . . . in a relationship of absolute fidelity to their
chieftain [who was the ritual server of the drink]. When, at his
command, they have gone forth to battle and fought without
flinching until struck down by the foe, they are said to have "paid
their mead."[7]

The warriors' honor, solemnized by the mead communion,
bound them to fight on. Alcohol and the spirit of *participation*
mystique in the group quelled the drive towards self-
preservation that might have urged them to flee. And by
fighting and dying heroically, they achieved immortal fame
for themselves and their chief.[8] Such fame in the emergent
patriarchal culture of the Celtic aristocracy gave each warrior
the recognition that nascent individual exhibitionism
required and confirmed primary allegiance to the idealized
paternal chief and the war god.[9] For example, the Ulster hero
Cuchulainn willingly took up his arms on a day that the
tribal druid augured would bring undying fame and only a
short life. He also fought to the death the only son born to
him, a brilliant young fighter named after his mother in the
poignant tale "The Death of Aife's Son." Carrying the dying
boy up the shore to his chief and fellow warriors, he claimed
his terrible victory for the glory of the impersonal father
principle and "for the honor of Ulster."[10] Doing so, he
sacrificed the personal paternity that had once been his
dearest wish.

The Gododdin, a Welsh epic of the sixth century
AD, is full of references to the "wine drink and wine talk of
the soldiers"[11] who "went down to Catraeth to pay for [the
war leader's] drink"[12] with the willing sacrifice of their lives.
Indeed, the value of their lives was considered equal to their
feast of mead. The bard, one of only three survivors of the
bloody defeat, tells us the warriors "drank yellow, sweet,
ensnaring mead." Here the mead ensnared them "because it
was the symbol of a bond that led to ineluctable disaster. This
was a bond of the warriors' own choosing. For them renown,
achieved at whatever cost, was the supreme good."[13]
Although they all died, their poet extols the warriors even as
he laments them, and he praises their chief. In one stanza he

compliments the war-maddened leader as a "death hound" and "butcher":

After their drinking,
before the broad-chested charge of their horses,
this death hound
piled raven meat
high on the skyline.
Princes falling like cut green barley
butchered in clover.
The best of the wine cellar
kept us lively
before that. [14]

Among poems attributed to Merlin by the neobards of the 12th and 13th centuries is one that tells us of the close ties forged over *medb* between war chiefs and their druidic advisors:

I have drunk wine in a shining goblet
with the chieftains of the cruel war.
My name is Myrddin, son of Morvryn.
I have drunk wine in a cup
with the chieftains of devouring war.[15]

Celtic warriors—male and female—used alcohol then as a communion to bond them in sacred loyalty to their war chief and to the tribal deity whose passionate infusion granted them the immortality of which the keepers of the heroic oral tradition would forever sing.

The wine they drank was also a battle stimulant and enhanced their capacity for fierce actions.[16] It inhibited their debilitating fear and lowered their consciousness of pain. Thus Maeve's consort Aillil commanded, "Give wine to any . . . [warrior] who comes—it will give him courage."[17] The *medb* also helped to unleash battle frenzy—an altered state of transformative rage induced by another potential intoxicant, the hormone adrenaline, itself a source of extraordinary power with a potential for creating experiences of *exstasis*. In Celtic myth the Ulster hero Cuchullain asked his charioteer on numerous occasions when he flagged in battle to induce his adrenaline rage, called his "warp spasm," by shaming his honor with insults. Then he was physically transformed into a terrifying and invincible warrior. Such wildly possessing rage turned the human fighters into demonic/divine beserkers, avatars of their fiercely guarding totem animal deity—the death hound or wolf.[18]

In psychological terms we would say that the *medb* muted the boundaries between the warriors' consciousness of mortality and the powerful, eruptive affects and timeless, magical consciousness of the archaic self.[19] It infused the Celtic warriors with its powers to instill and compel actions based in divine grandiosity.[20] It inflated them. The *medb* put them in touch with daemonic transpersonal energies that enhanced their already trained capacities to battle. At one with the war goddess through their ritual ingestion of her as the *medb*, the warriors became filled with the unimpeded focused power drive that supports fearlessness before death and heroic action against an adversary.

The still common outbreak of fighting among the younger males at the end of Irish rituals—wakes, pilgrimages, weddings, and fairs (and now hurley and soccer games)— harks back to the ancient mead-feast. The intoxicated participants often finish their celebrations with rowdy fights from which even today the children must be protected.[21] The bishops through history have protested these contests of strength and the "obscene" games[22] and "lewd songs and brutal tricks" of their drunken parishioners, calling them "immodest [and rough] games, which suppress the memory of Death in the minds of those present" and detract from "the sacred rites of the Church."[23] Like those in other cultures who participated in ritual funeral battles, the Irish may unconsciously maintain the orgiastic pagan forms to express and celebrate a fuller spectrum of exuberant life energy. Thus not only do these fights allow for vivid communal participation among the males to express the anger and anxiety often connected with loss, they also provide balance for the solemn rituals of mourning.

In the modern world many soldiers use drugs and alcohol during duty at the front. One of my clients became addicted to marijuana while fighting in Vietnam. Another became alcoholic while serving his term with NATO forces in Germany. On the business front where pressures to perform and fears for survival can also feel massive, many individuals also resort to drugs and alcohol for purposes similar to those of the Celtic warriors.

Kinship Ceremonies

Celtic tribespeople used the medb in their seasonal festivals to celebrate and motivate their work to ensure nourishment from the earth and herds, which were all also aspects of the divine nature goddess Maeve. The great Assemblies brought the people together at their sacred grove, wellspring, riverside, or hilltop. The freely flowing drink helped to cement their kinship as much as the communal sacrifices, dances, games, competitions, displays of music, poetry, and storytelling, and the trade and legal settlements that also took place.

Alcohol blurs the sense of individual boundaries and separating differences and thus serves to enhance feelings of sacred and convivial incorporation with the whole tribe. It relaxes inhibitions and heightens the mind's attunement to revelry. In each drinker it creates an experience of *participation mystique* with the community and makes a communion of souls who partake together of their divinity—the very concrete mead or *medb* that is the goddess Maeve.

Seasonal and astronomic time, which is an aspect of the goddess' cosmic cycle, structured the tribespeoples' participation in the sacred feasts. Poet-musicians sang the stories that mirrored the people's sacred history to themselves and provided the music for their impassioned dancing. The rulers who provided the abundantly flowing mead were judged stingy and satirized if their mead halls were not bountiful.[24] Druids performed the rituals, and druid law forbade criminal offenses during the feast periods when close communion and altered consciousness required safe containment.

Besides the seasonal communal feasting, the Celts had a specific professional class whose high rank depended on their providing food and drink to any traveler desiring it. These hospitallers institutionalized and secularized the ancient rituals of hospitality. They welcomed and abundantly feasted all who came to their "great drinking halls" [*midchuairt*] just as the kings entertained guests at their courtly mead halls.[25]

Modern carousals honoring the year-king consort of the goddess, John Barleycorn, who is planted, grown, cut down, and threshed to make ale, take place at the festival of first plowing in Britain. Echoes of other customs honoring the goddess as the earthly source of mead survive also in solstice rituals and in the modern peasantry's secular but orgiastic participation in harvest frivolity. Until the mid-20th century in Ireland, there was abundant dancing around and over the bonfires on Beltane, Lughnasa, and St. John's Eve.[26] We may still have a blast, go out on the town, load up, and drink our fill to participate in the New Year or St. Patrick's Day.[27] Such patterns of binge drinking often start in adolescence. Many students in high school and college today feel they need a drink and/or some drugs to blur a sense of separateness and make it easier to bond with their peers.

Behind all of these modern orgies are the ancient and sacred seasonal rites. Their numinosity is still honored albeit unconsciously and often negatively. We still may partake of the *medb* to mark our accomplishments and to celebrate our harvests and the rituals of hospitality when we commune with one another in the full seasons of life. Like the ancient Celts, we take her spirits into ourselves to honor the expansive powers of the fertile goddess, who grants our bounty and our struggles and also supports our ease and our efforts. The Neolithic pattern lives on under later suppressions just as childhood patterning persists throughout our lives.

Analogously, we release ourselves in such social situations, sometimes with the assistance of alcohol, from responsible adult behavior and return to childish or childlike abandon and to a sense of *participation mystique* with the whole group.

Druid-Poet Initiation

Celtic druid-shamans and poets knew that "[i]ntoxication has . . . given humans sights to see, voices to listen to, thoughts to ponder, and altered states of consciousness to explore."[28] They knew that "Wine expands, unites, and says Yes," as William James wrote. "[I]t brings the votary from the chill periphery of things to the radiant core; it makes him for the moment one with truth"[29]—the truth of a unitary energic reality underlying and suffusing the multiplicity of its sensed discrete forms. In many mythologies this apperception of "the wisdom and spiritual exaltation that transcend[s] reason"[30] was equated with an elixir of immortality. In Ireland the divine ale was brewed by the god Gobniu, in Wales by the goddess Ceridwen, in India by the gods together who churned *soma* from the cosmic ocean.

Like shaman-priests in many cultures, the Celtic druids and *fili* were described as going into trance so that their bodies might be taken over by the inspiration that speaks through them.[31] They may have used the sacred *medb* and analogous substances to stimulate visions as well as for ritual purification, mystic communion with the supernatural, and the attainment of wisdom and prophetic powers that such widened and deepened consciousness brings.[32] Stories of Bran's Company of the Wondrous Head, of Finn, and Taliesin describe potions that bring mystical knowledge. Whether they were libations in great god Bran's skullcup, the broth of the magic fish caught from the sacred well of knowledge, or the goddess' cauldron brew, these drinks initiated the participants into vastly expanded and intensified states of consciousness. The companions of Bran shared an initiation ritual, communal bliss, and perhaps the knowledge of druidic mysteries. Finn and Taliesin acquired the language of animals and the magical skills to shapeshift, view distant events, and discover truth.

We can still find literary evidence in medieval Celtic lore of the druid-poet's ritual communion. The fairy queen served her kiss and an apple to Thomas the Rhymer, enabling him to see with otherworld vision and to express the wonders he glimpsed in poetry.[33] Taliesin drank three drops from the goddess' vat of steeped herbs and gained magic and mystic powers permitting his rebirth as a magus or druid.[34] He sang of his vision of being present throughout world history and of his capacities to move into the future and shapeshift after his initiation. Still drunk with the grandeur of vision and the love of words, images, and poetry itself, he sings of his consciousness as it has been identified, we would say, with a trans-ego perspective or "integrated . . . in a universe beyond time and space."[35]

Primary chief bard am I to Elphin [the young king]
And my original country is the region of the summer stars . . .
I have been in the galaxy at the throne of the Distributor . . .
I have been loquacious prior to being gifted with speech . . . .
I am a wonder whose origin is not known.[36]

I got poetic inspiration
*   from the cauldron of Ceridwen . . .*
And I was moved
*   through the entire universe;*
And I shall remain till doomsday,
*   upon the face of the earth.*
And no one knows what my flesh is—
*   whether meat or fish.* [37]

Celtic bards were often rewarded with wine as well as gold by the chiefs whose praises they sang. An eleventh-century ecclesiastical scholar, honored in terms of the older tradition that equates the druidic singer with the godhead, was praised as "a magical mead-sage who quaffs ale."[38] Writers still sing of the value of wine to enhance artistic and spiritual vision of cosmic truths that are obscured by rational consciousness—"to light up our lives with chemical glimpses of another world."[39] "'Alcohol' in Latin is *spiritus*," Jung wrote to Bill Wilson, co-founder of Alcoholics Anonymous, "the same word [we use] for the highest religious experience."[40]

The names given to the Celtic otherworld— *Tir inna mBeo* (Land of the Ever Living), *Tir Tairngiri* (Land of Promise), *Tir na nOg* (Land of Youth), *Mag Mell* (Plain of Delight), *Mag Da Cheo* (Plain of the Two Mists), *Tir inna mBan* (Land of Women), Isles of the Happy, etc., all point toward experiences of a state of timeless bliss. William Butler Yeats describes the Irish story-teller's

mind [that] constantly escaped out of daily circumstances, as a bough that has been held down by a weak hand suddenly straightens itself out. His imagination was always running off to Tir na nOg, to the Land of Promise . . . . His belief in its nearness cherished in turn the lyrical temper, which is always athirst for an emotion, a beauty which cannot be found in its perfection upon earth, or only for a moment. . . . His art, too is often at its greatest when it is most extravagant . . . [reshaping] the world according to his heart's desire . . . not troubled by any probabilities or necessities but those of emotion itself.[41]

Medieval voyagers to the otherworld discover islands of glass, miraculous castles, chambers of the sun, or cities under the sea where they are granted remarkable visions and regenerative cures.[42] They find orchards where the fruit is ripe in every season. They find chambers of crystal having inexhaustible cisterns, "though they were never filled they were always full." Beautiful women welcome the voyagers with superb food and drink and loving embraces. In their otherworld sojourn the travelers may acquire new strength or find their soul's otherworld partner. While recent commentators have equated these islands of bliss with the realm of Platonic essences, the Golden Age, the ideal happiness of lovers "in glorious isolation," and the blissful maternal womb,[43] Irish poems describing these realms of archetypal ideals also suggest the marvels encountered during experiences of mystical ecstasy. One famous early medieval account of such a visionary voyage describes a series of islands strung out like jewels across the sea. On each one the traveler

enjoys a different variation of the inexhaustible pleasures of
the senses heightened and intensified to their most exquisite.
Throughout this voyage the mortal limitations of age,
sickness, and decay are unknown; instead joy reigns. One
island is called "the fairest land throughout the world." It is
supported by four pillars of gold and has a silver plain "on
which the hosts hold games. "

On another island the traveler finds that

Colours of every shade glisten
Throughout the gentle-voiced plains:
Joy is known, ranked around music . . . .

All that would rankle or distress is named and banished from
this paradisical trip.

Unknown is wailing or treachery
In the . . . well-tilled land:
There is nothing rough or harsh
But sweet music striking on the ear.

Without grief, without gloom, without death,
Without any sickness or debility . . . .

On still another island

Wealth, treasures of every hue
Are in the Land of Peace—a beauty of Freshness:
There is listening to sweet music,
Drinking of the choicest wine . . . .

The traveler will see the sun (feminine in Celtic lore though
not in this medieval poem) riding across the sea at sunrise
with a vast host that

. . . row[s] to the shining stone
From which arises music a hundredfold.
Through ages long unto the host
It sings a strain which is never sad.

On another isle there are "thousands of many-hued women"
watching the games and listening to "the voice of music
[from] a chorus of birds." Everywhere in this land of bliss the

events and aesthetic beauty that would bring joy to an Irish
heart are described. Wine, women, and song share the stage
with sports, travel, the pleasures of good health, and the
loveliness of nature.

There comes happiness with health
To the land against which laughter peels:
Into the Land of Peace at every season
Comes joy everlasting.[44]

In the description of another voyage to the
otherworld we are told of

Delightful fairy music, travel from one kingdom to another,
  drinking mead from bright vessels, talking with the one you love.
We play with men of yellow gold on golden chessboards:
  we drink clear mead in the company of a proud armed warrior.
Der Greine [the goddess of the sun], daughter of Fiachna is my wife,
  and to tell all there is a wife for each of my fifty men.[45]

Still in 1899 Yeats writes of the Irish longing to
recapture the ideal Otherworld that once existed just over the
sea wave or under the sidhe mound or in the depths of a
spring. He reminds the modern world that into the present

The host is riding from Knocknarea
And over the grave of Clooth-na-Bare;
Caoilte tossing his burning hair,
And Niamh calling Away, come away:
Empty your heart of its mortal dream.
The winds awaken, the leaves whirl round,
Our cheeks are pale, our hair unbound,
Our breasts are heaving, our eyes are agleam,
Our arms are waving, our lips are apart;
And if any gaze on our rushing band,
We come between him and the deed of his hand,
We come between him and the hope of his heart.
The host is rushing 'twixt night and day,
And where is there hope or deed as fair?
Caoilte tossing his burning hair,
And Niamh calling Away, come away.[46]

Even the ancient Celtic initiate is warned,
however, to "Sink not upon a bed of sloth! Let not thine
intoxication overcome thee! Begin a voyage across the clear
sea, if perchance thou mayest reach" the Isles of Bliss.[47]

While "a chief poet had to understand not only innumerable kinds of poetry but how to keep himself for nine days in a trance,"[48] all visionary travelers had to know that one hazard of the use of inebriants for creating altered states is that consciousness will succumb before it can gain the fruits of vision. The voyager must have support for the intensified awareness that inebriation brings. In the actual training of Celtic druids and poets, which sometimes lasted as long as twenty years, traditional masters supervised the complex and multifaceted process. Through experiences of isolation, trance, incubation, and the memorization of vast quantities of sacred, traditional lore, such training created structures and purposes through which the ritually induced states of altered consciousness could be channeled.[49] The fruits of the magus' vision were expressed in poetry and prose that conveyed legend, historical and calendrical lore, rituals and spells. Although the poetry might be created in trance, it had strict rules of meter, alliteration, and repetitions with rhythmic syllabic patterns, and the rhyming of vowels.[50] The free and passionate imagination was held, thus, in precise aesthetic forms and balanced by the massive quantities of traditional lore that created the vocabulary in which to express the individual's visionary material to the community.

Within the framework of such teachings and precisely ordered rituals, the *medb* and other trance-inducing methods were used to prepare and expand the initiates' consciousness, enabling a spiritual leap[51] to a transcendent and cosmic perspective.[52] Liberated from identification with his or her person and previous personal and social relationships, the trained master or magus could then see "from the eye fixed in heaven"—from the pleromatic perspective that has been called "the pole star center of the whirling mill of manifestations."[53] Identified with the divinity[54] they had ingested and carefully trained to hold and express their mystic vision, the druids and poets could be sent "reeling drunkenly out of the world"[55] to explore past, present, and future in timeless, spaceless trance. Such visionary capacity was called *imbas forosenai* by the Celts and was highly valued as a means of divination.[56]

The druid-poets could also sing incantations that empathically identified their consciousness with all aspects of creation—a mystical fusion with the cosmic "intelligence underlying both the world and oneself"[57] that they celebrated in their myths of shapeshifting and in their ecstatic "I am " poems.[58] One of the best known of these is the incantation sung by the poet Amairgen claiming the land of Ireland for his people through identifying himself with different manifestations of the unitary, transcendent energy coursing through all of them:

I am a wind on the sea (for depth).
I am a sea-wave upon the land (for heaviness).
I am the sound of the sea (for fearsomeness).
I am a stag of seven combats (for strength).
I am a hawk on a cliff (for agility).
I am a tear-drop of the sun (for purity).
I am fair (i.e. there is no plant fairer than I).
I am a boar for valour (for harshness).
I am a salmon in a pool (for swiftness).
I am a lake in a plain (for size).
I am the excellence of arts (for beauty).
I am a spear which wages battle with plunder.
I am a God who forms subjects for a ruler.[59]
Who explains the stones of the mountain?
Who invokes the ages of the moon?
Where lies the setting of the sun? . . . . [60]

With his right foot upon Ireland as he recited this incantation, Amairgen made himself a bridge between sea and land, nature and culture, the gods and humans. From such a state of focused communion with the energy underlying a vast range of forms and attributes, the masters sought what Jung has called the mystic's "particularly vivid experience of the processes of the collective unconscious. . . experience of the archetypes."[61] Intentionally in touch with what we have come to call "implicate reality," they could work magically or shamanically for the tribe's benefit. From this perspective, they were said to be able to read the signs in what we would call synchronous events, to prophesy, shapeshift, heal, control the weather and the optimum timing of human activities, attune to animals for hunting and the stars for guidance, master the arts, transform materials, and advise chiefs.

A modern participant in a Mexican peyote rite expresses the ecstasy that may accompany such altered, mystical consciousness:

Your body lies in the darkness, heavy as lead, but your spirit seems to soar and leave the hut and with the speed of thought to travel . . . in time and space. . . . What you are seeing and what you are hearing appear as one: the music assumes harmonious shapes and colors, giving visual form to its harmonies, and what you are seeing takes on the modalities of music—the music of the spheres . . . . All your senses are similarly affected . . . . The [participant] is poised in space, a disembodied eye, invisible, incorporeal, seeing but not seen. In truth he is the five senses disembodied, all of them keyed to the height of sensitivity and awareness, all of them blending into one another most strangely, until, utterly passive, he becomes a pure receptor, infinitely delicate . . . . [Guided by the shamanic singer] your body lies there, your soul is free, with no sense of time, alert as never before, living an eternity in a night, seeing infinity in a grain of sand. What you have seen and heard is cut as with a burrin in your memory, never to be effaced. At last you know what the ineffable is, and what ecstasy means.[62]

Hallucinogens to produce religious trance have probably been used in cult activity since the Upper Paleolithic period.[63] "Religious communities that use drugs teach their members how to switch from the intoxication to the religious trance,"[64] and as we have seen, they have ritual and art forms through which to mediate visionary consciousness. In the peyote rite, a spiritual master presides over the sharing of the intoxicant and may guide the participants through their otherworld journey with song and music. In Celtic lore we have a suggestion of a similar practice in the "Company of the [god Bran's] Wondrous Head." A Mabinogion tale tells us that a small group, returning from across the otherworld sea with their leader Bran, enjoys a long period of joyful, ecstatic trance together with his decapitated talking head. Not only may they have received instruction from this godhead, but their intoxicating, initiatory libation may have been drunk from his skull cup, a vessel used for sacred communion in Celtic as in Vedic lore.[65] We may never know what they learned in their years of isolated service and communion with the transcendent spirit, but we can surmise that the community was not unlike the sacred grail societies and small participatory groups of other mystery religions.

In India the hallucinogen *soma*, fermented or churned from the primeval ocean by the gods, is considered a gift of the goddess Lakshmi. Ritually connected with a skull-cup communion, it is celebrated in the Rig Veda as the drink providing knowledge of otherworldly realms. An ancient hymn proclaims

We have drunk the Soma, we are become Immortals,
We are arrived at the Light, we have found the Gods.
What now can hostility do to us, what the malice of mortal,
  O Immortal Soma![66]

The prophet Jeremiah equates drunkenness with religious ecstasy: "all my bones shake; I am like a drunken man, like a man overcome by wine, because of the Lord and because of his holy words."[67] In Sufi and Taoist teachings too, wine and its drunkenness are central symbolic images to suggest what slakes the soul and gives direct imaginal experience of union with the divine. Sufi mystics sing of the "inner intoxication of contemplation" and call for drink to "drown me in an ocean of wine before my thin barque's caught and broken on the Wheel of Time."[68] Such self-annihilation in the *kharabat*[69] (tavern) enables the Beloved, at one with God, to see "even at night . . . the Sun's fountain" and to experience the mystic's "mad" paradoxical harmonies:

I know, drunk on you,
This world is harmony—
Creation, destruction. I'm dancing for them both.[70]

Writer John Blofeld describes his experience with a sacred mind-altering substance that provided him with a glimpse of Buddhism's paradoxical truths:

I was plunged into a state of ecstasy in which dawned full awareness
of the . . . great truths I had long accepted intellectually but had
never experienced as self-evident, now all of a sudden, they became
as tangible as the heat of a raging fire . . . .[71]

Blofeld also puts the use of the intoxicating *medb* or, in his case, mescaline, into perspective. These substances may help the apprentice learn to cross the threshold to experience transpersonal consciousness.

*Using it once or twice, with proper preparation and under suitable
conditions, might benefit newcomers to the path; on the other hand,
its continued use would be disastrous—bliss so easily attainable
would be likely to reconcile them to life as it is and induce them to be
content with drug-induced experiences instead of actually treading
the path.*[72]

Both from treading the path and from
psychotherapy, we learn that consciousness is not merely a
function of ego. There is also what Erich Neumann called the
"consciousness that is not yet, or no longer, effectively
centered in ego." Primitive, early childhood modes are not yet
centered in ego. Mystic consciousness is no longer bound by
the categories of ordinary experience, for it reaches backwards
and forwards in timeless openness to the objective psyche.
Neumann called such visionary consciousness "a fundamental
category of human experience."[73] He describes it as

*the experience of the numinous Self [that] . . . always brings with it
the intoxication that comes of a changing and heightened feeling of
Self, a change in the ego position and in consciousness.* [74]

In modern transpersonally oriented therapy, we
experience both modes of beyond-ego awareness, because
much of consciousness and even memory involve the whole
organism, which includes body and psyche. We find
increasingly in therapies of body and psyche that trance,
deep muscle and breath work, and other consciousness-
altering experiences enable us to shift from habitual and
parochial patterns of perception and cognition in order to
evoke healing transformations and atonements within the
psychic and somatic whole.[75] Through such experiences we
have come to understand the integral unity of body and
mind and the subtle forms of awareness that arise within this
organically coherent and multiply aware totality. We now
distinguish between pre-ego and dissolving-of-ego, or post-
ego, dissociations in our therapeutic work, attributing the
former to archaic emotional states of awareness out of which
the ego coalesces and the latter to the states we associate to
"spiritual emergencies" and mystical experiences in which
consciousness of a separative identity dissolves. As we work
with capacities for awareness of our pan-psychicsomatic
states, therapists of the body and the psyche know that we

need to try to discriminate between these levels in order to receive and process accurately the many non-verbal (Alpha, Delta, and Theta wave) messages they convey.[76]

Because the experience opens consciousness to a vastness far beyond the felt limits of the body ego, a safe alternative containment is necessary. The holding environment of therapy substitutes for secure parental mediation when the pre-ego is coalescing from its diffusions and fragmentations. Its security permits the releasing of hitherto unapprehended aspects of awareness that create an ego that can function effectively but still remains open to the vastness of consciousness and the passionate intensities of emotion experienced in pan-psychicsomatic states. The new explorer of beyond-ego states requires the presence of an experienced guide who appreciates the sensations, who can accurately read the participant's reactions and the symbolic material in which the experiences are usually conveyed, and who can secure the opening and closing portals of the ritual into trance. Then the fruits of the *ecstasis* can be tasted without debilitating fears of annihilation and defenses preventing or skewing the experience.

Whenever we are able to step outside the ego into the all-containing matrix of animal, body, Self, godhead where there is no split between body and psyche, we can flow in field consciousness with what is commonly experienced in separatist consciousness as an inner or outer otherness. Such whole, body-Self knowing permits deep intraspecies, and even interspecies, communication. It is common in the vivid experiences of early childhood. It is necessary to the empathic intuitions of the healer. Its passionate and visionary sight fuel the creative obsessions that propel the artist and enable us all to do our creative work. The *medb* is here a symbol of the intoxicating psychic and somatic intensities that attune the human servant with the energies and images of what we call "experience of the archetypes" and what Taliesin called our "original country . . . the region of the summer stars."[77]

Regal Initiation

Celtic rulers also had to drink the *medb*. Tribal chiefs had to be able to dare and endure inebriation in order to undergo a ritual transformation of consciousness.[78] In Irish myth the goddess served each of her royal consorts a libation before his sacred marriage with her. The drink served was the *medb,* the sacred red liquor of royal initiation. Drinking her wine from her cup empowered and established the king. In Celtic ritual the *feis,* or sacred marriage between the clan chiefs and the queen who embodied the goddess of the land, repeated this *medb* communion along with the ritual sexual intercourse of the sacred marriage.

In psychological terms, the communion separated the chosen king from his ordinary life and symbolically dissolved his old identity. Filled with an inebriating substance that represented expanded consciousness, he then symbolically and, perhaps actually, metabolized attitudes and emotions that had been outside his previous awareness. This expanded consciousness supported the creation of the new psychological structures that accommodated and sanctioned his identity as ruler over the whole clan, embodying the capacities of the other three classes as well as those supporting regal dominion. Filled with the ecstatic experience of the goddess of sovereignty in actual communion with her as substance and as sexual partner (since both paths to ecstatic expansion were ritually granted to the Celtic chief), he was thus prepared to embody his divine role as the new, virile, and wise partner of the cosmic life force that was revered as the matrix of the tribe's prosperity.

We could say that regal authority results psychologically from being able to integrate the experience of archetypal affect and grandiosity and to transmute these into the life-enhancing, conscience-bound wisdom and assertion needed to manage daily affairs. When evoked and metabolized in a communal ritual, the primal affects become less dangerous and inflationary because they are themselves subject to containment, mediation, and rule. Thus the Celtic chief could reign as Maeve demanded of her consorts, "without jealousy, without fear, without stinginess" and with expanded consciousness. Ritually freed of diminishing partiality, the chief could then reign justly over diverse factions whose battling might threaten the stability of the clan. Similarly the ruling function in each of us must support, mediate between, and rule over the diverse portions or factions within the personality without identifying with only one or flailing back and forth between opposing parts.

Like the druids and poets, the rulership function in each of us relates directly to the transpersonal source of sovereignty and life and "speaks from the truth that nourishes," as one analysand in recovery expressed it when she began to claim her own rulership over the previously dissociated parts (or complexes) in her psychology.

Then I don't need an outer person to mirror-and-mommy me [in order] to feel all the fragments held or [another person] to fight against to bind the parts of myself together against their common enemy.

The Irish ritual of marriage and communion with the Earth and Mare goddess symbolizing sovereignty is spelled out in all its concrete details by Gerald of Wales, a churchman who "delighted in the scandalous behavior of the Celts."[79] He witnessed an eleventh-century AD inauguration in north Ulster. In this late vestige of a Neolithic ceremony, the king mated with the goddess as a white mare. The horse was then killed, cut up, and cooked to convey her substance literally as meat and broth to the new ruler.

The whole people of that country being gathered in one place, a white mare is led into the midst of them. He who is to be inaugurated, not as a chief, but as a beast, not as a king, but as an outlaw, embraces the animal before all, professing himself to be a beast also. The mare is then killed immediately, cut up in pieces and boiled in water. A bath is prepared for the man afterwards in the same manner. He sits in the bath surrounded by all his people, and all, he and they, eat of the meat of the mare which is brought to them. He quaffs and drinks of the broth in which he is bathed, not in any cup, or using his hand, but just dipping his mouth into it round about him. When this unrighteous rite has been carried out, his kingship and dominion have been conferred.[80]

Representing an ancient Indo-European theriomorphic hierogamy, the event expressed the ritual identification of human with beast, a destructuring of human consciousness that reaches back farther than human infancy to the totemic animal itself.[81] For the Celts who divinized the animal, such identification was not a *lowering* of consciousness or regression. It was a sacred initiation to encompass the animal's powers. As stallion and sexual partner, as infant colt baptized in the cauldron womb of the mother and fed with her actual substance, the ruler-to-be was recreated as the destined equal of the Earth and Mare goddess. The experience of this ceremony sanctioned the king's rebirth. By filling him with the goddess' substance, the ritual dissolved his old identity and changed him, altering his status so he could embody the archetype of prosperous divine kingship and become the sacred king.[82] Thus he was inaugurated before the tribe. Like the Mare goddess of this Ulster ritual, Maeve was the divine mare, the mother and bride of her consort kings. Her mead was like the Ulster tribe's broth. It, as much as her equine form,[83] was the means of initiatory transport from one state of consciousness to another. We still find this dual transport dimly recalled in the folktale of Madge (see page 30). There a broomstick-horse ride whisked her man James through the air and into the distant castle where he landed astride a stallion, partook of the festive libations, and ultimately achieved the sovereignty that enabled him to escape his captor's sentence of death.

The very body imagery of the rite enacted in Ulster transports us to an archaic level of consciousness. The images are similar to those expressed by clients during deeply regressed or expansive phases in analytic work. The body symbols created and discovered both in the ceremony and in therapy convey the activity of psychoidal levels of the psyche—the profoundly deep levels where matter and spirit are still conjoined in the activity of the body-Self to enable radical transformation. One strikingly analogous example occurred in the dream and ensuing active imagination of a recovering heroin addict after he had fearfully expressed both dependency and separative anger. He dreamt, "I am like a tiny child, sort of like a fetal tadpole. I am swimming up into your vagina to be safe in the dark waters inside. But you are huge like a horse." Working further on the image with a growing capacity for self-observation, he realized, "I am surprisingly not afraid . . . . In fact after a long time I can come out different and not be so afraid . . . . I am big enough." This powerful image, which gripped him for some time, gave him his first experience of blissful safety and containment that was not connected to his addiction. He had a psychotic mother who had given him up for adoption, then taken him back, and abused him with neglect. Experiencing consciously his own communion with his infant self in the safe and shared space of the therapeutic container enabled him to begin to ground himself in life and express his intense feelings. Over time his acceptance and valuing of his own emotional truth helped him to begin to trust that he could "speak his own word" and survive. He had then an alternative to the flight from anxious pain into the womb-like regressions that his addictions expressed. Thus he could begin to venture forth to rule his life from a Self center.

One man's drink is however another man's poison. Like the *lapis* of alchemy, which can cure or kill, the royal cauldron bath or drink might transform and regenerate, or it might transform and destroy.[84] Irish myths tell of both consequences. Maeve, as leprous hag, used her powers to bind and kill disrespectful claimants to her kingdom. The Irish goddesses Dierdre and Grainne used drink to put their obsolete and unwanted marriage partners to sleep while the queens eloped with newly chosen younger consorts.[85]

To avoid the potentially entrapping and toxic effects of the regal libation, the Celtic king was carefully chosen. His properly attuned, even destined, fit and his human adequacy to fulfill the forms of his role had to be assured in both supernatural and human terms. The chief's destiny was mandated by the goddess and her human representative, the queen. Thus the feminine put her fated call [*geis*] upon him and/or tried him with riddles and challenges to test his wisdom, skills, and worthiness. The druids of the tribe also affirmed this fate with special tests or ritually induced prophetic dreams. In the story of young Niall, he indicates his capacity to bear the tasks of kingship by choosing the anvil from a burning smithy. Like the sturdy support against which red-hot metal can be pounded, his choice expresses readiness to face the fire and sustain the harsh trials through which regal authority creatively forms tribal factions into a kingdom. His brothers' choices of hammer, straw, and bellows foretell their different future roles in the land.[86] Through such tests the tribespeople sought to determine the leader who was most physically able, mentally capable, and magically destined. While such ordeals of selection may have symbolized victory in a war between tribal factions or, later, tribal election, all such trials ensured the new ruler's destined primacy among the people of the clan. Before his inauguration *feis* with the goddess-queen was undertaken, he had proven his capacity for leadership and could thus undergo the initiation by which Maeve affirmed his destiny and divinized him.[87]

A particular set of special magic ordeals was part of preparation for the high kingship at Tara. Called the Tara tests, they are a beautiful example of the qualities inherent in being destined. Administered by druids to the high king, these were analogous to those that the smith gave to Niall and his brothers preliminary to the *feis* with the goddess-queen. The four Tara tests are psychologically significant for us because they describe what happens to confirm us when we are on our destined path. The regal aspirant passed the first test if his chariot did not fly up and throw him, and its horses did not attack him. Passing the first test signifies that the individual is traveling towards a goal that the Self supports, a goal that feels destined and right and is supported by instinctive energy to carry forth and facilitate the aspirant's intentions. Things feel easy. For example, a woman in recovery from alcoholism who wanted to try to write a novel and expand her sense of herself to include the risking of her creative capacities found she was able to get up while her household was still sleeping to gain two hours of writing time every morning. She discovered untapped reservoirs of energy. Their effects spilled over into her regular job, where she felt more efficient and less harassed by issues that had previously bothered her.

In the aspirant's second test, the cloak of kingship must fit. Often bestowed by the queen-goddess, the king's cloak represents the social and spiritual role that requires filling. If the individual is too small in a real or sensed incapacity, he cannot carry the regal authority that will be required for the task of self-rule. On the other hand if the candidate is too bloated with his own importance and inflated with defensive righteousness and his own perspectives, personal narcissistic issues will stick out from under the new identity and spoil it. The ruler will not be sufficiently able to heed the requirements of the transpersonal purpose and guidance that he must serve humbly. Nor can he attend to the multiple factions within the tribe that require just balance. When the cloak is right, there is a fit between the purposes of ego and Self or destiny. In our example, the woman realized that her writing, which she had postponed for decades out of fear of her own incapacity to carry her sense of a writer's necessary greatness, was not the mammoth undertaking that her idealization had made it seem. It was, as she put it, "a vast relief to be finally doing it, but also no big deal—just daily hard work."

In the third Tara test the stones will open to let the chariot through if the aspirant is destined to rule. The stones have the same names as the Tara druids, the shaman-priests who shapeshift to incarnate divine forces. This implies that the transpersonal path is opened. No longer impenetrable, the way feels right and clear. The sacred and natural order of the *unus mundus*—the primeval unity before the opposites are separated—now opens to make a gate. This division permits the time-bound, incarnated, and true king to pass. The woman writer felt increasingly that her work flowed, and in its unfolding her creativity opened further.

In the final test the *lia fal* or stone of kingship and knowledge will shriek in affirmation when the rightful king steps upon it. Still standing at Tara, this coronation megalith was identified with the penis (analogous to the sacred *Shiva lingam* of India) of the god-king Fergus, son of the Great Horse and consort of Maeve. It represented the sacred creative energy of the transpersonal principle of kingship that blessed the temporary human king fulfilling the archetypal role. The blessing is similar to the baptismal benediction that the Christian god bestowed on his beloved son. Not with words but with a primal shriek, it conveys the deep sense of entitlement and charisma that others intuit and cooperate to support. Thus the woman, who was increasingly engaged in her novel, was given a raise at work and offered a summer cabin by a colleague who knew nothing about her creative intentions. When the book was finally published, it received a good review that enabled her to begin to assert her new identity as she restructured her life.

The successful completion of the Tara tests implies psychologically that the true ego has come forth in the Self's image and with the Self's blessing. This ego is not a fraudulent usurper identified with power, nor a pretender wearing a defensive persona ego. It stands in a coalesced, creative, and validated position to serve the whole superordinate center, not just a partial and particular feeling-toned complex. Thus this validated sense of identity can rule over conflicts and complexes serving the whole until its day is done and a new ruling attitude is required. At that point the felt sense of identity may have to sacrifice itself and pass into the underworld to be regenerated for the next phase of life. Then it may emerge in new form to meet a new set of Tara tests.

In modern psychological terms these ordeals imply that the partner of the goddess, who is chosen to imbibe her sacred mead-feast for expanded consciousness and/or expanded behaviorial capacity, must feel destined by the call of his or her fate. He or she must also be competently stable, skillfully trained, and reverent in service to the collective and its transcendent spirit before risking the ordeal. The individual cannot escape the rigors of personal development nor attempt to leap from pre-ego states of infantile omnipotence to regency as is often attempted today. No more can those destined to deal with druid issues evade the discipline and shadow integration required to build a valid container to receive and channel the spiritual *medb*.

Modern Ego Functions

The purpose of each of the four tribal functions in Celtic society is to mediate an aspect of Maeve, or life energy, into tribal life. Each therefore involves ritual and *medb*-supported identity with the archetype, but each conveys a particular shading of the ecstatic, altered state experience that such identity brings. Warriors overcome their fear and swell with aggressive affect beyond their personal limits. Farmers and herders form the large kin groups that come together in tribal assemblies. Their mutual *participation mystique* is analogous to an ecstatic symbiosis within the containing community and the body of its tribal land. Druid-poets identify their consciousness with visionary imagination to enable them to work with archetypal energies and symbols. Rulers claim ecstatic expansion beyond their personal limits to encompass the demands of sovereignty itself.

Today we can view individual ego functions as analogous to the collective tribal functions in Celtic culture. The archetypal pattern underlying the four initiations in the culture of Maeve's Irish worshippers thus still provides us with a blueprint for the initiatory structures that bring forth a balanced identity and ensure that we develop capacities for a strong, self-valuing, permeable, just, and creative sense of ourselves. In daily life each of us must function and continue to expand in all of these modes to survive and thrive and contribute to our society. Like warriors we need to guard life and to assert and claim our needs, staying in touch with transpersonal sources of strength and honing our skills to ever greater effectiveness. In the service of the individual Self, we may have to stand our ground, to refuse to cooperate, even to become adversarial and do battle. Like farmers and herdsmen, we need to nourish our individual styles and take care of our biological, emotional, social, and spiritual needs in celebration of the powers of the fertile and fallow seasons of life that grant them. Like druids and poets, we need to relate to the overarching, transcendent dimension and its guidance and to serve and express its truths creatively and as clearly and objectively as we are permitted to see them. Like chieftains we need to rule over all of these functions held together in our own lives in harmony with the sovereign processes of our individual destiny.[88]

When, like the process of Celtic kingship itself, we can permit old structures of consciousness to dissolve as they are no longer relevant, we may return repeatedly to the matrix of the Self in order to become ever more what we are meant to be.[89] This permits transformation in the service of our creative individual development. Much of therapy and life itself involves such destructuring of old structures— outworn defenses, attitudes, and ideals—that impede the individuation process. Thus Maeve, as the sacred font of dissolving and initiating spirit, guides us throughout life and is central to much analytic work. Her multiple powers to loosen, support, and expand consciousness are vital at all stages of individual and cultural transformation.

While we struggle to fulfill all of these roles in order to attain a sense of authentic individuality, we are not to identify with them. Instead, today, we need the ability to allow and endure the surges of ecstatic union with Maeve's energy in the different modes through which it comes into us. We need also to disidentify or step aside and see its rhythms as aspects of a transpersonal developmental process. Without this capacity we lose our balance and fall into the addictive patterns connected with each function, as we will see in the next chapter.

Reflecting on our own experiences of "drunkenness" may help us to disidentify from their grip and also tell us where we have found and still find the expansive body and mind alterations brought about by the *medb*. We need to consider that which inebriates us—the substance or mind-altering emotions, activities, or objects that enable (or substitute symbolically for) our contact with transcendence.

Many paths can lead us to ecstasy. They point to areas where we have needed and may still need to expand our sense of identity in order to fulfill our individual potential to function as warriors, caretakers of life, wise visionaries, and just authorities in the realms granted us. Participants in one workshop provided the following activities as paths through which they had experienced inebriation. In considering them together, several individuals realized that each activity had held a vital clue about where they had then found access to the Self. In some cases the participant had only seen the inebriating activity as negative. By pursuing the deeper symbolic meaning of that activity, individuals were often also able to discover its purposeful meaning in their lives and the still latent ego function that the activity supported. Here is their list:

Feeling secure enough to let go completely, like falling backwards and feeling held.
Surfing on the Internet.
Playing Solitaire. Doing cross-word puzzles—and mindlessly compelled to keep on.
Having sex.
Feeling the thrills of raw sensation, like sky-diving and skinny-dipping.
Eating foods that taste enchanting. Good drug trips.
Having everything under control. Feeling triumphant power.
Feeling totally helpless and having to let go into it.
Feeling infatuated with a specific (idealized) figure or having a crush on someone special (from a guru with endless wisdom to an infant with endless potential or a new lover with endless empathy and endowments).
Adoring some place in nature or an object (that evokes sacred values in projection—from holy images to beautiful crystals or fabrics).
Seeing or engaging in creative activity like music, art, or poetry and feeling swept away into the process. Taken over by the frenzy of it.

*Meditating, when I have melted into the vast paradox of the void
   holding everything.*
*Forgetting time and space in the reverie brought about by seeing a
   face or a flower that holds the life-flow for a moment of
   transfixing poignancy.*
Feeling merged in a group or with a lover.
Swimming or skiing until I am completely one with the flow.

Almost any enthralling emotional state that seizes
us can enable such transcendence. The affect may range from
joy to panic, from passionate sexuality to aggressive rage.
Joyful excitement no less than anxiety, abandonment-panic,
anger, shame, guilt, sorrow, risk taking, and empathic fusion
may all propel us into states of archetypal emotion that
transcend ordinary consciousness, even as they also change
our hormonal balance. Power and powerlessness, fervent
cleanliness, passionate ambition for success or fame, righteous
contempt, and aggressive/fearful perfectionism may be as
potentially addicting as drugs, gambling, alcohol, cigarettes,
television, etc. The qualities of timeless trance experienced in
their grip and hence attributed to them fill our consciousness.
These and other activities and states may also lessen pain.
Rather than bringing a sense of active expansion, they may
bring the melting relief of comfort as they hold us safe or
numbed from experiences of chaotic fragmentation and
misery. The potentials for divine attunement symbolized by
the *medb* may thus appear in many forms. We may find
ourselves beside and beyond ourselves in many ways. While
any of these experiences may open our consciousness to a
larger dimension, these same forms can merely reconcile us to
life-as-it-is and become like a fetish and the focus of an
addiction.

Often the inebriating values and sources change
at different stages of life, but inevitably the intoxication
involves an experience of wondrous Otherness that comes
from an influx of ecstatic, embodied, emotional attunement
and expansion. While the Otherness may feel positive or
negative, often it arrives with a sense of paradox and a shiver
that makes us gasp as we are gripped and carried beyond the
accustomed haven of our sense of ourselves or plunged into

awareness of the larger matrix holding us. While often bliss filled, such transport may equally fill us with terror as we are shifted out of ordinary and limited personal reality (and often out of our accustomed sense of bodily integrity and solidity) and forced to experience the larger dimensions with all of their potential to shake up and enhance or deform our lives. Thus even the onslaught of joy-filled excitement may be frightening when such joy has previously been unconscious and humanly unmediated. The relief of feeling held in someone's positive regard may seem as overwhelming as an attack of shame. In a poem Emily Dickinson tells us of one of these experiences of the *medb*:

I can wade Grief—
Whole Pools of it—
I'm used to that—
But the least push of Joy
Breaks up my feet—
And I tip— drunken—
Let no Pebble —smile—
'Twas the New Liquor
That was all! [90]

Initially we may even experience upset and panic and seek to flee the experiences that may lead us beyond our familiar and hence seemingly safe sense of ourselves. This is why Jung wrote that an experience of the Self is felt to be a defeat for the ego.[91] In an experience of the Self's vast expansiveness, the old structures with which ego consciousness is familiar are dissolved or shattered, and we are made vulnerable to suffer what feels an unaccustomed assault by the influx of what we are meant to become. We are carried beyond ourselves. When we can process these experiences consciously, feeling their intensity and finding their place and meaning in our lives, we may as individuals be able to find the potentials for expansion that are analogous to those that the ancient Celts underwent in their cultural rituals. Instead of having traditional ritual forms through which to assimilate these experiences of the larger matrix, we must today often find our own vessels for mediating the *medb*. We must undergo our own initiatory processes.

Chapter 3

Maeve as Toxin

Men will get drunk on wine and forget heaven in favor of earth.
The stars will turn away from them and obscure their course.
　　　　　　　　　　　　　　　　—Merlin[1]

In every culture human beings have sought altered states of consciousness to achieve transformation and revitalization. Among the Celts and peoples of other magical/mystical religious traditions, experiences of euphoric elation were considered divine and honored in communal rituals. "Our greatest blessings come to us by way of madness—provided the madness is given us by divine gift," Socrates said to an already dubious fourth-century B.C. Greek audience.[2] The Celts would have agreed wholeheartedly. A Gaelic word for insane means "close to god."

Cultural Issues

Unfortunately, however, the main exoteric Judeo-Christian and Muslim religious traditions and much classical and Western mythology have not supported individually experienced vision-seeking nor embodied ecstatic passion.[3] Unless the visions are congruent with dogma, they are branded as heretical threats to the power of the religious hierarchy that wants to maintain "its monopoly on legitimate access to the supernatural."[4] Perceptions achieved through

altered states of consciousness also threaten the seeming
objectivity of much Western science. Thus many of the Celts,
Native Americans, Africans, Australian Aborigines, Slavs, and
other predifferentiated and wholistic cultures whose ancestors
have been severed from their Stone-Age shamanic
celebrations have experienced painful dislocation. The
modern descendants still bear the painful scars of those
broken roots. When they have not secretly continued the old
rituals to support and enhance states of altered consciousness
that might rebond them with traditional wisdom and self-
esteem, they have often tried to medicate themselves with
alcohol.

Among the Irish this is particularly true. The
primacy of their ancient earth religion, which honored the
powers of the goddess of nature and her rituals, came to
coexist in what Marija Gimbutas has called a "hybridization of
two different symbolic systems."[5] One was goddess based; the
other originated in the cults of the warrior gods brought by
the waves of tribal invasions that came from the East.
Although the old religion of the earth goddess was "by turns
absorbed, transformed, and negated"[6] by the religion of the
masculine solar god and the heroic ideals of the warrior
chiefs, it survived remarkably intact in Ireland. It was saved
from the Roman incursions that conquered southern Britain.
The early and Patristic Christians remained tolerant of native
sensitivities and allegiances. They maintained women as
priests and the druid tonsure for male priests, and they
eschewed the doctrine of original sin. Starting in the eleventh
century, however, the primacy of the old religion was slowly
dominated by particularly severe forms of antilibidinous,
Norman Christianity and foreign, patrifocal, hierarchical, and
feudal customs. The Irish penchant for euphoric, embodied
participation with the *unus mundus* (unitary world) was
denigrated by the new authorities using bipolar Roman and
Judeo-Christian logic and the force of repressive dogma. The
alien value system split body and psyche and disparaged the
feminine and the mystical communion with all of nature. It
sought to destroy essential interconnections with the source-
ground of life (what Joyce McDougall calls the "primitive

mother universe"[7]). The process of marriage with the goddess of the land was replaced by overt attempts to subjugate her. With the rise of patrifocal authority and the new kind of consciousness it supported, the Church sought to diminish the image of the female godhead whose cultural presence in the landscape, the kinship system, and the mythology supports each individual's internal representation of a secure holding environment and the constant-enough, receiving, and bountiful matrix. We are meant to turn to the father god instead. Even Mary and the other ancient goddesses, whom we now recognize in the figures of the saints, receive validation only because they are said to mediate between humans and the higher masculine powers.[8]

While folk traditions kept the old ways alive into the present century, many of these customs were not officially supported. Sometimes local priests and English authorities tolerated them, but often the people performed them in secret.[9] Thus the same fate met the old cultural mores that meets individuals hiding their true selves under socially adaptive facades. Just as individuals operating out of a persona ego or false self lose touch with their original nature, so the people began to lose touch with the deeper significances of the older rites. Just as individuals suffer loss of self-esteem without access to their authentic core, so whole groups came to feel excluded from the security that results from a living experience of the matrix represented by the goddess and her sovereignty over the land and its nature and culture.[10]

In the nineteenth and twentieth centuries more direct affronts battered the vestiges of earlier forms of worship in Irish society. With the flight of so many family members from the occupied and starved land and with the derogation and repression of the Gaelic language and its rich culture, Eriu, Banba, Fodla, and Maeve's island were threatened by English authorities with their own forms of economic exploitation and ethnic cleansing. Irish identity was further dislocated with the renaming of the geography still vibrantly alive with local and mythic history. What was once the body of the goddess on which the tribespeople lived became a system of coordinates and Anglified names on ordinance surveys. Everywhere the sense of rootedness in clan and place was disrupted in spite of Yeats's Irish revival movement. With the advent of the radio, the need for local storytellers and communal festivities diminished.[11] Many Celts were wrenched from their sacred relationships to each other in community, the tribal land, mythic history, and the rich aesthetic/spiritual otherworld. Granted inadequate economic and spiritual means to maintain their participation with the unitary world, they, like other peoples in similar cultural and personal distress, have suffered "anomic depression."[12] Thus they have been particularly prone to using secular buttresses for individual security.

In many cultures increased substance abuse is associated with the pressures of cultural change just as it most threatens individuals during crucial transitional periods in the life cycle when loneliness and alienation may be prevalent. In ancient Ireland the patterns sanctioning the sacred use of the *medb* aided those experiencing societal and individual transition. Initiatory rites supported enlarged consciousness and eased the passage from one state to another with structures sustaining both individuals and group. The same archetypal pattern underlies modern secular variants in Ireland.[13] The pub took over the function of the ancient mead hall as an unhallowed gathering place. Today whole families find their comfort and nourishment in this vital institution of village life. In the pub local adults commune together with Guinness and music, seeking to fill the voids where the old roots once grew strong. Under British rule, *pocheen* (the powerful home brew) became readily available because moonshine production assumed an important part in the rural economy. "Drinking and 'getting rowdy' . . . [became] both a pastime and a sort of informal initiation for modern [Irish and] Irish-American males."[14] While children are not allowed much drink, starting in adolescence Irish men in Ireland and their adopted countries drink hard and boisterously to prove their manhood and express their Irishness.[15] Local festivals from St. Patrick's Day to Puck's Fair rarely resonate with their sacred meaning as ancient tribal assemblies. Today they are more often reduced to unholy invitations to indulge in ethnic pride, alcoholic binges, and trade. The secularization of the *medb* has resulted in widespread virulent and compulsive behaviors, and alcoholism has become a serious social, economic, and spiritual problem in Ireland as it is in much of the modern, secular world.

We have learned a great deal about the economic and social stresses that play their part in creating the problem of addiction. Loss of a job, frustrations about unemployment, dropping out of school, and living where it is easy to get drugs and alcohol but hard to get quality treatment all correlate with tendencies towards addiction.[16] Social, racial, and gender insecurities accompanied by a sense of inferiority, inadequacy, and/or powerlessness, dysfunctional family dynamics (including marital and child-rearing problems), social phobias and learned hopelessness, inabilities to identify, express, and process emotions, fears of success or failure, of old age and death, of boredom, loss of an important personal relationship or social role, and loss of meaning and direction may turn us towards addictive solutions. There are peer and family pressures to use substances to support gender roles that may also be factors in any addiction. We are coming to realize then that the addict is an individual caught in a web of cultural, economic, genetic, chemical, psychological, and spiritual tensions.

Ecstasy Demonized

The polymorphous experiences of the body and its ecstasies, which we know from childhood, are part of Maeve's rites. But patriarchal religions consider them demonic or at best a dangerous source of heretical perceptions unless they can be made to fit into already revealed Church dogma. Mystical sects and individuals who discover their own visions and connections with the matrix of life coexist precariously within, for example, the larger frames of Judaism, Christianity, and Islam as separated offshoots, which the orthodox institutions may seek to co-opt and control or may even persecute.

In one medieval Celtic description, individual cosmic wisdom is specifically ascribed to the demonic outcome of passionate but illicit sex with a girl, whom we can see has some of the qualities and gifts that once belonged to a great goddess like Maeve.[17] In the story the Welshman Meilyr, "who could explain the occult and foretell the future," is said to have obtained his gift from "a girl he had loved for a long time" when he was finally "enjoying himself in her arms and tasting her delights." She was at that moment transformed from a beauty into the repulsive hag form of the goddess (rather than the other way around as the older mythology knew the process—see chapter 9). The Christian legend tells us that poor Meilyr lost his wits and "became quite mad." He, however, also acquired quite mad oracular sight through the euphoric orality and lovemaking with his shapeshifting goddess. He was deemed to be possessed by "unclean spirits" or "demons," for only with such damnable "help" did his contemporaries feel he could prophesy the future so well.[18] In spite of the demons, he was consulted as a sibyl by many people including the churchmen of his day. Meilyr's story tells us that the profound capacity for initiation and visionary experience acquired through the body in the arms of the goddess had become demonic in religions of the book. Thus Meilyr was temporarily rid of these illicit but useful presences by placing the Gospels in his lap. The holy book on Meilyr's sexual organ is an apt image to signify the attempt in what became the dominant Western culture to repress his ecstatic, mystical vision and its "unclean" blissful source.

Although such vision is individually valid and may be recognized, as in the "mad" Welshman's case, as possessing a measure of objective and prophetic truth even by the contemporary churchmen who consulted Meilyr, it is at variance from what parishioners are taught.[19] As we have seen, in all societies valuing mystical experience each individual may participate directly to perceive the supernatural even though such multisensory experiences may be dosed, supported, and understood within traditional ritual frames. The main tenants of exoteric Western religion, however, are based on the sacrifice of individually sensed bodily attunement. They require obedience to already revealed and written dogma and socially adaptive propriety, which are considered valid, good, and godly. This obedience has too often replaced the individual's search for a vision of truth because the exoteric forms of institutionalized patriarchal religions attempt to create followers with a limited and obedient ego, with a disciplined, sentient, and mortal sense of identity that devalues original, expansive, and imaginal individual experience.[20] The elation that the *medb* induces destroys both conventional established form and patterns of compliance and self-control. Maeve encourages individual embodied consciousness to taste its own transcendence.

Without living, embodied, emotional, and ecstatic participation with our larger matrix, all of us are left alienated from the original and interiorly experienced security in community and cosmos. "By age eight," writes Morris Berman, "the magical [non-alienated, kinesthetically perceived] . . . world is finished for [most modern] children; participatory consciousness becomes the exception rather than the rule."[21] Maintaining or reestablishing a ritual connection to such matrix consciousness is indeed a difficult task when our culture does not inherently provide one.

Maeve herself and her magical, nonalienated, kinesthetically perceived participatory consciousness with its power to transcend and transform the individual have rarely been granted the blessing of the churches. Although shunted aside, those powers are nonetheless sought and honored unconsciously and in secular aberrations of the old rites. This separation of secular and sacred patterns of ecstasy poses a major problem for the more permeable and, perhaps, ultimately mystical and creative—though too often unprepared—modern individual ego. Lacking the ritual containers that support the participant's consciousness and mediate any substance's powerful and mind-altering effects, we suffer problematic relations to ecstasy and expanded consciousness. Many today seek these in foreign religions from Tantra to Voudon. Others find them in secular aberrations of the religious spirit. Thus young addicts speak of "getting wings" when they are first introduced into the use of a needle and talk of "giving wings" when they introduce another to drugs.[22] They claim the addiction with the compelling allegiance once granted to a deity. For them the shooting gallery, the bar, and the lonely room have become places where each one may participate in a dark desacralized ritual, but one that erodes rather than enhances collective life.

Maeve as the Loathsome Death Goddess

When we confront Maeve consciously and with reverence, we can see that she represents a pattern of wholeness underlying health and expanded awareness. When we fall unconscious into her energy field, these same patterns can be found underlying dissociation, disease, and toxic destruction.

The Celts knew the ravages of drink. We have heard Roman comments on the besotted incapacitation of their Gallic adversaries. The Christian scribes who wrote down the great early Ulster epic in the twelfth century also suggest a subtext in *The Tain*. Along with other slights to the goddess, they imply Maeve's scurrilous use of wine and sex to enlist the previously unwilling support of her champions. Many a warrior Maeve and Aillil sent forth was bribed, flattered, and finally given "wine until he was drunk" before each would agree to battle alone against Cuchullain.[23]

The Celts told another story to illustrate the terrible and deathly powers of Maeve when she was not honored as the spirit of a transcendent process by appropriately prepared seekers within a sacred ritual space. It is an apt metaphor of addiction. Maeve of Cuala, they say, became angry at five brothers who were sons of a king. They sought to take over her lands, deciding to become kings in their own right without revering Maeve as the earth goddess and principle of sovereignty and without enacting the sacred marriage ritual to become her consorts. In retribution Maeve changed her shape into that of a leper and appeared to the false kings where they rested from hunting. Then she seduced each of the brothers who had spurned her. One by one the usurpers went off eagerly to lie with her, and she bound and killed each one.[24]

Just as the arrogant kings sought to overturn the ancient law of the land, so in response to them, the goddess of the land overturned her own ritual. Instead of leading the brothers to regal initiation through the holy marriage rite, in this tale she seduced them and led them into slavery and death. By the oldest law of justice—the revenge that balances hurt by inflicting equal injury—the goddess, whose kingdom, power, and glory were in danger of being killed, killed.[25] She sent to their deaths the ones who would negate and fragment the matrix that she represents.

Culture—in this case the new forms of patrifocal kingship represented by the five usurping brothers—attempted to ignore, subvert, and control the processual order that is represented by the goddess. It is an order of trans-species relationships that underlies all earthly life including seeming chaos. It is perceived through subtle embodied awareness that attunes with the human and animal group mind, synchronous event patterns, and the energies of the earth's geography itself. The kings of the story did not want to acknowledge this deeper order. They sought to repudiate matrix consciousness and forego Maeve's initiatory gift of the ritually heightened awareness that might attune with it. No longer submitting humbly to the transcendent process that relativizes their dominion, the kings signify the then new forms of consciousness that felt threatened by and became defensively superior to nature and the old religion. This new consciousness fosters a sense of individual entitlement and possessions and an illusion of permanence. It is based on attempts to polarize against, negate, and ultimately control the experience of being merely embedded in process and its cyclic transformative rhythms. Such consciousness separates itself with a sense of objective order and seeks to dominate what seems threateningly irrational and chaotic. It makes its own discriminations, fragmenting the original pattern of wholeness to which temporary kings were subordinate. It creates abstractions and oppositional concepts: good and bad, virtue and sin, above and below, mine and yours. It fears the loss of clear boundaries and lacks the humility required to live with paradox and flow. It fragments reality to claim rule over it.

We can see such development as a necessary step in the evolution of consciousness similar to the growth of new forms of cognition in childhood. In this case culture supports the process of evolution towards what may eventually create an integral form of consciousness.[26] The development is expressed in several Celtic myths in which the goddesses, representing matrix consciousness, gave birth to twins, representing the oppositions inherent in rational consciousness. After birthing the new potentials, the goddesses withdrew to enable or even support the culture of their progeny. Thus Aranrhod and other once great deities vanished to their island castles, only to be seen at magical intervals by heroes granted the vision. The agricultural mare goddess Macha suicided to become the foundation sacrifice of patrifocal Ulster and was buried under the newly created mound where the chiefs assembled their tribespeople and trained their warriors.[27]

The story tells us that in response to the threat of the usurping brothers, Maeve turned herself into a leper. She boldly embodied her new role as outcast and confronted the new kings with their rigidly derogatory attitude toward the old religion. In leprosy, areas of the skin become scaly, ulcerous, and numb. Ultimately, afflicted parts of the body rot and disintegrate. Leprosy is thus the disease of fragmentation.[28] Like Meilyr's girl who became ugly to the new cultural rulers who wanted to demean her powers, the leprous goddess expresses the psychological fragmentation facing those who would blithely oppose matrix consciousness and the goddess' authority. Emboldened by their heroic ego ideal and urge to dominate, the kings become adversaries of the goddess and lose access to the security and spirit of the whole process of life in transformation. Separated from their original matrix[29] in identity with power instead of relatedness, they suffer psychological fragmentation. Thus Maeve shows the five kings the only face of her unitary order that they can now see.

The energies of the goddess nonetheless remain powerful. Even though they are outlawed or psychologically repressed because they are equated with chaos and eventually with sin in the new consciousness, they stir us. They claim each of our five senses. They excite the irrational depths that still live passionately under simplistic binary controls and attempts at dominative autonomy. Leprous and fragmenting as she is, the diseased goddess holds the seductive fascination of the outcast or repressed opposite even to the kings who represent the dominants of heroic culture. She lures, seeping under the new culture's hybris when its kings are "resting." No longer goal directed in their hunting, they relax the purposive actions that ensure maintenance of the new self-controls. The kings let go, the way any contemporary worker or executive might after hours. Entitled now through the virtuous accomplishment of their performance, they indulge in what they would otherwise spurn and yet cannot do without. Today such strivers might feel finally released by age or ill health from a lifetime of performance and lose the emotional intensity of performance ambition that has supported their capacity to embody the heroic ideal.[30] Then feeling depression's fragmentation and abandonment, they and modern warriors reaching retirement may refuse to honor the goddess of nature's organic transformations and find themselves instead susceptible to Maeve's powers in the addictive forms through which the heroic ego often attempts to regain illusory control of her processes.

We know that most individuals who become addicts ignore the reality of Maeve's leprosy. They do not see the defensive fragmentation and dissociation in themselves that make them initially susceptible to seduction. As do these kings, they go off with her in denial, as if there could be no problem with such lovemaking. They begin their relationship as a mere dalliance, sure they are in control, sure there is no danger. With a sense of delight, ease, relief, enlivenment, and relaxation, they take up with a substance or behavior that seems to be only an aide or enhancement for living. The part of them still longing for unity with the matrix is unconscious, and they cannot discriminate between regressive or expansive and growth-enhancing means of relinking to it. Thus they can be seduced into using addictive substances to survive a misery or to become temporarily part of the social matrix from which many heroic individualists are emotionally alienated. Even after they are deeply enmeshed, they may deny their enslavement.

Leprous Maeve tightens her grip as the user falls increasingly under the control of the addictive substance or behavior and becomes ensnared by its compulsive grip. The addictive source increasingly serves as a pseudo-matrix without which the addict feels unable to live. So negatively focused, the addict becomes increasingly inert and abandons further potentials for development. Finally, fully revealing its malevolent potential, the dalliance turns into a bondage, holding the addicted one out of life, a bondage that cannot be undone even when the participant tries.[31] "Alcohol changes from a harmless or enjoyable substance to a deadly poison . . . and becomes for the alcoholic the embodiment of death itself."[32] As an executive in recovery put it,

> *I began looking for social effectiveness and relaxation, the kind of ease where I could feel at home. Pushing so hard in life, that's never been easy for me to find . . . . But seeking paradise, I ended in hell. Even when I realized it was the wrong track, I couldn't stop until it got me all the way there.*

With his very syntax the former addict revealed the ineluctable power of the now leprous matrix in which his heroically striving and separated ego had thought he could dally to find the comforts of home.

We know that if our existence and capacities have felt worthless and shameful, we remain partially unconscious of ourselves and are thus susceptible to feeling powerless. If basic drives like dependency, sexuality, and aggression are made to seem disgusting to repress their lure, they attract us more powerfully when our guard is down. We may then become so obsessed we waste time and energy in righteous contempt of the behavior, or captivated by our attention to the person who indulges in such "sin." We may even inadvertently encourage such outlawed "shadow" behaviors in another, as was the case with the confessor of a therapy client. The client remembered that in his early youth he had learned all about masturbation and alcohol from his priest, who had shamed his budding sexuality and asked him prurient and overly explicit questions. Later in life while struggling to live abstinently, he found himself ineluctably drawn to experience what the priest had called sin. In spite of his best intentions he felt compelled to sneak off to look at prostitutes. After every orgiastic bout he felt suicidally guilty, and he used therapy at first only to comfort himself and reconstitute his self-esteem through an idealizing, positive transference to his therapist. Recovering somewhat from shame, his consciousness relaxed. Since shame and guilt represented consciousness for him, however, his behaviorial controls lapsed without the vigilance that self-blame supported, and he found himself again compelled to revisit what he called "the dens of iniquity." Like the arrogant kings, he had been brought up to deny the goddess and the necessary "friendship of her thighs" even as he unconsciously submitted to her seductions. Without any deliberate alternative and creative ways to claim and honor the pull of sovereign nature on his loins and to rule over his own life with its blessing, he fell back repeatedly into the leprous bindings of his sexual addictions.

We know that without reverence for the higher power in the *medb* and without consciously observed rites to honor and channel the source of the concrete and transformative energies of the goddess, righteous churchgoers can become sex and power addicts, social drinkers can become alcoholics, and medication users can become substance abusers. Then the mind-altering energies and substances may create passionate attachments that are stronger than the ego itself and stronger than any superego controls over them. The addictive substances or compulsive behaviors thus acquire godlike powers, and modern addicts may even unconsciously confuse them with gods, or as poet Jimmy Santiago Bacca says very directly in his poem "El Gato," "Crack is god [because it] transforms despair into heaven." Users are thus seduced, captivated, and bound into dependency on the *medb*, and Maeve's sovereignty is reasserted, albeit in secular and perverted form.

We can say from a psychological standpoint that the tale of the usurping kings also poignantly represents the fate of the person—or particular complex or part personality—that tries to grab transpersonal power illicitly. It tells us the fate of tricky hybris that would steal power without respecting the goddess' rituals and the authority of her processes. Rather than initiating the new ruling dominants of consciousness, the goddess as the addictive *medb* becomes then powerfully captivating, and Maeve's capacities to alter consciousness become a leprous and fragmenting disease and deathly danger. She becomes the deity of fragmentation and death. As addiction, her forces undermine the disrespectful ruling dominants and impel their return to unconsciousness. As addiction, her powers become the focus of life, giving it meaning and structuring a mode of existence devoted to getting high. In our inner cities this drug culture has evolved into a world in which its denizens are committed to the death goddess since they have no other purpose in life. Like Cuchullain, they expect to die young. Unlike Cuchullain, they are willing to destroy themselves and their communities to support their habit. Proudly they call themselves drug fiends.[33]

Applicable to all those prone to addiction, this story of Maeve's power over the false kings also warns us to be wary of arrogant assumptions, to be wary of claiming more than we are fated to gain and able to sustain. It expresses a legitimate, even necessary fear for all of us who seek power, authority, and the enlargement of consciousness. We cannot always be sure if some siren-hag is luring us to death through righteous omnipotence or to transformation through our partnership with transcendent processes. This quandary must be the humbling companion of all societal and political endeavor as well as of all inner psychological work, since there is inevitably a shadow aspect in what we are trying to do. For help in making the necessary discriminations, we will need continually to search our consciences and attend to the messages our dreams convey as they mirror our current psychological and spiritual reality.[34]

Acceptable Indulgence

Certainly not all drug use is addictive. It may even today be part of a sacred ritual, as is the wine of Christian communion or the peyote mushroom of the Native American Church. When its use seems purely secular, a potentially habit-forming drug may be thought of as a temporary response to a stressful situation in a medical emergency or combat zone— and the combat may be in war, business, or even a school-examination crisis. Sharing a joint or line or bottle of alcoholic beverage with social peers may be a recreational activity. It may be part of a brief experiment. Thus adolescents may try out the currently popular mind-altering drug to feel what it "does" for them. Or seekers of an experience of ecstasy may try to open the mind's doors with drug assistance. Scientists have used drugs like LSD and marijuana to support research on fetal and birth memories and for the alleviation of pain. When any of these lead to intensified and compulsive use, however, we speak of toxicomania and addiction.[35]

To survive within the stresses of the modern world, probably most of us participate at some point and to some extent in addictive behaviors. Fortunately a wide variety of them are not life-threatening, although even those with a gentler grip on us have the same outlines as others that may be lethal. We all too easily find ourselves possessed by needs that claim us compulsively and cannot be gainsaid or ended without withdrawal symptoms. These may be life-enhancing, "positive addictions" or they may be life-threatening because they are dangerous in themselves, because they lead to lowered physical functioning, or because they become overwhelmingly obsessive and destroy our psychic and social equilibrium. We may be subject to cravings for specific mind-altering substances, for certain foods, for drugs and alcohol. Prescription drugs, nicotine, caffeine, alcohol, and sweets are all commonly used and misused to mitigate stress and assuage depression and anxiety. Cannabis, amphetamines, cocaine, and heroin are readily available in the streets and at many social gatherings.

Rather than depending on substances, we may find ourselves dependent on states of emotional and hormonal soothing and arousal stimulated by sex, romance, rage, gambling, threatening crises, power, loss and rejection, exhibitionism, risktaking, caretaking, fasting and bingeing, worry, meditation, exercise, work, activity, and even depression, guilt, and self-hate. Panic itself has a dissociative "adrenaline high" that can become addictive even though it is experienced as painful. As one client explained over several therapy sessions:

I easily fall into terror and helplessness. It keeps me small and quivering, filled with a familiar abyss-feeling . . . . It happens to me, and I've always thought it was my fate to suffer it . . . . I begin now to see this panic as an addiction. It is my oldest, clearest [emotional] place and power. . . Fear was my safety, my caretaker. It sweeps me away in its arms. . . . When I was scared, my mother couldn't attack [me] further. She'd have to take pity and stop . . . Maybe she liked driving me to terror with her stories of sin and the slappings. But I learned I was safe in the fear. . . . It prevented my learning to express myself or think, but I could float in it, completely "out" . . . . It's a pull that feels consuming. Like a drug.

Even the more benign addictions are stronger than habits. Called repetition compulsions or neurotic habits, these unconscious methods of managing stress are usually psychologically useful. Few people are therefore addiction free. Some of our compulsions may even be culturally sanctioned. Exercising, house-cleaning, dieting, watching television, shopping, smoking, playing cards, gossiping, scapegoating, ruminating about one's body, one's finances, one's political security, or one's family, working long hours, or even attending church are all supported in various segments of society. They can, however, all become compulsive. When the activity evokes no shame, although it is felt as a commanding necessity for living comfortably and structuring one's behavior and emotions, it may be considered a socially approved "normalized" addiction. Workaholism, for example, is called "the addiction most rewarded in our culture."[36] Sharing such mutually acceptable, compulsive, ritualistic behaviors bonds individuals into groups and thus has an important social function.

The Spectrum within Addictive Behavior

I feel that the nonchemical root of all such dependency on compelled behaviors for stress reduction and stimulating arousal lies in the same primitive areas of the individual psyche in which are found the existential insecurities and cravings of the full-blown substance abuser. The difference is one of degree rather than kind. Along this continuum no one can afford to be judgmental. But all of us need to become aware, for one of the hallmarks of any addiction is its capacity to evoke an altered or trance state where we lose access to ordinary perceptivity and rational thinking and assessing functions. The trance may be relaxing, a kind of holiday from stress, or blissfully intense, but we need to know when and how we enter this state, for in it we are beside ourselves and hence susceptible to compelled behaviors, cognitive distortions, and even to suggestion.[37] We can easily find ourselves open to manipulation by forces we would normally dismiss. In our present secular culture, advertisers of products and political candidates spend millions on research to discover how best to fan our addictive propensities and excite us to collude with their purposes. Like con artists they learn to take full advantage of our compulsive tendencies. A recent obvious case is that of the tobacco companies, which pitched their ads to lure us towards the easily aroused fascinations of sex and power even as they adjusted levels of additives and the amount of physically addicting and consciousness-altering nicotine in their products to ensure our pleasure in the enslavement.

The wide variety of disparate addictive behaviors arises, I think, from the same set of underlying factors that structures the patterns of the alcoholic and drug abuser. Whether we are totally ravaged or only partially caught in ritualistic behaviors, all of our unconscious bondage to such compulsions has biological as well as psychological and spiritual components. The interrelationship has become somewhat clearer in regard to alcohol and specific drugs where the issues of neurophysiological motivation and changes in the patterns of brain-rewarding circuits during addictive highs have been studied. The relationships between the more subtle addictive effects of adrenaline, dopamine, other endorphins, and naturally occurring hormones and opiate-like brain substances need much more exploration, as do the stimuli arousing them and the behaviors that are in turn further aroused by them.

Some of the complex interrelations can be seen in an example from a client who was dependent on drugs and masturbation. He decided to say "no" to his addictions and reach for what he called "a higher solution." He entered a six-month meditation retreat with a religious group where he knew he would have no access to his previous addictions of choice. He did not consciously realize that he was simply switching one addiction for another. He became as dependent on meditative "highs" as he had been on drugs and sex. Meditation, which he pursued for spiritual enlightenment and

psychological calming, also alters endorphin levels and
changes brain waves and cognitive and autonomic nervous
system patterns. The rewards of all of these changes sustained
him and enabled him to maintain the arduous routine.
Indeed at the end of the retreat, he felt the concomitant
withdrawal of emotional and physiological rewards as "a
terrible return to old misery." He had simply switched his
"drug" and been able to sustain himself with the newer
rewards as long as he was in an environment that deprived
him of pot and held him to the meditative focus. Without that
containment he relapsed, returning to his previous
compulsive use of marijuana and masturbation. Faced with
evidence that the underlying factors predisposing him to
addiction had not been dealt with, his spiritual advisor told
him either to return to the monastery or enter therapy.
Increasingly, transpersonally oriented psychologists and
teachers of meditative practices are recognizing the need to
work at establishing the fundamental personal, emotional,
and social stability required to create the groundwork for an
authentic spiritual journey.

Although the current use of the term
"addiction" implies vice and self-harm, the word itself has
both secular and sacred meanings. *Addicere* originates in the
Latin word *dicere*, which means "to speak or declare" from
the Indo-European root *deik*—"to pronounce solemnly" as in
judgment—and the Latin prefix *ad* or "toward." In Roman
secular custom *addicere* meant to make over goods to
another by sale or legal sentence and/or to assign debtors
into the service of their creditors as slaves. The original
addictus was thus brought to court and sentenced into
slavery because he could not pay his debts. He was forced to
become devoted to his creditor. *Devovere* means vowed away,
promised down to the gods of Earth and the underworld, or
consigned to doom. Addiction's wider definition—giving
oneself up to a habit or unconsciously consenting or being
devoted to some pattern of mind-body behavior—thus
reflects more than secular usage. In the ancient world one
solemnly declared oneself to the gods by bearing witness to
their powers.

Among the Celts such devotion and readiness to sacrifice was exhibited through the wearing of a *torc*, a round collar that was the emblem of aristocracy and of certain divinities. Often it was made of a precious metal. We find such *torcs* on a Roman representation of a dying Gallic warrior, and many golden ones have been retrieved from troves deposited in sacred lakes and springs, in man-made shafts, and on hilltops.[38] Thus *addicere* also implies the religious devotion or declaration of allegiance to a deity by whom one is then possessed, just as a debtor is assigned or sentenced to the service of his or her creditor.[39] In addictive behaviors as we know them, the addict unconsciously and compulsively seeks to invoke a larger power in and through the mind-altering substance, emotion, or behavior. Like the usurping kings in Irish myth, he or she is also enslaved, possessed, and sentenced to serve the power habitually. We will be following the interweavings of this bivalent meaning pattern throughout this book.

Addicted Modern Warriors

We still use intoxicants today to gain the effects that Celtic culture invoked for members of its four social groups. We still find alcohol and other substances used to anaesthetize us against the pains and anxieties of life; to stimulate an illusion of magically omnipotent control, self-sufficiency, and power; and to reduce inhibition against intense emotions like fear, joy, rage, grief, and shame. Celtic warriors ritually used the *medb* for all of these purposes. Modern alcoholics who may struggle to feel assertive find that the *medb* sometimes enlivens because it depresses the severe superego inhibitions that take the place of authentic authority in their psyches. The mind-altering substances may also serve as a stimulus to outbursts of powerful-feeling sadism. Cocaine addicts find that their *medb* enhances access to energy and emotionality. "Crack" and "ice," which are cocaine and amphetamine derivatives respectively, cause especially volatile expressions of aggression. But modern *medb* users have no ritual training with their mead and no loyalty to Maeve or even to a princely leader whose activities serve the whole of society. Instead they are liable to elevate to divine status the addiction or the criminal leaders in charge of their supplies or societal models who seem strong and ruthless. To these they grant loyalty and from them they seek a mirror of the individual value and honor they cannot otherwise sustain.

Often those prone to addiction suffer a sense of self so fragile and easily bruised by the responses of others (or the lack of response) that they require nearly constant affirmation to recognize themselves and thus to feel that they exist as a font of perceivable, valid, effective, and shared experience. The source of the addiction itself, the attention of addicted buddies, and illusions of fused relationship to their powerful heroes temporarily support such a sense of existence. Dependent on these outer supplies, lacking hope for any future without pain, without a secure interior sense of self, and feeling increasingly unable to live up to the standards of their ego ideal, they may try to cover their deeply pervasive shame and despair with denial, bravado, rage, and/or charm. But beneath the tough and trickster facades, they are often racked with needs to gain honor by becoming perfect, all knowing, and fully in control of events. Often they are so easily made anxious they unconsciously eject painful emotions onto others whom they can then blame and use as adversaries to restore a temporary illusion of their own goodness, strength, and cohesive integrity. Inevitably they are self-absorbed and eventually may become psychopathic as they slide further into addiction and the focus of life revolves increasingly around their craving.

In such identity with the archetypal emotions of the archaic Self, addicts can also fall into states where they can easily act as omnipotent beserkers against anyone who offends their aggravated emotional sensitivities, even against their own children. They then embody the aroused warrior who is in unconscious identity with the war goddess aspect of

Maeve and terrify those on whom they act out their fury.
Children of addicts are well aware of this maddened warrior,
a depraved slave of the death goddess, whose addictive binges
have led to child abuse, lying, cheating, stealing, and the
killing of relationships.[40] An Irish-American client
remembered:

*[Mother] raged and shrieked like a banshee,[41] out-of-control and
warring against her kids instead of against the cruel system that had
made her have ten of us, or against the real problems [we had] . . . .
[She was] stealing from the house money, and always lying about
her drinking . . . . Usually drunk fathers terrified my friends, but
my mother, who prayed so much, was a holy, abusive terror for the
sake of the drink.*

Mary Doyle Curran gives us other portraits of such rages in
her depiction of the protagonist's uncles and brothers in her
novel *The Parrish and the Hill*.[42] Not only are the children of
addicts victims of parental-beserker energy, but most of the
violence in our society and even in our schools is related to
addiction. Drug-related violence has spilled over inner-city
boundaries into more affluent suburbs. "Addiction and
incarceration are common partners in crime" reads the title of
an article. A prison superintendent reports, "Close to 99% of
my inmate population was high on something when they
committed the crime responsible for their incarceration."[43]

Without internalized communal or transpersonal
guidance in dealing with aroused impulsivity and in the face
of the *medb's* anesthesia of superego inhibitions, the berserk
addict may feel helpless panic at the eruption of the primitive
aggressive drives that mark the appearance of the unhonored
and uncontained war goddess. There is no felt psychological
space between the emotion and its release into action, just as
there is no felt space between the craving and its being acted
upon. Since frustration and anxiety are still no more tolerable
than they are for an infant and because affective and symbolic
expression is blocked, the eruptive aggressive energy can
reverse and sour easily into suicidal rage against the Self and
the painful life process. As one person abused in childhood
and prone to addictive relapses explained:

I still feel so helpless . . . [and] my anger is totally ineffective to stop
them [the hurtful and frustrating others whom she could not find
focused strength to confront] so I turn it against myself and what I
need and my own mind. I go numb and feel like I should die . . .
find oblivion, but I never do it, [I] just fall towards it and find
myself needing a hit.

Caught between the illusion or acting out of
omnipotent power and the fear of that power, addicts
increasingly depend on their mind-altering *medb* to both
stimulate and soothe. As one typically sensitive addict
described her dual allegiance to toxic substances for both
arousal and calming,

There's so much pain and excitement. Life feels like a dentist's drill
on raw nerves. I crave the intensity, because I don't trust anything
that's not intense. But then I can't stop it, and I need the novocain
that alcohol and drugs provide.

Possessed by transpersonal energies that enhance and
frighten, those prone to addiction lack positive relations to the
matrix where they might have developed internal structures
to contain, filter, and mediate raw experience and their own
helplessly raging responses. The lack of connection to the
archetypal ground may be due to genetic propensity, fetal
traumata, cultural or personal factors leading to early
deprivation of attuned care and/or childhood abuse. Many of
the addicts on inner-city streets are themselves children of
addicts and grow up in a society without hope for any
alternative future. Any of these causes may result in an
inadequately or destructively constellated relationship to
mediating maternal functions, which then creates what
Jungians call a negative parental/child complex imaged as a
death mother like leprous Maeve. Not seeing their value
mirrored and lacking opportunity to develop adequate
internal structures to support self-esteem and functioning,
addicts seek containment and manage life defensively with
repeated self-medication. With a dose of such help they can
dissociate and lose awareness of pain and shame and/or
identify with emotion to fill up the empty core. The client
above drowned in her familiar habit of suicidal ideation. It
seemed preferable to grappling with her own access to the

aggression she had found so intolerably sadistic in childhood when it was used against her and her siblings. Another recovering client felt her mother escaped a chaotic family and drunken husband into the trance induced by "rotely saying her rosary and calling on the holy saints." Both of these women had used addictions that felt virtuous, thus proudly honorable and good, because they understood their religions as supporting an ideal of masochistic submission. The cruel withholding power expressed as neglect of the children by the rosary-sayer was hidden and not even in the client's awareness when she reported her mother's behavior and acted out a similar pattern in her own.

The addictive search acts on body and spirit to prevent the addict's dealing more creatively with frustration and primitive drive energies. Symbolically then, these impoverished modern weaklings using their *medb* to become quick and impassioned proud warriors are seduced and bound, and their capacity for fruitful living is killed.

Addiction in Modern Kinship Ceremonies

In their Assemblies the Celtic tribespeople used the *medb* to celebrate the divinity of the harvest in festive communion. In the modern world the net of spiritual and societal interconnections is often invisible or broken. Loss of communal connection with land and kin is assured by industrial economics, political fragmentations, and by the cultural ideal of independence. Thus the modern "user" of mind-altering substances or mind-altering emotions and behaviors often indulges without reverence for the seasons and service to Earth—simply to loosen the boundaries and inhibitions that create feelings of alienation and the painful anxiety that is called social phobia. The modern addict—whether addicted to drugs, behaviorially induced hormones, or to the exhilarating and painful relationships of romance, intimacy, or sex—attempts to infuse the sense of being a lone and lost individual with a sense of harmonious security in cosmos, community, and libidinal power. But often because of severe problems in the early fit between caretaker and child that enables satisfactory bonding, such addicts both crave and fear personal intimacy. The craved intimacies, when they are then created through addictive substances and relationships, become dangerously engulfing—like a deathly "regression to . . . [fusion with another] wherein it is impossible to distinguish where Self ends and Other begins." Hence the addict often only reexperiences "the ultimate horror . . . of collapse back into the abyss"[44] of suffering similar to that which has been experienced in childhood through intense and intimate relatedness with misaligned caretakers.

Not surprisingly, we are discovering the links between addictive behaviors and psychologically damaged personalities as well as with dissociative and borderline levels of parts of the psyche.[45] Individuals who become addicted are often particularly sensitive humans, opened very early and/or with repeated traumata to the experience of overwhelming emotions with which they could not learn to cope.[46] Because in their personal lives universal needs for caring relationships have not often enough been satisfactorily met, they experience legitimate but heightened needs for safe and meaningful relationships to others, to themselves, and to mediated transpersonal emotional energies. When stressed, they are susceptible to reexperiencing early chaotic feelings and regressing to more primitive structural stages of identity. A pub drinker in Frank McCourt's novel suggests this link to infancy when he says, "This [stout] is the staff of life. This is the best thing for nursing mothers and for those who are long weaned."[47]

Concrete substances and altered hormone levels provide a partially controllable and seemingly constant object that ensures immediately soothing gratification, easy enlivenment, and reassuring spaciness.[48] Through drink, alcoholics seek an experience of what Erich Neumann calls uroboric bliss. Michael Balint puts it, "[t]he yearning for this feeling of harmony [that the womb provides the infant] is the most important cause of alcoholism or . . . any form of addiction."[49] Unable to bear the long hard work of living because the addict still feels so terrified, possessed by extreme emotions, despairing, enfeebled, and existentially alone, the individual returns repeatedly to self-soothing and self-stimulation "in an attempt to reassure itself that it is alive, even that it exists at all."[50] The addiction thus functions as an inner mother (or selfobject). In bonding to it, individuals prone to addiction also remain bonded to the potentials of infancy that they have not yet been able to grow into and out of.

Such a bond to primitive patterns and concrete consciousness-altering substances and behaviors have prevented more encompassing, symbolically and spiritually developed satisfaction of needs. Instead the addictive solutions have remained in or restimulated the fused, literalistic, and immediately gratifying levels that are typical of early childhood. Actually altering consciousness and providing somatic effects, the addictive solution is not a delusion, but neither is it adequate to satisfy the changing needs of reality. It serves, like a fetish, in a realm between need and material actuality, between psyche and soma, to create a transitory focus and stopgap relief. Indeed, from the perspective of extreme developmental lack, the search for enhancement and relief that leads to addiction can be seen as a desperate creative act. It is an illusion constructed by the infant that is comparable to the terry-cloth cover for the wire mother used in maternal deprivation experiments.[51] Harry Harlow studied the effects of early bonding and separation on baby monkeys. One group of little monkeys left in a cage with a wire sculpture shaped like an adult mother monkey suffered irretrievable developmental harm even though the wire figure provided milk and they were given practical care. Those with a towel-covered dummy mother did somewhat better in that they could recover some of their capacities for relationship and social behaviors when they were returned to their animal families.

Humans with addictive behaviors are often trying, with some desperately seized comfort, to medicate extreme sensitivity to cover despair and the painful gaps in their nurturance. They have grabbed at various mind-altering solutions when no others were available to provide a kind of security-blanket relief from the raw fears of annihilation and the despairing raging depression of abandonment, from the agony of needing a warm parental holding and instead finding only the emptiness and cold wires of an armature. In the face of the caretaker's palpable absence or lack of fit (rather than secure-enough presence) in all or certain particular areas of bonding, the addiction serves as a peculiar kind of transitional object between the archetypal mother, the energic structure we are here calling Maeve, and the needs of the child. It is created or discovered—not in the safe space between human caretaker and infant but in the humanly unmediated gap between the transpersonal mother and the infant. The potentials for assuagement and stimulation come from the great mother of nature working through the psychic and biologic substratum of life—the child's body-mind-spirit, or wholistic consciousness. The infant accepts the comfort and enlivenment as its own creative discoveries and clings onto them.[52] But rather than developing within a trusted human relationship that can mediate archetypal energies, this infantile grip cannot open to grow flexibly and seek more widely. Instead it remains rigid with a desperate craving that prevents further creativity in the very areas of greatest need where dependency on addictive solutions takes over. Even when we fall into actively addictive patterns only later in life, I believe they arise in those areas of deepest need that have never been adequately mediated and that are stirred to desperation by current stress.

We are finding that many psychotherapy clients with early structural damage to their psyches use various addictive behaviors and substances to soothe and enliven their fragmented, enfeebled, and alienated selves and to replace absent and deformed parental introjects. Both the solace and stimulation created through addictive habits provide a substitute for the effective self-soothing, self-esteem, and self-motivation that were not sufficiently fostered during early development and/or that are not again currently available due to the catastrophic stress of present circumstances. Rather than being able to learn how to seek for the satisfaction of long-term intimate relationship and career goals, for example, energy is bound into the immediate acquisition of the next "fix" to assuage the immediate stress.

Because this infant part of the addict has not found a way to internalize a sufficiently sustaining primary relationship to the archetypal ground—one that could support development—it remains paralyzed in the grip of archetypal need and hopeless regarding fulfillment except in relation to the addiction. Desperate for such attuned sustenance, it also fears to abandon the particular scripts created in the originally misconstellated caretaker-child relationship. Even when these patterns have been negative, there is an inertial pull to remain in their familiar matrix. Even when they can be seen as masochistic and self-destructive, they have the implacable attraction of home. Sometimes the therapist is given a glimpse of the overlap of the complex and the addiction. One still-active addict expressed it with typical boundary and time distortions:

I'm not afraid. I just know that I want to go back into the arms of the Stuff. That's where I find myself anyway. . . . It's like the pull to give myself over . . . and having a connection that makes me feel I'm home . . . . Like to my mother. . . . She was the only mother I know. Yes, mean, but I never remember that in the beginning. I only feel the ecstatic joy she got when she drank and then felt her power to abuse us. I can merge into her and even savor the feelings she got from beating us. . . . It's a crazy high . . . like I'm on [cocaine].[53]

Along with feeling this symbiotic merger with the destructive matrix in a terrible bond to the death mother, the addict also fears to reexperience the unbearable terrors of annihilation that suffused his or her awareness in infancy. As one recovered alcoholic put it when therapy touched this level:

The fear [inside myself] is like a silently screaming infant in my chest. I am too afraid to let go and let god [in the Twelve-step phrase]. . . . This infant was never held. I am afraid to move, even to take in my own breath. . . . I could use a drink.

At a similar point another realized:

I still despair just like my father did. It's in the genes. . . . [As a child] I abandoned myself just like [I felt] he abandoned me when he was full of drink and terrible . . . . I abandoned myself to the addiction, but to save myself from feeling the pain that would have killed me then. I guess that's why I had to hit bottom, to see it wasn't such a great solution after all. Once, it was the best I had. And it felt easier than this [therapy]. . . . I know now, with my head at least, that it [binge drinking to blackout] isn't easy. It's also a killer. But going [in therapy] into the old pain feels closer to death. It's full of rage and hate and despair.

Originating from the time when the child was still bonded within the archetypal matrix and when that matrix carried transpersonal powers that were constellated for the child in severely negative and life-threatening form,[54] such existential terrors and abandonment depression continue to feel both compelling and unbearable to the adult addict and constitute a potent regressive lure even for the client in recovery. Addicts "use" substances in order to feel infused with power as well as to find a means of quelling their fears of annihilation and abandonment.

Using drink or drug or hormonal arousal releases archaic, unmediated, and unfocused drives and affects that may feel momentarily compelling and grand. These fill the empty, depressed core of the addict's sense of identity with stimuli that have the intensity of those known in early childhood. Thus there is an urge to seek and fuse with emotional intensity—"the force of it all, the raging, pummeling, inebriating power of passion" as one recovering alcoholic and cocaine addict called it. Another asserted:

I hate mundane. It's flat. I crave intensity, a soaring bliss or a plummeting agony . . . a hit that sweeps me up and fills me up . . . . Even now [in early recovery] I like to have my emotions straight, all-or-nothing, just to get those inebriating extremes.

This client drew her sense of the "soaring bliss," depicting herself as a bodiless head carried off in the grip of a winged demon-lover. The drawing suggested her own identity with the emotion/breast as a gratifying part-object and her dependency on the demonic inebriant to achieve this merger. This woman had been deprived of necessary care in infancy by an overburdened pregnant mother and the sick sibling born when she was eleven months old. Seriously depressed, she had medicated herself for a decade with amphetamines originally supplied by a physician to help her study. For many years her substance-supported emotional font, like a substitute breast, filled up her emptiness and never disappointed her—as long as another "fix" was available.

Medb users may gain some comfort through partaking of substances that lower their inhibitions against opening themselves intimately to others or even performing in social situations. Indeed "the first effect of intoxication is invariably the establishment of a feeling that everything is now well between the [participants] and their environment . . . . [T]he yearning for this feeling of 'harmony' is the most important cause of alcoholism, or for that matter, any form of addiction."[55] Dependent on social drinking, a drug prop, or quick sex, users may get through a social ordeal, but their relationship is to the addiction, rarely to the persons involved. Thus they can only find shallow, sentimental companionship with binge buddies as they celebrate getting through life's tasks and anaesthetizing the sorrows of bad times. They may seek an immediate and illusory beloved or peer group into which they long to sink as into the arms of a bliss-giving mother, but because they suffer a loss of basic trust and an inadequate connection to others and to their own existential value, they are unable to create enduring or deep relationships even with the help of the various forms of the *medb*. Instead, the addiction itself serves as the object of constancy. As one recovering borderline addict said,

My despair and vodka are always there when everything else goes away and I am as afraid as I am in my [repeated] nightmare of falling forever.

Addicted Modern Visionaries

The druids' and poets' ritual use of the *medb* is likewise perverted by modern, secular usurpers. Celtic use of the *medb* enhanced the sense of at-one-ment with the source-ground of life and attuned the trained magus and poet to explore mystic visions of the unitary world. Sacred inebriation permits ecstatic union with the pleromatic whole. Thus Jung wrote to AA co-founder Bill Wilson that the "craving for alcohol is the equivalent on a low level of the spiritual thirst of our being for wholeness."[56] A recovered addict expressed the same thought: "I was looking for *something* [to fill me up], and I found it in drugs, even though I didn't feel good about it."[57] Another said:

In the culture of the streets there is no sense of future except pain. Drugs give people a reason to believe in something. They give each day a purpose—to get high.

A journalist studying substance abuse concluded:

Substance abuse in general, and crack in particular, offers the equivalent of a born-again metamorphosis. Instantaneously, the user is transformed from an unemployed, depressed high school dropout, despised by the world—and secretly convinced that his failure is due to his own inherent stupidity and disorganization. There is a rush of heart-palpitating pleasure, followed by a jaw-gnashing crash and wide-eyed alertness that provides his life with concrete purpose: Get more crack—fast![58]

Thomas Wolfe writes in 1929 of his character's first experimental and intense experience of drink. It gave him "a moment of great wonder—the magnificent wonder with which we discover the simple and unspeakable things that lie buried and known but unconfessed in us. So might a man feel as he wakened after death and found himself in heaven." "Why," he asks, "when it was possible to buy God in a bottle, and drink him off, and become a god oneself, were men not forever drunken?" Modern addicts may start out as explorers like Wolfe's character Eugene Gant, seeking for the something "that lay in him . . . that could not be seen and could not be touched, which was above and beyond him—an eye within an eye, a brain above a brain, the Stranger that dwelt in him and regarded him and was him, and that he did not know."[59]

Millions of individuals around the globe are consciously in the process of seeking new centers of devotion and patterns of identity.[60] These seekers are, inevitably, the very people who have a sense they do not fit within their families of origin and/or conventional society. They are called pathological or black sheep from within the old system's frames. They often feel ashamed, worthless, crazy, and homeless. Beset by social (and often economic) peripheralization and emotional fragility, they feel alienated or exiled. When this sense of alienation is accompanied by powerlessness to effect their future and lack of self-esteem, it is unbearably painful. Thus often before these alienated individuals can be conscious seekers, they become bonded to addictive solutions that they sought only to make existence more tolerable.

The epidemic numbers of addicted individuals who seek solace, harmony, and enlivenment because they cannot fit within their familial and collective contexts and are not yet strong enough to create appropriate new ones provide terrible evidence of a deep cultural change in the making. These individuals have been forced to discover makeshift structures and sources to sustain themselves. Nonetheless their inadequate addictive quest for deepening and healing highlights issues that require attention in all of us. As David Stewart has said, alcoholics "simply express the ideals of every sensitive and imaginative human being in his depths."[61] Unfortunately the misguided creativity that gets co-opted into addictive solutions cannot deeply enough satisfy the quest for those ideals or the quest for deeper meanings.

Seeking an experience of the omnipotent and omniscient Self through ingesting concrete substances, addicts often end as escapists. Like Wolfe himself they may binge on food and alcohol to overcome regressive longings and allow the venting of impulsivity, only to find themselves trapped in the seductions of the *medb*.[62] Usually they "space-out" or "get wings" to medicate and buffer their extreme sensitivities in the face of a present reality that feels too painful to bear. In part because of this fragility, in the areas medicated by their addiction they have not learned reliable verbal and relationship skills to protect their vulnerability, to discriminate emotions, and to mediate their expressions of affect effectively. Like panicked and paralyzed children, they have instead developed the habit of dissociation, fleeing even to unconsciousness, to "far-far" as one recovering addict put it, "just to numb out." There they seek to evade pain, fear, despair, and shame in a regressive, magic bliss defined by illusions of ease and perfection. The addictive trip serves as a surrogate in the place of maternal solace and spiritual meaning.

Celtic visionary travelers voyaged to the otherworld, as we have seen, to glimpse the mythic land of everlasting youth, joy, and beauty where there were no limitations, no sickness, aging, nor death. Sometimes they were sought by their supernatural counterparts to accomplish a task and were rewarded for their service, or they went to bring back knowledge of other realms. Some stories, however, tell of adventurers who were lured away to this state of boundless bounty by the call of a goddess or who undertook their journeys without adequate preparation and consciousness.

Inevitably when the travelers returned to ordinary life, whole centuries had passed, and like our Rip Van Winkle, they were strangers. One voyager longed to revisit his homeland, and when his foot touched its solid earth, his body turned to dust "as though he had been in the grave for hundreds of years."[63] Bran's Assembly of the Wondrous Head lived for four-score years in timeless bliss until one of their company opened the door towards their homeland and its painful reality. "And when he looked, they were conscious of every loss they had ever sustained, and of every kinsman and friend they had ever missed, and of every ill that had come upon them, as if it were even then it had befallen them."[64] Neumann puts this return from a voyage into psychological terms:

[T]his transcending of the limit is a seizure that carries the mystic out of humanity and the world, into an inhuman sphere outside of the world. When this occurs the ravished ego falls back into a hostile world fraught with uncertainty and anxiety.[65]

This kind of journey is common in addiction. Each time the fragile high with its illusions of perfect comfort and peace ends, the addict must return to Earth as a stranger, again forced to suffer what seems a total opposite of bliss-out: a painful, very imperfect, yet familiar horror. Illusions of strength and wisdom crumble to dust, for there is a lack of internal structures to support and care for a constant-enough personality that could weather the highs and lows of ordinary life and mediate what is often a potential medial and visionary gift. Indeed, denial and dissociative avoidance make it impossible for the addict to learn how to proceed step-by-step through reality. The propensity to identify with the ideals of the archetypal otherworld also prevents exposure of the individual's ordinary incapacity. Thus the possibility of learning brings with it fear and shame for not already being perfect, for being the very opposite of perfect.

Returning from the "trip" is often felt as an excruciating lurch emotionally as well as physically. While this felt disintegration may also be masochistically and pseudo-spiritually enthralling, it evokes a repeated craving for "bliss-out." Stuck then in a compulsive search for what Freud reductively called "oceanic feelings of the earliest preverbal gratification,"[66] modern addicts pursue an illusion. This serves as a temporary substitute for experiences of the safe-enough matrix where care feels truly bountiful, where criticism and painful demands do not exist, and where painful encounters and emotions have been sufficiently buffered by adequate maternal shielding.

Devoted to chemicals that lower consciousness of differentiations and create a sense of expanded vision, the addict is often enthralled with the fruits of imagination. Yet without the skills to serve the divine muse and her forms and rites, and without ways to maintain or regain her or his own boundaries and to accomplish the hard, slow work necessary to support individual potentials, the addict cannot transmute vision into healing exploration and art. As one recovering client complained, "A lot of poets and writers drink a lot and some use drugs . . . . I have beautiful ideas, but they never seem to work out." He was experiencing his disillusionment when the marvelous visions of his drug trips vanished in the light of day because he had no idea how to engage with them in the artistic struggle for their incarnation.

Just as escapism cannot be transmuted into art without effort and relationship to the whole Self, rarely can the addict transmute his or her passionate devotion to fragments of experience into poetry. The Celts saw every part of life as a manifestation of the supernatural. The vision that sees the intensity of the whole in every part needs a disciplined aesthetic or religious overview and a concomitant sense of self-coherence and respect. Otherwise the moment's fragment becomes the whole. For the modern addict such magical-level thinking makes the individual's identity feel lost and scattered like the beads in an unstrung necklace of aimless intensities. Or when the negative fragment becomes the whole and only focus, he or she, in identity with that part, feels lost in a totally pain-ridden world or in a limitless wallow of shame and self-hate.

Addicted Modern Rulers

We know that modern perversions of the Celtic sacred regal initiation also occur. Because the person prone to addictions has never felt adequately special to an attuned caretaking and ideal figure in childhood or has been misused and abused as a substitute parental or sexual figure by caretakers who themselves lacked a life-enhancing relation to their matrix, the addiction-prone individual lacks an adequate sense of self-esteem. To compensate for this, the addict still craves the experience of particular specialness and controlling power, even fearing and detesting what might be "merely ordinary and temporary," as one man put it. He said,

I had a terror of excess but a greater love of it . . . . I drank when things were good to bring [myself] down—to dull the excitement, when I felt so overstimulated I might burst, and used drugs to get out of myself when [I was] depressed. I lived big.

Like this client, many people prone to addictions use the addiction to feel "big." One man confessed a secret wish to be "a king baby." But such a king cannot relate as consort to Maeve to foster development. Instead the addict's wish is to remain fused with and/or to fill up with the archetypal emotions of the undifferentiated, archaic Self. Like the woman who drew herself as a round head flying off in the hands of a demon-lover, the addict participates in the Self's grandiosity and identifies with its completeness and omnipotence to foster the illusion of being superior and special. As we have seen, this compensates a pervading sense of emptiness, shame, and inferiority and substitutes for the development of adequate, though limited, psychic structures to mediate personal identity and effective self-rule.

One man, who repeatedly fell back into masturbatory bingeing, put it strongly: "I don't want to be born out of my habit. It's all I know, and I made it up myself." His braggadocio covered fear to leave the only safety he could count on and control, what he hoped was his kingdom. Others proclaim, "I can survive. I can stop any time I want. I'm stronger than the addiction." Such bluster arises from the compulsion to push oneself to the edge to find the reassuring proof that one can survive dissolution and even be reborn out of it. Thus it reveals the addict's illusory bravado in the face of the archetype of life and death. It denies fears of dependency on the addictive substance and, more importantly, on disappointing humans who have been experienced as death dealing in their abandonment or emotional and physical abuse. Its cockiness reminds us of the boasting matches of the youthful Ulster warriors who sought to claim the champion's portion at the feasts and of the defiant assertion of power by the messenger that started the Cattle Raid of Cooley (see page 177). It is similar to the invulnerability we associate with adolescence that makes many addicts act as if they were immortal. Thus they can indulge in dangerous activities and relationships, seeming to live on the brink of survival yet oblivious to or denying the perils of that abyss.

There is even something akin to grandiosity in the addict's habitual though despairing fixation on neglectful, depriving, and abusive sources, which compulsively repeat early negative experience. To wrest any reward from such relationships requires nothing less than omnipotence and omnipotent denial. One woman whose parents misused her child's polymorphous erotic attentions to soothe her workaholic father's sadistic outbursts grew up feeling both as "worthless as a prostitute" and dangerously "more powerful than" her mother. She explained:

If I admit I was powerless in that romantic, incestuous love, I'd have to admit to fear of his rage and my mother's abandonment of me. I'd have to see all my seductions as tricks to get care, to get a mommy and daddy.

She had suffered an addictive sexual craving for male partners that had led her to play the same romantic games with them that she had learned to snare her father from his black moods. She promised everything—the kind of care she secretly craved for herself—and misused her own energy, eroticism, and generosity in the service of an illusion that she might thus fill her unmet dependency needs. When the men—including two therapists—failed to repay her boundless devotion with what she considered adequate rewards, she rejected them abruptly and retreated into lonely depression, glutting herself on binges of sweets and wine in an attempted communion with what she came to call "easy goodness." As she emerged and pledged to go straight, starve herself, and exercise four hours a day, she was drawn to another seemingly powerful man to entice and take care of until she again realized her resentment had outgrown her romanticized omnipotence, and she withdrew to wine and sweets.

At least I'm in charge [she told herself and her new therapist]. If I admit I'm powerless over this, I'd have to think and live differently . . . . It would be death to me to believe I'm a weird addict just living out something I was hooked on. The shame would be killing.

In beginning sobriety the defensive facade of bravado and omnipotence may continue. Still projecting her painful experience of being "parentified," needed as a Self authority by her own parents, the same client said,

I should be able to go into a social situation and bear it . . . prove I won't be seductive or drink . . . . It is too painful to accept that I'm not a superwoman, bigger than the craving and everything else. If I'm only ordinary, no one will ever want to be with me.

The awareness of shame and meaninglessness in the addict usually precedes the addiction itself. More primeval, it arises out of a lack of adequate connection to the holding, receiving, and accepting personal maternal matrix, the child's first incarnation of the goddess and of the individual Self.[67] Sensitive and needy, the infant sees its reflection in the eyes of the neglectful, abusive, or ill-matched parent and internalizes the sense that it is not worthy of good attention. Inevitably it then feels its sensitivity and needs are themselves shameful because they are associated with abandonment and pain. Because the parent cannot be held accountable by the desperately needy and dependent infant, the child assumes responsibility and feels itself shamefully flawed to have brought such pain on itself. The lack is thus defined with a typical reversal that serves to maintain some illusion of omnipotence and control in an otherwise unbearable situation.

Fear of losing such control even when it is only manifest in the power to feel the cause of his or her own misery often makes the recovering addict flee from the conscious acceptance of ordinary reality and ordinary generosity and relatedness. Although the ideal of all-generous caretaking is secretly craved and unconsciously even expected, it falls outside of familiar experience and is therefore frightening and resisted. As the woman above confessed,

I'd rather feel bad, evil, even hateful than [feel] that my truth is painful and like other people's—that I'll never get everything I want—that I'm afraid to really take in anything.

The person prone to addiction has usually had to develop—like this woman—so precociously in a dysfunctional family or deprived social and economic group that she or he is caught in the enforced external adaptation that cannot support individual felt experience from within. The true or authentic self has been hidden behind a falsely competent facade or persona that tries desperately to cope with life. With seeming regality this bravado-ridden defender manages, soothes, charms, bullies, and tricks those on whom the addict fears to be dependent. But deeper learning is blocked. As an alcoholic woman in recovery who had nonetheless gone far in her profession said:

I'm very smart, but only about other people and their needs . . . . I managed to climb pretty far up in the world. That's not hard. I knew I had to be accomplished or I was nothing . . . . About myself though I haven't been able to learn because I've always had to pretend I was fine and wonderful. That grandness hid real well the pain of how I felt, even from me. But I couldn't really support it when I got too close to the top. It was terrifying, [I could finally feel it as] a house built on sticks. That's when I crashed all the way down.

Heroic omnipotence may feel familiar and "necessary," but it is also subtly alien to personal identity. This woman's "false self" of persona super-competence and invincibility was a terrible burden to maintain. Another client expressed his similar suffering:

I act like I am the bionic man who can handle anything, but I feel like I am buried in a quicksand of helplessness, trying to crawl out and not having any idea how to manage even that, certainly not able to ask for a hand.

The addict's "true self" hidden and lost behind these fraudulent, precociously usurping ruling powers and bionic grandiosity remains a fragment of dependency bound into unconsciousness by the leprous Maeve. In her vengeful grip it nonetheless seems to receive a modicum of holding and care. Thus it remains inert, radically dependent, and unable to learn to claim real sovereignty over personal life. The addict's illusory omnipotence then alternates with and is undermined by the secret shame of intrinsic inadequacy. Without positive-enough connection to the individual identity and the guiding Self, which develops in relationship to the early caretakers and on which ordinary self-esteem is based, the person prone to addiction continues to seek the solace of illusory power and care evoked by the leprous Maeve and the addiction. He or she may even feel in control of some security since the simple act of bingeing can gain the illusory omnipotence of ruling a kingdom—at least for a moment and until the stakes are too high as they were for the woman who "crashed." Blind to the addiction's seduction and denying dependency on its shoring up, the addict is equally blind to seeing it is a leprous disease that will revenge this arrogance with inescapable seduction, bondage, fragmentation, and even death.

From a Self perspective we could define the principle of sovereignty that queenly Maeve represents psychologically as self-rule over our own lives and bodies. In addiction this principle, like the usurping kings, seeks to arrogate divine powers. In the process the addict's consciousness loses touch with the underlying process of life and becomes split. Then the person prone to addiction (and those addicted and dissociated parts or complexes of all of us) becomes ruled by two impersonal authorities.[68] One master is the seemingly limitless drive for the addictive solution. The other is a principle of order and limitation constellated as a rigid, sadistic, superego or ego ideal. This ideal is derived from a desperate need to adapt, and thus it is based upon internalized standards felt to belong to the early caretakers or to those whose approval is most feared, albeit needed for security, in the present. Both opposites function autonomously as desperate though divergent claims on the individual. Because they are polarized along collective lines and not connected to the individual authority of the Self, they are unrelated to the subtleties of specific situations and to the deeper processes of life's changing patterns.[69]

With power equal to the addictive craving, the rigid superego authority (the negative, society-based animus of both men and women in post-Jungian terms[70]) enforces its ideal standards and oozes poisonous contempt for anything less. This makes the addict feel abject shame for dependency. Instead of admitting needs because they are defined as weakness and self-indulgence, the addict must deny both need and dependency. The contemptuous animus perpetuates the addict's original deep sense of inadequacy and proneness to panic. Some individuals continue to project such authority onto parents, partner, police, or therapist. Then they live with a compulsion to adapt dutifully to or rebel against those authorities and suffer a painful sense of inferiority and even criminality in relation to them. Others suffer an inner splitting: "My badness is the real me; I never get anything right," one substance abuser in early recovery and still negatively inflated assured the therapist. "I have to run back to feeling bad about myself because that's so familiar, and I know who I am there . . . . It's hard to remember who I am [otherwise]."

This client had repeated dreams in childhood of being a rubber balloon that would fill ever fuller and make him feel terrified that he would explode. He had been physically abused by both parents and had little experience of emotional mediation and holding. Thus he was identified with his affects as they coursed through him. Unable to discriminate their intensity and to relate to them, he tried to manage his fear of being overpowered by rage and other spontaneously flowing energies by holding himself to perfectionist standards. This attempt at ideal control alternated with eruptions of rebellious acting out as if he was invulnerable. He would then binge with drugs and alcohol to feel free enough to indulge in random sexual encounters with sadistic male partners. On these strong men he projected the embracing Self-authority he craved to hold himself together. Seeking it addictively, he needed ultimately to find this strength symbolically and within himself. First, however, he had to find safety and self-acceptance within the therapeutic transference in a positive relationship to a parental figure. As this relationship formed, he slowly began to recognize and acquire structures within himself through which to channel the powerful life energies that were part of his intense personality. For a long time in therapy, however, he expected his female therapist to embody the authority his father had held in his family of origin and provide similarly rigid rules for behavior. At the same time he also defended against such expected rigid authority with diffusion, passive-aggression, lies, and reports (that were full of both pathos and bravado) of his dangerous drug and drinking bouts and liaisons. These defensive behaviors were modeled on those he had experienced in his mother, who had bound her to him seductively while alternately infantilizing him and berating him for incompetence. Through the reports of sexual acting out and drug abuse, he sought both to elicit the masochistic infantilization and negative judgments as familiar forms of holding and to transform the sadistic rule-maker into an adequate caretaker. After months of working on his projections of both parents onto the therapist, he dreamed of

a queen, looking like my mother. I think she will require me to kneel and kiss her hand to get some gift, but she doesn't, and I discover I don't want it now anyway. I want to go to the king, but I don't know where he is.

He woke conscious for the first time of a yearning desire for a warm and supportive father. From within the dream's feeling intensity, he could begin to resist the automatic fear and placatory appeasement of the sadistic inner authority that had ruled his life. In the transference he began then to express and claim his warriorlike resistance and the self-coalescing he could feel behind its shield. In the following months he dreamt of positive strong male figures, whose qualities he learned to see were within himself. He gained courage to join a men's group where he found a peer community and male mentors. After an introduction to meditation in therapy, he enrolled in a meditation course that helped him to focus on breathing when his emotions threatened to overwhelm him. Through experiences gained in all these arenas, he was finally able to overcome his habitual fear and shame to form a relationship with his biological father, a man he could now see realistically as narcissistically flawed, frightened, and angry, yet not without some goodwill towards his son.

Often unconscious but nonetheless a powerful force in the active addict, the sadistic authority to which he or she is bonded becomes a palpable obstacle in recovery. Because a brutal tyrant rather than a benign ruler occupies the position of inner authority, the recovering addict's sense of identity is neither adequately defended and boundaried nor connected in service to a center of positive self-rule. Thus the individual must remain an obedient and passive victim or a rebel against all authority. Because the rebel is often timid, it may appear as a trickster, and this mix of hiddenness and power may play a strong part in the defensive system of the false self. The trickster operates in reaction to the unrealistically high ideals and concomitant shaming of the harsh superego, which is projected wherever there is anxiety to be contained. Automatically then it slides into evasiveness, charming, wheedling, lying, or throwing forth threats and guilt. The weak boundaries of the addict's sense of self easily permit adapting to and blending with others in the relational field to intuit what they most need, value, and hence will fall for. Offering a promise of this currency, the tricky con artist seeks to gain protection from shaming as well as to gain the necessary emotional and physical supplies. While such essential supplies may be forthcoming for a time, they are based on false premises because the addict's capacity to sustain a relationship is undeveloped. Eventually the psychopathy in the maneuvers becomes palpable; the gullible partner feels entangled in a counterfeit racket and may become both canny and resentful, no longer willing to be duped. When called to take responsibility, the trickster addict without a capacity for relatedness based upon deeper resources usually then feels victimized and betrayed and becomes more openly arrogant and aggressive. Unless the partner is again willing to succumb to the tyranny of trickster controls, the addict abandons or destroys the relationship—often without any prior communication to the partner.

In reaction to the lack of a just inner authority, the person prone to addiction may unconsciously induce or try—sometimes with great subtlety—to elicit imperatives and prohibitions from the therapist and other care-takers or to find absolution for behaviors that are hurtful to self and others. Like the tricky usurpers in Maeve's myth, the addict tries thus to ignore the need to discover and create a locus of true inner rule. Instead he or she projects the authority in a primitively split form and tries to steal it back from the person on whom it is projected. As if trying to evoke judgmentalism and shaming, the client like the one just described brings accounts of endangering and moral transgressions from acting out in bingeing and theft to sexual promiscuity and self-mutilation. Presenting such evidence of a legitimate need for admonishment and care, the client lures the therapist and others in close-enough relationship to feel the induction to become codependents and surrogate saving authorities. As long as this ploy is played out rather than confronted and made conscious, it serves as a defensive replacement for the painfully slow struggles required to develop adequate self-care, inner authority, and interpersonal responsibility.

Acquired through relationship to a weak, unsupportive, and/or sadistic parental complex, the superego and its ideals of perfection cannot work to inhibit the self-destructive behavior nor the compulsive force of the addiction. Its prohibitions only make the recovering addict feel more ashamedly secretive or more rebelliously antagonistic. Driven by two separate and demonic powers, the beleaguered addict cannot find an inner point of coalescence or a central and authentic authority. Instead both drinking and its driven inhibition—"going on the wagon"—may alternatively possess the drunk with the force of divine compulsions. The addict, like the borderline, is lurched between these split and opposite imperatives without psychological structures or space to find an inner authority derived from the balanced completeness of the individual Self. In the depths of the addiction, beleaguered consciousness is fragmented and reduced to ineffectual passivity. It becomes the ravaged battlefield on which the craving and the ever-weakening prohibition struggle against one another for the addict's soul.

One man in early recovery was struggling to find some point of safety against both the addictive habit and the introjected habit of sadistic shaming. Made to feel even more inadequate when tempted to return to his addiction to assuage emptiness and guilt, he realized:

Rules Not-To are no help . . . . I feel like I'm trying to play against the devil, but if I'm already sitting at the table to be given the rules, that's already a defeat . . . . Nothing humanly made can stand against this compulsion. It's like a dragon that wants to grab me, a siren that's irresistible . . . . I can only put myself in the hands of a Higher Power, and hold to that with everything I've got . . . . Just holding and calling you or my sponsor for help in holding is the best I can manage. You don't make me feel even more awful. You are just there for me—a me I can't even find [by] myself.

This client was aware that the very feelings of primal shame and the guilt used in an attempt to prohibit his obsession had the opposite effect of "eviscerating [him] further" and reevoking his need for drugs.

Mark Twain expresses this quandary in his description of a man who

had often taken the pledge to drink no more, and was a good sample of what that sort of unwisdom can do for a man—for a man with anything short of an iron will. The system is wrong in two ways: it does not strike at the root of the trouble, for one thing, and to make a pledge of any kind is to declare war against nature: for a pledge is a chain that is always clanking and reminding the wearer of it that he is not a free man.[71]

As we have seen, the *medb* in intoxicating form serves to create an illusion of care and support for the weak and beleaguered person prone to addiction. Without an alternative source of empathic support in an accepting and confronting human relationship, he or she fears to separate or be born forth from the addiction. Instead the individual is sorely tempted to return to dependency on the addiction's repetitive soothing and arousal whenever the stress of change and its requirements to separate from old patterns and relationships recur as they are bound to throughout life. Thus at the beginning of any new phase or at any threatened disruption of an old pattern when regal initiation into a new attitude might be called for, the addict, the recovering addict, and even the normal neurotic is most vulnerable to feeling abandonment and being drawn again to the substitute maternal support, including addiction, found in the old defenses against psychological pain.[72] As one therapist colleague puts it cogently, "When in stress, we regress." Thus while the addiction may change from booze to sex, cigarettes, food, exercise, rage, or anxiety at any stressful transition, the recovering addict lives with the danger of resubmersion instead of rebirth and the temporary rule of a new kingdom. This danger, hopefully, can foster the creation of a balanced ego with its potentials for consciousness and life-long self-development in relationship to the guiding Self.

For even in the addict's bravado that he or she can survive the ravages of addiction in identification with the Self lies the potential for trust in that higher power. With the slow development of such trust, the addict may be able to transform the defensive omnipotence into a sense of attentiveness to the individual Self's guidance and the personal responsibility to heed it—both vital aspects of the gifts and requirements of a fated devotion to Maeve.

Chapter 4

Processual and
Fragmenting Maeve

Like the ancient Celts, who passed their knowledge "from
mouth to ear," many people whose cultures are based on oral
traditions have a keen awareness of their sensory and
spiritual participation in the natural universe.[1] Each individual
feels enclosed within the world of nature and its geography,
melded via permeable, participatory consciousness within the
human and non-human environment. For these tribespeople
attunement with the flow of matrix consciousness is ongoing.
Individual volition seems to depend on what we would call
intuition or mood. Time is not seen as an abstract grid into
which to fit activities; it is felt as an ongoing cycle with which
human activities must be aligned. Health is defined in terms
of attunement and integration with archetypal processes
operating throughout nature—a matrix that modern physicist
David Bohm calls the "implicate order."[2]

Finding and maintaining the balance and ordered
relationship within these processes sustains the flow of
human and non-human life. Thus individuals and the plants
and animals taken for food live, die, and survive or regenerate
as part of the whole matrix. Individual dreams can be used
for the community's well-being and guidance. Because the
individual soul exists in intimate mutuality with others in the
group and the environment as an organ exists within a body,
so-called native peoples seem to steer by signs invisible to
rational facilities. They rely on intuitive sensations of

correspondence between outer and inner energic patterns. The subtleties of earth, waters, climate, animals, and vegetation are perceived with sensitivities and traditional knowledge to which most of us have lost access.

Such attuned awareness of the ever-shifting balance of relationships in nature made possible the alignment and construction of marvels of Stone Age architecture. It permitted travel along geophysical energy paths that connect far distant centers (called ley lines in the British Isles and song lines in Australia). It fostered awareness of astronomical and earthly cycles. It enabled hunters to find their prey and gatherers to find food and healing herbs. It created therapeutic methods in tune with subtle field patterns of information and energy, herbal and geographic potencies, and the focused emotional intentionality that we call magic. Traditional healers in many cultures still honor this attunement in daily life and ritual. Our own culture is finally beginning to revalue the use of such methods and to study native herbs and energy medicines, such as acupuncture, homeopathy, electromagnetism, as well as the use of visualizations and other shamanic methods. What we now call field theory and ecological consideration are becoming commonplace in many modern disciplines.[3]

We know the attuned, aboriginal mind intuitively in our own lives. It is perhaps most accessible to us personally in our memories of childhood, for then each of us is close to its modes of mentation. As infants, we still exist in a state of participation with others and can pick up the subtle energy shifts in our environment. We are dependent for our survival on empathic rapport from our caretakers, and we must influence them in turn with emotional clues and behaviors that come directly out of the organismic level of functioning. In spite of marked individual variations, we react within the parameters of such embracing fields and the archetypal energy patterns or deep structures inherent in them. Although awareness of these energic realities may fade when it is not valued and named in our culture, we continue to react to the influence of these energies subliminally throughout our lives.

Knowledge of attunement with these subtle energies was considered part of the sacred lore of the earth deity. It survived among the druids, for the early Celtic invaders of Ireland lived within and still valued the Neolithic perspective. Even after the druidic order waned in the sixth century, there were close correspondences between the new hermit monks and the earlier shamanic priesthood. Thus a monk's gravestone in St. Malachedar's churchyard (Co. Kerry) has a vaginal hole carved into the stone, telling us that early Christians in Ireland still imaged the portal to heavenly rebirth as the *yoni* of the goddess. Other vestiges of the ancient lore remained in folk traditions through the generations, and they are being revalued today. Into the present century Irish and Cornish children were passed through special holed stones to cure various ailments. Now we find the stones and megalithic circles have electromagnetic frequencies that modern science assures us have effects on human health.[4] While the medicinal and symbolic power of herbs and holy wells is still acnowledged, many of their effects are also finally given scientific affirmation. Medieval Celtic stories tell of rituals of healing, of prophetic and shamanic knowledge reached through visionary attunement. Sometimes medieval texts point directly to a fragment of old wisdom telling us that even the shifts we today might call oppositional lurches find their balance and meaning within the ongoing interrelated processes of the matrix. In *The Mabinogion*, for example, the young grail hero Peredur is shown the mystery that a white sheep jumping across a stream into a herd of black ones turns dark, just as a dark sheep jumping into the herd of light ones turns white. Modern practitioners of energy medicine are reasserting that maintaining such dynamic balance is essential for health.

Among the early Celts, initiatory rituals, including those brought about through the use of *medb*, heightened awareness of the energic matrix beneath the constantly changing ebb and flow of events. Maeve, the divinity, thus signifies both that deeper order and the processes through which it unfolds. While she changes the faces she reveals to us, she asks us to stay attuned to the underlying reality and to bear the changes that accompany rebalancing. As warrior goddess, Maeve does not stave off death but exacts it as the price of communion and transformative regeneration. As everlasting queen of the land itself, Maeve abandons one kingly lover for the next one when change is required to support the demands of a new era. She is the constancy in which we may find our security, but she does not offer comfortable permanence. Instead she stands against fixation and for the whole cycle of gaining and losing that underlies life's transformative processes. Tasting such impermanence as an aspect of the larger matrix of ever changing life can optimally lead the initiant to sense the spiritual interdependence of all states and all seemingly separate, discrete perceptions. The early Celtic heroes still knew that the experience of "me" here and now changes in relation to what is "beyond me" just as a wave changes, even disappears, but is still part of the ocean. What is constant is change itself. Jung puts it: "All true things must change and only that which changes remains true."[5] Within such fluidity what might be feared and rigidly resisted as death and annihilation for the separatist heroic ego becomes a means to learn that every transient state is only a part of an oceanic fullness that embraces all divergent forms. It is from this perspective, perhaps, that the Celts were described by the Romans as philosophers and admired for their fearlessness before death.

As the heroic ego in both men and women develops, it repudiates its original participation in the matrix to coalesce its sense of separate identity. It seeks mastery and learns discipline to rule over nature. With this separation it also begins the fragmentation of matrix consciousness that we have seen carried to its adversarial extreme by the usurping kings in the story of leprous Maeve. For while the separation permits the burgeoning of masculine dominative power and new forms of objectifying and abstracting consciousness, individual effectiveness, and self-control in the face of opposing impulses, it also brings about the defensive devaluation of the participatory awareness of our personal and cultural origins. This can lead to the derogation of the goddess of nature, women in her image, and all those who depend on matrix consciousness. Not only are so-called primitive peoples then looked down upon, so are women. They are carriers of the fearful potencies associated with childhood vulnerability and with change itself. Women remain more closely connected to participatory embodied consciousness through the cycles of their menses and through the hormonal shifts occurring in pregnancy that permit attunement with their infants, thus making them susceptible in heroic society to depreciation and/or envy.

While we have evidence in the myths that many Celtic heroes were still chosen, taught, and initiated by the goddesses, the increasing strength of the patriarchy caused the eventual disregard of the ancient goddess and her initiations. They seemed to threaten nascent individual power and autonomy, just as, psychologically, the bond to the mother and all relationships of mutual interdependency may be seen as inhibiting a boy's full expression of phallic aggressiveness. The child allied with the now excitingly powerful patriarchal fathers finds it seemingly safe to abandon the bountiful mother. Thus to the heroic kings dissociating from the older rituals of the matrix in our story and bent on proving their prowess, Maeve seems a minimal threat when they spurn her.

The loss of participatory consciousness is central to patriarchal culture. From the perspective of Maeve it is the original sin that cuts us off from the matrix and cuts up that matrix in order to prove that we can control, dominate, and rise above it in identity with the sky gods, who are now masculinized and separated away from earth.[6] Patriarchal culture severs our ties to the encompassing environment, both geographic and maternal, and to the aboriginal consciousness that knew security in community and cosmos. Henceforth the isolated patriarchal ego may no longer feel and find the original bonds that enabled the sense of meaningful unity with and within all of nature. As the Irish archetypal hero Cuchulainn killed the son of the mother for the glory of the father chief, father god, and the father's sons who are his peers, so each hero of the patriarchy must repress personal vulnerability and dependency on the matrix.[7] However, the heroic ego's very separateness engenders a sense of alienation that makes the unconscious quest to restore the lost unity all the more potent.[8] Secretly craving a way to reconnect, the heroic ego is susceptible to the seductions of Maeve. Thus although she has lost her sovereignty as the initiating goddess for the five brothers, Maeve easily reasserts her power when she adopts the vocabulary that the new kings will understand. She comes to seduce them, luring them one by one to connect intimately with her when they are resting from heroic, phallic endeavor. She reassures them in their relaxation by arousing the very organ they are most loathe to have threatened. But she also double-binds them. She comes as the loathsome damsel whom the Celts equated with sovereignty to lure each of them to embrace her and claim the kingdom with a sense of victorious accomplishment. But her invitation mocks their fraudulent power. She shows them the leprous face representing their own separation from the matrix and the fragmentation the new consciousness has wrought. Instead of granting the potential gift of the authority and joy of power that the Celtic goddess of sovereignty still holds, she punishes their disregard and kills them. Thus Maeve in the patriarchy becomes the endangering, seductive death goddess. She brings the embrace of sexual bliss, bondage to addictions and emotional possessions, unconsciousness, and death—all prime ways in which the hold of the matrix is still experienced in the world of alienated heroes.

The Defensive Purpose of Leprous Maeve

In the story of Maeve and the five kings (see page 107), we saw that Maeve transformed herself into a seductive leper. In another tale of the patriarchy we will find that she becomes a fiercely competitive warrior. In the story of Madge (see page 30), we saw her transformed into a witch who stole back her own *medb* to carouse in an English lord's wine cellar. All of her shapeshifts in the patriarchy are in defense of her original powers. Thus the energies of the ancient goddess evolve into a system of defenses of her original meaning, a system that is antagonistic to the heroic ego and its separated individuation. From the perspective of the development of the masculine ego, she represents an inertial or regressive pull, the entrapping arms of the death mother. But there is purpose in her shapeshifts. It is as if her drive energies force us to regress to the level of the first chakra, the lowest spine center from which radiate the capacities ensuring survival. She fragments, attacks, addicts, and even becomes wildly outrageous and sociopathic in order to reassert or maintain the values of the matrix that were initially so threatened by those of the patriarchy. Like the feminine aspect of the Self in individual psychology, she becomes powerful in the assertion of her own sovereignty and against the values of the separative patriarchal ego. This is why the figure of the witch, the preserver of the Old Religion in Europe, is so often paired with the half-orphaned and abused girl child in fairy tales and dreams.[9] Appearing in the absence of the bountiful mother, the terrible witch is fearsome and must be served. Then her role as a secret ally or bestower of gifts to the orphaned daughter in the patriarchy becomes clear.[10]

To use Winnicott's famous phrase, we can say that Maeve shapeshifts to defend the state of "being" that must precede that of "doing" and performing in order to allow the true self to be born into the world.[11] In each of us growing up in the patriarchy, she initially operates as the numbing denial, the regressive inertia, and the fragmentation and dissociation that seeks to protect the hidden kernel of integrity endangered by development of the heroic persona ego. Thus she serves to maintain or restore the relationship of that dissociated part with the matrix. By guarding and holding the level of participatory being that is anterior to doing and heroic performance, she remains the matrix and holds our place in it against the patriarchy's heroic incursions, refusing to allow the deintegration of what does not find adequate reception for its development. She guards the true self against unthinkable pain, keeping it in such deep hiding with her in the archetypal world that

consciousness can feel it only as a dead place in the overall
psychological geography. Then consciousness may even
forget the still-infant self's longing to be born. At other stages
in the service of guarding its survival, she closes the newly
incarnating true ego off behind armor and the repertoire of
the defender. Throughout she uses the possessive,
dominative, separative, adversarial, and tricksterish forms of
the patriarchy itself. Sometimes she cuts us into parts so
some bit may stay unborn, still fused with the matrix, and
forces us to return to her if we are to discover more of
ourselves.[12] Sometimes she snares us with addictions and
possessions, with denial of our experience of inner and outer
reality, with dissociations that serve to defend us from
consciousness of the abuses to matrix consciousness under
the patriarchy until we are ready to bear the knowledge and
strong enough to join the struggle to redress these abuses in
our own lives. Sometimes she battles against development,
turning envy and aggression against parts of ourselves to
keep us fragmented and besieged beside her. Sometimes she
forbids our submission to the ego ideals and superego of the
heroic culture to ensure that our outbursts and carousals and
our rebellious psychopathy will keep us in her camp.

All of her holds on us are the concomitants of
early pathology, but they also show themselves in adolescence
when independence and rebellion against collective authority
make the young adult ego susceptible to her lures, and they
may appear in mid-life when we feel unable to function as
heroically as our ideals require. Her grip on us both snares us
and serves the survival of life itself. Sometimes, as with denial
and addiction, our earliest defenses seek to buffer us against
the pains of abandonment and abuse when the goddess of
nature has been demeaned and the women in her image,
who have taken on the role of mothers, cannot function
adequately to hold, receive, and tend our infant selves with
the mutuality of attuned matrix consciousness. Sometimes
these defenses bind us outside of life, keep parts of us unborn
in the patriarchy, and forbid development when it starts from
the wrong premise and lacks reverence for the matrix and the
feminine principle that are our earliest caretakers.

Seeing primitive defenses as assertions of leprous Maeve has profound effects on therapy with severely damaged and addicted clients. It makes the therapist more patient with their power and slippery resistance to entering consciousness and with the client's profound distrust of human relationships and therapy. The addictions, the denial, the envy, the attacks on linking, the raging contempt, the sadistic and masochistic maneuvers, the delusional idealism all intend to save the true self even when they are attacking it to keep it fragmented and away from the possibility of healing relationship. They have served survival. Although they may no longer be as necessary or helpful as they were when the client was subject to unthinkable suffering as a vulnerable child and although they now operate against the therapy itself, they are to be respected even as they are repeatedly pointed to and confronted. Seeing the defenses as an aspect of Maeve removes them from seeming to be the responsibility of the pre-ego, which causes unnecessary shame for further failed omnipotence in the client. The wording of an interpretation would not point to *your* denial, *your* rage, fear, and greed, *your* envy, *your* addiction, but the *archetypal* denial, rage, fear, greed, envy, and addiction *in you* that operates to protect the ego and to keep it connected with the derogated matrix. This way of seeing the problem obviates sadistic definitions of the person. Instead it points to the psychological landscape in which the client's consciousness is still caught. Only when dreams and countertransferential feelings later suggest that the client clings to the defenses out of inertia and in defiance of the process, then an empathic challenge of personal responsibility is appropriate.

To redeem leprous Maeve one must serve Maeve in her original nature and for her transpersonal purposes. In therapy this implies service to the client's wholeness in its processes and relationships with all of the capacities of rational consciousness (including objectification, hierarchical ordering, and confrontational focus) within the context of the intimate, empathic attunements of matrix consciousness. Indeed, a function of Maeve's leprous defenses is to ensure that therapy not become part of the patriarchal system that will foist theoretical interpretations or pathologize and pigeon-hole the wounded client apart from and beneath the superior healer. For the therapist this means recognizing on a deep level the danger to therapy of incursions of the power drive that is part of our competitive culture and thrives in each of us even when that drive seems to be in the service of healing and helping the client get better.[13] It also means recognizing that therapy in the service of Maeve or the Self is more than a means to ensure collective adaptation to patriarchal institutions and definitions of health.

Throughout the work there will be many challenges to determine if the therapist will claim illegitimate authority from the process rather than trust in the messages from dreams and the unified field of the transference and countertransference, which require for understanding both objectivity and the subtle attunements of participatory consciousness. In this process the therapist may become as intensely bonded with the client in the service of Maeve as are those in a kin group and must nonetheless resist acting out this intimacy for personal relief or gain.

The therapist is also called to avoid the seduction of focusing defensively and adversarily on fragments of the client's personality rather than the whole person in the interpersonal and intersubjective field.[14] Only then can the raging, addictive, seductive, or overeating fragments that are symptoms find their balance, and the therapist not join leprous defensive Maeve in attacks on the linkings of each part to and within the whole. Such deep wholistic work requires the skill, humility, and self-monitoring that help the therapist to avoid being identified with those heroic and powerless people who scorn Maeve. While the therapist must see and point out and even stand against colluding with the seductions of leprous Maeve in the patriarchy, she or he cannot claim the ultimate authority or power to oppose her. This power belongs to the guiding Self supported by the matrix of life that we are calling Maeve herself. As the therapist firmly holds to this dual perspective and its processes through the years of work, it almost seems as if Maeve can feel her sovereignty respected again. The capacities of the kings are again relativized to serve the life process. Then she may change her face and allow the pre-heroic core of the personality, which she has held out of life, to return for development in an environment where her original power and purposes are revered.

The Experience of Leprous Maeve

When we have an insufficient cultural and ritual context in which to find and value the numinous, multiform matrix, we cannot integrate our own personal experiences of life and death, bliss and terror, bounty and deprivation within a transpersonal context. There is no archetypal image to stand behind the inevitable vicissitudes of life to give them meaning. Overly fearful before the pains and pleasures of fusion as well as those of separation, our consciousness is made impermeable to the flow of the deeper reality.

When we have had insufficient personal experience of constancy in the arms of a secure and self-valuing caretaking figure who represents the cosmos to the infant, we may also experience our matrix only through its fragmenting lurches and lack of stability. Our inevitable awareness of abject neediness is not helped to grow beyond its fears of abandonment and/or engulfment to find or trust any deeper constancy. Unable to develop beyond binary awareness when we are forced too early in life to try to control the pain in this malevolent attachment, we find that the experiences of the actual caretaker mirror and solidify the perceived split between the craved, blissful, all-rewarding one and the feared, unholding all-depriving one. Tossed then between our dependency and the persecutory terrors of being annihilated, we nonetheless become focused on the inconstant caretaker with the tenacity we associate with all such intermittent reinforcement.

Just as we cannot find the constantly holding matrix, so we cannot find our consciousness of self in relation to the disparate incongruities we experience. Fragmented, we cannot discover or create an identity to hold our awareness of shifts and enable a sense of our own continuity. Our sense of coherent me-ness then drops as if into an abyss of nothingness, into the maw of the death goddess. At that point we withdraw, terrified in shame, or we overly attend to finding ourselves in the other and hurriedly developing the skills of adaptation that would make such outer matching possible. Thus we build up the false selves that enable us to survive in the world, and we leave the true selves invisible and unconscious, still in the realm of the archetypal powers.

Without a human caretaker to mediate the potent archetypal energies and enable trust in our own validity and wholeness, this hidden core cannot develop. Without human help to enliven and shape potentials and soothe frustrations with the limits of concrete reality, development and differentiation cannot occur. There can be no adequate transitional bridge between the original matrix necessarily projected onto the caretaker and separate, incarnate existence protected and nurtured by that caretaker. Then without the humanized link between matrix and individuality, each transition may only be experienced as a painful disruption that opens the primeval gaps in consciousness and makes us feel the stress of too much illusory hope or too much fear, misery, deprivation, and rage. Unable to find the possibility of encompassing order, serenity, or bounty in the universe and in ourselves, we cannot trust that we can discover and/or create a meaningful, inclusive pattern from within the seemingly chaotic changes and a meaningful identity for ourselves. Knowing no real alternative to the needed but death-dealing goddess and even fearing the new experiences that might bring us an alternative, labeling them dangerous or foolish indulgences or fantasy, we find ourselves then not bonded to the whole process but in bondage to its fearful, "leprous" fragmentations.

Such bondage tends to have a magical aspect. We feel loyal to the death goddess, for there is a macabre bliss in the familiarity of the horrors to which we are habituated. "The old habit of horror is home," one borderline woman in recovery put it. "Abandonment, rejection, fear, even suicide have a weird ecstasy that fills me up." Another affirmed,

I know myself as the tortured one; so I end up in relationships that hurt . . . . How can I leave that world? . . . I have my proud, stony, inner hate and my carbohydrates when I get hurt. I have never built up the muscle for anything else; though I might if a rescuing prince arrived . . . . But either I wouldn't recognize him, or I'd know the rescue could never last. The torture will just start all over again because that's what's most real.

This woman was often angry with her therapy because

it seems to lure me out into relationship [with the therapist], where I may get hurt, and then I'd want to collapse and binge again . . . . I'd rather stay with despair and deprivation, even if that's being loyal to the opposite of what I have to blame and resist you for wanting me to seek because I cannot want it myself yet in therapy.

Over time her "ecstasy of horror" in the bonds of leprous Maeve began to transform into new curiosity as she felt more secure in the participatory companionship of the therapist and could bond with the therapist's attitude of observation and acceptance. She dreamed:

I see a woman from a mental hospital, very depressed and despairing—like the way I felt in early sobriety, like the way I feel when I'm separated from you [during vacation], like the way I feel because I'm separated from any mother. In the dream the crazed woman sets herself on fire and I am horrified.

The night after the dream and her feelings were discussed in therapy she dreamt:

I meet an explorer who can guide me to Machu Picchu. I don't know the person or even if I can go; though I want to. I seem to be on the trail.

The mentally ill woman in the first dream despairs in her abandonment and yet from the association cannot fully claim a personal relationship any more than the dreamer can fully stand for her need for connection to the therapist, who is after all only one among "any old mother." The dreamer associated the dream figure to her mother when she beat the children and, equally abusively, ranted that she hated to be alive and had to be their mother. But, said the dreamer, "she is also like those Buddhist monks who set themselves on fire . . . in a sacrifice for peace." She represents the dreamer's rage about the therapist's impending vacation separation that felt as crazily unrelated to her own needs and as abusive as her mother's ranting. Heating up and expressing the burning passion directly to the therapist is a sacrifice of the dreamer's identity with mute despairing deprivation. The image is thus a reevaluation of her habitually adaptive masochism, a conscious sacrifice like the monk's for a higher goal. The figure's burning suicide (in fiery death—one of the ritual means of killing the cast-off Celtic chieftain) suggests a potential transformation of energy. The figure's return to the unconscious via the transformation of death releases for its new incarnation the libido that was previously bound into horror and depression. In the second dream, the figure of the exploring guide suggests that the released energy might develop into her relationship to curiosity—a new and wider kind of desirousness than any the dreamer had previously known. The dreamer mused that the guide could help her "to learn and be strong enough to deal with the hazards of the journey." Wanting to go to "Machu Picchu peaks of experience" where, as she said, "the Incas hid from the conquistadors, in a holy city," indicates she is still somewhat grandiose. Nonetheless, she is beginning to sense there might be a place of safety and structure that enables a perspective that could let her be less identified with the enthrallingly bifurcated emotions and the familiar desires that made up what she called the "raw horror of home."

Until such development is made possible, we tend to stay loyal to the intensity of our own dread and with it to the magical omnipotent fantasy with which we might seduce the death mother herself to change. Like the false kings, we harbor the hope that we might be able to manage and even gain bliss from the leprous Maeve. Here we seek for ourselves the expanded potential we intuit in the archetype of the goddess herself. Like children still fused with the mother, we assume we have seemingly omnipotent powers to transform reality. We may then wait passively for the longed-for nurturance. Or we may struggle fiercely to transform the destructive person or substance into its opposite only repeatedly to realize our inadequacy. Between hope and despair, power and collapse, duty and rebelliousness, need and fear, we find ourselves addicted to the bipolar process with the same literalistic fanatic devotion that seduces and binds alcoholics to their *medb*.

Both soothing brew and death mother replicate the infant's exciting and destructive experience of the dichotomized mother, which Melanie Klein named the "good" feeding and "bad" persecutory breasts. In the areas of our addictions we are compelled to live that infant experience onward through life.[15] When, however, we can experience consciously the excitement of those raw emotions in a new psychological container without being overwhelmed, we may be able to open our awareness and reconnect to the originally uncontained infant and consciously share the intensity that matches and mirrors its own suffering. In this we have the opportunity to become mirrors and even mediating caretakers for the infant self who was not adequately regarded and protected and still exists within us as a potential for future development. As one recovering alcoholic expressed this,

My child self was blasted off into space. Its umbilicus hangs in empty air. It feels only despair and fear. Those are its food, its poisoned milk . . . . When I can let myself feel those feelings now, I connect with that infant for a moment; then that is too awful and I forget again . . . . I even want to forget so I feel a strong pull to binge . . . craving a box or two of crackers and enough chocolate to blot me into a sugar high.

This woman was experiencing the bipolar swings within the maternal-child archetype. One part of her, newly modeled upon her still idealized and untrusted experience of the therapist as a constant-enough holding figure, dared to attune for a moment to the terrorized child. A much larger part was frightened of being overwhelmed again by archetypal emotions. This part was still symbiotically fused with her experience of an inadequate mother in infancy. In identity with what she perceived as her own mother's fear of life, it despaired and wanted to flee, returning to the momentary sweetness of her defensive addiction to hold her fear. Over time as she was able to forego gorging on sweets and grain products that had warded off repeated alternations of terror and empty despair, she began tentatively and consciously to suffer the bipolar extremes of the mother archetype. Eventually she discovered that she could find a survival point outside her identity with the two alternating poles of the archetype. From this small gap of cleared space she struggled to witness and disidentify from them and begin to build her own abiding sense of existence, her own kingdom.

Like the extremes of the borderline mother, leprous Maeve can represent such momentarily blissful states alternately with states of annihilating, enraging, and depressing abandonment. This is her intoxicating power. In the addict—as in the borderline—the search for ideal, all-soothing comfort, which is heightened by its alternate deprivation, becomes a compulsion to hold the transcendent moment and to avoid an inevitable fall back into the limited, time-bound, pain-filled experience. The craving for unattainable and delusional ideals of perfectly met need becomes the core obsession of life: "get more crack—fast." With the intensity of desire momentarily satisfied and inevitably lost, those dependent on addictions become focused on increasingly hopeless frustration and increasing refusal to live with the realities of the body and the emotions. Sacrificing the capacity to live within the ordinary dimensions of time and space and addictively dependent, such fragmented awareness can neither mediate the supernatural into natural life nor hold sufficient awareness of bountiful and ecstatic encounters to ameliorate daily stress. Conversely, it cannot hold memory of ordinary and bearable pain to offset the chemically induced manic flights. Then terrible and seductive Maeve binds us. Enslaving us to our addictions, she asserts her possession fully.

Refinding the Matrix beyond the Fragments

Without granting the absolute security that our deepest fears and experiences of alienation and suffering crave, Maeve forces us to endure change. In our addictions Maeve may pick us up and grant ecstatic communion, holding and possessing us like a bliss-bestowing mother. But she does not offer the kind of total security in "an everlasting merge-fix," as one man in recovery expressed it, that our frantic, existentially anxious, and unmet cravings desire. Caught by them, we nonetheless scramble avidly for the security of the matrix that our culture has fragmented and devalued.

We are no longer like the Celts in being readily able to experience or even believe that the ordinary world and daily life are infused by the *unus mundus* or unitary, supernatural world. We suffer from our culture's splitting apart of the realms of nature and the supernatural—just as we suffer from too extreme a splitting of the experiences of good and bad when we remove the shadow and pain from the deity and relegate their cause to a demonic force outside god or only inside human nature.[16] Weakly grounded by this dichotomous consciousness, we can either feel dispair and rage at the tragic separation or we can struggle, play, and work creatively to bridge the gaps. After tasting the bliss of expanded and unitary consciousness, we may then learn to return to ordinary separatist consciousness, both to suffer its mundane realities and to bring into its limited world the mystically experienced truths and energies we have received in the other.

If we can experience the alternations between opposites including those of transcendence and ordinary reality, we may acquire a larger perspective.[17] Then good and bad, high and low, inner and outer, spirit and matter reveal themselves to our ecstatically transparent consciousness as a numinous and paradoxical unity that also manifests as diversity. Then the shifts between expansive potential and the experience of limits, even the fluctuations between joyful well-being and painful deprivation, between peace and

conflict, order and chaos, all can be perceived as great and
powerful communions with the matrix source in all her full
and empty otherness. In Jungian terms this fluctuation is
paralleled by alternations in the organic processes in the ego-
Self cycle between states in which the ego feels merged in
identity with the Self and states of alienation in which the
ego feels cut off from its matrix.[18] The oppositional poles can
stand as markers for us to experience and explore ever
widening vistas of life. They enable us to experience with two
kinds of consciousness, comparable to what the alchemists
called Luna and Sol, or to what Freud called primary and
secondary process, and what I am here calling matrix and
separative-ego consciousness. The alternations themselves can
be like the rhythms of breathing or, more aptly, of labor. They
carry us through our psychological and spiritual births,
deaths, and rebirths. They bring us ever closer to an
appreciation of the new kind of integral consciousness that
enables us to value and find meaning in the rhythms in
which we participate.

Although our embodied emotional experience of
the matrix where we feel wholeness and intimacy with all of
life can be held only fleetingly, we can become secure in our
knowledge (*gnosis*) of its existence and of our own attuned
integrity as we survive through its onslaughts and
manifestations. We can then abide more trustingly in the
emotional spaces between the highs of ecstatic communion
and the lows of abandonment depression to find our value as
creative witnesses to the wonders of many phases of a
transpersonal process. We can sometimes experience that the
ten thousand things, as Buddhists call the separate
manifestations of reality, have their ground in an implicate
and unified order. Such ability to accept change and
separateness and their inevitable peaks and chasms as our
"stabilization in God,"in Etty Hillesum's poignant phrase, is
the gift of many forms of spiritual practice.[19] It is also the goal
of any adequately deep healing of the wounds to the sense of
self and relationship to the Self that have brought us to
addiction and all our pathologies.

Part II

The way back home passes through that one place—that one hell—we want most to avoid.

—Albert Camus, *The Fall*

There is always a certain condition of psychic need, a sort of hunger, but it seeks for familiar and favorite dishes and never imagines as its goal some outlandish food unknown to consciousness.

—C. G. Jung, *CW 12*[1]

Healing involves turning what was blind bondage to archetypal factors into conscious participation in divine purpose.

—Edward Edinger, *Lecture on Jung CW 14*

Chapter 5

Towards Healing

Ending Addiction

Breaking the bondage to addictive substances and gaining
control over addictive behavior are essential steps in the
healing of addictive dependency. For some individuals this is
relatively easy. Studies have shown that "Just Saying No" is
effective with some low-risk youngsters in low-crime areas.[1]
We know that for others such simplistic prohibition cannot
work. Even those who have completed short-term drug
treatment programs have a high rate of recidivism. Indeed
some addicts use the treatment merely to temporarily lower
the dose of addictive substance they require to get high. Thus
they can start off buying less when they are back on the
street. For them, "Just saying No" is as irrelevant as saying no
to a volcano. They have no reason to believe that anything
else will hold equal comfort, power, or meaning. Twelve-step
programs can be very effective in ending the specific
addictions on which they focus if the individual in recovery is
sufficiently motivated to remain sober, go to meetings, and
work the steps. Nonetheless, even after the addict has
managed to gain enough control of a compulsive dependency
to stay sober, there is usually much further healing to be
done.

Some of this change must come through efforts
to effect the economic and social environment that breeds the
conditions leading to shame and despair and the addictions

that numb their pains. Some of this healing must also be done by individuals seeking to transform the personal, psychological, and spiritual conditions that led to and supported addictive habits. For them recovery is a life-long journey. Many of them seek therapy with a transpersonal perspective.[2]

Towards Healing

Initially through encountering within a relationship the empathic acceptance of painful affects and obsessions, addicted individuals may feel their burden of loneliness lifted. With a therapist or trained mentor on whom they can project the role of healer, authority, and even redeemer, they may go further to relax the anxious blockages of body and mind that beset them and allow those old structures to dissolve in a dependent transference. Automatic and defensive fears can then slowly soften to permit more perceptual clarity and the possibility of self-reflection. Slowly within the safely companioned sensory field of therapy, they can then learn to witness more deeply their own stories and the experiences of the therapeutic relationship. They can feel more consciously connected to the pains they have already suffered and the distorted relationships that caused them—even as they also become aware of themselves as observers.[3] Slowly they may also become aware of the patterns underlying their pains and the healing processes at work among them.

Archetypal Patterns

What are these patterns? They are certainly not only personal, nor reducible to personal history. Jung called them archetypal form potentials; recent science calls them information fields. They underly the processes in which we— and all life forms—are held and moved and also move. They inform all aspects of existence. We know them as the energy patterns in living creatures and the developmental patterns infusing plant and animal growth. We seek them in the linguistic structures that underly all languages and in the misalignments of pattern in psyche and soma that create disease.

We have seen how the archetypal forms in Maeve's mythology and rituals support creative access to basic energies and expanded awareness. We have also seen that when we cannot relate consciously and reverently to the energies we image as Maeve, we may find ourselves drawn unconsciously into her field and caught in "blind bondage to archetypal factors." From a Jungian perspective, we know that for healing to occur we need to address our relationships to basic form patterns and the processes through which they manifest in our lives. We know that when therapist and, eventually, client are able to perceive and relate consciously to the archetypal energy field underlying the dis-ease, energy and self-esteem and meaning may flow more adequately into life.

Jung has stressed that we can become aware of every archetypal energy field via its imaginal and energic aspects (including somatic and emotional ones). While we can perceive archetypal processes through their grip on our embodied functioning and emotions, such awareness becomes more subtly honed as we allow the energies to intensify into emotions and thoughts and then find their symbolic representations. With this more conscious access to the archetypal energic processes, we may discover how to relate to the patterns within them as they structure matter and mind, body, and spirit. Thus we can begin to learn to work with and within the physical, emotional, mental, and spiritual potencies as these manifest in our lives.

The symbolic image reveals the structure of the underlying archetypal energy pattern that creates health and potential meaning when it is relatively balanced. Equally it provides clues to rebalance the skewed complexes built around the archetypal core that embody the disease. Through the symbol we can thus gain access to the archetypal patterns that support health just as they may express our distorted relationships to life energies. The Bible tells us that when the wanderers in the desert reflected on the image of their fiery resentment, they became conscious of their misalignment with the processes of their destiny. Through the image of the brazen serpent, they were made to look afresh at their pain and defensive anger to recognize the archetypal significance behind it. When the suffering was thus held in the vessel of meaning, they could disidentify from its grip to find a new relationship to their disease. They were healed by being restored to self-acceptance and more harmonious functioning as they wandered on their long journey from bondage towards the home that was ahead of them.

In similarly reflecting on the symbolic image of the goddess-queen Maeve, sustainer of tribal life and initiator of warriors, kings, and shaman/druid poets, we have identified an underlying pattern that supports health and the possibilities of expanded consciousness when it is balanced and addictive disease when it is distorted. Through her stories, we will look again at some of the processes over which she rules, trying to see how to work with the distorted archetypal pattern to find its significance and rebalance its energies in consciousness. Connecting in these various ways to the images of Maeve initiates healing, because it enables us to begin to view the archetype as a transpersonal force with which we can relate more consciously. It also allows us to somewhat separate from our unconscious enslavement to Maeve as well as to gain some inkling of the purposes of her grip on us. As Edward Edinger has put it beautifully, "Healing involves turning what was blind bondage to archetypal factors into conscious participation in divine purpose."[4] If we can accept the significance of this participation, we can better bear the fate that destined us to experience its processes with the special sensitivities that have brought us so much discomfort.

Indeed it has been my hope that we might find in the mythological images of Maeve and her lovers a medicine analogous to the healing substances (called *simillimums*) that homeopaths use so successfully to enable the immune system to restore the individual's balance and thus heal all kinds of diseases of mind and body. These curative substances are used in doses that both desubstantiate the physical material and release or potentize its energic and information patterns. This is analogous to releasing the spirit of the archetype and then assimilating it through a specifically prepared communion. For the healing remedy is created from the same substance that can, when given repeatedly, produce symptoms similar to the total disease gestalt in healthy persons.[5] It thus provides a precise correspondence to the disease pattern. Finding the *simillimun* to the disease in the individual and giving it in the potency required constitute the basis of healing. In undertaking this work I set out to discover if the structures in Maeve's mythology could provide a *simillimum* between the toxic effects of the disease in individuals prone to addiction and the archetypal energy patterns underlying the emotional and symbolic realizations that can inform and effect a curative process.

The more I have looked into issues of addiction and Maeve's stories, the more I have felt the striking similarities between this Celtic archetype and addictive behavior. Nonetheless what we can learn through studying the correspondences between Maeve's mythology and health, disease, and healing can also be generalized. It can help us see the particular field effects of any archetypal pattern on psychopathology and health. Exploring the relationship of this one pattern clustered in images around the figure of Maeve may even help us learn to search for the deep structures underlying all the vicissitudes of our histories and daily life.

Healing from an Archetypal Perspective

Without awareness of the name and qualities of the archetypal processes in which the addict is caught, he or she is captured by the powers of the concrete substance *medb* and

consigned to unconscious servitude, dissociative
fragmentation, and death.

To find healing, the addict and those addicted parts
of all of us must awaken to conscious appreciation of—and
conscious devotion to—the many aspects of the archetypal
field that we glimpse through mythic images of Maeve. Her
pattern holds both the disease and its cure. Thus for addicts
and the addicted parts of us, Maeve represents the *alpha* and
omega, the wild cravings and the mediating structures that
transform craving into desire, the fragmentation and the
integration, the problem and its redemption.

One of her stories even tells us that through her we
may get a hold on our compulsions. For addictive disease is
analogous to Maeve's rampaging pigs in the tale. These pigs
poured out of the underworld at Cruachan from a cave called
Ireland's Gate of Hell. So greedy were they that wherever they
foraged, they killed off the potential for any vegetation to grow
for seven years. And like addictive craving, their voraciousness
was invincible. They even evaded human ordering. They refused
to be counted, racing across the land to wreck their havoc in
another place whenever someone tried to determine their
number. Finally Maeve herself came along with her consort.
This suggests that her image provides the perspective from
which to see the whole herd. She is that perspective. Not only
did she count the pigs, bringing cognitive order to encompass
the size of the ravaging menace, she also seized one as it jumped
over her chariot. Not taken over by its frenzied appetite, she
grabbed the problem instead. Holding onto the devouring
creature, exhibiting the kind of muscle required, Maeve stood
her ground. And the pig left her with its skin and hind leg in her
hand. She gained its hide for her use and also the champion's
portion, the favored haunch that goes to the tribal champion at
the start of any feast. The wild herd itself then left the lands over
which she ruled in her queenly human form.

As we summon or invoke the symbol of Maeve
in its fullness, we also may be able to grapple with the

problems of ravaging addictive greed to find the strength, the access to integrated wholeness, and the healing that she can bring us. To discover such an adequately deep and broad perspective, we return now in Part II to the mythological sources. In them we have already found evidence of Maeve in her many potencies. We have seen already that she is battle goddess, earth mother, inspiring muse, sovereign process, loathsome hag, inebriating drink, passionate appetite, and sacred vessel. To all of these aspects of the goddess in us, the addicted personality must consciously discover new relationships, accepting them as necessary for life and also seeking among them the balances that can support creativity.

As we connect psychologically to Maeve's pattern of wholeness, we may also be able to find our own sense of multifaceted integrity. From its center we may learn to assess and deal with the energies that unconsciously and hence destructively overran our inner and outer landscapes. Instead of suffering the onslaught of destructive energies as wild as Maeve's pigs, we may invoke her as battling goddess and learn to use the aggression for life. Instead of being held unconsciously in the grip of archetypal affects, we can struggle to hold them in consciousness and balance the desires and feelings in us. As the complexed or diseased structures in which we are caught can loosen, we may thus discover the spirit of the equilibrium inherent in the archetypal potentials. We may even find new meaning and direction for the underlying energy to flow creatively into our lives.

In this process the figure of Maeve may function as a healing image—a beacon guiding us towards deeper understanding of the archetypal pattern that apparently destined us to experience addictive cravings. Since she also provides us with a structure of meaning to mediate our relationship to archetypal need, we may find through her the source that adequately slakes our thirsts and enables personal transformation.

An Individualized Interlace

Each individual working today with the processes imaged by
the figure of Maeve will probably need to undergo aspects of
all of her initiations to come to full functioning. While each of
our paths and styles of connecting to the various aspects of
the image will vary, each of us may find that the lines of
contact with the goddess' patterns tend to overlap and spiral
in a unique interlacing design. Thus capacities for assertion,
for example, may depend also on our relations to the
maternal ground; awareness of creative vision may weave
into capacities for sword-like discrimination and a sense of
maternal ground; the capacity for self-acceptance that permits
self-rule may be intimately entwined in all the other
processes. In Jungian therapeutic work, we are specifically
guided by each client's individual Self processes as they
manifest to direct the unique individuation journey. They
reveal themselves through dreams, all manner of life events,
and the unfolding transference and countertransference
relationship between analysand and analyst.

Many of the issues addressed in this section
inevitably arise in any deep psychotherapeutic process. All of
us need to work with our assertion, our parental complexes,
our multilevel cognitive processes, and our capacity to
embrace the loathsome shadow. Nonetheless the four-fold
pattern of Celtic society is particularly relevant in recovery
from addictions. Following it takes us back to circle once
more through the ego functions that are analogous to the
cultural roles that the ancient Irish once created and
supported through their ritual uses of the *medb*. This time in
Part II we look at material relating to the goddess Maeve as
the deity behind the four initiations to help us find clues to
healing our addictive propensities. Finally we consider
Maeve's stories as a paradigm to harness and refine archetypal
appetite and to discover and cocreate the vessels of our
individual identity through which to relate to the libido that
empowers life.

Chapter 6

The Battling Goddess

In the famous medieval epic *The Tain Bo Culainge* (*The Cattle Raid of Cooley*), considered to be the Irish equivalent of *The Iliad*, Queen Maeve is described by an Ulster hero whom she has gravely wounded:

"A tall, fair, long-faced woman with soft features came at me. She had a head of yellow hair and two golden birds on her shoulders. She wore a purple cloak folded about her, with five hands breadth of gold on her back. She carried a light stinging, sharp-edged lance in her hand, and she held an iron sword . . . over her head—a massive figure. It was she who came against me first" [the dying warrior, Cethern, said]. *"Then I am sorry for you,"* Cuchulainn said, *"That was Medb of Cruachan."*[1]

Here we are shown the goddess as a massive, beautiful, well-armed, and deadly figure. With her regal garments and golden birds, she fights boldly at the head of her armies and sends her many warriors to combat Cuchulainn. Maeve's desire to capture a giant bull to maintain her sovereignty, which was threatened by the rise of patrifocal religion, turns her into an ambitious warring queen. She uses her aggression and her militant sexuality with effect. She propels the epic's action.

We need now to look at Maeve as the embodiment of an energy that underlies biology and culture. Neutral in itself, the energy we call aggression can be felt as either negative or positive; it can be used destructively or for life. Unlike the distended rages of the maddened addict, assertive urges can operate in the service of survival. As wolf, Maeve represents the drives towards aggression, territoriality, and protective guarding. Within the overarching balance of nature, these function to support and preserve the life of the individual and the pack. Maeve the battling goddess represents basic urges for primacy, possession, and effective power already honed for struggle. These function to ensure that the tribe will have its basic needs supplied and its safety guaranteed. In the emerging patriarchy, skillfully used aggression also ensures that the youthful heroes will have their proud place in the mead hall after the battle and the enduring praise of poets in the tribe.[2]

For the addict or the individual prone to addiction, a new relation to aggression is inevitably an issue in healing, as we shall see.

The Boasting Match

The story of Maeve's war starts with "pillow talk." The goddess queen lies on her bed with Ailill, her current husband, a king representing the new patriarchal aristocracy. He wants the ancient goddess of the land to admit how much better off she is now that she is his wife. She answers proudly from the old tradition that she "was well enough off without" him, for she outdid her five sisters in "grace and giving and battle and warlike combat" as well as in land and property. Asserting her own self-esteem further, she tells him "if anyone causes you shame or upset or trouble, the right to compensation is mine . . . for you're a kept man."[3] Ailill, upholding the new values that demean matriarchal custom and the female, protests. But Maeve, not to be outdone, avers, "It still remains . . . that my fortune is greater than yours." In this response we can see that the ancient goddess is already partly caught in the snares of the patriarchal construction of authority fostered by the invading Celtic tribes from mainland Europe and the later scribes who recorded the story. She no longer blithely abandons cocky Ailill as she did previous royal consorts throughout the land's mythic history. Instead she joins with him and appeals to the terms that became medieval Irish law. Under these, either wife or husband might control household affairs and the partner, depending on whomever had the greater fortune.[4] Far more lenient to the female than Roman and Greek custom and law, this construction expresses a transitional balance of matristic and patristic authority that persisted in Celtic culture until Norman churchmen came to power. Nonetheless its emphasis is on the individual's material fortune rather than on the customs of matrilineal succession that in older sovereignty rites asserted the clear primacy of the queen over the land and all its products.

The boasting match itself is an outgrowth of survival urges that have turned competitive to assert individual need and worth. We see such assertion in two-year-olds with their claims of "me" and "mine," and we associate it also with adolescent-turf fights and divorce cases. It becomes fierce and adversarial in an atmosphere of threatening scarcity or when domination is held in high regard as a cultural value. Thus such competitive encounters are rampant in any hierarchical, militaristic society where the champion must prove his or her mettle by battling to the top. Since much of our Western society derives from early Bronze and Iron Age heroic cultures, not surprisingly many of us can still resonate with such struggles for pride of position from the narcissistically inflamed phallic-aggressive levels in our own development. Even as adults, we can get caught obsessively in the need to prove ourselves worthy of parental love, society's acclaim, and even God's grace when those affirmations have been made conditional on our winning performance. Because this same pattern of motivation is too often also fostered in school and the workplace, it may obsess us throughout life with frantic addictions to power, perfection, possessions, fame, and the hard, competitive work that supports these goals.

Accounts of proofs of strength were already dear to the Celts. Thus early Irish storytellers extolled the exploits of heroes in the Ulster cycle to their aristocratic listeners. In the epic *The Tain,* the boasting between Queen Maeve and her consort escalates to actual comparisons. Since in Irish law a wife could rule her own and her husband's affairs if she had more possessions than he, the issue is not mere petulance but an accounting to determine sovereignty in the royal household in an age when the goddess' dominion was under threat from the rising patriarchal Celtic aristocracy.

All their possessions are brought before the royal couple "to see who had more property and jewels and precious things" and also to provide opportunity to express the love of explicit, detailed description and finely massed accretions of the storyteller's art. The values, measured in the terms of the Bronze and Iron Age Celtic herdsmen and later Christian scribes, are vested in metal and male animals, not on the fecund mares, sows, and cows revered in earlier eras as embodiments of the sources of plenty and transcendent power. Essential worth is still measured in bondmaids, not liegemen, however.

Their buckets and tubs and iron pots, jugs and wash-pails and vessels with handles. Then their finger-rings, bracelets, thumb-rings and gold treasures were brought out, and their cloth of purple, blue, black, green, and yellow, plain gray and many-coloured, yellow-brown, checked and striped. Their herds of sheep were taken in off the fields, and meadows and plains. They were measured and matched, and found to be the same in numbers and size. Even the great ram leading Medb's sheep, the worth of one bondmaid by himself, had a ram to match him leading Ailill's sheep. From pasture and paddock their teams and herds of horses were brought in. For the finest stallion in Medb's stud, worth one bondmaid by himself, Ailill had a stallion to match. Their vast herds of pigs were taken in from the woods and gullies and waste places. They were measured and matched and noted, and Medb had one fine boar, but Ailill had another. Then their droves and free-wandering herds of cattle were brought in from the woods and wastes of the province. They were matched and measured and noted also, and found to be the same in number. But there was one great bull in Ailill's herd, that had been a calf of one of Medb's cows. Finnbennach was his name, the White Horned—and Finnbennach, refusing to be led by a woman had gone over to the king's herd (emphasis added).

This last phrase expresses the whole shift in cultural authority taking place at the time of the Celtic warrior tribes' invasions into Stone Age and matrifocal Ireland.

*Medb couldn't find in her herd an equal of this bull, and her spirits
dropped as though she hadn't a single penny.*[5]

To restore the balance Maeve sets out to borrow
the Brown Bull of Culainge to have a match for Ailill's bull.
She offers a fine price including land, chariot, and her own
"friendly thighs." The brown bull's owner accepts. But he
reverses his decision in rage when one of the messengers sent
to ask the loan undoes the bargain with a haughty sneer that
they would have taken the bull anyway, "with or without . . .
leave." Throughout the tale, many characters display this kind
of bristling hypersensitive pride and massive competitiveness
to shore up the delicate but primary sense of individual honor.

The Power of Insult to Arouse

Indeed throughout the epic, the warrior Cuchulainn, who is
the guardian warrior of his tribe against all foes, calls on the
power of insult to arouse himself to greater feats. Whenever
he is flagging in battle against an adversary that would
threaten his life and/or thwart his duty as guardian, he orders
his charioteer to berate him. Inevitably the affront to his
honor triggers an influx of rage that infuses him with fiery
ardor and makes him go into his famous "warp spasm." Then
with his face and body contorted, he becomes a monstrous
manifestation of berserk energy. Fully in identity with
aggressive fury, this warrior guardian of his tribe is rendered
through inhuman distortions as a divinity, able even to stand
single-handedly against all Maeve's forces. He is terrifying and
invincible:

*A monstrous thing, hideous and shapeless, unheard of. His shanks
and his joints, every knuckle and angle and organ from head to foot,
shook like a tree in the flood or a reed in the stream. His body made
a furious twist inside his skin, so that his feet and shins and knees
switched to the rear and his heels and calves switched to the front.
The balled sinews of his calves switched to the front of his shins, each
big knot the size of a warrior's bunched fist. On his head the temple
sinews stretched to the nape of his neck, each mighty, immense,
measureless knob as big as the head of a month-old child. His face*

and features became a red bowl: he sucked one eye so deep into his
head that a wild crane couldn't probe it onto his cheek out of the
depths of his skull; the other fell out along his cheek. His mouth
weirdly distorted: his cheek peeled back from his jaws until the gullet
appeared, his lungs and liver flapped in his mouth and throat, his
lower jaw struck the upper a lion-killing blow, and fiery flakes large
as ram's fleece reached his mouth from his throat. His heart boomed
loud in his breast like the baying of a watch-dog at its feed or the
sound of a lion among bears. Malignant mists and spurts of fire—
the torches of Badb [the raven goddess of war]—flickered red in the
vaporous clouds that rose boiling above his head, so fierce was his
fury. The hair of his head twisted like the tangle of a red thorn bush
stuck in a gap; if a royal apple tree with all its kingly fruit were
shaken above him, scarce an apple would reach the ground but each
would be spiked on a bristle of his hair as it stood up on his scalp
with rage. The hero-halo rose out of his brow, long and broad as a
warrior's whetstone, long as a snout, and he went mad rattling his
shields, urging on his charioteer and harassing the hosts. Then, tall
and thick, steady and strong, high as the mast of a noble ship rose
up from the dead centre of his skull a straight spout of black blood
darkly and magically smoking.[6]

Following in the pattern of Cuchulainn's warp spasm, modern cultural heroes transmute physically into their powerfully rageful aspects to defend the people and values they hold dear. The mild reporter Clark Kent becomes Superman by removing the ordinary clothes that hide his true identity as the salvific and indestructible hero of his city. A television character undergoes bodily distortions similar to the transformation that represented Cuchulainn's influx of divine rage. When angered by threats, he becomes "The Hulk" and is able to achieve extraordinary feats. While combat training seeks to transform ordinary civilians into fierce soldiers for their country, such behavior in daily life is called aberrant. We would call such hulkish outbursts defensively omnipotent, explaining the grandiose behavior as an impulsive identification with the Self's primal rage in reaction to perceived threat. If the behavior is habitual and the threats not currently realistic, we would hypothesize the existence of what we call borderline or narcissistic personality features, such as those we find often in individuals prone to addictions.

In early patriarchal Celtic times, however, such eruptive behavior was the heroic standard. Embedded in clan loyalty and extremely reactive to omnipresent transpersonal forces that required orderly, collective ritual mediation into human affairs, personal identity was still a fluid and precarious construct.[7] With the beginnings of the hierarchical order under clan chiefs and with ideals of dominative power, it coalesced around the archetype of the warrior hero. Thus when *The Tain* was first sung, what we would call the phallic narcissistic and grandiose ego was a prototype, not a pathology. Nonetheless, this sense of identity is structured and defined according to collective cultural roles, relationships, and norms, rather than balanced through conscious participation in the multivalent processes of the individual Self as these interact with societal demands. I would see one-sided identification with the adversarial hero in modern adults as identification with a role—a persona ego. It represents a nascent and partial stage in the development of true individuality.

The Hero

The struggle for power between the ancient omnipotent goddess and the aristocratic Celts forms the background of *The Cattle Raid of Cooley*. But *The Tain* is primarily an epic tale of the heroic individual who emerges through a series of extraordinary combats in his battles against the armies of the goddess. While his own Ulster comrades are laid low by their mare goddess' vengeful curse, the ardent young warrior proves his mettle in one battle after another against single warriors and whole hosts—all those Maeve sends against him. Aided only by his charioteer, his supernatural father, the god Lugh, who takes his place for three days so he can recuperate, and the delaying tactics of his foster father, Maeve's lover Fergus, this guardian Hound of Ulster Cuchulainn distinguishes himself with mighty deeds displaying his skills-at-arms, his courage, will, boldness, invincible strength, and his "three talents of sight and intellect and reckoning."[8] "It was no easy thing facing Cuchulainn on the Tain" comments the storyteller sardonically as every man sent against him meets with defeat.[9] Even his own beloved foster-brother Ferdia, who had trained with him and knew all but one of

Cuchulainn's feats and who had a skin of horn that no weapon could pierce, is roused to combat by Maeve's false reports of Cuchulainn's insults against him. In this closely matched encounter Cuchulainn inevitably prevails, proving that no human being and no human relatedness can stand in the way of his trained passion. The three days of battle with Ferdia allow the poets to extol more marvelous heroic deeds. Indeed descriptions of Cuchulainn's prowess not only fill the epic and its songs, they are also celebrated in the names of landscape features that honor the events of his battling: The Ford of Yielding, The Stream of Blood, The Skill of Chuchulainn, etc. Not lacking the capacity for bold self-praise, the Ulster warrior himself sings: "none of human birth, until the day of doom, can ever match the heavy, high deeds that I do against Connacht [Maeve's territory] with shield or shield-rim, sword or dart, draughts or chess, horse or chariot."[10] Cuchulainn notes that "the mighty Medb has had carnage and renown with all the warriors I've slain." He seems to acknowledge that Maeve made him a famous hero as surely as Hera made one of Herakles. In battle with her forces he comes into his own, standing for the heroic capacity required of any youthful individual to withstand Maeve's challenges in the repeated, seemingly endless, psychological and spiritual battles to which the goddess of life consigns us.

The sad toll of battling is also sung poignantly in one early medieval interpolation into *The Tain*. Cuchulainn's lament for Ferdia expresses the limits of heroic grandiosity and the full force of remorse—the other side of the single focus on domination required for the hero to prevail. Its inclusion in the epic gives a human depth to the hero and makes us realize that although the poets could extol battle furor, they also knew the painful cost of heroism. Its price is the loneliness and misery incumbent on anyone who stands against the enmeshment that the goddess holds us in, pushes us out of, and reclaims us into through heroic death. As Cuchulainn clasps the body of his foster-brother, he sings: "My friend, why should I rise . . . and this one fallen by my hand?. . . You are dead and I must live to mourn my everlasting loss."

Ill-met, Ferdia, like this
—you crimson and pale in my sight
and stretched in a bed of blood,
I with my weapon unwiped,

. . . .
Our famous foster mother bound us
in a blood pact of friendship
so that rage would never rise
between friends . . . .
Sad and pitiful the day
that saw Ferdia's strength spent
and brought down the downfall of a friend.
I poured him a drink of red blood! . . .
Misery has befallen us,
Bravery is battle-madness!

. . . .
It was all play, all sport
until Ferdia came to the ford.[11]

In this Ulster tale honoring the heroic ego that is created through opposition to the powers of Maeve, there can be no outcome except terrible carnage. As Cuchullain sings it:

I have slaughtered, on this Tain,
three countless multitudes:
choice cattle, choice men,
and horses, fallen everywhere!
. . . slaughtered in my savage sport.

The story ends with the giant bulls of Maeve and Ailill killing each other and Maeve's armies in rout—even though she "took up her weapons and hurried into battle . . . and three times drove all before her."[12] The ancient land is ravaged by the fighting bulls. Countless multitudes are killed in the war, and the primacy of the goddess over the land and its rulers is successfully challenged.

As the magnificent poetry extolls Cuchulainn, it also derogates the goddess. With irony and mockery the Ulstermen and the monkish scribes, who left us the written tale, snipe at Maeve. She is portrayed as an ultimately doomed manipulator who, with sexual lures, entraps her champions into impossible battles. She is made to seem dependent on her "general" Fergus. He is no longer presented as her otherworld consort but rather as a king defecting from the enemy camp to become her lover and war chief. At the end of the war he even belittles her saying, "We have followed the rump of a misguiding woman. . . . It is the usual thing for a herd led by a mare to be strayed and destroyed."[13] Her armies are ultimately defeated by the single, glorious hero, whose immortality is won in the story of his resistance to her.

Maeve as Warrior

Like the relatively peaceful cultures of goddess-worshipping Neolithic peoples that were overrun by the aristocratic Celts, Maeve herself was dominated. Her earth-goddess nature originally encompassed the creative and destructive cycles of life as a continuum affecting and affected by humans through supernatural, magical powers.[14] With the rise of the patriarchy Maeve became also a representation of the principle of adversarial action and the dichotomized aggressive principles by which the army of Ulster chief and its champion, Cuchulainn, fought against her ancient powers.

As male warrior gods climbed to the top, Maeve was not raped, as were many goddesses of Old Europe to demonstrate the brute power of the masculine deities and their militaristic invaders. Still too potent, she was only flouted with mockery, reduced with insult, and fought against as a scorned adversary. In this early stage of the patriarchy, she thus came to represent an aspect of the feminine that refuses to be dominated but is already changed. Maeve adapted to threat by embodying the combative ways of her opponents, thereby joining and sanctioning them. While she reasserted her triadic processual rhythms at the end of the great raid by loosing three rivers, Maeve in *The Tain* gives us a glimpse of the warrior goddess. In the epic she uses the warlike means of the Bronze and Iron Age usurpers of her ancient powers against themselves. Passionately guarding her sovereignty, her people, and the old religion, she transforms to meet the patriarchy on its own terms. Seizing the offensive against the Ulstermen, she turns the plowshares and scythes of the fertility goddess into bronze and iron age spears and swords. Although the storytellers of the new patrifocal culture used *The Tain* to glorify masculine prowess, the epic also portrays Maeve as a fearsome adversary. "The greatest warrior is Medb," an Irish text proclaims.[15] Cuchulainn says as much when he commiserates with the dying Cethern.

In spite of the medieval literati's disparagement of her divine fury and capacity to wage battle, in spite of the defeat she is made to suffer in this epic, she still reminds us of Inanna of Sumer, Sekmet of Egypt, and Durga of India, great goddesses roused to battle to maintain the order sanctioned by all the gods. Taking direct part in the war with skillfully employed weapons instead of the magical methods more commonly used by the ancient Celtic goddesses, Maeve here represents active feminine force co-opted into adversarial and aggressive forms. She signifies the feminine power to take arms and act assertively to fulfill life's need. Maeve's warrior form deifies female capacities to stand fiercely and effectively against threat. This war goddess shows us that women living under threat in the patriarchy must also be capable of direct and powerful assertion.

Several other goddesses in Irish myth exemplify such capacities as well. They were the women warriors who taught battle skills and led their own troops. The goddess Scathach had a special camp where she trained warriors. She taught Cuchulainn his most potent battle feats and earned his gratitude.[16] Otherworldly warrior women, called "witches" in the later written tales, trained the heroes Finn MacCumail and Peredur.[17] We also know, from historical evidence, of at least one female leader of a youthful war band [*fianna*][18] and of several ancient queens who led their own armies. Boudicca, queen of the Iceni, rose up to avenge the rape of her daughters and the theft of her dead husband's land by Roman conquerors. She invoked her people's goddess of war with gruesome rites and led the successful battle herself. She was one of the few British rulers who were victorious for a time against the phalanx forces of Rome. The powerful Celtic women, who defended their homes beside their men, gained

Roman respect and awed comment.[19] Only in the seventh century AD were Irish women finally forced by edict to lay down their arms and their right to take part in battle. From Celtic lore we can see that the capacity to use rage effectively for life, to become both warrior and guardian, and to train others in assertive skills is not gender limited.

Addicts into Warriors

Modern addicts know Maeve the war goddess unconsciously in projection and as possession. They may feel and identify themselves as the helpless victim of Maeve's battling power, known through their early intimate caretaker's attacks on them and then continually re-projected and feared in all of life's later relationships. Too tortured and sensitive to bear further discomfort, they may then seek to avoid all other-directed confrontation and express anger by turning it back against themselves and their own bodies in self-hating impulses and masochistic dissipation. Then they may seek to gain a sense of power through surrender to the carriers of their projected aggression or to their addiction, perpetuating the negative specialness first experienced when they were physically or emotionally abused. On the other hand, as we have discussed, they may also find themselves in identity with such transpersonal aggression, possessed by sadistic eruptive rages that readily destroy anyone who thwarts their fragile self-esteem or their compulsive quest for the drug on which they depend. The craving for power itself may become addictive since it correlates with aroused hormone levels on which the person can become dependent for an exciting rush. Further, because addicts often lack conscious relationship to assertive energies, they may be bombastic bullies or sly and ruthless manipulators whose strategic capacities are bound into the pursuit of their drug or getting others to care for their split-off dependency and self-disciplinary needs. Often they have developed a bully-like bravado with which they hide and disguise their vulnerability. This cover may appear in various guises: as passive aggressive, as automatically and rebelliously fierce like a brat, or as bitterly rejective of all relationship. It operates defensively to ward off expected abuse, but it alienates others and maintains the status quo by forbidding and frustrating new possibilities. Thus it can readily destroy all potentials for transformation until it has been made conscious and warmly affirmed as a once life-saving defense.[20]

Inevitably those prone to addiction have to begin to relate consciously to the capacities represented by the battle goddess and her heroic enemy Cuchulainn as soon as they can realize that their position and existence are worth defending. This interwoven validation of existence in turn is dependent on Maeve's maternal and mirroring functions as they are incarnated through the transference (see chapter 8). Initially clients need to respect the value of old, even counterproductive, defenses as attempts to claim and assert their survival. Then with a sense of valued existence, they can begin to develop more adaptive and strategic individual capacities for active heroism. They can restructure their relation to aggression, consciously learning to be worthy adversaries, to separate, to reject, and to defend and shield themselves. Like Cuchulainn they may learn from the war goddess, trainer-in-arms, the very "feats" of war skill that even enable her own defeat. Psychologically, this implies reaching deeply and consciously into and through the paralysis and eruptive outbursts that are defenses against early experiences of destructive care to rouse the rage of passionate aggression again and to train it well in group and individual therapy to protect and serve life.

In such therapies and the Twelve-step programs, recovering addicts who have felt powerless against the circumstances of their life and the control of their addiction can learn to become warriors.[21] While recognizing the power of the addiction, which operates as a negative numinosum compelling their devotion, recovering addicts can learn to assert that they are not still helpless victims. They can end their denial of the life and death contest in which they are caught and begin courageously, as survivors of the death fields, to take part in the struggle. They can find help to rally their will and find the heroic strength to abstain from the substance or action that has bound them.[22] They can battle against the shame that has covered their deeper emotions and learn together to express the truth of their intense feelings. Thus they become warriors. Like siblings-at-arms in communion with each other and the Higher Power, they learn together to fight against their enslavement to the literalistic lower forms of spirit. They can then begin to serve the Life Spirit that also motivates their intense cravings and find other, more creative avenues through which the ecstasies and defenses provided by alcohol can become integrated into life.

They use the qualities of Maeve, the war goddess, and the war hero who stands against her to battle their cravings for *medb*, the concrete substance. In intuitively affirming this context for the struggle of recovering addicts, AA has brilliantly evoked one healing aspect of the archetype behind addiction. In Twelve-step programs addicts learn to convert their personal and life-long fear of annihilation in the arms of the death mother into willingness to struggle heroically in the face of death. Because they can share a transpersonal purpose and meaning—the salvation of other addicts—as part of the company of those in recovery, they can find the courage to become heroic together. In this struggle they heed Jung's words to AA co-founder William G. Wilson:

Alcohol in Latin is spiritus *and you use the same word for the highest religious experience as well as the most depraving poison. The helpful formula is "spiritus contra spiritum."*[23]

As we continue to explore this spirit-against-spirit aspect of Maeve's image, we can see that the battling queen's sword is a basic human tool for cutting, separating, and dismembering. It can destroy an adversary. It may clear the way and provide discrimination of boundaries and parts of the whole to create order from the chaotic tangles of addiction. The image of the sword represents the powers of confrontation and clarification that can offset the addict's predisposition to symbiotic fusion with others and to cognitive and affective confusions within. Very often the addict's capacities for thinking, feeling, perceiving, emoting, and self-valuing are in such fluid interpenetration, they remain irrational and/or unconscious. Thus battling for abstinence also involves issues we will discuss in chapter 9 when we deal with Maeve as process.

Battling for Abstinence

One alcoholic in early recovery was using the sharpening edge of thinking to clarify the chaotic mixtures that ensnared her and prevented her even knowing what her adversary was. As she began to learn how to use mental faculties analogous to a mental sword to discriminate and do battle with alcohol dependency, she expressed the chaotic mix that had kept her unable to function:

Drinking is like a pimp that lures me, or a drug dealer inside my own soul. I've always thought I was it, or it was me. Because being bad and feeling bad—upset, ashamed—got all mixed up. As mixed up as feeling high and being good and worth something. Sometimes I know now that it's my crazy father-complex that makes me feel so bad I'd do anything to feel good, so I'm vulnerable to that pimp . . . . Sometimes now I can make a discrimination and hate the addiction rather than the craziness and shame—[that represent] the chaotic me that falls into it.

Slowly she began to separate from her identity with the addiction and the shame that seduced her in order to develop a sense of herself as a constant embodied presence who could stand against its seduction. As adversary, supported by the therapist and her Twelve-step group, she began to feel she existed. Much later, when her self-esteem was more available, she could also begin to take practical steps in the world to support her own life.

The various Twelve-step programs can help in the initial clarification process. They distinguish between the negative power of the addictive substance and the positive

Higher Power to which they appeal for help to sober addictive behaviors. They begin to transform the addict's unconscious and acted-out capacity for powerless submission to the *medb* into a conscious relationship to a Higher Power.[24] This divinity and the community gathered in communion with its power support the addict's consciousness as it separates from bondage and coalesces *against* the negativized siren of the destructive brew to develop the heroic, nurturant, regal, and expressive integrity that can sustain pain, emptiness, passion, grief, and responsibility. Battling with Maeve against the chaotic snares of the *medb* provides a first birth for the addict's acquisition of the disciplined controls that Celtic society itself provided with its ritual initiatory communions.

These disciplined controls are required by Maeve herself. Like all Celtic heroines she would "never tolerate self-abasement or self-contempt. . . . She wants a man [or woman] conscious of his [or her] responsibilities, and worthy of her esteem and love."[25] She requires proven battle skills even as she tests them in repeated battles. Again and again she urges individual warriors from her armies to go forth heroically, and she motivates their passion with the offer of "her own friendly thighs." She makes them put their lusty hearts into their heroism to earn renown in the songs of the tribe and to gain their sacred status as consort of the battle queen if they succeed in battle. With every battle she also honors and elevates the hero who stands against her forces. Thus she refocuses energies of desire and exhibitionism to motivate courage. Valued and enjoyed, the warriors of Maeve find pride among their peers and renown on the lips of the poets. Cuchulainn becomes an image of the qualities and skills of the intrepid individual who can successfully stand against the overwhelming powers of the *medb*. But he is an ideal representing the principle of heroism. He is fated from birth to accomplish his task and help to usher in the patriarchal heroic age.

Heroic qualities require rallying in the addict. In the Twelve-step programs there is acknowledgment that one may have to hit bottom in the battle for one's very life to find sufficient rallying power to motivate the assertion required for the long struggle towards recovery. Battling then against the *medb* leads over time to successful abstinence. Abstinence becomes part of the addict's warrior discipline, and sobriety anniversaries are part of the renown to be celebrated. The process cannot be rushed, however, and temporary losses in the fight are expected as they would be in any war. Slips from abstinence are rallying points from which to try again, just as pride in one's lengthening span of sobriety supports an honor that helps to guard it further. Marking anniversaries of sobriety in AA is thus a potent ritual acclaiming the addict's rebirth into the new company of the sober.

Other assertive energies that require assimilation into the addict's enfeebled, early ego include active self-guarding as well as the quieter capacity to stand firm. Here the addict needs to learn to use the warrior's shield. Not only can it ward off attack and prevent fragmentation in the stresses of life, but behind it the hero can begin to feel coalesced and whole. It sets a limit against imploding energies picked up from others in the psycho-social field. Usually the sensitive addict has had to process these unbounded energies since early childhood in a fused and dysfunctional family system and is left with a sense of pervasive doom and hopelessness. The shield also represents the capacity to set a limit against eruptive reactivity from within. Then emotions can be seen more objectively and assessed for their relevance to past and/or present and for the best strategies to clarify and embody their messages. Like a safely guarding parental arm, the shield can begin to give the recovering addict a means of self-protection from outer and inner attacks, one that permits integration. Rather than erupting wildly, disappearing into addictive behavior, or shame, despair, and self-hate, the person prone to addiction can, as one man said, "clear the space to begin to see and want my own life."

The skills with sword and shield are learned by standing against the lure of the drink as well as the habits of weakness and rebellion in the face of any seemingly strong authority. In the relative safety of individual and group therapy, confrontation and challenge can be received, defended, and dealt out. The warriors can learn that self-affirmation and anger may have the desired effect of stopping or at least confronting what feels abusive—a stand recovering addicts report was rarely respected or possible in childhood. Yet the effective assertion need not destroy relationships to other people; instead it can enhance intimacy. Like the warriors at the mead-feast, those who practice battle skills together can become as close as siblings (they were called "foster-brothers" by the Celts) because they know and respect each other through battling honestly together to express their own reality.

It is not surprising that young addicts sent to detox centers often refer to their time there as being in boot camp. One client spoke of attending his detox group as "going to karate class." In such struggles recovering addicts can build their personal strength and refine their capacities to use sword-like discriminations, lance-sharp confrontations, and appropriate self-guarding shields against their comrades-at-arms and against their own raw emotionality and addictive tendencies. Over time such therapeutic practice enables the squashed, eruptive, and often reversed instinct of self-assertion to flow effectively into mastery skills and self-esteem.

One man, afraid of powerful women like his sometimes-abusive mother, drank and misused Maeve's sexual powers to conquer his "enemies" by taking them to bed. When he began to resist the habitual mix of power and sexuality that possessed him, he needed a training ground to practice alternative skills and strategies. From under his veneer of polite seductiveness, he began to indulge in sniping accusations, insults, challenges, and mockery, sounding very much like the scribes who demeaned Maeve. As he learned to enjoy taunting his therapist, who could appreciate most of the assaults non-defensively, he also began to try to control the therapy. He demanded changes of time, told the therapist how to respond, criticized the office arrangements and even her person. This felt to the therapist like a restoration of healthy omnipotence in a relational setting even though it was mixed with long-repressed rage. Thus the therapist initially accepted each incident at face value and discussed its merits, not interpreting the issues of control and transferred anger until a dream suggested that the dreamer was ready for confrontation. As he felt more secure that the therapeutic relationship could survive his attacks, the client encouraged sparring matches. At one point he asked to role-play the more effective and subtle battle skills he needed at his job. Trying various methods of confrontation, he gained confidence and began to take pride in refining his techniques. After nearly two years of such a therapeutic "mead-feast" in which the therapist was given the roles of the destructive Maeve as well as the trainer-at-arms and the foster-sister, he was often able spontaneously to experience his instinct for self-assertion that had once been squashed into unconsciousness. Gradually he gave up his older, habitual masochistic and sexualized defenses because they provided less gratification than direct confrontation. He welcomed the flow of battling energy and found he could enjoy the strength and self-discipline it required. Because he could fight well when he had to, he found one important basis of self-esteem. As he celebrated his own value and found he could defend it, he slowly became able to feel genuine empathy for others, to be able to apologize for hurts he had caused, and to develop effective strategies for self-assertion that respected the others' needs. Then he began to enjoy a wider variety of options for relationship.

The recovering addict in the boot camps of AA and therapy abstains from the mead itself and thereby begins to exercise the strength among peers to confront reality.[26] This process involves facing up to old fears of annihilation, engulfment, and fragmentation, to old loyalties to negative parental complexes, old depression, masochism, and low self-esteem, and to the old habits of defensive numbness and denial as insulation against pain. The warrior in recovery battles by courageously becoming aware of and reflecting on newly awakened sensitivities and the boredom that constellates when borderline addictive excitements are sobered. By learning to stand separate from powerful emotions and consciousness-undermining complexes, the recovering addict gains a sense of mastery over the once-swamping inner and outer world. This sense of mastery coalesces the feeble and fragmented consciousness of the addict. No longer overpowered by compulsive cravings and numbing escapes, the warrior can discover, as did the client above, the strength to exist and even to thrive on the psychological battle fields of life.

Because, however, the addict has been predisposed towards paralysis of will, even when he is a bully, he or she initially has little muscle for becoming a real warrior or ruler. Hence while AA stresses fighting the addictive substance by open disclosure, it does not allow confrontation in its meetings. Standing and speaking up is a first step in building muscle for social relations. Just to "show up" and declare oneself in a supportive environment is a triumph. Similarly, the initial stages of therapeutic work often require enormous courage and energy. Because sessions can be so momentously hard and fatiguing, the work must be dosed carefully. "Seeing reality is such hard work, I'd like to sink back into my muddlement," said one man, beginning to know that if he did not stand against it, such "muddlement" exerted an inertial pull that drew him back into addictive patterns. He had a series of dreams showing him increasingly able to resist an evil seducer. Sometimes the seducer was imaged by the figure of his needy and neglectful mother when he had to face his own fears of abandonment. Sometimes the seducer was a powerful intruder when he had to connect to the assertion that had been unconscious in the shadows of his own personality.

Another recovering addict spoke of needing to "cut the umbilicus" to the original misconstellation of the maternal archetype in her psyche, her personal mother complex. Loyal to her mother in spite of continuing contemptuous abuse that the client had initially denied, she was masochistically turning the other cheek and persisting in the fantasy that there might be a magical reconciliation. As she repeatedly cut herself free from her own illusions, she became able to sacrifice her hopes that she might still omnipotently cure her abuser. She was surprised that she could bear the pain of the loss, for as many recovering addicts, she had experienced herself wedded to suffering and despair. Everyone's pain impressed her, and she had felt unable to challenge anyone or herself if she expected discomfort from the encounter. Gradually she came to realize that she even exaggerated pain because her traumatized childhood sensitivities and fears had received neither respect nor care. Still hoping for empathy, she had kept them alive. As she felt the concern of her therapist and group, she began to see that she was now "tougher than [she] thought." Not quite like the Ulster warriors who accepted wounds proudly as emblems of their struggles, she nonetheless learned that she could sustain pain, empathize with it, and still survive.

Very often the addicted person's parents have themselves required care from their child, as this woman's mother had. Very often the parents have given concrete things to the child instead of empathy, thereby reinforcing the young child's literalistic tendency and encouraging the need for concrete and immediate gratification. Or the narcissiistic parents have overtly or subtly neglected the child's own feeling needs and failed to provide affirmative mirroring of the child's separate and particular identity. Thus the addiction-prone individual feels personally unwelcome on Earth. Fearing to acknowledge this orphanhood and the child's terrors of annihilating abandonment, even defending against such admissions by extreme and unrealistic loyalty to ungiving and unseeing parental figures, the addict blames him or herself for being unlovable and turns to the substitute maternal nourishment through an umbilicus to the addiction.

Often the addiction's bonds are also experienced in images of a deathly womb or mummy casing from which the person in recovery must struggle to be born. Without psychological muscle this feels almost impossible. The famous "learned helplessness" research tells us something about this numbed state. In one experiment a group of dogs had been tied down and shocked when they could not escape. They were subsequently unable to jump free from the torture even when they were untied. Since their capacity for active self-preservation had been thus severely damaged, they had to be retrained to protect themselves. As traumatized children in situations from which they could not escape, those prone to addiction often have suffered the same loss of ability to take assertive or guarding action on their own behalf.

When a positive therapeutic transference can form to a therapist, sponsor, or "recovery kin" group, recovering addicts may find a necessary magnet of hope, motivation, and encouragement. Even then the pressure towards emergence from the deathly embrace of Maeve may alternate with a desire to stay safely dead. During periods of stress, emergence from the *medb's* anesthesia threatens pains that seem far worse than her grasp. Then the therapist may also be perceived as the enemy midwife and avoided. Sometimes emergence is impossible due to old habits of flight from pain. Sometimes it is impossible for the time while the sword flails wildly and seemingly autonomously in the hands of the negative complex. Without focused intention such unconscious violence threatens the new bonds rather than the older destructive ones. As one client described it:

What you call "the spoiler" destroys our bond and even the links in me to my own mind and memory. . . . I lose all sense of my body. Breathing is scary . . . I lose all sense of who you are. And [then] you are someone else who is dangerous—my mother, maybe—someone not like yourself . . . . In fact I can't remember you from session to session, nor my own intentions, nor anything but what is right now. . . . Everything gets chopped up into pieces I can't hold together. Because the attackers are stronger than anything I can hold . . . . This is how it used to be when I was on drugs, but then I said it was drugs. Now I see it's some horrible defect in my own will. That's much more frightening.

This severely borderline man was close to the psychosis he had used drugs to manage. There was also some medical uncertainty about the degree of damage his reliance on toxins had done to an already very damaged and immature core. Although there seemed to be moments of potential healing, the underlying fragmentation remained relatively unchanged throughout years of therapy. In loyal identification with the abusive system that had made reality a terror, this substance-sober man could only manage to assert himself through fear and self-hate, and these held a masochistic and addictive excitement for him. As expressed in his comment, he used his fear as a perverted club to tell the therapist she and therapy were terrorizing, but he was gratified and at home in the terror and found all attempts to separate from it were thwarted. As he and the therapist could both see, healing was continually defeated by such profound mistrust and despair that it amounted to an existential and spiritual problem that could not be resolved within their therapeutic relationship. Although he discovered a love of painting and was able to create a series of self-portraits, he did not want to learn more about his craft and became repeatedly disheartened by what he called his "own ravaged face." Still he did not want to put his energy into painting anything else. The therapy terminated after eleven years when the client moved away to a somewhat better job than the ones he had previously been able to hold. He wrote that he functioned within the structures of his work and went regularly to AA meetings but was not ready to become a sponsor. He knew and was grateful that the group's steady sustenance maintained his fragile grip on life.

Even when there is a stronger possibility of healing transformation, there is also real danger in emerging from the "Coffin Haven," as one client called it. Having lived within a bifurcated world of extreme terror and the muffled illusion of comfort, the naive addict may have no sense of real danger, no appropriate fear to evoke a sense of self-shielding, and a paucity of life skills. Thus the therapist or mentor may need to model an approach to reality as a parent might by expressing dismay and fear for the recovering addict's safety and existential value in situations of real danger. One recovering woman walked the New York city streets alone at night. She was unaware of danger until a cop accosted her and told her to go home. A man in recovery continued to pick up men for casual sex as if he had never heard of AIDS. Another gave away his savings in a con game. In each instance these particularly self-destructive behaviors occurred after an experience of self-value that challenged the addict's habitual identity as a woeful reject. This new experience created a valuable potential for learning, but it also disturbed the status quo and engendered a sense of chaos into which a backlash of the destructive addictive and negative parental complexes intruded with envy of the new potentials. The old defense of naive bravado reconstellated in its magical omnipotence, and along with habitual masochism, it propelled dangerous behavior. By feeling the therapist's (and policeman's) concern and seeing that the behaviors eliciting such concern were part of a backlash collusion with old spoiling abuse, the recovering addicts could slowly reorient to begin to find value in self-protection that was real and not a repetition of escapist patterns.

Initially as we can see, part of the energy released with abstinence must be used to guard against the destructive pull of old patterns, which underlie the need for addictive behavior. These occur, as in these instances, through attacks on the new experiences of value, validation, and bonding. The attacks restimulate a desire for intoxication, because without its anesthesia the addict is very susceptible to habitual emotions of fear, abandonment, shame, deprivation, boredom, depression, rage, and/or self-hate. Slowly the client may become aware that there is a pattern of automatic backlashes from the original abusively constellated parent/child complex. These occur regularly to spoil positive, new experiences. The backlashes repeat the original spoiling, which undermined bonding and thriving when the addict was a child. They also reawaken infantile defenses against such attacks. They therefore bring important material for analysis as well as provide an image of an adversary that can be challenged in battle. Learning to stand against backlashes functions as a training ground for refining intrapsychic aggression. In this phase clients also often express rage against family members whom they will later be able to see and accept in a larger context.

Often the backlashes reconstitute old attacks of doubt or shame, old habits of disconfirmation of perception and emotion, old perceptual splitting, or single-minded focus on fragments of experience that are globalized and distorted. Sometimes they manifest through unconscious merging with negative parts of self or others. Sometimes they manifest as perceptual reversals in which a negative quality belonging to another is instead felt to be one's own. Since the backlash attacks are fused with the rage, panic, and extreme dependency needs of the infant, psychotic moments may occur in the transference until the addict has some awareness of the backlash pattern and can learn to disidentify from its automatic attack on new experience. Only then can the aggressive urge begin to be channeled to serve and protect life. Then the images of the spoiling attacker and the endangered "little one," a figure representing the addict's sensitive inner child, can operate in consciousness, and the client in recovery can learn with the therapist's help to take the "little one's" side against the automatic brutal attacks. In time the urges of the attacker may also be claimed as part of oneself. Gradually the development of ego-syntonic assertion shifts energy away from the old compulsion to spoil and becomes adaptive. This allows the spoiler's old victim to transform into a sensitive consciousness that can explore and thrive.

Ultimately as embodied aggressive and defensive drive energies awaken out of their unconscious spasms and paralytic helplessness, the recovering addict can begin to acquire warrior skills and learn self-guarding against inner and outer adversaries. In a dream image a man discovered his role in choosing a new assertive courage to struggle. He dreamt:

I am walking along a beautiful seashore, but there are a lot of boulders. The going is very tough for me. I have a desire to fly, and start willing myself into the air like I used to do. I am about to lift off when I see a small dog struggling along through the stones. He's a mongrel, but I decide to stay on the ground with him.

Faced with emotional boulders in his life, the dream ego recognized his desire to flee into old, omnipotent and escapist patterns. "I wouldn't ever drink again," he said, "but I could stay out of work and feel guilty and hate myself and get into a depression and hope that someone could rescue me."

Instead the dream image of the dog reminded him of another potential in his psyche, the still small instinctive capacity to struggle. Now the boulders seem only stones, and he chooses to ally with the humble determination to wrestle with life's inevitable adversity, as he said, "one stone at a time."

The capacities for abstinence from escapist flight and for new and genuine mastery give the recovering addict weapons and muscles with which to guard life and to confront problems effectively. But acquiring these skills cannot be accomplished by sheer macho grit. Otherwise the abstinence is motivated only by fear-driven duty to another severe superego, which will be undermined rebelliously as soon as the next craving overcomes its brittle demands and prohibitions. Abstinence and self-assertion need to be taught, welcomed, and incorporated within a containing environment, much like that of the Celtic mead-feast, where the warriors were housed, fed, and trained together by the male or female authority figure who held their personal allegiance and guided them in acquiring battle skills. Then the new learning can be mutually suffered and supported. Then lapses can be tolerated as inevitable, not viewed from a perfectionistic vantage as contemptible. The necessary tough gentleness is modeled in AA and psychotherapy. It is expressed in some of the Twelve-step slogans: "One day at a time"; "Easy does it"; "Just for the next five minutes [staying sober is possible]"; "Keep it simple"; "Think the drink through"; "Just show up"; "When Daniel got out of the lion's den, he didn't go back for his hat"; etc. These, like mantras, can often sustain individuals in recovery through the habitual fears and spoiling attacks of what would undermine them and tempt a return to the illusory solace of addictive habits. Learned together in the mead-feast, the slogans can reevoke the communion with fellow warriors and with a higher, caring and not shaming authority. In this context the archetype of Maeve provides leadership and training as well as the opposition that can impel true heroism and growth.

Chapter 7
Maternal Queen

Knocknarea

On the west coast of Ireland in Sligo near the boar-shaped hill called Ben Bulben,[1] there is a truncated mound visible for miles above the landscape. It juts against the sky northeast of Carrowmore, the largest and oldest group of megalithic tombs and stone circles in Ireland.[2] Swept by intense winds, the stony cairn stands on the crest of Knocknarea. Climbing to its top, a traveler can see the holy white quartz mountain of the ancient harvest goddess, formerly called *Cruachain Aigle* (the Pillar and/or Eagle of Cruachan), now named Croagh Patrick, and far beyond to other heights and the western sea. Eastwards, north, and south stretches the land that once belonged to Maeve's people. Called Maeve's cairn and thought to be the goddess' grave, this massive heap of stones is still held sacred. Pilgrims today venture up with faint remembrance of the ancient rites. They may carry a small rock to symbolize their troubles and lay it on the breast of the great earth mother, not unlike the way Twelve-step practitioners learn to turn their struggles with addiction over to a higher power.

Knocknarea was probably not constructed only as a grave although ruined satellite tombs lie nearby. Thirty-five feet high and two hundred feet across, containing forty thousand tons of stone, this cairn is thought to contain a passage chamber like the ones in the Boyne River Valley, a sacred core to which we have lost the physical entrance.[3] The folk of the region have prevented attempts to excavate the site for its mystery remains alive.[4] They seem to fear dire consequences if the spirit of Maeve should be disturbed from her slumbers. The homophonic sounds of the mountain's name suggest multiple significances. It is a level hill (Knock na Re), a striped or furrowed hill (na Riabh), the Hill of Royalty (na Ri), and the Hill of the Moon (na Rea). From a distance, from the tombs at Carrowmore, the heights of Carrowkeel, and many sites in the plains below, we can see that the cairn marks the protruding navel of a huge pregnant earth belly. On closer view, we see that Maeve's mound itself echoes the shape and position of Silbury Hill, a temple built in Somerset near Avebury. There the ancient architecture with its partially surrounding waters also suggests the belly-womb of the earth goddess within an arrangement of forms created in the landscape to celebrate many aspects of the great mother of life and death.[5] At Knocknarea, nearly surrounded by the Sligo bay far below, Maeve is much more than the death mother, and her great patterns are not buried except perhaps in modern consciousness. Her mound recalls the ancient worship of the fertile earth and sky mother and the alignments between earthly and celestial events that humans have held sacred from the Stone Age. The massive cairn rises on this commanding site to exalt the abiding and fecund life process through all its seasons and to represent the vessel of life, death, and rebirth. Appropriately placed near the western sea where the ancient Irish located their Islands of Joy and the Ever-Living, it stands as marker of the setting sun and harbinger of reborn light. It may also mark one of the beacon hills of Ireland. Along these crests the bonfires lit on special holy nights could be seen from height to height, orienting the different tribes to their common calendar and linking them across space in a single kinship celebrating their seasonal festivals together.

We know a great deal about the agricultural assemblies honoring the beginning of summer (May 1, Beltane) and the harvest of first fruits (ca. August 1,

Lughnasa) held at similar sacred sites all over Celtic lands from Stone Age times into the twentieth century.[6] Thus we can surmise that such ancient festivals also drew the original clans and later inhabitants from miles around on pilgrimage to Knocknarea and its surroundings. It is a center to steer by, rise to, and revel on. The cairn's position encourages circumambulation and communion with the elements of earth, fire, sea, wind, and stone. Here Maeve is not a warrior goddess; she is the deity of all of nature. She is the link between mountain and sky, setting sun and Earth, the guardian of the waters, the belly of the fertile land, the focus of strong winds. Encompassing the whole natural world, she is the generative and powerful force that supports, heals, and feeds her people in some seasons even as she blights them in others.

Just as the human mother is the holding and transforming environment of early infancy, Maeve at Knocknerea represents the cosmic goddess as the archetypal matrix underlying the ever-changing life process. In another form as divine mare, she symbolizes the energy that carries that process onwards and sustains our bodies, our society, and our work. As the human mother of seven sons, who are sometimes equated with the days of the week,[7] Maeve still represents the matrix underlying the cycles of time in which we live out our existence.

Such cycles are both constant and inconstant, as we have seen. They may be fraught with anxiety unless we can feel the spiritual ground that supports all processes below the temporary surface turbulence. At this deep level our perception of Maeve as the great mother grants perspective and functions as an elementary holding environment for our psyches in both space and time, just as it did for the ancient Irish. By analogy Maeve's image suggests the archetypal matrix lying beneath our personally experienced basic faults, the cosmic net that can catch and comfort us when we fall into life's unthinkable terrors, the endlessly bountiful cornucopia that can fill our sense of deprivation, the ever-present breast that can assuage our inevitable experiences of neglect. Throughout life we can let ourselves relax into this matrix to find again our existential security. Maeve is one representation of the fulsome, ambivalent mother of life and transformation, beyond, below, above, and only partially visible through the personal mother. When our needs are gratified and we feel well met and received, she represents the archetypal principle behind the personal mother that grants our necessary sense of specialness as divine child. When our needs are left to suffer and become greed, she represents the archetypal mother as terrible maw with which we are merged and then feel in identity. In these original bonds to the mother, we live out our deepest primal scenes and shape many of the structures that pattern the perceptions and reactions of all of life.

Maeve as the Principle of Maternity

The sense of Maeve as the impersonal, archetypal principle of maternity persisted from earliest times. As a triune goddess in human form, she bore three sons in a single birth to her divine lover Fergus Mac Roech.[8] In later Celtic culture she became the principle of maternal queenship that created, sustained, and received back her tribespeople and their chiefs. In still later medieval literature a mythic queen with the same name as Maeve's daughter[9] is described as the maternal ideal:

Just as the wise master teaches young children, my lady the queen teaches and instructs every living being. From her flows all the good in the world, she is its source and origin. Nobody can take leave of her and go away disheartened, for she knows what each person wants and the way to please each according to his desires. Nobody observes the way of rectitude or wins honour unless they have learned to do so from my lady, or can suffer such distress that he leaves her still possessed of his grief.[10]

Centuries after patrifocal Roman Christianity claimed dominion, this chivalric queen is represented as the font of wisdom, prosperity, sovereignty, strength, honor, and emotional well-being. She reigns within the ancient Neolithic and Celtic tradition as the embodiment of the goddess of the tribe. Thus through the position of the medieval queens who stood in her place, the earth mother and her mythic patterns continued to be revered alongside the dominants of the newer warrior and knightly religion. Similarly we can see that the goddess lived on in the medieval rites of the Grail castle, in chivalry, among the troubadours and the assemblies of courtly love, and even in the cults of the Christian virgin mother of god and the female saints.[11]

This description of the goddess-queen expresses the ideal of a comforting and teaching mother of her people. She represents the nurturing side of the archetypal maternal source-ground, which we can experience in the many forms of support that we require throughout the various stages of human life. This fully gratifying one also expresses an ideal that lies beyond the capacities of any merely human caretaker. It is an ideal of beneficence separated from the ambivalence of reality. It is also an ideal made more poignant in cultures that have demeaned the role of women. Because the archetype is first incarnated through the personal mother, each child of the patriarchy is born into a double bind. In order to become heroic, the developing ego must repudiate its matrix and manifest its separate destiny, rule over nature, and achieve conscious self-discipline. Such development forces the ego to become alienated. In turn alienation cries out for reunion. This can be a conscious individual search, but it can also be a powerful incentive to addictive illusions and delusional fusions.

Since all individuals prone to addiction lack adequate connection to the maternal archetype as parent, Self, body, and psychological ground, they endlessly and obsessively (often unconsciously) yearn for a symbiotic, harmonious merger with this all-good matrix. Yet they seek for such perfectly attuned support in addictive substances and in other unrealistic and inconstant sources, ones guaranteed to provide the more familiar experiences of dread, discomfort, and deprivation. The ideal thus compensates the equally polarized death mother or "bad breast," a destructive

amalgam of the individual's painful experiences of the misfitting and/or abusive caretaker on whom he or she was once dependent and the persecutory emotions of fear, envy, unbearable greed, shame, and rage resulting from those miserable experiences. This split of the archetypal maternal ground into good and bad is typical of the early, magic-level functioning of those prone to addiction. Fostering development to encompass ambivalence becomes a central issue in treatment, as we shall see.

We invariably perceive relationships to human and even non-human objects as if they expressed or embodied archetypal patterns. Our perceptions may change. Thus we are only partially bound to the biological personal carrier of maternal experience. Our preexisting requirement to relate to an encompassing and supportive source when we feel vulnerable and dependent can be released through any relationship that provides or even intimates the possibility of a steady-enough holding and nurturance. Thus the projected image of the mother (or any other archetype) can be discovered and will meet us in many incarnations. Children whose biological mothers were unable to relate to their clues with constant-enough, attuned, empathic attention and to adequately mediate inconstancy, limitation, and separation often learn early in life to bond with another person, if one is available, or even with a non-human carrier of the parental archetype.[12] For example, one severely deprived, depressed woman who was addicted to panic for its adrenaline-driven excitement and to sex for its sheer physical comfort told me she had bonded to her bed as a small child. Then she could not sleep anywhere else, and the bed had to be taken everywhere the child traveled following her harassed mother's theatrical career. She still spoke of it with poignant emotion. We spoke of the little bed as her "crib mother." This furniture was not a transitional object in the usual sense (between child and personal mother), for it stood in the empty space where she had no other early experience of warm holding. It replaced her experience of the emotionally destructive caretaker who had written of distress and annoyance when her attempts at abortion failed and who seemed barely able to tolerate her daughter's presence thereafter. We could say in Jungian terms that while the bed itself symbolized the securely holding aspects of the archetypal mother, it served concretely for the little child as a transitional object between her body-Self's needs and the otherwise unconstellated aspects of the maternal archetypal pattern.

Other clients have come to recognize that they had "intellect mothers" (when they could realize how their precocious minds had provided a holding environment for their childhood) or "panic mothers," "rage mothers," or "masturbation mothers" (when they saw how the familiar primary affects and behaviors had provided comfort and stimulation). These individuals later also discovered addictive solutions to provide some relief from the sense of frightening void within and the lack of holding experienced from without.

Because archetypal patterns can be filled with different contents or seemingly transferred to other concrete forms that symbolize aspects of them, we can hope to find and even pursue substitutes to carry their powers into our lives. Sometimes a bed, an emotion, a comforting/arousing behavior, a lover, or a drug has provided a partial or illusory stand-in to embody the missing maternal support and stimulation for us. Optimally a therapeutic relationship can better fulfill the same maternal functions and allow us to experience consciously our needs and disappointments in relation to the adequately balanced qualities of the maternal ground. Then the therapy may restimulate the parent/child archetype into consciousness. If the archetypal relationship can be served devotedly and skillfully by the therapist and with courage and commitment by the client, it can provide a safe holding for the dismantling of destructive defenses and for the regressive experiences necessary to restructure the client's personality. In the process the ego's relation to its individual matrix, the Self (the core, completeness, and guiding source of individuality posited by Jung) can transform as well. As Jung put it:

Regression if left undisturbed, does not stop short at the "mother"
but goes back beyond her to the prenatal world of the "Eternal
Feminine," to the immemorial world of archetypal possibilities.[13]

Through the holes in the personal mother complex, we are forced and enabled to fall into the arms of the archetypal maternal form pattern when this archetype can be well-enough incarnated to release its hitherto unmet and latent possibilities. In the conscious human relationship through which the release is stimulated, dis-eased emotional experiences may be relived in all their suffering, relativized in the safe holding environment, rebalanced by hitherto unreleased archetypal energy patterns, and reformed as viable structures in our lives.

As we have seen, however, the focus of the addiction itself may initially serve as a surrogate parent; it is similar to a maternal power in that it picks up, soothes, and sustains the addict for a time.

I always got a fix—in a drink or the nearest man's arms. I had to
fly away to that safety, leave my body and its nerves, never let myself
fall into the pain, that black hole.

To begin recovery, addicts must consciously accept that the moments of bliss in the arms of the addiction mother who seduced but then bound and killed nascent creative individuality are only temporary. The addictive substance or behavior functions so poorly as a maternal source that the one loyal to it will inevitably be lurched between the extremes of hope and despair. But the individual who lives with some degree of bliss alternating with the misery has staked out an early sense of home that often feels isomorphic with the seductive/rejective experiences of early caretaking, thus comfortably familiar and real. As a man in recovery explained:

I lived for the highs; and the crashes just gave me reason to get
another high. . . . They go with the territory. . . . I've known that
[pattern] all my life; that's been my base camp: home sweet home.

In recovery the qualities and existence of the original and addictive sources need to be consciously addressed and slowly discriminated. Initially the infant requires the mother's body and physical/emotional care. Addictive behaviors represent a similar search for such basic gratification in equally concrete/emotional forms. With abstinence, when the individual can finally forego addictive gratification, he or she usually finds that the need for another adequate and embodied substitute becomes paramount. As one woman in recovery said:

I have to have someplace to go, someplace that feels like a home that fits me if I give up bourbon and fast sex and my blissful, horrible binges.

At another time she said with irony and bravado partly veiling her need:

My life has been devoted to battling and cutting up and cooking and even eating dragons. In childhood they were my abusive, alcoholic parents, then all the crazy, rejecting partners and booze. . . . That's not exactly health food . . . . I guess it's my ecological task to clear the space to become me. But I have to find a place to make it worth it [to do the work]. I'm looking for that like a fierce dog hunting . . . but of course, I don't trust anyplace or anyone. Why should I?

This is a common cry among recovering addicts. When the cravings once held by the addiction are loosed, they seek alternative quarry "like a fierce dog hunting." This may simply cause a switch in addictions. Even so the ability to switch is essential to the healing process. While some severely damaged individuals remain dependent on stereotypal and compulsive repetition of their frustration alternating with delusional gratification, others can learn to experience the potency of the maternal archetype in different and less wrenchingly polarized incarnations. When these are both similar enough to and yet somewhat different from the original constellation of the seductive/rejective structures, a gradient of development can form. The images that mark its path (or images of the defense itself) will thus be both feared and needed, both defended against and felt to draw the individual towards the goal of deeper fulfillment. While the recovering client may not see the path, an analyst can read the images symbolically to see the double, Janus-like potentials of each step. As these are transferred into the relationship with an adequately conscious and trained therapist, the pains of the original dysfunctional patternings can be felt and discriminated from new kinds of sustenance and empathic companioning. Thus in therapy along this gradient, the individual in recovery can slowly begin to experience the immense range of the maternal archetype until he or she can, hopefully, meet Maeve in her archetypal fullness to catalyze a basic restructuring of consciousness, a rebirth.

The Gradient of Recovery in Therapy

The description of the queen named after Maeve's daughter suggests the degree of empathic attunement and constancy expected from the therapist to begin to "make it worth it" and to create a "home that fits" the client. Only in such a psychological space can the feeble and fragmented, infantile and orphaned pre-ego of the addict begin to open towards trust in a human relationship without again feeling the shame of believing that its needs have destroyed its source-ground and its sensitivities brought on rejection. Yet this very space rekindles the client's envious rage, which attacks the potentials in the new bonds like the genie in the fairy tale that was released by the fisherman after thousands of years in its bottle. Instead of expressing gratitude, the genie threatens the poor fisherman with death, roaring that if it had been set free during the first thousand years, it would have given a reward, and after the second thousand it would have granted an even larger boon. Now it is so possessed by fury, it can only seek to annihilate its redeemer. In the face of such envy the therapist (or to some extent also the Twelve-step sponsor) must survive, maintain empathic acceptance, and conduct carefully dosed explorations of the client's expectations of delusional gratification and hate-filled rejection. This work, in turn, requires that the therapist attentively monitor and resist acting out the inductions of the habitually expected destructive reactions in the countertransference. Over time the client may gain awareness of the envious genie and begin to struggle courageously to be freed of its looming presence. Temporarily the raging envy may submit to returning into the bottle as it does in the fairy tale. This clears the therapeutic field and allows trust in a safe-enough containing environment to grow. Then the client may begin to let go of the defenses shielding the traumatized inner infant to explore and receive the possibilities still latent in the archetypal mother-child relationship because there "is somewhere to go."

Initially, however, once the primary addictive behavior is sacrificed, the original structural holes and painful emotions that such behavior has hidden begin to be palpable to consciousness. With the returning hope that these can be met and companioned and/or with the equally powerful hope that their pain can still be evaded, there is the potentiality— as well as challenge—that the therapy itself can become the focus of addictive longing.[14] Most addicts in recovery do become addicted to therapy (as they may to Twelve-step meetings). Like methadone for recovering heroin addicts, a replacement "fix" of therapy or a secret part of it becomes a daily necessity and seems to offer the means to evade the frightening affects now threatening to rise into consciousness. The greeting handshake, for example, may become the focus of the client's longing for erotic bliss, which stokes old cravings for merger in delusional ways; or the defensive battler's secret or overt thwarting of the analytic process can be the expression of an addiction to power to ward off fears of engulfment that such craved dependency stirs. Sometimes clients may come to therapy to get repeated shots of enlivenment or reassurance from the therapist (who may not yet even be conscious of the maternal caretaking role induced in her or him). Separation for a weekend or a change in schedule may thus feel as catastrophic as missing a dose of craved substance. These possibilities need to be addressed both directly and gently in therapy, for the individual in recovery has yet no symbolic structures to exchange for the seemingly concrete benefits provided by the primary addiction and may feel profound shame at having its therapeutic replacement discovered.

Nonetheless, the compulsion related to therapy (and group meetings) is a necessary shift along the gradient of similarity and difference. It both perpetuates the addictive process and allows the disease to arise in a similar but (hopefully) significantly more conscious and less damaging form. It gives the client an opportunity to experience vividly the raw, unmediated sensations and affects and the suffering that led to addictive solutions in the first place. But in the therapeutic relationship, the intolerable affects can slowly be metabolized and allowed to develop towards awareness, differentiation, and symbolic expression. Thus the suffering feels first lifted, as if by another drug, and later companioned. As a woman in early therapy put it,

It's awful to cut loose and be an orphan again. I'd rather stay dead and live off my fantasies . . . and I am gone, floating off anyway, a lot of the time, as you keep pointing out. . . . But if I didn't think you were perfect for me some of the time I'd be really gone.

This client admitted that she only came to therapy for "the attention" and didn't "want to work at it." She was passive, indulging in fantasies that were not unlike those she had once woven around her addictive solution. She wanted a "perfect" fix, a "perfect" analyst to take care of her. Nonetheless there was an important shift. She hoped and expected that her therapist should embody the archetypal, bliss-granting mother into whose embracing attention she could safely regress and remain regressed. While the regressive need required the therapist's acceptance and support as long as her process (monitored through her dreams and the images and emotions of the transference and countertransference) demanded, its delusional and infantilizing aspects soon needed confrontation. Thus the client could not just remain passive in her misconstruction of infant behavior. As she began to trust that her needs and behavior were effective communications that the therapist took seriously in the relationship, she began to voice her grief and anger at disappointments without fearing retaliation. She could then begin to accept that "perfection" came "only some of the time." While initially this made her furious, she found that she could begin to differentiate the severity of her pain along a scale of one to ten. She realized she could bear some of the inevitable disappointments without clamoring "at every tiny discomfort because," as she put it, "I am not just the princess who feels every unbearably bruising pea under the twenty-four mattresses."

Slowly we came to see that her initial addictive idealization of the therapist as an all-good source functioned in several ways, often simultaneously. First, it served as a defense against her inner void and deep sense of abandonment and rage. As she said,

If I once lost my hope, my ideal, I would only feel that everything is flat, blank, inarticulate, and there's no life anywhere. I'd feel empty and unseen. I'd also feel furious.

Second, the idealization was also a defensive disguise of her need to experience safe dependency. She had learned in childhood to fear and hate as shameful any expression of vulnerability or need, and she still sought to avoid her own feelings. The idealization thus effectively functioned to "make" the therapist into the perfectly attuned giver of care, who should automatically intuit what the "infant" needed and supply nurturance without the client's having to voice and thereby acknowledge what she had come to feel were her own abjectly "wicked" dependency needs. She could thus avoid her fears that she might disappear into the combined image of child and death mother, a "stupid infant, blubbering into a pool of tears and melting in the water like the wicked witch [in the Wizard of Oz]." Third, she could distance from her own terror of retaliation. She feared that if the therapist were merely human and imperfect, she might be like her mother. Then the client would again have to manage the kind of wildly emotional sensitivities that had precipitated eruptive attacks on her very existence. Fourth, she was afraid she could not influence or control anyone without providing doses of gratification, for she had not been able to control her mother effectively (as she had delusionally felt she could control her addiction). By feeding the therapist's presumed need for idealization, she could assure herself that this would

be a safe person on whom to depend. Fifth, she felt there was less danger of venting her own destructive hatred and rage at an exciting ideal. Instead of protesting when she felt hurt, she could rationalize that the therapist was always in charge, and she could turn her aggression back on herself. Thus she felt her discomforts in the therapy were merely part of a lesson she was supposed to learn, and she was bad because she hadn't learned it. If she only tried harder to acquiesce and work at it, she would be rewarded.

Sixth, if the therapist were perfect, the client could split the archetypal parent/child relationship and remain bonded with her personal mother as well as to the fixed delusion that it was only her own hateful badness that had deprived her personal mother of being a good-enough and powerful parent. This was familiar negatively inflated or masochistic ground that did not disturb old structures, but it seriously threatened the therapy process. Its vicissitudes could seem to be under her own control and a result of her own intrinsic badness. She thus tended to turn the hatred she felt for never having received emotional companioning in childhood and in the therapy (at separations and therapeutic blunders) against herself in a subtle loyalty to old patterns. Seventh, while the idealizing maintained a pattern of magically powerful self-hate early in the therapy, later it also permitted extraordinary expressions of abuse. As the client came to verbally express her envy of the therapist's bounty, she treated the seemingly non-human (because idealized) therapist as abusively as her mother had treated her, venting emotion in the style of the very impersonal eruptive outbursts that had so traumatized her childhood. These had the benefit of enabling her to test the therapeutic bond and to learn that the actual therapist and the therapeutic relationship was not as fragile as she had herself felt before maternal attacks.

Lastly, the idealization carried the projected goodness and power that were still latent in the archetypal mother-Self. While the client's hidden power complex could not bear openly acknowledging these qualities as potentials in herself any more than her mother had tolerated her own individual specialness, dependency, and infantile omnipotence, they represented the return of a capacity, badly damaged in infancy, to find supreme value projected into a human relationship rather than onto her addictive substances. She could begin then to fuse with the valued carrier of the Self-projection in the transference and could open to the possibility that the therapist's regard might mirror back to her positive aspects of her own value. As she perceived the maternal archetype and transcendent Self in the idealized therapist, she could begin to sort through her pathology and to relate to an ambivalent human carrier of the transpersonal source that both gratified and frustrated.

Towards the end of a long therapy, she was able to accept the fact that she was indeed stuck with her own life. She mourned the years lost to pain and addictive solutions and discovered a way to comprehend her destiny that made even those years bearable. She turned to the source-ground or Guiding Self, accepting that it had given her the problems and frustrations of her life as well as the energy to defend against pain when it would have been too much for her fragile psyche to bear. She decided that it had also "been a kind of guardian angel," saving her life many times over even as she had acted out the ravaging compulsions of her addiction. She came to feel profoundly related to this source and chose to take the responsibilty to live what was left of her life as fully as she could.

The Trio of Infant, Defender, and Addiction

Another recovering alcoholic came into therapy ostensibly to further her already successful career. Instead of overtly idealizing the therapist, she controlled the sessions with non-stop accounts of her business problems for which she demanded concrete solutions that she dismissed just as she politely belittled interpretations that pointed to her defenses. She concealed her addictive problems and her emotions. Guarding her inner world fiercely, she resisted the therapeutic relationship with the aggressive and avoidant habits of a lifetime by making therapy seem superficial and inane. Although she later confessed that she had felt relief at the few flickers of acceptance that she could allow herself to receive, she gave only rare indications that she even acknowledged my existence in the room with her. As she began to relax, she complained sweetly that the sessions and the therapist were "usually not very helpful" to her. While she came to the sessions out of what she called duty—"we do have a contract, don't we?"—she was continually preparing to leave. Increasingly she expressed anger at my attempts to connect with her or, as it felt to me, to exist in her presence. It was clear that she was avoiding her underlying despair and shame, instinctively fearful that any hope for a healing experience of a good-enough maternal environment was inevitably doomed. Secretly she expected only to unearth again the original abusive parental/child complex in the transference, and this complex was indeed induced in the countertransference.

For months, the projected expectations had their effect. I felt inductions (through projective identification) of rage at being abused in ways similar to those that the client had been and of hate for the perpetrator of the abuse. These were manifest within me as an impatient desire to have the client leave therapy or to get down to the inner work required to deal with the deep and painful issues she was avoiding. I struggled to metabolize the affects, needing more work on my own familiar terror, shame, hate, and rage. Since I could sometimes make an interpretation that mirrored the client's reality and was not often deflected by the client's needs to resist such intimacy in the grip of fear and spoiling envy, the therapy could at least survive. Finally the images of the single dream that the client reported in the second year of analysis penetrated her defenses as no interpretation had been allowed to do:

I am standing in my crib in a satin nightgown, throwing everything that is in it at an empty chair where my mother might have sat. As it fills up, I sense there is someone there, rocking, maybe looking at me, waiting for me. I want to get out, to climb over the bars.

Initially astonished to see that the dream placed her still in her infant crib, dressed as she thought would be seductive but still raging at neglect, she was relieved to have its images reflect a truth she had fled from as shameful. She opened to begin to acknowledge her deeper reality.

Yes, it is like that, but I've never let myself fall into the pain. I hid it so well I lost it, too. I'd run out of the house, later take a drink, go off and do things. I don't know a different way to survive . . . . I don't ever want to fall back into the black hole where I'll be obliterated. That hole isn't drinking. This hole is under everything. . . . It's a vortex . . . . I've always tried to leave those feelings.

At the core of each individual prone to addiction lies such a felt void around which the personality is poorly and negatively constellated, riddled with terror, shame, despair, and desperate raging need. As this woman explained,

I hate to feel like this. I've always tried to leave this pain. It's a baby—weak, terrifying, disgusting. And I hate that baby. If I don't, I'll have to wonder why I do. How did I come to feel that way?

Around the hole, which contains and expresses the needy and suffering infant part, the addicted client has inevitably created/discovered a pair of surrogate guarding and soothing inner figures. While these enabled psychological and sometimes physical survival in infancy, they remain as impediments to further development. One of this pair is the precocious, seemingly omnipotent, fierce and tricky inner defender. The other is the illusory, short-term maternal substitute projected into the various addictive mind-altering substances, "love objects," and behaviors that we have called the *medb*. With either or both of these, the frightened raging infant part may fuse.

We have seen that these early defensive structures of defender and addiction are both aspects of Maeve. The defender uses the aggressive vocabulary of the patriarchy to protect the threatened values of the besieged matrix. Like the war goddess, these archetypal protections guard what once could not survive in a threatening and competitive world. Sometimes they have even attacked or fragmented the part still requiring a matrix in a desperate attempt to save it from "emotional meltdown" or outer savaging.[15] Sometimes they have hidden it behind their blustering ferocity. Often one aspect of the defender becomes a precocious persona that functions in the world of competitive striving and domination as it did for this woman. For her the defender identified with the ambitious and competent role she held in society. Other clients have come to discover the image of the defender part in therapy as "a fierce adolescent," an "alligator," a "superman" (or woman), an "invincible quarterback," "Mrs. Atlas," or a "clown, always painted." Functioning as one or a variety of "false selves" or "persona-identities," this part has often enabled the individual to function in the world, even to be moderately successful.

The defender both holds and hides the traumatized infant. In identity with the negative parental complex and/or some other powerful authoritative structure, it fears and hates the infant's hypersensitivity, dependency, and ever present cravings for integration with a constant and safe-enough matrix. Rather than tenderly holding that dependent part, it watches it critically. The aggressive contempt evokes old defenses from blank dissociation to the compulsive habits of shame, guilt, and other addictions. Rather than companioning the vulnerability to relate to the situation at hand, the defender part attacks it aggressively, surging contemptuously against the dependency within or against intimate others outside on whom similar dependency and weakness are projected. The angry lashing out and superiority seem temporarily to obliterate the void at the core of the addiction-prone individual's sense of identity; thus the invincibility defense is continually reinforced.

This omnipotent, controlling defender part, which has survived with a style that includes precocity, over-responsibility, and perfectionism as well as carefully managed ruthlessness and many kinds of adaptive trickery, is often overwhelmingly proud of its survivor skills. It sometimes even seems, like a bristling Celt, to nourish itself on pride alone. With fierce arrogance, the "super-person" defender fears and

fights against change or new learning because this might
result in its losing the precious controls that have maintained
it. Thus it spoils or breaks apart relationships that threaten to
stir it from its rigid defenses. Usually, because real change
only comes about through experience of what is hitherto
unknown and hence seemingly unsafe, it assumes that all
change is bad or illusory. From its perspective there can be
only miserable replications of the past doom or worse if its
vigilance relaxes. Habitually contemptuous and belligerent (or
subtly passive aggressive) out of deeply hidden fear to trust,
its bullying usually evokes the very rejection it was created to
withstand, as it nearly did in the countertransference here. It
spurns any empathy offered to melt its barricades as
weakness, even as it continually tests to ensure that any
perceived acceptance is not fraudulent. Its attacks are
ultimately purposeful—in the service of determining if there
is a safe-enough matrix or holding environment to permit a
hitherto unborn and healthy infant part to incarnate into the
therapy.

Needing to feel detached and unsupported to
maintain its existence, the defender defense does however
respond to the therapist's genuine appreciation and respect
and is even secretly grateful for the acknowledgment of its
long service as guardian of the client's very survival. After
repeated testing of the therapist's acceptance, it may subtly
begin to modify its goals. Then this defender part, once a
sadistic caretaker-attacker of the inner "wimp" in identity
with old aggressors, may become an effective guardian of the
newly born true self with an adaptive capacity to set limits
against excessive demands from inner eruptive emotions and
outer others.

The abused infant part without its umbilicus to
the addiction feels the painful vortex of emotions—raw
dependency and helpless rage—that were its initial lot. Its
acute sensitivities, no longer swaddled under the pall of
dissociation and denial, begin to awaken and experience the
all-consuming anguish and cravings we connect with extreme
early childhood distress. When allowed to climb over the bars

of its crib cage or through the defender's grip, long-hidden fears come to consciousness—fears of abandonment, of the seeming omnipotent destructiveness of both its hunger and its hate, of its helpless and shame-filled inadequacy to affect a caretaker, and of its despair. While the stoic defender still jealously watches over this charge, seeking to prevent expression of the primal pains in new relationships by shaming them with contempt, it often attacks the infant, envying and fearing the vortex of its opening need and its emotionality. The infant part easily collapses, experiencing itself again terrorized and punished for abject dependency or for striving to become independent of the omnipotent source. It reverts to its regressive position, still safely and masochistically encompassed by the defender's cruel strength.

The lure of the addictive solution is always present to assuage the agony of such inner mayhem. As a renegade tendency to evade unbearable torment,[16] this defense of the abused infant part of the individual is understandable. Nonetheless the habit of dissociation may also propel the client to evade the painful work of healing. Then the client may switch addictions or find new ways to escape and become passive. The evasions may be as subtle as an abject and meaningless agreement with all therapeutic interpretations, or as overt as splitting the therapeutic work between different caretakers to maintain an illusion of control and circumvent the hard work of becoming more integrated. Such defensive behaviors need appropriately timed and supportive therapeutic confrontation that respects and companions the painfully slow work of learning to be aware and responsible. AA has enshrined anniversaries to celebrate sobriety. It also values working with others who are addicted. Both of these support motivation to wither the addict's renegade tendencies.

Ultimately the infant part of the recovering addict may become a capacity for perceptive attunement with others and the emotional environment. Like a young child, it is especially sensitive because it functions on the magical level of consciousness and attunes to preverbal dynamics. It is also fragile because it has experienced disintegration in fearsome identity with archetypal emotions and bears the fault lines of such turbulence. Sensitive and fragile, it may become a valuable potential for discernment. Then as one client discovered, "The hurt child place in me is like an incredibly calibrated instrument. It picks up everything." Another found the analogy of "lock-picker's fingers that have the skin rubbed so thin they can sense what is hidden." Never losing the scars of its initial misery, this vulnerable part also remains susceptible to stress and injustice throughout life. Its care becomes a function of the rest of the personality that can learn to parent its ever fragile and heightened susceptibilities.

In the initial entanglements of this terrible triad of defender, addiction, and agonized infant, there is little space for a merely human agent to penetrate. Thus while the addicted client needs ultimately to discover the possibility and value of good-enough human parenting, the process is both long and difficult. Fortunately the addiction to therapy is so similar in structure to the original problem that the addictive switch can often slip into the mix, where, if the gods are willing, it may initiate the beginnings of a process of transformation. Then as the tight triadic system begins to shift, the therapist and/or detox staff will not only need to be willing and able to receive the full force of the regressive transference exacerbated by the passionate furies of the defender attacking the new linkages, but also be able to avoid the dangers of false appeasement that might cause only an easy, fraudulent, addictive merger.

At the beginning of sobriety when Twelve-step group and therapy may function as substitutes for the addiction, the treatment will require heroic steadiness and unswerving empathy in the face of the client's hate and demandingness. The therapist will also need the capacity to process a large portion of induced rage and despair in the countertransference. Seven times over, like Maeve with her seven sons of the same name, those in the position of therapist will receive the force of the need for and projection of the archetypal matrix. This is a hard phase for all concerned. The demands on the therapist to survive in the face of desperate ferocity and need are so extreme that a treatment center is often the place of choice for early detoxification. There the various fragments of the personality can aim their projections at different individuals and be held securely within a community matrix or "boot camp," as one recovering adolescent put it. Spread out and yet confined, the parts can be seen more clearly by the primary therapist, whose job it is to begin to help the client integrate and work them through.

After initial detoxicification the recovering client may be able to use one therapist to stand for an adequate-enough maternal holding environment. Then the split between the longed for dependency in a soothing fusion with a regressively seductive ideal and the rageful detachment and precocious independence in reaction to a dismissive, frustrating, and hateful death mother can be worked with as alternations in the relational matrix formed within the transference and countertransference field. Here the exciting polarization that mirrors early experience of the archetypal matrix may develop into a trusted-enough human relationship in which hitherto unborn aspects of the client's psyche can incarnate. Dreams of a healthy new baby alongside a sick one may indicate that the therapeutic bond feels secure and trustworthy-enough to support such renewal. The inevitable frustrations in the work help to maintain the human reality of the therapeutic attachment. They permit grudging, then mournful acceptance of both the therapist's empathy and limits. They also serve to build the new internal structures that foster authentic independence as the recovering addict gains experience and trust in him or herself.

Maeve as the Primordial Mound

When the unborn part begins to be released from its dissociated defenses into consciousness, it may initially be experienced fused with the defender, the abused infant, and the archetypal matrix itself. Dreams may represent it as a repulsive or grimly sick infant. Since the new life is often threatened by attacks from negative parental complexes and the defenses that operated to dissociate consciousness from body sensations, it may be experienced as shameful and repellent. Without the drive to conform to a collective ideal and also lacking the furious greed that is part of the abused, neglected, and now addictive part, it may seem irrelevant or lifeless.

In fear of such renewal, the client may experience the no-longer barren psychic landscape as dangerous or disgusting, breeding forth horrors from which the client wants to flee. Images of the body/Self matrix as something akin to a "gooey blob," a "lump," a "fat sow," a "weak mess," or a "slug" appear to indicate that the earth level, Maeve as the primordial mound, is coming into awareness mixed with the client's defensive aversion. The mound, however, represents the somatic and psychoidal levels of consciousness returned from their dissociative defenses and still in partial merger with the womb-breast of the matrix. This mound symbolizes a quality of being antecedent to performing that lies in the psyche as fields and mountains do in the landscape, and as a neonate lies on its mother's body. The metaphors of basic matter and earth emerge into consciousness to fill in and transform the islands of illusory bliss where the unborn part lived, sustained by defensive ideals of perfection and the addiction.

Often dreams about trees or plants or maternal animals living in or on the soil appear as the client emerges onto the earth and body plane. The structure and pace of this material level and the slow grounded perceptions and actions that arise in it mitigate the frantically driven anxiety and mental effort in the defensive parts of the individual prone to addiction. Such basic vegetative and animal processes of being are central to infant survival. Too often they have not been respected by early caretakers and by the defender part of the client in identification with those caretakers. Thus returning to claim the embodied, earth level is both painful and

profoundly transformative. As one food-addicted client
remarked when she began to accept her body shape stripped
of its ideal of nearly immaterial thinness:

*This state feels weird, scary. I feel like a blob, just fat and just
there. . . . Is it depression?. . . I feel so fat and ugly and [as]
endangered as the mountains that might be torn up into strip mines.*

Through drawing her body forms, she began to see they were
indeed like the landscape. She could begin to identify with a
human body image that resonated with the soft curves and
mounds of the great earth mother. She began slowly to
experience her own body and that of her lover's as
"geographies" and learned to love their undulating forms.

The concern for reclaiming bodily well-being and
care has other aspects. There is some evidence that alcoholics
and perhaps other addicts, especially in early recovery, have a
problem metabolizing sugars. While this may be part of the
genetic background of those prone to addictions, it
nonetheless requires practical attention as well as allegoric
understanding. Addicts in early recovery often need to change
their diets and shift away from refined foods, coffee, and
sugars to whole grains (high in B vitamins), proteins, and
vegetables. Unfortunately, while many of our economically
disadvantaged abusers have neither the means nor the ready
access to such foods to replace the drug nipple, nonetheless,
attention to diet needs to be a major concern in treatment
facilities and follow-up.

Such care of actual nourishment establishes the
client as a caretaker in a role requiring attentive, empathic
regard for the needs of the body-Self. This has profound
effects. Attention to the altered diet for the body has helped
some recovering addicts to stay sober. It also has a profound
effect on the psyche, for it transforms part of the old defender
modality and introduces a new and positive incarnation of the
maternal principle in the individual's consciousness into the
care required to maintain physical health. Taking
responsibility for healthy supplies activates a positive maternal

function, thereby lessening the client's self-image of impoverishment. One cannot be merely worthless and bad if one is caring for health. Such capacity also implies that a necessary fusion with a reliable and empathic caretaking other has taken place and been internalized. This identification permits acceptance of the caretaking function, first as a way to appease and please the therapist or group and finally as an aspect of the client's service to Maeve and the individual Self.

Dietary change is not a panacea, however. Like all the other means of effecting endorphin levels (exercise, music, meditation, etc.) and giving a drug-replacement "high," the health-promoting activity may become addictive. The individual may feel depressed without daily doses, sometimes in vastly increasing amounts, and may become obsessed with the activity, becoming a devotee of the nutritional or exercise pseudo-religion. Nonetheless, these means of self-care can provide an ongoing sense of well-being and a relatively safe means to restore it while the rest of therapy proceeds.

The psychological and spiritual concomitants of this physical care also need work. Often the sugar craving and hypoglycemia of the newly recovering addict are an expression of difficulties in the assimilation of life's sweetness. Usually those prone to addictions cannot discriminate concrete from symbolic sweetness. As the symbolic capacity grows during the course of therapy, the physical cravings for sweets and alcohol, as well as difficulties in metabolizing sweets, will sometimes change and diminish. While these somatic and psychic interconnections need further exploration, I have seen examples of the changes that can occur. One client recovering from drug addiction became obsessed with his diet, carrying sprouts and nuts to stave off what he had diagnosed as hypoglycemia. When he fell into a needy eroticized transference, he found he was easily able to eat a widely various diet, which included his childhood's favorite cookies. With the vicissitudes of the transference, his "hypoglycemia" reappeared and vanished, but he began to be able to gain literal and symbolic sweetness in increasingly various ways. The somatic concomitants of the process disappeared altogether as he became able to reach for and claim deeper personal relationships and entered training for a satisfying career.

Certainly the metaphor of oral assimilation is powerful in the recovery process. "I have to drink and eat you into me," one client in recovery said demandingly after three years of testing her analyst's capacity to abide. After long resistance to any expression of dependency, she put forth her need angrily. It came forth mixed with the defender's omnipotent protective vigilance. It also came forth in starkly oral and concrete terms. At this level of infant-mother dynamics, fusions of inner and outer, infant and mother, self and other are the norm. Here, too, we find expressions of primary fusions of substance with spirit and symbols with concrete actions.

In this shared field much communication is therefore carried on by inductions from one psyche/soma to another. Presymbolic, affect-laden, mimetic discourse engulfs both client and therapist, who must tune in to the client and the mutual field with hovering consciousness, much as a mother attunes to her exquisitely sensitive, cranky, and dependent baby. At a later point this client put her sense of her relationship to her therapist in terms that are a mix of child and adult grammar reflecting her own state:

I am beginning to learn a relationship [sic] to a mother that's good for life. It solves my mystery. . . . Finally I can feel what it's like to have a mother the way my kids feel about me.

After several more years of working together, she expressed her communication more symbolically. She said, "I have needed to drink you into my soul." This poetic description of the archetypal transference is strikingly like the vocabulary of mystics, like Rumi and the Psalmists, who used oral imagery to describe their craving for spiritual attunement.

Community

Recovering addicts may acquire a sense of maternal support and psychological nourishment through the attuned human companionship of their Twelve-step or therapy "group of kindred souls." The group can function as a collective maternal figure.[17] In its embrace basic acceptance and mirroring can permit the discovery of who we are, what we need, and the fact that we can assert our perceptions and needs and still feel valued. With a particular sponsor or therapist and together in the new group, recovering addicts can learn the life skills that permit self-expression, coping with adversity, and new forms of honest (but not abjectly self-victimizing) relationship. Without the development of such capacities, there can be no way to thrive beyond addictive dependency.

The rituals of therapy, and of AA and other Twelve-step programs, thus begin to address the addict's need to establish enduring connections to an initiatory caretaker and the human community as adequate-enough carriers of the maternal aspects of the deity and the Self. Like Maeve's queenly daughter, they embrace the addict within warm, accepting, generous, and empathic human bonds. This enables the recovering addict to transform shame and impotence into shared humanity. AA and the therapy group thus provide for resocialization experiences, for education in constructive ways to meet assertive and dependency needs, for detoxifying guilt by sharing it in mutual confessions and by making amends, for transference to an ideal (the AA group itself or the Higher Power) that can provide a model to repair structural deficits in the ego.[18] They support the transformative "religious conversion" Jung described as necessary for healing by fostering the shared acknowledgment of a Higher Power as the basis of spiritual communion. Over time and within the constantly holding, accepting, maternal community, the addictive cravings for *medb* are then able to be converted into desires for communion with other sufferers and with the antitoxin of a Higher Power. These desires support and nurture the addict's impetus to break the bondage of intoxicating compulsion. They begin to turn the recovering addict toward new sources and styles of self-care. In touch with the Higher Power and empathic human caretakers, those prone to addiction can begin to forego trying to get "the impossible blessing" from parental figures who were unable to give it or their addictive surrogates.

The warm embrace of such groups may also have a negative aspect, however, in that it can enable a kind of stagnation or inertia. Long-term and true believers in such programs often fail to develop their own individuality. Comfortable with the group's lack of individual challenge beyond the need to stay sober and remain in its company of similarly afflicted members who continually reaffirm their solidarity with one another and the disease, they may even find themselves subtly addicted to group norms and processes.

Spoiling

In the positive transferential relationships to therapist and group, there are inevitably inductions from the client's negative complexes, the spoilers, that seek to reconstellate themselves and even deepen the old patterns and wounds. Acutely sensitive to lapses of empathy and separation, though these reactions may not be verbally acknowledged, the addict readily lapses into old patterns to manage stress. Since these patterns include the old fears, dissociations, loyalties to abusive parental complexes, and spoiling attacks from the defender that kept the addict's individual consciousness enfeebled and fragmented, they provide a backdrop against which new learning can take place. In psychoanalytic language these backlashes are called resistances. They are more fully understandable as loyalties to now outdated habit patterns that make the client resistant to new learning. We can imagine the client as a victim of childhood abuse who cannot leave the abuser until trust in an alternative caretaker is built up. Until that time, as we have seen, the defender

complex encompassing all the old power modalities attacks
the new bonds and new learning[19] and requires the
therapist's non-defensive survival and tireless reconstitution
of therapeutic linkages. Even then the old habits need to be
carefully disentangled from the familiar psychic ground, like
rootlets from stony earth, in order to permit safe transplantation. The repeated attacks on the forming therapeutic
relationship have the paradoxical effect of ensuring that the
transplantation process, if it can occur, will be slow and
careful enough to ensure that the new ground is sufficiently
safe and stable for development to proceed.

A particular difficulty for the therapist in
companioning recovering addicts is the need to withstand
the manipulative, psychopathic seductions at which many
addicts are so proficient. Addictive clients will repeatedly test
the "tough love" of the one who companions them with
subtle demands for special attention beyond the limits of the
usual therapeutic frame, with subtle and overt appeasements
and threats that touch the therapist's own most vulnerable
abandonment fears and early needs for fusion. Each situation
needs to be carefully weighed and responded to in its
particular context.[20] Collectively determined rules often feel
only like betrayals of the necessarily individual bond with
the addictive client, part of whom is allergic to the
dominative, impersonal superego masquerading in the guise
of parent and also acutely sensitive to his or her uniqueness
through having felt an outsider. By contrast the therapist's
realistic limits, conveyed with empathy for their effect on the
client, can generally be tolerated. Nonetheless, these
boundaries may first be accepted abjectly and masochistically,
making a new manipulative collusion, and/or they may be
tested in every possible way in order to make conscious any
regressive dependence or omnipotence in both client and
therapist.

If the therapist, and eventually the recovering
client, can become aware enough of these spoiling and
attacking pieces, space can be cleared from their grip for new
learning to begin. Within the safe and supportive-enough

container of therapy and group, the addict and therapist can then watch the interweavings of the underlying life energy as it moves from old patterns of concrete, immediate need-satisfaction and eruptive emotionality into the seemingly more painful gaps and "unknowings." During this process the client must sometimes withstand raw batterings of backlash because there are still too few inner structures (and sometimes only the transference as an other-related one) to channel the needs and energies.

A Transformed Parental Complex

Slowly new psychological forms are created and discovered from the balanced maternal/child archetypal pattern, which emerges in the emotions and images of transferential dynamics and dreams. Such profound forms can help to mediate the acquisition of a transformed parental complex within the psyche that can effectively support a new courage to risk self-care and objective as well as compassionate self-mirroring. All addicts (and many of us in this age of cultural change) have to learn afresh through various therapies the skills to parent the inner undeveloped infant self—not only the orphaned infant of childhood but also the newly emerging and tender parts of each of us that are inevitably unknowing and unprotected before the repeated challenges and onslaughts that appear at every transition throughout life.

A woman sober from addictions to marijuana, sex, and "sugar daddy" relationships realized after much inner work that when such images came up, they signaled the gravity and import of the situation underlying her current stress. "It must be a bigger step than I thought," she said after dreaming of figures from her adolescent drug scene.

I know I was dealing pretty well with the current anxiety [triggered by a career choice that required that she assert her regal authority and self-esteem], but I forgot the old fears it triggered off and that I have to care for them, too. I didn't realize I was beginning to space out and not take the step-by-step work seriously.

In her dream she found herself

baby-sitting for a scared little kid when X and Y come over. I leave the kid alone and go outside to smoke with them. Then I feel paranoid that we'll be caught smoking dope by the parents, who have very strict and high standards.

The dream told her that her primary responsibility as caretaker for the frightened baby is endangered by the lure to old pacifying, addictive patterns. The baby, she says, "has a legitimate need for a pacifier, but I don't need that kind now, even though part of me still wants it." As a child, this woman had to undergo traumatic surgical procedures to correct a congenital malformation. Because she had felt "abandoned" for the most upsetting times in the hospital and also "overindulged by [her] parents" when they were anxious, she had not learned to deal well with frustrations. Stress still frightened her terribly, and she felt pulled to her old, once useful defense of "flowing out into the void" in dissociation. At each major step on her individuation path, the fearful infant and the addictive pull to assuage its pain returned to confront her and to force development. In the dream her fear of the parental authorities represented the unclaimed (and therefore still projected) discipline and high standards that she needed in a more empathic version. Work on the dream enabled her to begin to see that she needed to find her own relation to discipline and her own goals and standards in order to deal with all the aspects of the large change she was contemplating.

In individual and group psychotherapy the transference can create a whole spectrum of mother and child bonds. The long process requires an attitude of acceptant companioning.

"The patience [with which you] companion [me] through all of the shit is a miracle," one recovering man said to his therapist.

Through all the mistakes and falls back into chaos . . . I remember once seeing how a mother teaches her child to drink out of a cup—with patience and through all the refusals and droppings, just steady and there. And it takes a long time . . . . Well, that's what I need: someone to stay there even when I refuse or drop the cup, or [when I] can't help [it] and even want my failures to smash the process. Then the problems can just be temporary mistakes, not the essence of my badness. I need you to be there through it all for when I can try again. "One day at a time," not, "One strike and you're out."

Built upon the emotions and images of transferential dynamics and dreams, like a recrafted boat in the shipyard, the new structures can keep the recovering addict afloat. On the relatively safe planks, new life skills permit the recovering client to maintain the ship, to steer carefully, and to explore.

At various points in the therapeutic transference, dream and meditation images may portray an archetypal image in the guise of the figure of the therapist or connected to the therapy process.[21] Sometimes this numinous image represents a parent-like authority figure; sometimes it is a sibling or a lover; sometimes a plant, a helpful animal, a mythological personage, or a combination of these. At various points the images may be profoundly frightening. The loathsome Medusa or a devouring monster may meet the client in the dream therapist's office. These images can represent the way the therapist appears or behaves to the client. Thus they can help to sort out what powerful positive and negative forces are being enacted in the therapy as well as point to the projection of a transpersonal dimension that carries messages about the client's history, current transference, and countertransferential inductions. Because they are archetypal, they also suggest the client's ultimately positive potentials for relationship to the powers they represent once the ego is stronger and more integrated. At other times the archetypal images present images of energy that are so benign they may be equally discomforting and distant from the client's ego position, hence still unavailable for personal life.

One man, for example, recognized aspects of his analyst in a dream figure that looked like the fecund Venus of Laussel. She was carrying a horn-shaped cup of what the dreamer thought was milk and blood (for him the food of fetus and infant and also of young Masai warriors separated from the tribe during initiation). He was reoriented through the image to the possibility of maternal support for his heroic separation from the burden of caring for his suffocating alcoholic mother, and by projection, also the therapist. He began to claim the transformative aggression of the warrior with the Great Mother's blessing. Another client, habituated to outbursts of rage that she could not contain that made her feel illicit power and shame, found herself sitting on the huge lap of a figure. It reminded her of her analyst, hence it represented here the therapy process. In her own lap she held her young feisty son. She thought of the large figure as Saint Anne, the great earth mother of Christianity, who held Mary, who she said, "had suffered, holding everything in her heart." To her child she associated a loving feistiness she was finding help in therapy to embrace and make its potential her own.[22] Another woman dreamed that there was a wondrously colored bird outside the therapist's office that flew in onto her shoulder. Another dreamed of her therapist as a gardener who repotted, watered, and fertilized plants and removed destructive insects, carrying the seedlings inside and out as the spring weather changed until they were sturdy enough to be planted in the garden.

Such experiences of the archetypal transference are a necessity on the path of deep healing. While they must invite the therapist to address the countertransference and to question whether there is a tendency to identify with the great mother in her destructive or creative forms, or with some passionate and airy animus, they also invite shared appreciation of the numinous symbolic images as manifestations of the divine spirit immanent in life and available for guidance. Thus they appear to provide balance to the personal misconstellations of the archetype suffered through the intensely negative experiences of the death

mother that led to the client's propensity for addiction. They also help to resolve the idealizing transference, often appearing to complement or compensate actual experiences of the therapist as frustratingly less than ideal, or to grant symbolic significance to an event of the previous session(s) in what is never merely a relationship of persons. Their mysterious qualities thus shift the analytic focus to the transcendent dimension on the one hand and to a more realistic view of the human-enough therapist on the other, allowing the client's ego to grow with roots in both personal and transpersonal dimensions in order to become slowly capable of sustaining the ego/Self relationship through what one client called "finally, just ordinary-scale difficulties."

When the spiritual hunger underlying an aspect of idealization is set free, the craving requires experience of such archetypal form patterns. These provide the focus for ever necessary experiences of non-pathological union with the mother-beloved-cosmos, which restores the ego's bond to the matrix of the individual Self. They serve to give meaning to life's lurches and function as conveyors of safe access to a mystical experience of vastness commensurate to and balancing the void hidden at the core of the addiction-prone client's personality. Indeed they enable appreciation of the emptiness, "as part of my fate, and ultimately as the space in which to receive the vastness," as one woman in recovery put it. Such an expansion of boundaries in safe-enough ecstatic bliss allows the adult individual to feel again at one with the universe and him or herself. Sustained by direct experience of this expansive and supportive spirit, the recovering addict can rest, melt in joyful awe, and find the security of home in the larger matrix—"like a drop of rain, falling in the ocean" as a chant to the goddess puts it. This allows a letting go of once habitual fears of shame, loss, guilt, self-hate, rage, and loneliness and of defenses against previously unconscious energies, expanding the individual's creative repertoire. Thus he or she is enabled and empowered to grow, nurtured from transcendent sources.

Learning to Contain and
Restructure Eruptive Exciting Emotion

The addiction-prone client faces the particular problem of
having to learn to contain and restructure eruptive exciting
emotion. Adequate adaptive structures were not learned in
the original caretaking environment, and often the
impulsivity itself has come to feel like home. We have seen
that hot affect can provide a temporary filling for the empty,
hungry core. As any addictive behavior, such enlivening,
archaic impulsivity resists transformation through the
repressive injunctions of a sadistic superego. In the myths of
Maeve, as queen mother of her people, there is another
method of dealing with impulsive aggression and fear.

When the heroes of Ulster come into view before
her gates, Maeve realizes that their fiery energy may be
destructive unless tamed. She warns her people,

*"We will be ground into the earth and gravel the way a mill stone
grinds very hard malt—even with the men of the entire province
gathered round us in our defense—unless his anger and fury are
diminished." Maeve then went to the outer door of the courtyard,
and she took with her three fifties of women and three vats of cold
water with which to cool the ardour of the three heroes who were
advancing before the host.*[23]

The queen of the land confronts the furiously
possessed warrior with what we know from another tale[24] are
her naked breasts and those of her women. These confuse the
single-pointed rush of the invader, for she confronts rampant
and fragmenting rage not with more adversarial aggression
but with its opposite. With eroticism and nurturant empathy,
she evokes desire and dependency needs. These begin to open
a conflict within the berserk warriors and loosen their
identification with automatic adversarial fury. At the right
time, such queenly receptivity can begin the redirecting,
blunting, and ultimately the taming of aggression. (At the
wrong time it can only infantilize or engulf.) By providing the
radical opposition of acceptance, the exposure of the breasts
can bring about the remembrance and even the creation of

sexual and relational needs and begin to turn a person possessed by destructive rage toward considering her or his own behavior, need for an adversary, and even need to find an alternative to automatic combativeness. Ultimately, this conflict may open an interior space in which the warrior can discover an inner inhibition and create self-discipline.

In therapy the perception of such maternal concern (the "good breast") can also evoke, create, and model a vision of self-acceptance and empathy to mitigate automatic defensiveness and rage. With one recovering alcoholic, a man of many bar-room brawls, the analyst learned to move forward when he began to rage and shout. Instead of arousing fear and defensive distancing, which drove him further into abandonment panic, this empathic connection challenged his automatic belligerence, and he was so taken aback that he inevitably paused in confusion. Then a different level of communication could be opened.[25] Eventually this recovering addict turned over his gun permit to the therapist, a profound gesture marking his nascent trust in the possibility of being heard and of receiving justice as well as his commitment to the relational process of therapy and life.

In the myth the queen's three vats of cooling water quell the hero's maddened ardor by encompassing the one possessed by hot rage in containing, cooling vessels, symbols of the mother as a larger whole. When the individual identified defensively with one archetypal affect is thus held and the single obsessing emotion is relativized, the possessed one can begin to relax. We know from the parallel story that the first vessel splits, the second boils over, but in the third, eruptive fury reaches humanly warm containment. Thus it provides the bath of baptism into a new adaptive identity.

These vats are analogous to the large and safe-enough therapeutic vessel and its rituals. They provide the holding environment for the transformation of energy along the gradient mentioned earlier. Old hates and fears transferred into the therapy create an adversarial relationship. Then the rage of the berserk warrior erupts to try to destroy the therapy, and the splitting of the first vessel indicates the still-destructive effects of the possessing omnipotent power. The eruptive emotions result in acting out through abuse to self or others, through slips back into addiction, and through attacks on the therapy, for example by refusing to come to sessions and/or to respect the time and fee contract. If a reconstitution of the container, analogous to the second vat, can be made available, the therapy can continue. The material to create such a new vessel for each client is accumulated in part through the therapist's own analysis, her careful training and ethical practice, and her attitude of conscious service to the transpersonal source and meaning of the client's process.[26] The client's willingness to abide in the therapy and to struggle through the impasses to build new forms of relationship is also crucial. Because this requires some glimmer of trust, it often seems dependent on the Higher Power guiding the client's destiny.

The boiling over of the second vat suggests the intense affects aroused by the client's complexes within the therapeutic relationship. These reactivated emotions blind the individual in recovery and may also threaten to rupture the therapist's empathy and objectivity as they struggle against containment. The boiling emotions stirred by the client's process may activate a wide array of archaic emotions in the therapist from full-blown hate to oversolicitous, defensive care of the client. If these can be held, however uncom-fortably, in the therapist's consciousness and the client's commitment to healing while they are worked through, they will not rupture the vessel and break the therapeutic bond. Instead the overly heated waters rise as the client's abreactions, as the letting off of a life-long held geyser of steam, in the trust they can be endured and empathically met by another. The third vat signals the end of the client's possession by intoxicating, transpersonal affects and the transformation of wildly aggressive reactivity into appropriate, life-affirming assertion. In the third bath a warm and humanly scaled relationship can be born.

The triplicity of the vats also suggests—among many things—the need for multiple modes of therapy when working with recovering addicts, especially those referred to as having a dual diagnosis, the addiction augmented by severe early pathology. In other cases, too, more than one therapeutic vessel is often essential, since the needs of the recovering addict are so pervasive, raw, and eruptive. An in-patient treatment program can initially provide such a variety of containers. In my experience any single vessel cannot adequately contain the active addict in early recovery. It may break down under the stresses of the fresh addictive possession, and it may not be able to address itself deeply enough to the multiple dimensions of the underlying problems. Later, even with three or four weekly sessions, individual analytic therapy alone may not be enough. AA's frequent meetings and the human companionship they provide in daily life are of inestimable comfort and support to addicts, especially in the early stage of recovery. Medical and nutritional consultation is often necessary. Body work is essential. Often art and movement therapy are required to open avenues of self-expression. Group analysis and sometimes marriage counseling provide arenas to work through peer issues, confront authority, and internalize new social skills. Sometimes the Twelve-step group may take the place of group therapy. But even AA with its initiatory steps, its networks, and combination of work with both individual sponsor and group, is usually not sufficient for deep transformation. The Twelve-step group can hold, provide support, motivate, and inculcate self-awareness and discipline, but some of the turbulent depths that fueled the need for addictive substances and behaviors usually require commitment to individual psychotherapeutic work. As William G. Wilson put it in a letter to Jung, members of AA "following their recovery in AA—[have] been much helped by your practitioners."[27] In therapy the recovering addict can explore in depth the structural patterns in his or her individual psyche that predisposed the addictive escapes and discover their meaning and transformation.

Over time and in different contexts these supportive and confrontative therapeutic vessels can contain and mitigate the eruptive emotions of the traumatized addict.

In their embrace those once prone to dangerous addictions may learn the many forms of self-care and the many effective assertive and communication skills that are needed for a sober and creative life.

Another way to think of the three vessels is in relation to the maternal principle itself. The addiction-prone client inevitably reconstitutes his or her first personal relationship in the transference. With a reawakening of hope, extreme dependency, and idealization (even if it is largely illusory), the vessel forms. As the client's extreme neediness and legitimate rage at current frustrations resonate with early suffering, the negative transference blasts through the personal maternal complex—usually many times over. These expressions of rage at the loss of illusory and real gratification help to compensate the client's initial sense of powerlessness. They grant a mirror of effective aggression against an actual person, the therapist. They also, however, carry a deeply feared threat that the relational bond may be ruptured unless the therapist, acting for the healing process and in touch with the transpersonal source of holding containment and meaning, can metabolize the emotions without retaliation and continue to reassert the links of empathic relationship that create another vessel. Then as the client and therapist survive the attacks, fear of destructive rage may be transformed into explorations of linkages, emotionality, and effective assertion.

As the original misconstellation of the maternal complex is outgrown, a second vessel can form. It is analogous to what has been called the therapeutic alliance— a transferential realtionship of enough trust to enable cooperative work. Hopefully this container can abide steadily enough through the turbulent process between a client whose archetypal affects must be channeled and a safe therapeutic environment that must empathically mirror the client's reality, mediate explosive global emotions, and confront endangering pathology. In this second phase the client can gain experiences of having the emotional eruptions and cognitive distortions witnessed, held, sorted, and mediated in

a caring therapeutic relationship. As these experiences are repeated, there is the possibility that the client may learn from the therapist's attitude and introject different aspects of the maternal archetype from the therapy process itself, aspects that transform the inner mothering function to one that is closer to the description of Maeve's daughter.

The final vat is that containing the sober human being, warmed but not threatened by the archetypal emotionality that is an important aspect of the Self. One client expressed her sense of this as

the nest of emotions that is always with me, so I never again have to fear the desolation of abandonment. I spent years denying [affects] because I thought they were only painful. But they are always there, just like my body is. . . . If I don't judge them and try to erase their messages, or leap out of myself as if I am [in identity with] them, then they come through intense and rich and present, and I am full with them, and they are a nest for me.

Consciously experiencing but disidentified from the rich stream of intense emotionality, this woman in recovery learned that affect itself can function as a supportive and omnipresent source of life. It can be felt as an important aspect of the Self's internal mothering function. Acknowledging it thus with devotion, the once possessed and emotionally battered individual can step forth into life just as the Irish initiate did to receive the queen's cloak of honor.

The regal bestower of this embracing cloak is the representative of the archetypal processes through which the transformation takes place. She is also the holder of the vessels, the containing structures, in which it occurs (see chapter 11). In accepting service to this transcendent process, the client may discover that the discomforts and excitements inherent in the intense passions, which are inevitable in those prone to addictions, have forced a quest for the realm in which they can be adequately grounded. The meaning of their intensity may thus lie in their provision of yet another access to the spiritual dimension.

Chapter 8

Maeve as the Principle of Process

The Triple Spiral

One motif in the mythology of Maeve is the triple wheel of
the ancient triune goddess. It emerges in the description of
Queen Maeve as the source of three rivers, each pool so large
it can hold a turning mill. At the end of the medieval Irish
epic *The Cattle Raid of Cooley* (*The Tain*), this description makes
vivid the notion that the oppositional polarizations forcing
Maeve to become the warrior goddess have given way again
to the interconnected, transformative processes of life that
reveal the vast and ancient nature deity.

The image of Maeve's triple wheels in their three
conjoined pools harks back to the earliest phase of Irish
prehistory that has left extraordinary archaeological remains.
We can see the same triple spiral carved deep inside
Newgrange, the largest of Ireland's Stone-Age temples in the
Boyne River Valley. This egg-shaped mound heaped massively
over a long passage with three alcoves off a central chamber is
five hundred years older than the first pyramids. It was
traditionally the home of Maeve's eastern counterpart, the
cosmic white cow and river goddess, Boann.[1]

Placed on the north side of the entrance stone of
the deepest chamber in Newgrange, the carving of triple spirals
represents an essential clue to a mystery celebrated by our

ancestors. The same trispiral form is carved into the monumental stone that guards the passage entrance and on curbstone 52 at the back of the mound. The placements accord with the axis of winter and summer solar sunrise alignments across the huge circle. Most extraordinarily, the spirals at the center are naturally illuminated during the few moments of each winter solstice when the rays of sunrise reach along the floor of the narrow, vaginal corridor into the temple's interior. The golden glow brings their forms to life during the darkest days of the year, an event that must have been the culmination of some ancient incubation and rebirth ritual. Perceiving this awesome sight from within the temple chamber still fills modern participants with a sense of the wonders of nature and the uncanny wisdom of the mound builders.

While we cannot know precisely what mystery the triple spiral represented in its original Neolithic context, modern scholars have noted that its placements and carved patterns convey ancient knowledge of the interactions of cosmic energy and the astronomical mill wheels turning in the sky. Such knowledge is sacred in many civilizations, for it permits the shaman-priests to attune human activities with the same cosmic cycles that governed earthly seasons and celestial transits. Martin Brennan, a modern scholar and explorer of the Boyne River mounds, writes of these carvings:

The spirals are either centripetal, descending in anti-clockwise motion (as water goes down a drain) or centrifugal, ascending in clockwise motion symbolizing the creative force of fire (hence, the sun moves in a clockwise motion—opposite to water). These two can be combined to demonstrate the interplay of the two poles of energy. . . . A triple spiral . . . includes the third force, the play of attraction and repulsion between opposites. The unity of creation and destruction, the beginning and the end of all things is symbolized [by the geometry of Newgrange] . . . .The inner chamber at Newgrange is where the two extremes of the sun's movements converge, the place where opposites meet . . . [It is] symbolic of the centre of the cosmos in this gigantic scheme . . . representing the convergence of the three basic forces in nature.[2]

The image of three spirals, each around a center and interwoven together so the single raised-relief line moves from core to outer line and spirals in to another core, may indeed represent some clear and valid intuition about cosmic energy. Like a primitive face, it confronts us with the solar, planetary, and earthly cycles of time in which we form our consciousness and that were honored by the ancient Celts in their calendar festivals. It also represents the harmonious interpenetration and creative generativity of spirit and matter. Like the relationships of mother, father, and child, it is thus a symbol of the tripartite rhythms underlying psychological, spiritual, social, and physical life and development. Such interconnected processes expressed by the lights in an astrological wheel resonate through the seasons in nature and in our many births through life. Within their coils we move through our cycles from beginning, to full grown, to decline— then again to beginnings; through being held, to holding, to letting go; through receptivity and assertion to full synthesis; through deintegration, to reintegrating coalescence, to balanced relationship, and on to new separation and on again to new coalescence. Without embracing all phases, we cannot abide fruitfully through the changes that dictate the connections and destructions of old forms and the births of ever new ones. Acceptance of such rhythmic flow is thus central to the processual phases that underlie fertility in nature and creativity in humans. Inevitably, the personal discovery and reclamation of this transformational triadic process grounds us in a cosmic reality that also permits reattunement and healing.

Often in the therapy that leads to recovery from the cramping grip of addictions, we come to learn about our own individual relationship to this process. We may find that our own rhythms manifest a triple pattern that repeats at each new stage or venture through our lives. Sometimes we can see that the pattern initially tends to repeat the very processes of our birth whether we were ripped untimely in Caesarian section or came out with difficulty in breech position. The way we were born often remains as the under-girding mode of coalescing and pushing forth towards resolution through all of life's later discomforts and fears.

Similar patterns of passivity, resistance, struggle, reaching towards, acceptance, etc., that characterized our birth and infancy often structure all the births and nascent stages in our life. As we note that we encounter each new challenge in ways that are similar to that primal experience of facing into life, we may come to recognize its basic forms. Thus we may see that we are formed over and over throughout life with our own variations on the motif of the processual spirals. As we struggle to become aware, we may slowly move from blind submission to these patterns to more active cocreation of the events and products of our individual existence, a cocreation that celebrates and aligns with the triple spiral in ways that are not unlike those that may have been manifest in the ritual processes of Neolithic Ireland.

Spiraling Trines

For individuals prone to addiction who have not yet achieved recovery, the three wheels connote a noncreative kind of spiraling trine, one that functions to overpower the fragile and diffuse pre-ego. In its twists, issues and events either do not rise into awareness or else slip out of it without leaving a trace. Emotions seize intensely and are gone. Individual consciousness, flowing passively under the wheels of fate, cannot find more than a momentary perspective. Even though the individual may feel generally victimized and bewildered by the onslaught, the passivity permits evasion and prevents personal responsibility. Indeed the addiction itself forms a buffer to ward off the suffering and grappling with personal issues that are the concomitants of consciousness and growth. As one man put it:

As long as I was actively addicted, I could fend off pain. Like magic . . . I floated from one thing to the next in denial . . . [but that's] a no-win circling, like an airplane that circles and never lands 'till it crashes, out of fuel.

Other forms of the triple spiral are also common in those prone to addiction. They structure relationships to prevent seeing reality as it is and preclude learning to struggle with the sense of commitment to appropriate limitations that force us to develop and deepen. Sometimes the person prone to addiction remains in a bond to two perspectives represented as allegiances to different partners. Vacillating in commitment, the person becomes slippery and unreliable in relation to others and self. Often one bond repeats the loyalty to parental patterns that underlie familiar habits of shame and fear. Reverting to these can spoil the relationship to anything that requires a different attitude. Caught between two positions and unable to work with their oppositions, no action is possible. A dream image showed one food-addicted woman how what she called her "wobbliness" even created a problem in her perception of reality. She dreamed that she was facing a mountain covered by a fog that made the mountain look "terrible, frighteningly steep, impossible to climb." Far away on the peak she glimpsed the building in which she was to begin a new challenging job that in reality she was excited about and flattered to have been chosen to do. In the dream she says,

I stood looking up, feeling fearful . . . finally about to give up. I turn away. It's a familiar place between going and coming. This time when I stand still, I see that, the fog is slowly lifting. I see that the mountain is covered with gentle slopes that will make it a relatively easy climb.

She associated the fog to a memory of being driven home by her mother and to her orphaned mother's general panic whenever either of them had to venture out of the house. Here the pattern of response forged in loyalty to her mother temporarily shifted her view of reality and made her cringe from rather than commit to it. Thus she saw the job as too lofty, placed on an unapproachable pinnacle that could only make her feel despairingly inadequate.

In another form of relationship triad, the individual prone to addiction finds a single partner who incarnates radical alternations. Such a partner may shift between moods that are high or low, attitudes that are loving or cruel, or even physical presence or absence that is neither communicated nor mutually agreed upon. For the addictive person caught in the grip of the other's seemingly mutually exclusive alternations of mood, attitude, and connection and disjunction, the moments of intense intimacy shine through a morass of miserable losses. Hunger for connection reinforces a tendency to deny the pains that also exist within the whole relationship. Usually the person prone to addiction is willing to collude with the felt abuses because they are familiar and thus expected. Instead of standing firmly against them, he or she seeks to claim control of the misery by reverting to habits of self-blame and addictive using and/or by replaying old illusions of total responsibility and single-handed capacity to repair the relationship. This negative and positive grandiosity evades wrestling with the outer other and with inner conflicting pulls.

In another kind of triad the individual may remain in a bond to two actual partners. Usually the ecstatic high of impersonal sexuality and resonating, unexamined incestuous emotions may compel the initial connection and create the sense of having found exciting bliss with the perfect mate. This illusion prevents awareness of the reality of the partner's personality and the probability of being caught in a compelled, possibly manic and, hence, dysfunctional pattern of relationship. When relational problems begin to arise into consciousness, the addictive person can slip into despair, rage, and blame, and then escape into another fantasy of unencumbered bliss with someone "who will ignite and breathe life into me" and/or "*really* be there for me." The rejective shift may be rationalized with the excuse that the old partner is now boring, inhibiting, cruel, or just like a neglectful or suffocatingly stern parental-authority figure. The person identifies impulsively with the mood of the moment and either explodes in an exciting outburst and/or slides away from anticipated dire consequences. Here spontaneity is idealized and pursued in the exciting new partner while the limiting principle is polarized against and remains impersonal, rigid, and too constrictive. The principle of limitation is projected onto the waning partner where it can be both available and rejected. Pulled fluidly between the two projections, the weak ego fluctuates in a repetitive cycle that lacks the directionality of a dialectic and evades the task of creating an individualized consciousness and an individual authenticity and conscience.

Another kind of trispiral can be activated when the addict's consciousness remains fragmented. Its structure consists of an impersonal inner authority with demanding ideals, an inner rebel, and an obedient and desperate wimp. The authority critically judges events and persons, using the collective standards of childhood figures of power that have been accepted without question. This congealed *senex* authority instills fear, inhibits, and rejects everything. Sometimes in a seductive reversal, it sentimentally accepts everything. The eternally youthful inner rebel, bound firmly within the authority's perspective, refuses all discipline and erupts in the moment's mood, and/or it wallows in escapist, idealistic, or paranoid fantasies. Filled with hate of the abusive authority from whom it cannot free itself, it is reduced to ineffectual passive-aggressive behaviors or overt rampages that seek to dispel all authority including the possibility of its own. This rebel can, however, sometimes be passionately active and disciplined in rallying energy to caretake others on whom the projection of a battered victim is hooked. Then it can ground its fantasies and its ideals of freedom to serve the projected victim passionately. The third part of this triad is a needy victim, often an obedient fearful wimp fused with the aggressive authority within or seeking merger with projected outer authority, eagerly rationalizing or identifying with abuse, admitting its shame and flaws even before it is asked. Often however this appeasing victim, in a secretly heroic attempt to control and explain its misery, also takes responsibility all too readily for what was done to it by others. In the fusions and confusions of this triple misalliance, the addictive person's deepest reaction is despairing rage, which it tends to act out both passive aggressively and self-destructively. Having multiple centers, linked to each other but dissociated from a central consciousness of their interrelationships, the individual's sense of core identity feels terrifyingly empty and lacks cohesive effectiveness.

Dealing with these triads in therapy often feels to the therapist like confronting a shapeshifter or multiple personality. The client can exhibit or project one part or another in rapid succession and without awareness of the boundaries and differentiations between them:

You want me not to drink, so I have to drink or I'll be a cop out.

I hate you because you're not [an addict]. . . . I know you want to get rid of me because I'm a mess.

I want to stop [the addictive behavior], but I'll kill anyone who tries to make me . . . and you're no good because you can't help anyway.

Each partial statement carries conviction as the speakers slip from one perspective to another, completely in the spiraling intensity of the moment but managing to cover the field in seemingly chaotic succession.

Flow and Order

Visually we experience the lines carved into the great stones of the ancient Boyne River temples as combining both flow and exactitude. The forms curve, repeat, circle, play against one another to fill the spaces with a complex, mysterious geometry. On the megaliths there are spirals, lozenges, snaky lines, sunbursts, ellipses, diamonds; like the patterns of ancient hieroglyphs, they pull our attention across the surfaces and make us wonder at meanings we are excluded from knowing. We can sense a precision in the flow; there is a scale to the forms. Indeed the linear intervals in the patterns have recently been related to a standard of measurement called the megalithic yard.[3] The placing and spacing of the seemingly fluid array are so precise that the temple mounds and their carvings have been recognized as the manifestation of an ancient "scientific" system that presents a calendar and codifies the temporal order of cosmic cycles, including "latitudes, conjunctions of planets, moonrises and settings, eclipses, and a vast array of other information."[4]

Indeed, this combination of vast flow held in precise repetitive order, which is palpable in Neolithic carvings, appears throughout much early and medieval Irish visual art, such as the La Tene Battersea shield, the Tara brooch, *The Book of Durrow,* and *The Book of Kells*. It also manifests in the arts of music, poetry, and even storytelling. Indeed this style of union seems a goal of Celtic druidic-poetic consciousness. The ancient Gaelic poets (*fili*) melded the fruits of tranced consciousness with very exacting traditional rules of metric form and a "learned language" of metaphor to produce poetry and prose that are emotionally powerful as well as a "balance between delight for the ear and satisfaction for the mind."[5] The heightened collision of wild flow and precisely constructed form in medieval Irish art can, however, be unsettling to a more Romanized perspective. Thus historian Liam de Paol writes that the Celtic style

repels and fascinates because its order, barely controlling an explosive anarchy, allows us to glimpse the chaos at the heart of the universe which our own Romanized culture is at pains to conceal.[6]

Already only a decade since Liam de Paol made this statement, we know that such "chaos at the heart of the universe" has its own order, and we are amazed that the computer images of mathematically chaotic processes are so strikingly reminiscent of ancient Celtic art.[7] In both, coiling spirals repeat in different scales to reveal the beautiful and fertile tension between the flow of endless energy and the repetitive structures that express the regularities inherent within its apparent turbulence.

Maeve's Priestess and the Giant

There is a story about Maeve's chief priestess that suggests that the Celts recognized intuitively that this sense of deep order was an aspect of the goddess. Maeve had a sacred "comb and casket unsurpassed." Both profoundly feminine objects, they were symbols of her beauty and "divine sexuality." The round closed casket is a primary vessel of the great goddess. Such Irish caskets were "invariably made sealed up to suggest the unknowable *grianan* or "creation house" behind the face of the sun."[8] Symbolizing wholeness, the little drum encloses as does the womb and tomb. As does Persephone's phial of beauty ointment, it also connotes the otherworldly perfection of the deity and the perfection humans achieve only in potential and/or in idealization.

Perhaps originally a "plectrum for plucking lyre strings"[9] to celebrate the goddess in song, the comb is a complex symbol. In Greek the word *kteis*, or comb, means vulva. The comb represents a feminine and fertile means of ordering nature's chaos. In sea-faring cultures the comb is often an attribute of mermaids, who use it with a mirror to beautify their long sea-tangled tresses. By stroking with its parallel fingers, the comb allows what would otherwise be knotted and clotted to flow into sensuous and discriminated parallel patterns. Like a mother's hand it soothes and mediates confusion and raw emotionality into coherence. Like the tines of rake and plough, it opens the earth in ordered rows for seed. Like the metrics of poetry and the repetitive lines of Celtic art, it forms raw experience into beauty. In an Elizabethan play coming out of the ancient agricultural tradition, this life-giving potential of the comb is made clear. A sacred head in a holy well sings, "Comb my hair and smooth my head, And every hair a stalk shall be."[10] Like the harvest rake, the comb brings the rewards of bread, grain, and gold. Like the rays of the sun, too, its teeth bring light to earth; thus combs were found as grave gifts in the Bronze-Age tombs of the British Isles.[11] The comb represents a capacity for making thoughts and emotions "ordered, clear and conscious,"[12] but it is a particular means of fertile, feminine discriminating that seeks analogies and parallels, not oppositions. It supports fluid and lateral poetic thinking, not rational logic nor a goal-directed single aim.

In the legend describing the creation of Loch Erne, we learn that Maeve entrusted her sacred objects to the care of Erne, "chieftainess of the girls of Cruachan," her priestess.[13] Unfortunately "on a radiant evening in harvest," Erne and her companions were terrified by the "grisly shape and rough brawling voice of the giant Olca Ai," who had come out of his cave to fight another giant. The bull-like harvest god shook his beard and gnashed his teeth at them as he passed. Like children terrified by the loud voices of parental outburst into unthinkable panic, as if the noise were itself a murderous rage aimed at them, they "went mad" and fled, drowning in the waters of the new lough.[14] The comb and casket were also lost under the waters and Lough Erne got its name.

What can this story imply for us? Originally participants in the seasonal battle between the year gods for the hand of the goddess, the giants in this tale remind us of the druid gods who shapeshifted into bulls in an archaic part of *The Tain*. In both tales the giants represent an attitude of grandiosity, a ferocious braggadocio bullying that seeks to overpower and come out on top. Full of himself, Olca Ai is insensitive. Not quite a rapist, his power attitude is nonetheless cut off from its connection and service to the whole cycle of life. Rather than supporting the youthful Erne and her companions, he acts bullishly. He shakes his beard and gnashes his teeth threateningly towards them. His aggression runs over carelessly even towards the young priestess who might have been the virile harvest god's bride in a future sacred marriage. And in mad response to the raw and misplaced power, Erne and her friends are deprived of their sense of the old goddess' pagan power. No longer able to balance and contain, or battle against, a berserk warrior as Maeve did, Erne is reduced to a pallid and chaste maiden by the medieval storyteller. She flees towards *Ess Ruiad* (*ess* meaning boat, waterfall, and death; *ruad* meaning the dark red of blood). Before the god's phallic threat, her menstrual and brideshead blood lose their ancient potency and carry her off to death. Part of a pan-European process, the bullish masculine power becomes dominative and here, as in so many Irish tales, the representatives of the older, natural order suicide—into madness and the unconscious. They flee and drown under the waters of the lake. This represents for us a reversal of values and a loss of consciousness of the sacred order and the primacy of the goddess in the cyclic process of the year's agricultural seasons. With Erne is lost the mysterious vessel of our original containment and the comb that was the treasured means to discriminate what lay within the flowing and tangled intimacies that make up life's pattern of wholeness. Hence the comb becomes increasingly associated with a flight from "real" heroic life, with negativized primary process mentation and with women's siren wiles. When we want access to the goddess and her vessel, when we seek her comb's methods of ecstatic reverie and its poetic and intuitive lateral ordering of experience, we must go after Erne towards the unconscious.

The Opposition of Flow and Order in Addiction

Those devoted to addictive processes crave access to the mother's containment and ecstasies. But like Erne they have been scared out of life. Fleeing into unconsciousness, they have lost their bearings. Without conscious access to containment or any mediating comb, they are overly susceptible to the eruptive inspirations of the giant. They are thus readily open to cognitive distortions because affect can flood consciousness, which in turn defensively succumbs to a too rigid superego control. Conversely, overly strict controls create static polarizations, emotional repression, and the defensive longing for experiences of uncontained euphoria. The inflexible controls also enhance the potential for repressed emotions to erupt and flood consciousness. The result of the opposition widens into an adversarial relation between flow and order. It becomes an unreconcilable split between rampant impulsivity and power-driven control.

Addicted individuals seek the freedom of emotional bliss, primary process, and/or magical thinking through their addictions. But they are equally dominated by the need to use rigid, collective, and bullish patterns to hold their frightening freefall at bay. Until they meet the drug culture itself, they usually lack experience of flexible-enough traditional forms to mediate their experience of free fall. And they lack the ego consciousness and relationship to inner personal authority to wrestle chaotic flow into form and bridge these polarities in a more individual way. In this free flow, void of any individually asserted structure, there can be few felt priorities.

Further, when flowing emotional and mental processes have an adversarial relationship to inflexible form as is often the case in addiction, individuals may find themselves awash in the watery streams of primary consciousness that underlie and carry all cognition. In the vivid intensities Freud associated with childhood mentation, they may be swept along in the mood or daydream of the moment. Needing then to seek balm for their heightened sensitivities, active addicts may find themselves dissociated, caught under the spell of the formless flow of awareness and "spaced-out." Without mindfulness of present reality, they may drift passively with impulse or fantasy. In areas of life that stir anxiety and lead to addictive behavior, they may thus remain unaware of large portions of reality.

In attempting to establish control over the currents that move them, individuals caught in addictive behaviors tend to use modes of conceptualizing and evaluating that are like those of the giant. They tend towards simple oppositional bullying. They divide experience into simplistic all-or-nothing, either/or distinctions that are typical of magic-level thinking and feeling. When Maeve's casket and comb are lost and there have been insufficient maternal containment and stroking to teach us to feel our secure yet permeable boundaries, we are often beset with existential fears and shame that we are not worthy to receive such affirmation. We may then struggle to coalesce ourselves in the grip of the giant's rigid polarizations. There we can feel ourselves safe and valued only in opposition to another who is fearful and dangerous. The stranger anxiety of infancy and the tribalism of adolescence become intensified. Normal repression (of personality elements that are unacceptable to the social group we need to belong to) tends to become desperate and chaotic and linked to the underlying terror and shame. While we may try to attribute painful shadow aspects of ourselves to others and feel the good of the other in ourselves, we feel unsure of deeper self-value and easily reverse the process to fill our own identity with badness.

It is nonetheless with such simple division of experience that rational cognition comes into being. We recognize it in childhood and our own less developed rational functions. The simple categories support action. When consciousness remains on this level, however, it remains primitive, preambivalent, action-oriented, and tied to categories that prevent seeing all the shadings that are required for mature reflection. Such oppositional consciousness often lacks awareness of an underlying constant matrix that must contain paradox. In its grip the individual can perceive only fragments of experience or the emotions and fantasies of the moment. Gnashing and flailing like Olca Ai, such consciousness seizes on rigid categories and judgments, which are often remnants of the bullish controls valued by early socializing authorities or based on obscure personalistic dominants.[15] These form the basis of globalizations from particular instances to make only a brittle, exact, pseudo-order of fragments of experience, an order that has, nonetheless, a quality as compelling as the giant. Here a part may swell to stand for the whole or, conversely, specific present experience may seem to be endless and total. Gigantism reigns.

Often under the onslaught of such primitive persecutory affect, we find we have fled like Erne and her companions. We find our capacity for accurate perception has dashed madly into the lake, gone unconscious, and we have lost any sense of containment or mediating discrimination of the terrorizing onslaught. Instead we suffer extreme inhibition or even total loss of awareness. This is called dissociative denial. All of the attempts to control the wild and fearful currents that threaten to overwhelm us may confabulate cognitive processes and lead to severe limitations in the ability to attend consciously to reality.[16]

While such magic-level mentation is typical of active addicts and those in early recovery, none of us is immune to experiencing its effects. When we are caught in the depths of complexed functioning and/or are seized by gripping emotionality (as in falling in love, fear, rage, shame, need, or grief), any one of us may temporarily struggle to control our felt engulfment in unconsciousness with the most primal, magic-level means we have experienced.[17]

In traumatic areas of thinking and feeling, most individuals recovering from addiction function at this magic, concretistic level of consciousness with Erne and the giant. Lacking personal access to Maeve's casket and comb to structure and give wider meaning to their perceptions, they cannot meld tranced flow and form to produce art as the Celtic masters did. Instead the flow is a chaotic, often wildly idealizing fantasy. It produces illusions of supernatural bliss and ideals and images that avoid painful reality. These are often separated from the parallel need for limitation and order, which is associated with the all too familiar discomforts and responsibilities of daily life from which the addiction provides relief.

This is how one male addict with newly acquired and still unconscious ambivalence put his dawning awareness of the rigid polarization in his consciousness:

I stayed in the land of the archetypes where I got my drink and dregs
direct from the joyboy angels. It was perfect love.
I floated. . . . From there earth stinks with pain and abuse and fear.
I didn't know, or want to, about ordinary, whatever that is. It was
too dull and frighteningly empty even to contemplate.

This newly recovering alcohol and cocaine addict had no
conscious or effective awareness of the positive values that
are immanent within inconstant daily life; thus his
consciousness split away from a feared reality into fantasies
fueled by an escapist pseudo-spirituality. Like all addicts in
early recovery, he perceived either angelic bliss and/or
surcease from pain in the fantasy land of his "archetypes" and
only "stinking earth" in the fearful realm of daily life. He
could not hold bliss and pain together in his mind and
emotions. His perceptions were "either/or," separately fused
with either a "perfect" illusion or "the horror." In his
statement we can hear an unconscious capacity for
ambivalence beginning to form. "Dregs" have slipped into his
once enthralling drugs. A still unconscious part of him has
begun to see the problematic side of his "joyboy angels," but
he still knows nothing about the potential comforts and
balances in ordinary human life with its stabilizing limitations.

Images in a later dream helped him to begin to
work towards understanding the structure and formation of
his cognitive split:

I am kissing a truly beautiful woman in an airplane. She holds me
on her lap, kissing me. Then we come down on a field on the farm
[like the one where he was once attacked and raped]. I'm standing
beside her, but now she is hideous.

The truly beautiful ideal he associated to a fashion model.
That figure holds him in its positive collectivized values as if
he were a passive child. He has his containing lap, analogous
to Maeve's casket, but it exists only in the sky. When he
comes to Earth in a place where he is forced to recall the
traumatic abuse from which he had previously been able to
dissociate, the flying ideal turns abruptly into its opposite.
Indeed he felt himself hideous and worthy of abuse when he
could not escape into to his illusions. Later in therapy he was

able to see that the ideals he had kept safely abstract in the sky were fantasies to avoid reality, and he suffered deep mourning and "grief, that there was nothing real . . . . I've wasted years on illusions." He also felt the depression and "boredom of having to work soberly" to bring his dreams into reality. Only after several years of therapy was he able to recognize "the blissful creativity I adored in the clouds can perhaps live on Earth, so something can grow from real soil in daily life, in actual, daily writing."

Earlier in recovery when opposites are split rigidly to keep them under illusory control, each part stands for the whole, and each fragment has an all-or-nothing emotional power. This potency of parts keeps consciousness fragmented. There is no comb to permit the witness to move flexibly through the imaginal realm, feeling empathic identification with the vividly perceived parts to create or discover a bridging overview pattern. Instead, each piece of experience feels timelessly and globally consuming. As one alcohol and later cigarette- and food-addicted woman expressed this:

There are only literal, concrete, immediate moments, like beads with no string, parts with no background—each one, floating but ready to burst into exhilarating, dangerous intensity.

Her consciousness of psychic and bodily identity was "fragmentation prone."[18] Having never experienced an encompassing maternal lap to envessel all of her perceiving and feeling self, this client had never felt appropriately, constantly enough, and empathically responded to as a whole being. She did not therefore know how to encompass her own pieces of experience empathically, constantly, and appropriately within a larger whole. When they stirred fear and shame to stress her, she retreated to the intensity of fragments for reassurance.[19] Then she divided her world cognitively with simplistic either/or and good/bad polarizations to try to manage the intense emotions that flooded her. Like the previous client, who was also unable to contain the tension of these opposites in consciousness, she was forced to control her anxiety by splitting the opposites of any dyad and admitting only one side at a time. Thus in working with her, I tended to feel my own consciousness polarized, carrying the projectively introduced parts of the whole field that the client had ejected at that moment. Sometimes the mother/child dyad was split and tossed back and forth between us—sometimes, the desirous/inhibitory dyad—sometimes the good/bad dyad. Unless I was able to metabolize the splitting tendency and pointed out the various aspects of the whole field, the client reverted to the habitual, defensive, and bullish battling that gave her a feeling of power. This acting out of her power addiction spoiled the therapeutic relationship for her even as it gave her relief from therapy's demands for reflective consciousness.

Learning to shift her perceptual capacity from the moment's particulars to receive an impression of the ebb and flow of an underlying process in which the particulars were embedded was extremely difficult for this client. Every knot was enormous, and she had no idea of the process of combing or containment. Thus like most addicts she could not experience "consciousness embedded within a continuum"[20] but only her terror of each knot as it seemed to grow to a global size that threatened her with engulfment. In this persecutory chaos she felt awash and psychotic unless she grasped for what she came to call "posts to grip . . . ideas of thoughts or intense emotions to make sense of things . . . [otherwise I] have to go blank and let it all wash over me and maybe drown."

Between psychotic flooding and its "trance-out" state in which she had little sense of time and no priorities, she "caretook anyone who was there [except herself], ate any starch, drank any drink . . . ." On the other hand she was beset by "crazy details and judgments" that functioned as momentary anchors of her consciousness. Compulsive about chores, constantly in a hurry, and raging at trivial mistakes, she often felt frantic when she was not "spaced out." With little constant sense of emotional embodied experience to support her objective perceptions of world, or her identity as a whole, she had no sense that the self "does not exist as a discrete entity, but is in fact a process."[21] Between flood and irrelevant fragment, she felt an ever present undercurrent of danger and instability that she tried to control magically and through the self-medication of her addictions.

For her, as for many other borderline addicts, the grip of intense polarized impulses and emotions functioned as a magic, manic, holding maternal or Self experience. In the absence of an adequate personally experienced maternal environment, she was like Erne, susceptible to the giant's bullying. The power of the archetypal affects provided the comfort of encompassment as it possessed her. It created the stimulation that made each succeeding emotion into vivid drama. Each shouted intensity came with the delusion that it could last forever and that its grip might magically fill her inner void and/or encompass her severely enfeebled and fragmented self. The momentarily overwhelming traumatic emotions created a familiar seemingly strong bulwark against what another client called the "deathly abyss of nothingness"—an archetypal chasm, which she identified with "boring and ordinary life, what I've always most feared." Even though the emotions were themselves excruciating, she, too, was bonded to the exciting intensity of traumata that organized her cognitive life.

I know I think fear and rejection are more important than relationship or renewal. . . . Terror is the strongest thing I know— far stronger than anything—[stronger than] you or any slow thing like therapy . . . . It's my horrible haven.

At another point she said:

The sword is stronger than water. Power is my god. Nothing soft and yin. Nothing gentle has power comparable to destruction. . . . I would rather feel I am worthless or only negative because that is at least strongly horrible.

With the negative numinosity of destruction she sought to balance the blank despair that she suffered in her "endless moments" of near psychotic flooding. Although this woman had ended her multiple substance dependency, she was still in compulsive bondage to the strongest emotions she could find. They replicated her experience of bullying abusive parents with whom she now identified as she extolled aggression and split off her habitual terror of annihilation with its sense of victimization and shame. During this phase in therapy, her negative transference sustained the image of herself as strong as she tried repeatedly to destroy her analysis by acting out her impulses both outside and inside the sessions. Finally she disidentified enough from the rage to be able to let it out verbally. The therapy thus provided an arena for her to practice and eventually to modify the raw archetypal aggression of the grandiose self—as a berserk devotee of the war goddess. In the safe-enough analytic container she could also attain some sense of constancy as the analyst, the process, and she herself survived onslaughts similar to the ones that had traumatized her infancy and left her feeling dismembered. While the analyst accepted the outpourings of raw hate and aggression, the analysand began to feel some trust in the comparable power and integrity of forces that sustained life. In the language of mythology, the "naked breasts" proved their bounty and strength to be equal to that of the destructive berserker just as *yin* balances *yang*.[22]

A recovering multiply addicted client initially had a frightened reaction to the onrush of flowing libido as he felt his old rigid controls threatened. He found himself identified with the giant as well as terrified of its power. His experience underscores the therapist's need for careful and slow therapeutic dosage in the analysis of defenses, but it also may suggest the inevitability of this phase in some clients' therapy. As the therapy progressed, he dreamt of wild animals and of losing control and "pissing all over the floor like a river." Analogous to the ways he felt himself to be threatened, the therapeutic field between analyst and analysand was also repeatedly disrupted by abrupt aggressive attacks from his parental and power complexes or by the threat of his consciousness being submerged in the chaotic flood. These episodes nearly succeeded in undermining the therapy and twice sent him on dangerous suicidal binges. In a typical, defensive thought reversal, he feared the therapy was the cause of his upheavals, and he was sorely tempted to stop therapy to reduce his pain.

Over time he began to feel the analyst maintained the bond with him in all of his "wild states," and he began to accept more consciously his own connection to growing feelings of aggression and desire. He sometimes could see and release the rigid controls with which he had previously managed his life. As he then said:

I used to be safe living under my [inner] sergeant's discipline. . . . I always managed everything precisely with will and discipline—my sergeant. It was a weird comfort. Nothing could get too out of hand; though I secretly longed for the endless binge or endless years of a long vacation so I could paint. I even knew I could never do anything creative unless I had that "forever time." But it was dangerous, and the sergeant kept me safe. And sorry. . . . I see now he turns all I do into duty or makes me sneak around to get an alternative. That sneaking is still part of the illicit pleasure of drink or even of painting.

At another point he said:

The sergeant's way kills joy and creativity, but it's all or nothing with me. The sergeant still says there is no other way to be safe or to accomplish anything . . . . And I can't put the necessary chaos into that order, can I? . . . Sometimes I can feel that the force of the river is getting stronger than the little dish I have been dutifully using to scoop up each tiny, safe cupful of the water . . . . I don't feel too safe now. But I do like feeling fierce.

To balance and shape his fierceness he was relying on the therapeutic bond, which had withstood so many of his eruptions that he had begun to feel convinced that there was a potential for some form of ordering more flexible and attuned to life's tangles than his sergeant.

Only with such increasing trust in the reality of the strong reliable powers of casket and comb can the addicted pre-ego begin to sacrifice its flight into blankness or fantasy, its obsessions with magical fragments and drama, its feeling helpless in the volcano, and/or managing with superego-driven omnipotence to cope and perform, work harder, think through, force and structure and plan everything from a control center totally separate from events—all to avoid the volcano. With the therapeutic retrieval of Maeve's sacred objects and the processes they represent, the recovering borderline addict may begin to trust the life flow enough to participate in inner and outer, meaningful and sustaining process. He or she can learn for brief moments to "let go and let god," and even to let go and actively receive an analytic interpretation or discover a reflective attitude.

Constancy

After six years of therapy and abstinence that was repeatedly broken, one client began to feel trust in the bond with his therapist as one who could survive the repeated "attacks on linking."[23] At that point he said:

I can see and hold [my consciousness of myself] through events. Because I finally can see you are continuous. By that I mean you don't change much in spite of everything. I couldn't see that for a long time, you know. . . . And now sometimes I begin to feel continuous too . . . that life is strangely ongoing. . . . "Now" is part of a stream, so I don't so much have to be attached to the moment's particulars because I can feel the ebb and flow that is behind them.

Musing further in the process of his therapy during which he had assimilated some of the analyst's capacity for constancy and containment, he said:

I used to fear I'd go mad with intoxicating intensity. It's too much, I guess. I often thought I would burst, but I loved the intensity; I still do. It overrides everything and makes life lose its depressive dullness. But passion has broken me up into pieces . . . . You know, talking about this every session makes me feel it can be held . . . . Maybe I can even grow [to know myself as] continuous, not grip only on the savagery.

Looking back over the course of the process in which a client moves from swinging between inconstant opposites, we can see a slow progression. Initially each side of the polarity operates to attack or suppress the other, momentarily grabbing the allegiance of the addict's consciousness. Later they begin to exist as an either/or bifurcation, which the client can observe, even as she or he feels exhausted by the battle. Remembering that there is a polarity, the client can begin to mark out the images that define each side while standing somewhat separated from both.

At this point in his therapy a client in recovery had two dreams in the same night. In the first the mother superior of his high school was on her way to his house while he was in bed masturbating and looking at a photo of the singer Madonna. In the second he was driving in the rain and found that the windshield wipers were broken so he could not see the road. He could appreciate the humor of the first dream but was initially anxious about being discovered by the nun, feeling that she represented the superior virtues of perfectionism and "clean asceticism" that would shame him. The second dream helped him to realize that the space between and defined by the alternating and equal opposites needed to be clear for him to begin to find his orientation on the road of life. With help from the second dream he could then better evaluate Madonna as representing the positive exhibitionistic expression of his new creative career and the value of the flow of musings that fueled his erotic turn-on. His body Self was aroused by the image even as his habitual rationality valued the figure of discipline, a woman who he said had made him work hard enough to get into college. He was shown that he had a strong allegiance to both figures. Now without fear or shame about either side that might split them, he could begin to hold both sides simultaneously as a means of reaching a new consciousness. Just as the figure of Maeve represents both ecstasy and discipline, his dream pointed towards their coexistence in him. Thus with the dream images pointing the way, he began to repair his blindness by holding the opposites in a creative way: not as either/or but as both/and. He wrote a series of dialogues in which the nun and the rock star discussed their perspectives, ending up in a mutual collaboration for the benefit of his new career opportunity and his empowered and conscious life.

Time

We find in the myths of Maeve herself another image that we may relate to the forms of magical consciousness. Maeve renamed her seven sons with the same name. A late tale tells us this was to ensure her power to destroy an enemy. But when she sent them out together to battle, they were all killed by the hero Cuchullain. This curious image suggests that Maeve was the mother of the days of the week, the mother of a sense of time. But it is a sense that is both without adequate differentiation and also, in the myth, vulnerable to sudden violent endings.

Just so, those prone to addiction, among them workaholics as well as substance abusers, often lose their sense of rational, chronological time and fall passively into magic timelessness from which they are abruptly lurched again into frantic heroic scrambling. When they are passive, they are overly susceptible to the flow of moods. When they scramble in identification with heroic omnipotence, all sense of interior process is killed. In identity with the flow, the individual prone to addiction has a capacity for entering the stream of duration and losing all sense of life's earthly structures. Here submerged in flow, limitless non-egoic consciousness drifts in fantasy or stupor. Now seems to last forever. Hours and days can pass as if in slow motion, yet they are gone before their passage can be perceived, differentiated, and anchored to a sense of personhood. When the moment is full of helplessness, despair, or ineffective rage, we associate the duration that stretches from it with depression. In its dreariness there can be no change. Thus the individual may go on unconsciously expecting and projecting into the present experiences suffered in early life and compulsively repeating the early defenses against the feelings they evoked. On the other hand in identity with a childhood authority that seemed to require precocious heroism, the one prone to addiction feels he or she must always manage too much too soon. Then caught between passive drifting and percussive instants that have no thread to hold them together on a string of meaning and calm security, the person beset by addictions has a tendency to panic at pressure as if still alone in a universe full of dangers and demands from inside and out. He or she remains subject to frantic anxiety and the same kind of fear-driven and precocious struggle experienced in an infancy that lacked the weaving intersections of mutuality or companionship to mitigate its stresses.

In therapy and the Twelve-step programs, the recovering addict learns to appreciate the present—this moment's sobriety and this moment's reality. Rather than ideal success or failure forever, this focus grounds the omnipotence and illusions of total control that compensate despair and powerlessness. Here and now, simple, step-by-step experiences and actions keep consciousness focused. One client said: "Everything has to be like a Zen meditation—breathing each breath, just the one inhaling that is now and then the one exhaling." At first "excruciatingly dull and simple-minded," this focus, nonetheless, requires enormous discipline. Over time it makes possible the slow development that any process or project requires if it is to grow on earth.

After lengthy therapy one man reported his new insight:

Time feels fluid, so I don't need a rigid order to manage it. Life flows like a river and I have a boat. There's even a new constancy with my job and my writing. I can stay with the process every day just like I can hold you and other people and myself in my thoughts now. Images are steady. This must be what it's like to be normal.

With training and the learned security not to get lost or go mad, the addictive propensity for flowing with the stream of time can thus lead to aesthetic and spiritual experiences and a sense of the underlying processes of archetypal energy. Similarly, with security and training the learned fruits of precocious heroic grandiosity can be transmuted into competent mastery. The flow and forming can play together creatively to support the blending of these opposites that were previously split apart. Such creative play mitigates the sense of panic that one will be swept away by the unmediated pressures of time and/or by duration's cosmic "neptunian" flooding. The forms of the arts—music, painting, writing, film making, sculpture, dance—and the crafts and "domestic" arts like cooking all provide structures that many individuals in recovery report are helpful to anchor their fears and to help their beginning sense of flow fill with content and meaning. In the healing process commitment to these activities can hold loosened consciousness focused within the moment, structure and dose emotional intensity, and guide the flow. Then it is neither engulfing nor abruptly cut.

The Gap

Many clients in recovery hesitate as if at a felt gap after they have achieved abstinence but before their emotional energy has yet any new channels in which to flow freely. This may manifest somatically. A woman who finally stopped smoking felt for several months that her lungs were not taking in any air. Another who ended her compulsive sexual acting out felt depressed until she began to exercise two hours a day. Since at first this gap seems merely blank and hopeless, the addict is tempted to flee it and return to the old alternating split between exciting sado-masochistic indulgence and rigid superego control. "I'd like to go back to my polarized, exciting *yin* or *yang*, submit or dominate," one client said.

*Tossing between those makes me feel alive. . . . The drama of the
extremes—good/evil, me/you, love/hate—all that is shifting. Things
seems so strange: dull and "normal." That's a bad word for me. It
has no "high." I've always hated the thought of being nothing but
ordinary. It feels dead like depression—oh, I get it! That's my
[identification with the unmirroring and emotionally] dead mother
again.*

Sometimes before the recovering client reaches
such a capacity for insight and self-expression, he or she may
find a partner to help avoid the work of development by
colluding in the splitting. Even the therapist may be induced
into polarizing against the extreme position held by the client
rather than affirming both sides of the pairs of opposites. The
therapist may collude more dangerously by taking the bait of
the acting-out client and find him or herself drawn in to stand
as a surrogate judging superego against the compulsions of
the addiction and/or as a seemingly omnipotent caretaker
who might provide gratification of needs. The client's
attempts to polarize with the therapist need interpretation
and tolerant acceptance, for when such needs for
codependent relationships are unconscious and gratified,
recovering addicts are robbed of their opportunity to grow.

On the issue of polarization the therapist is tested
frequently. Sometimes she or he is defensively idealized and
lured to hold too much authority and/or caretaking
responsibility in old destructive ways; sometimes the therapist
is enviously dismissed and made to feel as inadequate as the
client in recovery had once been before the power of abusive
and/or withholding partners. Inevitably this stage requires
that the therapist has worked on his or her resonating
complexes in order to embody a skillfully enough blended
mixture of empathy and objectivity.

With repeated experience of surviving the
void and defenses against it, the recovering addict may learn
to endure and even to feel the seeming emptiness as an
opportunity to experience the creative process emerging
from an interior source. The client may then learn to see

the value of inconstancy and recognize the once
frighteningly open void as a space in which new structures
may grow. Emptiness may then be revalued and found to
be part of the long, arduous and invigorating drama of
creativity itself. Like the womb from which Maeve's rivers
flowed, its emptying can express the potential fertility of the
source.

Inevitably the new stage seems frightening.
Accepting the continuous flow of energy and emotion into
consciousness may feel initially more painful than the
numbness guarded by defenses against feeling. One woman
was overwhelmed at the rush of painful sensations she
began to experience when she gave up her addiction to
superwoman coping and the rewarding anesthesia of "a few
stiff drinks every evening." She began to realize that she had
concerned participatory companions in her therapist and
Twelve-step peer group. These listeners did not make her
feel foolish for complaining of her loneliness and suffering.
They did not tell her she was "wallowing in grief" and
"self-indulgent because you don't have it as bad as I did"—
phrases that stopped her self-expression in childhood and
made her feel she could not speak up unless she acted
cheerfully to support her caretaker. Instead the therapist
mirrored her emotional states by expressing her
understanding in metaphoric images that supported their
validity and meaningfulness for creative life. In AA meetings
others affirmed her experiences and told their own stories.
After a few months of pouring forth her stream of misery,
the analysand began to recognize how perceptively and
sensitively she herself responded, not only to others but
also to her own life situations. She began to experience
consciously the range of her emotions. Then she noticed
with amazement that she was always accompanied and even
sustained by the stream of affects and thoughts that flowed
into and through her. As she learned to accept and allow
this flow without identifying with and clutching at what
she came to call "the mood of the moment," she
realized:

*There's a stream of changing emotions and thoughts that can hold
and fill me. I don't have to feel ashamed and deny that stream any
more as I did in my old, dry house [of self-abandonment]. I don't
have to grab onto one bit either, as if it or I were a twig of flotsam in
the flood.*

The rich stream of affects became for her an abiding "self- object" that replaced her addiction. Slowly she began to sort what affects and thoughts belonged to the present and what were hypersensitivities and opinions living on as repetition compulsions from childhood, what she called "the old moldy habits." She came to feel that she had been protected, first by denial and dissociation and later by her addiction, from consciously experiencing the ravaging pains of early abuses when they would have overwhelmed her. She now wanted to sort her perceptions and to learn to trust and deepen them. As she began to wonder what might have "timed things to let [her] avoid [unbearable pain] when she had to survive," she marveled that there might have been some method in what she had thought was only her madness. She saw that even her defenses were part of a process that had companioned and sustained her. Now she saw that she was sturdy enough to open herself to experience this process. Like the source of the waters flowing across the landscape of our inner geography, its font of emotions and thoughts enlivened her. We can see that these are analogous to the waters pouring from the divine source that turns the three mill wheels of existential life.

Working through primary energy and emotion to include them as parts of a viable, individual creative life is a vast and complex psychological task. Sorting, disidentifying from, and channeling the energies creatively depends on the client's discovery and creation of new psychic structures that are appropriate to the time, the task, and the relational context. It requires willingness to struggle towards completeness and integration. It may even require the development of new kinds of consciousness and new structures of art and religion that go beyond those our culture has previously valued.

Maeve as the Rivers

Maeve as eternal queen of the land and divine source of the ever flowing waters provides an image to help in healing the distortions inherent in addictive "magic-level" consciousness. With her image we can move from the reality of intense and split-off moments, which hold consciousness in their immediate and compelling grip, to perceive the deeper reality of continuous process that is not a wild flood because it has organically formed boundaries. As one woman put it with alliteration worthy of a bardic apprentice, we can learn "to move from the fear of drowning that made me frantic, to flowing with the force of the river within its firm banks."

Maeve, the source of three mill-wheeling rivers and the principle of flowing life energy, was also the embodiment of the principles of sovereignty that supported the long flow of chiefs through time. She was, thus, the sovereign goddess of process and its destined unfolding. In her rituals she stood against permanence and fixation even when this meant the painful destruction of old forms. Through her rituals she empowered her people to relate to the whole cycle of life's functions and changes. For the Celts the feminine principles of being and becoming were sovereign; true rulership derived from the sanctity of the overarching life process.

This quality of being or existential presence evolves in its own "implicate order" to support what is meant to be. We see this sanctity of process represented in the image of another Celtic goddess who was the footholder of the Welsh king.[24] Unless the king was at war or "beating the bounds" of his kingdom to secure its safe boundaries, he was required to keep his feet in her lap. In actual fact the job of footholder was an important court office. The king represented the ruling principles particular to each stage. The goddess and queen as footholder represented the matrix of being that undergirds every stage of development as it unfolds to become active and change. The goddess thus grants and supports the principle of ruling authority. Psychologically speaking, our temporary ruling principles, intentions, attitudes, and perceptual frames have to suffer change and submit to relativization to maintain the principle of kingship in adequate relation to the process of life and its changing requirements.

As we have seen, change is an issue that is particularly painful to the enfeebled and fragmented consciousness of the addict. The defender part of the addiction-prone person resists it at almost any price. Indeed, for all of us change is difficult. It forces us to creatively confront repeated loss and chaotic destructuring as well as our fears of these agonies. If we identify with the temporary king's perspective, any shift can feel threatening and painful. The ancient king was actually dethroned. When the time of his reign was over, he was often ritually killed as the sacrifice ensuring new life.[25] When the time for a change comes into our lives, it is not surprising that all of us cling to old patterns, rigidly defending ourselves against the new. It is often easier to feel nostalgic for the familiar *status quo ante* and mourn its loss even when we found it excruciating. We may feel fearful and deny or hide ourselves from the challenges of the unknown that lie ahead. Into this new "unknown" we can project our fears of what is worse than familiar discomforts. Indeed many of the fears, guilts, thoughts, and conclusions we hold are defenses against not knowing. Thus the ability to tolerate not knowing is a sign of psychic strength. It attests to the development of basic trust in the matrix and its meaningful processes. Such trust enables transformation.

If in our therapeutic struggles we can learn to shift our perception to this underlying process of becoming—a metaperspective represented by the goddess and queen in the myths and the constant-enough inter- and intrapersonal relationships in the therapy, we can reinterpret the meanings of change to see each stage in terms of an encompassing pattern. Such perception can hold us and give meaning to the temporary upheavals so we may be able to feel a new kind of constancy. But this perceptual and cognitive leap cannot occur during the experiences of existential and irregular terrors that lurch into the active addict's consciousness, causing it to grab at whatever is near and seemingly strong, just as a drowning person does. Such emotional flooding is often concretized by clients in recovery in memories of actual near-drowning or submersion experiences (in drug trips and blackouts as well as in water or under general anesthesia). Sometimes the submersion was a dissociation of consciousness that enabled survival through the pain of a battering experience of physical and emotional abuse. Thus rape, physical attack, and/or traumatic abandonment are often triggering stimuli for alcoholism and substance abuse (including food abuse). Such experiences should be listened for when a therapist takes the history of any recovering addict.

As we have seen, too much anxiety about survival creates a hypervigilant focus on threatening particulars and the alert readiness for action that must manage and abate them. We know that nothing in us can relax to realize consistent flow when the holding environment has been an impulsively eruptive, overwhelming, and/or an abandoning one, and when we have congealed the flow of our perceptions with the terrifying expectation that these experiences will only repeat again and again. We require peace and constancy in some relatively safe regular environment to be able to perceive and trust the process of life. From Celtic myth we learn that when the king went to war or made the guarding circuit of his realm, he too lost his footing in the goddess' lap. Maeve's story tells us that she herself did not release her flowing rivers until the battles were done and she laid down her passion-driven weapons.

An alternative to fear can slowly grow into consciousness through the long and repeated encounters in Twelve-step meetings and in therapy where the recovering addict can learn to test and trust the human partner(s) and his perceptions of them. As one analysand put it:

The shift is forming in me from my fear-driven way to some [ability to] embrace the moments that make up the present and flow through time. From past on to now and maybe beyond. That's radical, you know . . . . [It's happening] because I know that I have been and am and will be held, the way therapy holds . . . . I begin to get a sense that I will be sufficient unto this moment now, and the next one, even if it takes learning. That [consciousness] lets me relax into something that is larger than me. . . . Nothing was reliable in my experience until now . . . . Worse, it was dangerous and humiliating. Yet I craved a place to trust as much as I craved liquor or sex. Of course, I know now there was no safety in liquor or that frantic masturbation, or even in my workaholism when I was saner and sober. They were all part of my madness . . . . But to give up my false mad safeties, to trust the whole, full, still scary process, feels as hard as coming off drink was. . . . I have an image of that process place as a fiery pink horizon. But I'm still not sure if it's the fires of war or the dawn.

Relatively stable psychological process is often imagined in therapy as calmly flowing waters. Overwhelming and dangerous water represents the unconscious affects and compulsions with which the individual prone to addiction has been flooded. These images remind us of Maeve's several connections to waters. An island pool was sacred to her as the place of her daily bath and renewal. She is the source of three rivers. Maeve thus represents the flowing life process as the waters of the earth.

A potent water image regularly appears in the work with most recovering addicts. It symbolizes a crucial turning point toward a new level of the work. It occurs both as symbolic image and as the motivation of behavior because it is one of the nodal points where the archetype of the deep feminine as process touches the client's psychosomatic whole. As the ego becomes stronger in therapy, the client often has a synchronous experience of rafting or canoeing on a powerful river that introduces the possibility of a numinous supportive force. Or the client is suddenly able to take up swimming, realizing that the terror of drowning, which hitherto prevented learning to swim, has been symbolically worked through, thus permitting an embodied return to the waters. The new trust in the powers of the flowing waters can serve as an orientation toward a sense of process that encompasses the old exciting polarizations. One woman realized that she could keep swimming through the spasms of fear of drowning that had always made her gasp and want to give up. Another recovering addict kept the image of the unsinkable raft navigating the rapids, which he had actually ridden, as a metaphor for his new sense of constant identity and a comfort when he reexperienced stress and wanted to reach for a drink and cigarettes. For him the therapist became like the river guide, and he learned he could call for help when emotional rapids threatened his stability.

Often the flowing water images occur in dreams. As he began to feel a potential for constancy in the positive transference, the man who had rafted dreamt:

The police station is being dismantled. I see what I think is an architect's drawing for the new building for the site. It's a picture of the rivers of the world. Then I am also making a drawing of the rivers myself. As I finish, a woman [like the therapist] comes, and takes me outside where we stand beside a river and look at the strongly flowing current.

The dream reveals that the structures that enforced collective rules of appropriate but repressive behavior in the dreamer's psyche are being dismantled. Therapy had effectively shaken up his sense of rote and deadening duty to a sadistically rigid superego (analogous to the sergeant's discipline described above). The dream gives him first a pictorial overview, then more embodied experience of new channels into which libido can flow. To compensate for what he had once feared as "pissing all over like a river," the dream image provides an artistic feeling control in which raw, emotional energy can flow, channeled into art. With a sense of such artistic form, he will then, the dream suggests, be able to look safely at the real river. Taking her clue from this image, the therapist suggested that the client try to do some painting to express the moods that came over him. He began to pour forth drawings and paintings, accessing the creative source in himself. He discovered that when he painted his emotions, he felt safe from drowning in them. They created their own form on the paper, and he had a way to express and objectify their turbulence. For this man painting became an aesthetic and spiritual discipline, very different from the discipline of his sergeant. He used it to honor, channel, and express the emotional intensities that the superego had found so loathsome and forced him to deny to consciousness—except when he binged on drugs and booze to repress its controls.

Another woman dreamt simply: "I see people learning to swim." The image brought up a flood of her own fears of actual water, her fears of drowning in her addiction to alcohol and anxiety, and her fears of eruptive passions in her emotional life. These passions she alternately indulged and controlled with adherence to the rote propriety she had learned in her family. Her relationships had, thus, been tumultuous and/or shallow. Synchronously, she found a poem by Philip Booth titled "First Lesson," in which a father teaches his small daughter to float. She brought copies for her therapist to distribute. The poem touched and expressed her own newly growing sense of trust in the therapeutic relationship and beyond it in the archetypal transference. It served as a beacon to light her way as she searched for a positive inner parental voice that knew and trusted in waters, one from which her own frightened and repeatedly betrayed child self could gain care and confidence.

Lie back, daughter, let your head
be tipped back in the cup of my hand.
Gently, and I will hold you. Spread
your arms wide, lie out on the stream
and look high at the gulls. A dead-
man's float is face down. You will dive
and swim soon enough where this tidewater
ebbs to the sea. Daughter, believe
me, when you tire on the long thrash
to your island, lie up, and survive.
As you float now, where I held you
and let you go, remember when fear
cramps your heart what I told you:
lie gently and wide to the light-year
stars, lie back, and the sea will hold you.[26]

Another recovering addict found a song calling on the River Mother to "carry me, home to the sea." She sang it

to herself as she worked through a stressful life change that
threatened to pull her back towards old addictive solutions—
no longer dangerous substance abuse but chocolate bingeing
and wildly irrational attacks of anxiety and self-doubt that re-
evoked the exciting and terrifying "highs" so familiar from the
crises of her childhood.

Both the chanted song and poem functioned to
evoke the trustful emotions we feel when sustained by
peacefully flowing waters. Such use of rhythmic sound and
music has been shown to effect the hormones in the body.
Music therapy is thus as old as the human voice. We know
how infants are calmed by the caretaker's voice and how they
learn to burble themselves to sleep. Celtic harpers played "the
sleep strain, the wail strain, the smile strain" as well as the
arousal strain to evoke, hold, and shape emotions.[27] Songs
universally have formed and sustained life. Like mantras,
prayers and psalms, and even the slogans of AA, their sounds
calm and stimulate. They both express and mold
consciousness even as they help to inculcate awareness of a
nourishing source that is worthy of trust. Maeve of the island
pool and the flowing rivers is one image representing this
source.

Rather than seeking to fragment or drown our
consciousness to control pain, addicts and the addicted parts
of ourselves may learn to live with the sustaining currents of
unconscious processes and constant-enough human
relationships. Over time these may come to be experienced as
available enough from the ever flowing archetypal source of
psychological, spiritual, and material life. This experience of
Maeve as the flowing waters is initially mediated through the
ongoing, trusted transference relationship and through the
endless series of dreams in therapy.

While human therapists can only be good enough
and are sometimes felt to be even disappointingly unreliable,
the communications and images evolving through the
sustaining therapy process provide evidence of the imaginal

flow that mediates between archetypal energies and the concrete world.[28] Its metaphors enable shared understandings, and its symbols reveal intimations of the unknowable transcendent realm through shapes, colors, sounds, sensations, and stories that we create/discover. This psychic level of analytic work, about which most of Jung's writings revolve, is constellated when there is finally a capacity in the analysand to move from concretistic to imaginal and symbolic thought.

One recovering addict vividly expressed her recognition of such relational continuity during a session after she had felt misunderstood and returned to try to communicate her feelings:

I can't go back to my old, proud, going-it-alone, as I've always done. I can't leave you even when I'm angry and feel hurt. That's never happened before—to hold a person or my ideas, or anything. . . . All the parts of me are tied to you after all these years [of therapy]. And all my dreams in one long line through them, too, like a rope . . . . My parents were eager to have me leave, and I've always held myself alone and apart as if not needing [them or anyone]. Except for a little dope that got me through . . . . But now I'm off that, and now I can't hold myself alone. I just can't . . . . I've been seduced into liking to communicate because I expect to be understood . . . . Sometimes it still makes me mad that you did that. All right, I wanted it. I did it . . . . So now I have to hold the relationship [to you and therapy] even when I think you are full of shit and stupid . . . . I know now I can hold the truth of what I see, even when you are blind. Because I know I can make you see what I need you to see. And you will admit it, eventually, or I'll see I was off, and we'll bridge between us again. Because we both want to and both care about telling the truth as we see it.

With pride in her own power to see objectively and in her learned trust in the other's willingness to be open to the truth between them, this client could sustain constancy and her own grip on the shared communicative process.

Being able to find adequately life-enhancing substitutes and to deal with the propensity to addiction itself depends on developing a constant sense of personal identity and a capacity for symbolic thinking. It also requires a relatively secure sense of feeling values. Thus another

essential step in the development of process-oriented
consciousness involves a move from a primitive morality of
simplistic ideals of good and bad to a more aesthetic standard
that can contain the balance of many relativized and
situationally determined elements. Such movement involves
the conscious sacrifice of duty to those rigid ideals, which had
seemed to offer safe control, and the metabolization of the
life-long rage (often—as we have seen—redirected against the
self as well as the offending other in the addictive personality)
that resulted from inevitable disappointment. It also requires
a capacity for self-forgiveness, an aspect of the embrace of the
Loathsome Damsel, which we shall see in the next chapter.
As one woman expresssed it:

*I guess I have to forgive myself for not being ideal or having ideal
control, matching the kind of perfection that has no mistakes, no
slips. That feels as hard as anything I've ever had to do. It means a
whole new way to think about, well, all right, a way to think about
others, but much harder, about myself.*

As she opened her feelings to find empathy for herself,
another focus and a new kind of responsibility came into
view. It was manifest in a dream with a stark and surprising
message. "Steer by Aphrodite now!" she was told. And she
was shown the image of a heart, not the bleeding heart of the
saintly figures on her mother's walls but the full heart of a
valentine. In reporting the dream she remembered another
from the beginning of her analysis in which she had given the
therapist her own heart to hold and wash, concerned then
that the washing water would not be too cold. This heart was
still somewhat sentimental, but the image and her
associations opened her consciousness to a need for more
personal feeling values. She mused:

*A valentine says I love you. And Aphrodite, she's the goddess of love
and beauty. . . . I guess my heart, with all its loving and hating, has
been washed and returned to me. . . . Saintly duty had a big should
attached. But this heart is so different, [it means] such a different
way to live.*

The aesthetics of feeling, which affirms both love and hate
and all the shades between the opposites, seeks to find the

forms expressing their interrelationships. Called to this from superego duty was indeed a radical shift and a new way for her to steer her life.

In therapy at this crucial juncture dream figures embodying a combination of primitive opposites often occur. One recovering alcoholic dreamt of "a piebald woman, her skin is dark and light in patches, but she's all right." Like Feirefiez, the mottled, step-brother of Parzival whom the Grail hero must confront and embrace in a final test of his readiness to reclaim the grail maiden and be king, this figure represents the opposites together but not yet fully subjectively assimilated and integrated. Another client, whose dangerous binges had been separated by weeks of total abstinence, found the image of "a beautiful child who looked like an old woman." Through associations the figure proved to be "both an innocent martyr, intent on being good, and an aggressive and passionate grabber, who tries to control life. How can all that be together?" she asked. Dream figures of the hermaphrodite may also occur as an image that points beyond simplistic categorization and toward the ever-flowing paradoxical affects contained in one pattern of wholeness. Such images, like that of the river of life, provide a glimpse of what Jungians call the Self—the encompassing dynamism that is the guide, support, pattern, and goal of the individuation process. We will take up this issue again when we look at the image of sovereignty as the loathsome hag.

Discriminating Positive Values in the Addiction to Find Meaning

The functions performed by the addictive substance are not only negative. Every compulsion also expresses values of the Self, or, as Jung put it poignantly:

this "slime" contains not merely incompatible and rejected remnants of everyday life, or inconvenient and objectionable animal tendencies, but also germs of new life and vital possibilities for the future.[29]

The Celtic hero had merely to avoid the toxin
and choose the life-giving cup that the goddess held, but the
modern addictive individual needs to develop a delicate
feeling discrimination and patience with unfolding
psychological process to sort the poison from the elixir.
Inevitably they come to us mixed and mixed differently in
different life situations. Thus we must learn to appreciate the
need for protection once afforded by our old addictive
defenses (even as we become abstinent) and to validate the
other Self needs once hidden within the toxic abuse patterns
that now require better support. Without such empathic self-
care, the attitudes and behaviors that received support in the
addiction easily create other dependencies. Thus many
recovering alcoholics during abstinence from alcohol and
drugs switch their addictions to food, sex, sugar, caffeine,
gambling, or nicotine. In AA these are tolerated as less
endangering than alcohol, but their containment has
spawned a host of other problems and Twelve-step
programs.

Initially it is not easy to perceive the positive
values held by the addiction. We have said that the addict's
consciousness tends to split opposites and to globalize
fragments. It also fuses and reverses poisonous and life-
enhancing aspects within a too fluid interpenetration. With
such splits, globalizations, fusions, and reversals, the addict
suffers from a radically weakened cognitive capacity to focus
attention in areas that are stressful. The combination of an
ever fluid and reversible consciousness with particularly rigid
and often distorted compartments is typical of the addict. But
we also find such forms in medieval Irish designs. The
writhing coils on the manuscripts from Durrow or Kells
entrance the eye, leading us along tightly interwoven, abstract
patterns. Suddenly a shapeshift confronts us with some
monstrous suggestion of a bit of animal and/or human
anatomy and this in turn is superseded by a sense of the
curiously distorting geometry that carries the suggestion of
organic form back into the linear pattern. Unraveling the
intricate interweavings demands a slow and meditative pace

and a stepping back to gauge the overall shape and colors of the pattern. These in turn may show us that the tight lines sprawl together simply to convey an initial letter that opens the reading of a Celtic gospel text. The close attention, the suspension of disbelief, and the alternations of focus required to unravel a magic Celtic interlacing to find its multiple meanings are similar to the requirements for making accurate assessments of the positive values hidden by and in the addiction.

One woman's reflections on her therapeutic process reveal some of the difficulties. In early recovery she finally named her habitual mode of cognition "Slippery thinking with stones." As she said then:

This new learning about myself and who I am and how to hold against the spoilers, all of that, falls into a lot of bits, and I have to start almost all over, gathering everything up again. Sometimes now all the bits slide around so I can see them, and that's even more confusing. . . . I can see when they are crazy. But sometimes I wish for the old blotto blindness just to get on with life in the old way. Even if it doesn't really work, I long for it because [now] this feels crazy. Before it was the only way there was and I didn't even notice.

In adulthood and against a background of pain and substance dependency, she was experiencing a flux comparable to what an infant may experience during early deintegration-reintegration phases. She was also beginning to discover through her sobriety, which allowed her to abstain from immediate action to alleviate stress, that she had her own satisfying and adult capacity for self-observation and what she called her "detective work." As she put it,

Before, I could never be curious because it was unsafe not to be sure. Now it's almost fun to be a detective, to discover and sort the clues like Colombo [the low-key, seemingly bumbling, television sleuth].

With this new found curiosity she then began to recognize that her drinking had contained the seeds of a capacity for self-respect and self-nurture, even as it still filled her with shame. During this early sorting phase she dreamt:

I am underwater. I follow M. who sets an ugly leech on fire. As it burns, I see it [the leech] turn into a crying baby who is hungry. I have to find a bottle to feed her.

Still submerged in unconsciousness in the dream, she follows M.—a figure with qualities similar to those projected in the transference—who represents tough love to her. The figure of M. respects the dreamer and refuses her demands for fusion in order to help her to stand for her own perceptions and authority. The leech felt to her "a sucking, wormy thing," "a vampire" like her own abject dependency on others and on alcohol. When it is burned in the dream—in a fire that reminded her of the anger she could now feel without denial when her demands were not immediately gratified—she discovers "[her] lost infant self" and begins to take responsibility to care for it. Since the bottle also recalled her alcoholism, she was again motivated to wonder how the addiction had functioned to keep herself alive. She realized that drinking had been a way to separate herself from her dysfunctional, alternately suffocating and rejecting, family when she was an adolescent. It had also allowed her to stay connected within the larger family context of alcoholism. In the dream she is, however, given a chance to find a more appropriate bottle to nourish the inner child. To this new nourishment she associated therapy, her dream journal, and a story she had been writing.

Just as the bottle recalled both addiction and infant care, so she still tended to mix up her alcoholism with her creative work. Her powers of discrimination remained quite flaccid, more like the leech than a pointer or sword. When she feared withdrawal of emotional support from her therapist or friends, or was frustrated by what she considered insensitivity, she turned against her own writing as if it were as negative and endangering as alcohol. Then she disparaged her creative efforts as "escapist and all illusion anyway."

In this long and difficult phase, negatively constellated shadow and neutral values of the Self coexist with typically borderline splits, fusions, and reversals. We can see this more clearly in the dream another woman had in early recovery. She dreamt:

The fine wine is mixed with cough syrup and dirt.

She happily decided that the dream was telling her that she was "definitely going to be able to be abstinent" because, as she reported, "I would never want to drink wine that way." In the early stages of her sobriety in AA, this interpretation helped her to separate from her compulsion.

Returning to the image again four years later in therapy, however, the dreamer found that it also illuminated some of the causes, results, and meaning of her alcoholism. The wine was no longer just a blissfully desired seducer and dangerous enemy. She had done considerable work on her own "dirt" and felt herself to be an individual with an interior identity and a shadow. She knew she had strength enough to withstand alcohol's old grip over her life. Its image, therefore, could function metaphorically to recall to her a "once very sensitive tasting capacity." She remembered then that the dream liquor was "an exquisite wine that I once enjoyed before I stopped caring about taste at all, but I would never touch it now because I am an alcoholic." Since she is no longer caught in literal addictive dependency, the image of exquisite wine can now function metaphorically and symbolically to remind the dreamer of her own perceptual gifts and the Dionysian spirit that led her to seek pleasure. In her dream this wine is mixed with a bitter cough suppressant. It reminded the dreamer, however, of a "bitter-sweet, red medicine" her mother had used to "punish [her child's] inappropriate behavior." The syrup—a sedative chloral hydrate—may have addicted her to soothing substances in childhood just as it (actually and symbolically) suppressed her natural, psychological immunity to the sadistic authority of convention. Mixed into the brew was also what she called some "dirt[y] aggression." To this she associated her own rebellious vengeance against all authority that did not indulge her. In working on the dream at this stage of therapy, she began to recognize that the automatic aggression also

functioned as masochistic spite against the authority of the
Self and as a spoiler of her own unique, aesthetically
discriminating and creative style. Several more years of
therapy were required to discriminate the positive and
negative vectors in each of these fused images, to restructure
the assertive drive, and to redeem her own taste and style.
She needed to disidentify from her old, habitual, spoiling self-
spite and to learn to use her aggression as the guardian of her
appropriately unconventional creative expression. She had
been crippled into addiction. But her addiction, even as it had
poisoned her life, had also hidden away and safeguarded her
individuality.

Another client, abused by his envious weak
father when he was a child, had introjected the father's
eruptive anger against his mother and himself. His depressed
needy mother had been unable to mediate his experience of
archetypal affects and urged him to "be still." In identity with
both parental complexes, he tended to explode or to split off
emotion and dissociate. He drank to soothe his rage and the
father's envy of his creativity, which he had introjected. He
also binged to release the expansive explosions he craved and
feared and to control them by numbing himself with more
alcohol and marijuana. As he became able to refrain from
drinking, he began to discover his fear, anger, and impotence
as well as the intense and frightening energy of his emotions.
After working in the safety of therapy for several years, he
finally allowed an image of the raw, frightening, emotional
energy to arise. He saw it as a huge bonfire. At first and
typically, he felt he was himself in the flames. With
encouragement he allowed himself to enact with dancing
movements and loud voice the excitement that this identity
with archetypal emotion—the bonfire—caused in him. As the
energy ebbed through his bodily expression of its power, he
experienced his body as constant and separate from the
energy coursing through it. At that point he was able to
imagine stepping out of the flames without fearing they
would be extinguished. He saw then that he tended to
sacrifice his consciousness of his own personal identity

masochistically in order to maintain a magical connection to transpersonal energy. At a later session he let the image of himself and the fire develop further. He then "discovered" a Native American, who stood beside the fire and let the fire speak to him, not as "killing firewater" but as "the Great Spirit." He also then associated the fire's voice to Moses' experience of Jahweh as the burning bush. Working with these images, he began to see that his addiction had expressed and contained a profound religious urge in perverted form. As he began to dialogue with his "inner fire," he discovered its authority and could attend to the fiery voice as the Great Father. Through contact with its messages, he began to feel motivated to undertake the difficult life task of providing the self-care, disciplined focus, and meaningful creative forms that could support and express his intense devotion to transcendent energies.

In therapy the recovering addict needs to be able to regress far enough to be able to restore access to a development in consciousness that was blocked in infancy. He or she may then be able to move towards capacities for symbolic thinking and emotional experiencing in those fear-ridden areas where there has previously been only concretistic and impulse-ridden intensity. Thus in one instance, an alcoholic writer could use metaphor in neutral areas of his life but not in the areas of his addictive substance or his obsessional interest. His obsession was large breasts. While he spoke as if he wanted to sink into them in sexual bliss, he behaved as if he wanted to destroy, devour, and drink from them as an infant. When he was repeatedly shown how he enacted these desires with the therapist's words, often glancing covertly at her body, he could dare to imagine what his behaviors might be like if he were to enact them. Taking his desires then into a shared active imagination, he described how he would tear and bite and suck the therapist's body. Confronting the imagined reality of his attacks and feedings made him realize that his aggression and need conflicted. How could he feed further if he had destroyed his source?[30] The stalemate initially made him feel depressed and cut off from the old nourishing excitement of his polarized intensity. After repeatedly holding the conflict and mourning his own sense of emptiness, he found that an interior holding space had begun to form within his psyche. In it he could begin to take bottle, drug, and breast symbolically. Then he could affirm the matching destructiveness and nurturance of "the Great Mother in the sky with emeralds,"[31] as he then called the archetypal feminine. This archetype, once known only concretely through the powers that had nearly killed him in childhood and during his active addiction and that he still craved symbolically for holding and inspiration, he could now find in a new symbolic image. It served to mirror his own wholeness.

Another recovering alcoholic who was further along in her therapeutic process finally also realized she could take her dreams of bourbon symbolically, not as what AA calls "drunk dreams" or enticements to drink again but as pointers to spirit and a supreme value around which to coalesce her identity.[32] After one dream in which she observed a full liquor bottle with a golden seal, she psychodramatically enacted the image. She realized how much power she had projected into the brew. Now held in its bottle, the liquor felt like "contained vitality." Somatically she experienced the image as similar to the excitement she felt when painting. She said:

I have the power of that drink in me, as if I've swallowed it, but deeper and fuller and secure. It's a miracle, this sense of flowing passion.

She could see and value its symbolic and transpersonal meaning. On the twentieth anniversary of her sobriety during the installation of her first museum exhibition, she dreamed that "A woman is ladling out some drink from a golden vat" for her. She associated the server to the exhibition's curator and to a therapist she had seen briefly during her detoxification as a hospital inpatient. To both she associated the capacity "to see and value and support [her] essence." Like the Celtic goddesses Maeve and Etain, who as we have already seen were the regal pourers of the wine at life's feast, the capacity for celebration is imaged in her dream as the server of the sacred spirit that she had once sought concretely in alcohol. Now she could appreciate its consciousness-altering expansion in the many fruitful ways she had learned to honor her own life and the transpersonal energies and spirit that flowed into it through her relationships and creative work. She said the dream image made her feel like kneeling and giving thanks. Similarly members of the peyote church worship the hallucinogen as the source of visions of the sacred primal state of wholeness with all of life that can turn their lives from despair and destructive addictions to health and creativity.

At such points in therapy recovering addicts may move on to a second birth as they experience the siren and the salvation as one and the same transcendent power. As one man expressed it,

*I thank god now that I went through that [drug and alcoholic crisis].
It nearly killed me 25 years ago, but it collapsed me into god. I can
see it was an agent of the same power, to make my life turn to find
its meaning.*

Fear, dissolution, and cravings to go berserk or to merge with the intensities at the source of life are unbearably gripping when the timeless and transpersonal font cannot be honored. These painful states may, however, bind us, compelling us to seek that source consciously and to value the sovereign goddess as guide as well as maternal comfort and inebriating ecstasy and expansive vision. Addicts, who originally seek spirit in concrete substances, must usually take up their spiritual and creative quest in different forms when they have recovered from addictive dependency. The divine appetite of Maeve will be satisfied with nothing less. We can see that experience of these states—too often first or only claimed through addiction—may be likened to a shamanic illness. It often foretells a capacity and talent for creative relationship with the inner and outer unitary world, the *unus mundus*, as the source of disciplined artistic and spiritual work. Then the ecstatic spirit can be held in the many forms through which we can live a spiritually meaningful and creative life.

Like the druids and bards of ancient Celtdom, the recovered addict's consciousness has a particular capacity for the magic of artistic creativity. In the story of Taliesin this is said to be the gift of the great goddess Cerridwen, Maeve's Welsh counterpart. In her cauldron she brews the mind-altering elixir that little Gwion Bach stirs faithfully for a year and finally tastes. It enables him to understand the language of the animals and to change into their shapes because he can so deeply identify with their forms and functions. Reborn through his harrowing experiences of the awesome goddess, Gwion Bach is renamed "Radiant Brow," Taliesin. He has the gifts of poetic and prophetic vision and magic that have resulted from his submersion in the unitary field of timeless and spaceless consciousness.[33] Another Celtic poet king, Finn MacCumail, received similar vision from one taste of the broth of a sacred fish cooking in a druid's cauldron of its own watery matrix. It came from the holywell source of the river (Boyne) named for the white cow and earth and river goddess, Boann, Maeve's counterpart in eastern Ireland, whom we have seen is also a goddess of the triple spiral.

Such fluidity of consciousness is common to those who have become addicted.[34] It may be innate in their characters (and even genetically determined). It is also powerfully enhanced by early experiences of unmediated emotional experience. The deprivations of infancy and early childhood and/or the derogation of the ancient sacred initiatory patterns precluded adequate parental and cultural definitions to circumscribe and mediate safe relationship to archetypal dynamics. Facing such raw depths alone and unheld within transformative rituals, their capacity for consciousness was flooded, and they were left with weak and culturally undeveloped, even aberrant, structures of perception and cognition.

Such lack of development, fragmentation, and capacity for the unmitigated experience of intense, archetypal emotions fosters the creation of an original, fluid, and intense consciousness in the ever healing addict. The potential for such culturally independent, subtle, and passionate consciousness is the other and beneficent side of the fragmentation addicts are heir to. It holds enormous potential benefit when it can be claimed consciously and channeled into the forms of art and religion.

As the initiated druid could understand the language of animals, so the sensitized and fluid consciousness of the recovered alcoholic so long condemned to what Freud termed primary process thinking can often now use its gifts to understand others. Almost as if from within them, this form of medial intuition can attune to the psychological field between perceiver and other. Such momentary merging of identity with the constellated field can be so accurately tuned and imaginally conveyed that it can seem to read from within the other. It permits extraordinary poetic empathy, feeling with and into the other—whether that be person, place, animal, or object.

The gift of the Celtic goddess' brew also provides a sensitivity to event patterns that may enable accurate visionary and prophetic sight. Like Meilyr, who won his vision in the bliss of erotic embrace, the recovered addict's capacity for such field vision results from the permeable boundaries that have remained open in the addictive-borderline levels of consciousness. It is very similar to the way children and animals are able to dowse the emotional feel of the immediate whole situation through the presymbolic resonances felt in their own bodies. Without a relatively stable sense of identity through these various shapeshifts, this intuitive gift can remain a curse. The individual prone to addiction can stay awash suffering fears and fragmentation or adapt defensively to human and non-human others and lose all sense of self. In adults with a more stable sense of identity, this empathic capacity shifts. It becomes an ability to suspend knowing and to loosen previously held categories of cognition. This capacity for relatively fluid boundaries enables the empathic perceiver to be present to the permutations of the other and the mutual field perceived through the parallel flowing of introverted and intuitive proprioceptive, kinesthetic, auditory, and visual images. While such intuitions underlie medial capacities, their powers invariably need to be honed with conscious practice and checked for objectivity. They may be further enhanced through learning to focus and direct such intuitive attention in various forms of meditation.

Experiences of surrogate maternal holding and mirroring and training in the warrior skills to separate from compulsivity create the necessary stablity in which ego consciousness can develop. Within this new context, the gift of bardic fluidity can then serve creativity. Because such perception is fluid and field sensitive, it can readily attune to the underlying psychological dynamics and spiritual depths that resonate through events and relationships. In artists this permits empathic attunment with many forms and characters and the creative, unfolding, imaginal process itself. In therapists it permits attunement with the many parts or complexes of the analysand and one's own subjective responses and countertransference. It supports attentiveness to the forces of destiny and guidance unfolding in the analytic process. Accepted and developed, Maeve's intense and fluid vision can thus nourish the profound, creative, and religious needs and gifts of the ever-healing individual who is prone to addiction.

Chapter 9

The Loathsome Damsel

Maeve is the Celtic principle of sovereignty. In early patriarchal times the cosmic goddess came to represent the power, completeness, expanded vision, and regal authority necessary to rule the tribe. In myths about the acquisition of sovereignty, however, her figure initially appears hideous, wild, and/or diseased. In this loathsome form she represents the final test that the "true king" must pass to demonstrate his capacity to rule. Already selected for surpassing his fellows in feats of strength and insight, he must also prove the wisdom of his heart. He must take the hideous damsel in his embrace and disenchant her with his kiss.[1] Transformed then into the beautiful "many-shaped" goddess of the land, she symbolizes the king's destiny to rule over it with truth and justice. In this form she bestows on her consort the cup of sovereignty and the "bounty of her own thighs."

There are several variations of this theme of the seeker's marriage to the earth goddess, who guards and serves the waters of life and grants the kingdom and the power and the glory of rule.[2] In one story that we already know from chapter 4, five usurping brothers deny Maeve as the principle of sovereignty and seek to evade the ancient royalty customs. Because they are irreverent, Maeve becomes leprous and loathsome. She then seduces, binds, and kills them. In this variant of the myth, instead of conveying rule, the death hag destroys the irreverent claimants, who represent a false approach to power.

A more positive version of the theme appears in
the story of the five sons of Eochaidh Mugmedon. They went
hunting to try their new weapons and encountered the
loathsome damsel.

*When they ceased from straying they kindled a fire, broiled some of
their quarry, and ate it until they were satisfied. Then they were
thirsty and in great drouth from the cooked food. "Let one of us go
and seek for water," they said. "I will go," said Fergus. The lad went
seeking water, till he chanced on a well and saw an old woman
guarding it.*

*Thus was the hag: every joint and limb of her, from the top of her
head to the earth, was as black as coal. Like the tail of a wild horse
was the gray bristly mane that came through the upper part of her
head-crown. The green branch of an oak in bearing would be
severed by the sickle of green teeth that lay in her head and reached
to her ears. Dark smoky eyes she had: a nose crooked and hollow.
She had a middle fibrous, spotted with pustules, diseased, and shins
distorted and awry. Her ankles were thick, her shoulders were
broad, her knees were big, and her nails were green. Loathsome in
sooth was the hag's appearance.[3]*

Just as the storytellers delight in recounting all the details of
form and clothing when they portray a beauty like Etain,
here they lavish their art on the specifics of ugliness. The
guardian of the waters of life first appears to the seeker with
all the distortions that might rouse aversion. Her hideous
figure is one well known in Irish and Scots lore as the *cailleach*
or old woman. Similar to dread Kali Durga in Hindu myth
and a favorite in fairy tales, she lives on as the frightful witch.

"Art thou guarding the well?" asked the youth.
"Yea truly," she answered.
*"Dost thou permit me to take away some of the water?" said the
youth.*
*"I will permit," she answered, "provided there come from thee one
kiss on my cheek."*
"By no means!" said he.
"Then no water shalt thou get from me," said she.
*"I give my word," he answered, "that I would rather perish of thirst
than give thee a kiss."*
*Then the lad went back to the place where his brothers were biding,
and told them he had not found water.*

Next Ailill went to look for water and chanced on the same
well. He too refused to kiss the hag, returned without water,

and did not confess that he had found the well. Then Brian, the eldest of the sons, went to seek water, chanced on the same well, refused to kiss the old woman, and returned. Fiachra then went forth, found the well and the hag, and asked her for water.

"I will grant it," said she, "but give me a kiss."
"I would give a few kisses for it."
"Thou shalt visit Tara," said she.
That fell true, for two of his race took the kingship of Erin . . . and
no one of the race of the other sons.

Here we learn that the hag has the authority not only to provide water from her well but also to grant it as the drink of sovereignty over Ireland. In accepting the hag's invitation to barter for it with a kiss, Fiachra wins kingship for two of his descendants. The tale undoubtedly gives mythic support for the fact that two of Fiachra's line did "visit" Tara to rule from the seat of Ireland's high kings.

[Nonetheless] Fiachra returned without water [for the others.
Perhaps he got some for himself alone. The scribe left this
unexplained.]
. . . . [T]hen Niall went seeking water and happened on the same
well.
"Give me water, O woman," said Niall.
"I will give it," she answered, "but first give me a kiss."
"Besides giving thee a kiss, I will lie with thee!"

Then he threw himself down upon her and gave her a kiss. But
then, when he looked at her, there was not in the world a damsel
whose figure or appearance was more lovable than hers! Like the
snow in trenches was every bit of her from head to sole. Plump and
queenly forearms she had: fingers long and slender: calves straight
and beautifully colored. Two blunt shoes of white bronze between
her little soft-white feet and the ground. A costly full-purple mantle
she wore, with a brooch of bright silver in the clothing of the mantle.
Shining pearly teeth she had, an eye large and queenly, and lips red
as rowanberries.

"That is many-shaped [beautiful], O lady!" said the youth.
"True," said she.
"Who art thou?" said the youth.
"I am the Sovereignty of Erin," she answered; and then she said:
"O king of Tara, I am the Sovereignty.
I will tell thee its great goodness . . .
Smooth shall be thy draught from the royal horn,
'twill be mead, 'twill be honey, 'twill be strong ale."[4]

*"Go now to thy brothers," she said, "and take water with thee, and
the kingship and the domination will for ever abide with thee and
thy children, save only with twain of the seed of Fiachra . . . and one
king out of Munster, namely Brian Boru—and all these will be
kings without opposition.*

*And as thou hast seen me loathsome, bestial, horrible at first and
beautiful at last, so is the sovereignty; for seldom is it gained without
battles and conflicts; but at last to anyone it is beautiful and goodly.
Howbeit, give not the water to thy brothers until they have granted
thee seniority over them, that thou mayst raise thy weapon a hand's-
breadth above their weapons."*

*"So shall it be done," said the youth.
Then he bade her farewell and took water to his brothers; but did
not give it to them until they had granted to him every boon that he
asked of them, as the damsel had taught him. He also bound them
with oaths never to oppose himself or his children.[5]*

Thus Niall wins the kingship of Ireland.[6] The
hideous animal-like female, who gives him the drink
affirming his right to rule, is the goddess.[7] She personifies the
sovereign majesty of the land with which the unblemished
and chosen king is to be joined.[8] She embodies and serves
him the draught of sovereignty and with it the regal power,
sovereignty, and good fortune, which are her gifts to bestow.
"High kings sleep with me, for I am the kingship of Alba and
Eriu," the fearsome hag tells king Lughaid Laigh, a king-to-be
in another Irish tale.

This loathsome damsel evokes both the extremes
of fear and fascination that must be embraced together by the
king. "None but the brave deserve the fair," an old Celtic
proverb states.[9] Only "the true king"—or an individual
consciousness brave enough to face the ugly, pain-filled
reality of the outer world and its own depths—is worthy to
receive the beauty that represents sovereignty. First he must
disenchant and transform the hag.

The hag represents the pre- or trans-ego
negative (and positive) shadow material that has been kept
from consciousness. Since personal consciousness is initially
shaped by the collective, its ego ideals are formed through

adapting to (or rebelling against) family and social norms. Shadow material is made up of those psychological qualities that have been devalued and excluded from the ego ideal. Because such material cannot be humanly mediated by those who ascribe to such ideals, it also remains dangerously encumbered with the unnamable dread of the unconscious itself, still projected and clinging to it. Thus the unlived and shunned parts of ourselves and of our society are represented as—what Jungians call the shadow—gross and hateful, laden with intolerable affects. These appear in ugly, monstrous theriomorphic images to express the revulsion of the consciousness confronting them.[10] They appear as the loathsome damsel, and her form also suggests the potential chaos and pestilence of the unknown. She arouses the fear that makes us viscerally reject any embrace that threatens such contamination. She disrupts our stability as she threatens the boundaries of our sense of identity and its congruence with standards that are ideal and safe.

The sovereignty hag represents those parts of actual life experience that we avoid and split off from consciousness with defenses such as dissociative denial and the anesthesia of addictive patterns. One of our defenses involves the repudiation of fearful psychological material like destructive rage or greed and its projection into our images of others, who inevitably embody some aspects of the projected material.[11] Because it falls outside acceptable categories and order, this material appears as intolerably ugly and evokes fear and contempt in us. Nonetheless, the material we repudiate is an aspect of our greater wholeness and necessary for life. We cannot live without it. Such seemingly horrid attributes are aspects of the "just-so" facts of existence—the matrix of psychological reality. Thus while at first we may only be able to recognize the ejected aspects of our own wholeness in projection, inevitably it is secretly fascinating. When we meet the shadow in projection, we can thus recognize it by the passionate reactions it claims from us. We grant it an excited, overdetermined, even anxious, attention. It gets under our skin, bothers us because while we reject it, we also need it.

The innate tendency to separate from and eject what has the power to discomfort us and to need and envy it in projection is a potent force in human conflict. This dynamic may help explain why the most savage violence is dealt to those who live intimately with each other. As carriers of projected shadow material, they are as necessary and familiar as kin, yet they can easily be feared, scapegoated, and attacked as enemy when self-esteem is reduced and seeks an easy outburst of aggression and/or revenge to refill its coffers. The conflict of need and hate can then open into realms of unspeakable, primal passion where the opposites clang together and erupt in wild, sometimes exultant, sadistic attitudes and actions. The needed and hated/envied shadow qualities can be projected onto children, partners, siblings, nearby factions, tribes, religions, races, and nations. Then members of the same clan or the same family may become veiled in loathsomeness and are seemingly fair game for persecution.[12] While many adults struggle to suppress and/or channel such sadism into non-harmful strategies of self-expression, we have seen it erupt in the violence directed against family members by those prone to addictions. Irish medieval history is filled with bloody eruptions within clans and between rival clans. Often family members indulged in aggressive battles when they were filled with alcohol after communal feasting. The ancient Irish knew that they required the mythic power of the goddess' sovereignty to empower a central, overarching authority and enable that leader to embrace all factions and hold them justly together in order to permit the tribal realm to flourish.

The shadow material is ultimately necessary neutral life energy that may be destructive, life enhancing, frightening, and/or acceptable depending on our relation to it. We have already seen that aggression can manifest as destructive rage, threatening what we hold near and dear, or it can be put in the service of the Self to guard life and support our legitimate claims. Thus while Maeve as sovereignty at first appears grotesquely ugly, she is also captivating. She has the potential to seduce us. For she brings awareness of Self stuff that needs to be sorted and lived with under the rule of conscience. If we can bear the disorientation and restructuring that her embrace inevitably holds, we can transform our habitual sense of identity and claim authority over our lives with a sense of expanded energy and psychological spaciousness.

The goddess Maeve invites us then to embrace her in her loathsome form and to drink from the inebriating waters of her own life's spring to gain the consciousness to see and move beyond our old limitations. Without such drink we are unable to empathize with and accept otherness in the outer or inner world, in others and in ourselves. Without such drink we remain fragmented and cannot coalesce our kingdoms around the regal cores of our own more complete identities. We remain under the authority of the old king and previously held collective ideals. Then we fail to develop the individual ethical authority of conscience, which is the voice of the sovereign or Self authority within us—the individual and inner analogue of the goddess of sovereignty for the Celtic tribespeople.

Today the loathsome damsel still demands that we claim expanded vision and authority over our own lives and the conflicting parts within us. To develop ourselves as fully as we can, Maeve still challenges us to confront psychologically what first appears to be repulsive and to accept it in an intimate embrace. Appearing at all the transition points in our personal development and at every stage of life, she thus confronts us with the next step of our unfolding destiny in a form representing the fearful difficulty of its assimilation. She expresses and forces us to embrace what we currently avoid and deny about ourselves. She forces self-confrontation. From the perspective of our fear and revulsion towards such still disavowed and/or unknown emotional states and parts of ourselves, this new view seems at first intolerable. Thus the goddess of our sovereignty initially appears to us as loathsome, the terrible other, whom we associate to all we have feared and despised and denied. According to old Celtic stories and modern psychotherapeutic wisdom, the hideous, untamed, and rejected parts of ourselves must be consciously experienced, accepted, and integrated into our self-image if we are to attain some authority over our lives and tap into the creative potential that comes from struggling with the many sides of individual wholeness. Like the hag, they all demand to be kissed, embraced, and known intimately.

For those prone to addictions, the task is particularly poignant because they are very sensitive to the unconscious, and hence often able to perceive the unconscious or shadow qualities in themselves and in those around them. Almost invariably they have developed with an early and primitive defensive incorporation of the caretaker's negative qualities into their own identities to maintain an image of that needed adult's goodness. Thus, swollen with negativity, feeling only negatively special, they easily identify all or essential parts of themselves with the rejected shadow of whatever community they are in. When stressed and in order to maintain some control over the discomforts they take so personally and feel so intensely, they often vent aggression back on themselves with attitudes of self-contempt and behaviors that are self-spiting. Due to magic-level cognitions, they often cling to an underlying and easily globalized conviction that they are worthless and rejected. "My badness is the real me," we have already heard one recovering addict declare. With this identity they often live out the roles of outsider and scapegoat. Since they are generally self-identified as loathsome, much of their own positive strength lies unconscious in what Jungians call the positive personal shadow. Initially, because it has remained unconscious, their self-esteem is still primitive and appears as an underlying omnipotence. From its grandiose unconscious perspective they may be very demanding and vengefully blame others when they do not live up to expectations. While such omnipotence contains the seeds of regality, it needs much work to be refined and developed.

Regality is not, the Celtic material tells us, a matter of secret grandiosity, but of demonstrating the three-fold capacities required to rule. The chief must be as strong a guardian as the warrior, as productive a caretaker as the farmers and herders, and as wise and wide-visioned as the druid-magus. Only then is he or she able to embrace the loathsome damsel of destiny and to rule justly over the many factions of the inner kingdom.

For individuals who manage intolerable affects with addictive solutions, all of these capacities are needed in order to acknowledge and bear intolerable states in their raw forms and claim the authority to rule over the many parts of their inner and outer kingdoms. They are essential in order to develop an adequately functioning ego. Thus while the first steps in *ending* an addiction involve the addicts' recognizing impotence before its grip and accepting sobriety, the first steps in *healing recovery* from an addiction involve their working ever more deeply on themselves. After learning to abstain ascetically from dishonoring spiritual power through its displacement into the addiction and dishonoring individual potential with unconscious and misplaced dependencies, recovering addicts still need to learn to become warriors and caretakers and visionaries on behalf of life. They need to find alternative maternal and spiritual containment for their battered psyches and learn cognitive skills to process reality more maturely and creatively. And they need to address the profound issues of regal authority.

Pretending to possess omnipotent control over their lives and addictions, addicts suffer failure, incapacity, and more shame as their attempts fail over and over again. Then they must remain dependent on the *medb* as tranquilizer, passion, and poison. They cannot be Maeve's regal partners.

In healing, addicts need to learn how to learn the wisdom of abstinence and self-acceptance. In healing they also need to develop—with human and divine help— something analogous to what the Celts called *firinne flatha*, "the king's truth" on which the justice of the ruler depends. This is a perspective that can provide a conscious and balanced relationship to all aspects of the whole personality including the previously repressed and eruptive transpersonal drives and powers. Rather than avoiding these intolerable emotions with addictive solutions, individuals working to claim their sovereignty need to face and appreciate them. Rather than fearing them as if they were still threatened children fleeing from Olca Ai, individuals may come to view the giant affects for what they are—awesome and neutral energies. With understanding gained through consciously experiencing the ways these energies have been misused and abused against them, individuals may be able to mourn for themselves. They may even awaken to the painful awareness that they too have misused these powers against others and even against parts of their own inner world and potentials. Recognizing that they have hidden away from finding conscious, personal, and productive access to these energies in their lives, recovering addicts may begin the process of turning towards the loathsome Maeve and embracing her with humility.

The Twelve Steps

With remarkable wisdom AA has evolved a framework to help alcoholics confront and embrace the loathsome hag. When we examine The Twelve Steps of Alcoholics Anonymous, we are confronted repeatedly with her challenge:

1. *We admitted we were powerless over alcohol—that our lives had become unmanageable.*
2. *Came to believe that a Power greater than ourselves could restore us to sanity.*
3. *Made a decision to turn our will and our lives over to the care of God as we understood Him.*
4. *Made a searching and fearless moral inventory of ourselves.*
5. *Admitted to God, to ourselves, and to another human being the exact nature of our wrongs.*
6. *Were entirely ready to have God remove all these defects of character.*
7. *Humbly asked Him to remove our shortcomings.*
8. *Made a list of all persons we had harmed, and became willing to make amends to them all.*
9. *Made direct amends to such people wherever possible, except when to do so would injure them or others.*

10. *Continued to take personal inventory and when we were wrong promptly admitted it.*
11. *Sought through prayer and meditation to improve our conscious contact with God as we understood Him, praying only for knowledge of His will for us and the power to carry it out.*
12. *Having had a spiritual awakening as the result of these steps, we tried to carry this message to alcoholics, and to practice these principles in all our affairs.**[13]*

The alcoholic, says the Big Book of AA, is like an "actor who wants to run the whole show."[14] He or she requires what AA's co-founder called "deflation . . . [to] smash the illusion" of omnipotent control over the addiction and its ending.[15] Thus in the first step we discover the most loathed and denied fact that any addiction-prone individual needs to admit into consciousness: true powerlessness over the addiction and the effective management of personal life. Such an admission cuts through the false pride and omnipotence that may have sustained the compulsive drinker when all caretakers and all other efforts failed, but it also fuels the shame and denial that prevent transformation. As one woman client in early recovery put it,

I have to face the shame that I am not in control. It is so huge and hideous I'd rather die or kill myself and everything I love or want for my life than reveal it. . . . That's why everything dies around me, and I give up. I can't care about anything as much as about hiding the shame.

Admitting powerlessness is not a portal to wallowing in self-abnegation however. It means confronting the reality of the compulsive addiction as a first step towards embracing individual fate. It permits wrestling with the bravado-driven illusions and secret pride of the defensive false self in order to begin building the real assertion, real self-esteem, real spiritual experience, and real self-rule that Maeve required of her lovers. Confronting what was unthinkable and loathsome, we can find release from the terrible grip of

---

* *The Twelve Steps are reprinted with permission of Alcoholics Anonyous World Services, Inc. Permission to reprint the Twelve Steps does not mean that AA has reviewed or approved the contents of this publication, nor that AA agrees with the views expressed herein. AA is a program of recovery from alcoholism only--use of the Twelve Steps in connection with other programs patterned after AA does not imply otherwise.*

shame. Since we can then begin to accept ourselves, we
will no longer project contempt; thus no one else can
shame us either.[16]

The second and third steps confront the addict's
previously feared, despised, and denied dependency needs
and unconscious spirituality. They invoke a spiritual power
equal to that of the demonic possession that can support the
beleaguered addict's newly admitted need. Turning with
humility towards this powerful new matrix can restore the
scale and sanity required for transformation and recovery. The
fourth through tenth steps confront the addict's entire system
of defensive denial and irresponsible acting out. They require
the addict to invoke the deep courage to become responsible
for working on his or her shadow. The eighth, ninth, and
tenth steps require making amends for previously
unconscious and acted-out loathsome and hurtful behavior
toward others. These steps also help to develop the capacities
for empathy and community, which have often been distorted
into dysfunctional patterns and callous opportunism. In
acknowledging openly what has been denied and hidden out
of ignorance and shame, we embrace the loathsome hag. This
embrace looms as a crucial task in the Twelve-step programs.
Only after such courageous self-confrontation can the
recovered addict adequately begin to know and carry out the
individual purpose of his or her life and go forth with the
personal authority acquired from inner work to work with
others as stated in the eleventh and twelfth steps.

Embracing the hag requires acceptance of the
shadow—all those infantile and raw emotions and behaviors
that seize us and get acted out unconsciously. Such work is
fostered in Twelve-step programs, and it is a major focus in
therapy where the subtle and deep discriminations that
consciousness and conscience can make are given central
attention. Most of us, when we operate on the addictive and
borderline levels of consciousness with their typical splittings
of consciousness, are likely to see the objectionable traits as
either only outside or only inside ourselves. We have no
objectivity. Those who deny and project the traits lose access

to their energies and gain only sentimental and fraudulent righteousness, which cannot relate adequately to the whole situation. Those who are identified with the rejected traits feel so overwhelmingly bad and loathsome they despair of being able to claim any authoritative sovereignty over life situations. Many addicts feel betrayed and rejected by human caretakers who did not enable them to enjoy self-acceptance. They shy away from any embrace. Unable to discriminate the siren who will bind and kill from the hag who wants a real partner and who will bestow sovereignty, they avoid all authentic intimacy.

As we have seen, experiences of fear, despair, rage, and shame are central aspects in the psychology of those dependent on addictions. Accepting these painful emotions rather than denying them is hard enough, for these loathsome emotions can feel so horrible, the addict would rather use the drug of choice or even "go psychotic" than have to face them. To embrace such material responsibly demands work on the underlying shame. This involves mitigating automatic and contemptuous judgmentalism to arrive at the king's truth, a truth that can see the reality of the facts in their larger inner and outer context. Because so many of the addict's ego capacities are in the positive shadow, these too need to be discovered, tolerated, and embraced although they, too, may initially feel ugly, chaotic, and shameful. Here cognitive therapy is often required to develop dormant rational thinking and evaluating functions. Clarifying assumptions and misperceptions, individuals can learn to become active, to describe and weigh all the relative facets of the situation as they are, here and now. They can notice how they globalize, chaoticize, rigidly bifurcate, and/or focus only on parts of a situation. Those of us with addictive issues can become aware that instead of learning to risk fresh assessments, we tend to depend on familiar prejudices. Daring to meet current reality honestly, empathically, and more inclusively, we embrace it and disenchant its horror. With such a kiss we gain a sense of regal and expansive authority in relation to the loathsome shadow within each of us. Parts lose their frighteningly global grip in our embracing consciousness; opposites lose their polarized intensity because we hold them within a larger context. Then we may gain a view of the situation's psychological reality as full of inevitably mixed blessings and banes.

Working through such intensely loathsome material in therapy creates the basis of the psychological structures that can support self-acceptance and an authentic sense of identity. Jung expressed such transformation of the loathsome hag when he wrote:

At first one finds contents that are rather disgusting and crude; then they reveal their inner value and one sees that they are really precious jewels.[17]

Working with the Loathsome Material

Niall, the king to be in the Celtic story of the five brothers, is reared in exile. As the child of a foreign princess who served as a slave woman in Tara, his royal father's court, he is threatened *in utero* by the jealous queen. She forces Niall's pregnant mother to do hard tasks "that the child might die in her womb." Neither aborted nor stillborn, Niall comes into the world on the green outside Tara, and he is immediately attacked by birds, which we can see as representations of the negative spirit of the queen, the destructive spirit of hate-filled envy. In Niall's story a stranger, the poet Torna, rescues and rears him, prophesies his future greatness, and helps him to withstand the further murderous attacks of the old queen. After returning to court, Niall elevates his own mother to her regal status and, passing all the shaman-smith's druid tests, goes on to embrace the loathsome hag and become the new king.

Both historically and mythologically, Niall's kingship was an unusual event. Niall came from outside the ancestral line, represented in his story by the figure of the old queen who sought to repel change.[18] With his inauguration a new dynasty found the support of the goddess of the flowing waters of life. Thus his rule represents the sanctioning of a new cultural order.

His capacity to embrace the hag that his stepbrothers rejected affirms the symbolic value and the sensitivity that is generated by being an exile and an outsider. It is impossible not to face one's relation to what is other and foreign when one has been rejected and forced into exile oneself. This is true psychologically. As one recovering addict who was beginning training to become a therapist said:

Out of my own sense of alienation, I can relate to what is alien and new. Because I have always felt awkward, I can often see through [other people's] awkwardness to what is, the core that is real and true.

Usually we repudiate and try to hide our experience of exile and alienation to avoid further experiences of abandonment. But the story reassures us that alienation, although it makes us initially feel vulnerable and suffer, also has a profound meaning. If we can embrace the fact that we are already estranged from the conventions others accept without question, we may find that the sense of exile can help us further the capacity to stand apart as observing witnesses. From this perspective we are better able to see impartially, turn towards, and empathize with the new and alien. We can then transcend the traditional ideals, which tell us what is supposed to be judged fair or ugly, good or evil, true or false in order to develop our own perceptions and our own standards. Since outer sources do not support us, we are also forced to turn towards our individual inner authority. Rather than mirroring the collective view as many of us were once forced to mirror our parents, we can learn to value our unique individuality. Then, like Niall, we may be able to discover and rule over our own inner kingdoms in partnership with the transcendent Self and with others engaged in the same struggle. Instead of suffering alienation, we become then engaged in the continual cocreation of our own destiny and can begin to feel the full and humble regality of our participation in this extraordinary task, which is the true basis of self-esteem.[19]

Too often without a sense of exile, we are like
Niall's stepbrothers in the story. We remain caught within the
bounds of familiarity, thinking its strictures will guard us from
loneliness. We maintain the old and collective categories for
perceiving and judging our experience of others and
ourselves. For us any step on the path of growth can only be
felt as hideous unless it is already collectively sanctioned.
Loyal to the community's fear and hatred of the new, we
collude in maintaining the status quo. Since the radically new
comes from a hitherto devalued place that we have learned to
hate and fear in ourselves and in others to sustain a coherent
sense of ourselves as good, we cannot recognize the values
necessary to create a new kingdom, a new life, a new age. We
usually have to suffer our frustration until it is strong enough
to make us loosen our old assumptions and ideals. Only then
can we risk going through consciously endured abstinence
from what has seemed to support us, feeling the concomitant
pains and depression of that loss to explore new potentials. Or
we may find some water bearer, like Niall in the story, who
has done the hard inner work. Then we can lean on him or
her. Unfortunately because we have not developed
confidence in our own creative and authentic vision through
personal experience, we are all too susceptible to following
false prophets and opportunistic gurus who pretend to slake
our thirst, offering new bottles filled only with self-serving
tonics and/or outmoded fundamentalism.

We need, however, a sense of exile that has
known good-enough foster care in order to gain experiences
of alternative means of safe and thriving survival.[20] Exile has
not been a safe and productive fosterage for the addict. Being
dropped outside any safe court or human context and being
beset by birds are apt metaphors of the abandonment
problems and endangering spirit that afflict those prone to
addiction. Although they are like Niall in having a life that
has often been threatened even before birth by genetic,
economic, social, and psychological malevolence, they have
not been rescued and reared in kindly fosterage. Instead the
addiction and the society of other addicts and their suppliers
have served as a precarious fosterage. Such illusory or

minimal care can only hold false prophesies of well-being and will not permit growth of the integrity needed to rule a rightful kingdom. Until those prone to addiction—and the unparented, potentially addictive parts of all of us—can find a strong and understanding foster parentage to affirm and validate individuality as a basis of identity, to reclaim the lost entitlements, and to help in acquiring life skills, the alienation only increases and may become permanent. Such unmitigated exile is torture, and the need to dull the pain of such alienation supports addiction.

Anomalous and living outside the bounds and structures of normal society, addicts then have a particular and frozen liminal status in relation to it. Addicts from privileged backgrounds as well as those barely surviving on the street belong increasing to a drug culture and experience themselves as living beyond the normative rules of the dominant society. As outsiders, they occupy a place that represents one phase of any initiation ceremony. Luigi Zoya has argued that the addict thus remains isolated in a marginal state that prevents his being reborn or brought back and reintegrated.[21] To be paralyzed in a permanently liminal status can lead nowhere. It prevents one from experiencing the transforming aspect of a rite of passage.

The addictive and borderline clients—and those levels in all of us—that have been left on the threshold to suffer outsider status usually continue to remain loyal to patterns and defenses established to survive with early negative caretakers. In the language of psychology, they remain in identity with those they experienced as aggressors. While such limitations trap them in the old perceptual and behavioral thimbles and cesspools in which they were raised, those miseries feel familiar and hence safe. They are clung to passionately. When deprived of adequate bonding, yet still craving harmonious symbiosis, and when deprived of learning to integrate new material, individuals prone to addiction remain within the intricacies of a dysfunctional family system and the defenses they adapted with a loyalty that is close to fusion. Ritualistically rather than ritually, they then suffer

Maeve's inconstant cycles as terrible and repetitive embraces
that do not lead to initiatory development. Bound by
contradictions they cannot subsume and fears of annihilation
they cannot assuage, they remain paralyzed in Maeve's
bindings, unable to undertake the ordeals that would let them
claim the creativity and authority necessary to usher in a new
phase of development.

Such loyal bondage is built into the structures of
identity. We acquire basic values within the embrace of the
maternal collective. We learn to turn towards the smells and
sounds of the mother even before birth. We are imprinted by
the archetype to associate our personal parents with life's
goodness—even when we experience them as negative. With
the development of stranger recognition at about 6-8 months
and with parental help in ejecting painful experiences onto
culturally suitable objects, we further coalesce our sense of
good parent-me and bad other-not-me. We learn very early
on a body level to shun what discomforts us and what does
not win parental approval. When there is no hope of such
approval and we try desperately to conform to find it, or
when those standards are too fearful and/or brittle, natural
curiosity may be damaged. Then we turn away automatically
from the call of the new by *perceiving* it—very naturally and
obviously—as aberrant, dangerous, revolting, and even
repulsive. Then, too loyal to the bonds and meanings created
in our troubled infancy, we can only shun the transformative
damsel. Her loathsomeness reminds us of old and loathsome
emotional pains and early loathsome, fascinating prohibitions.
She feels as frightening and overwhelming as they did.
Affecting us viscerally, on the psychoid level where body and
mind, matter and spirit are still one, revulsion grips our body-
psyche with the intensity of our earliest perceptions. If those
earliest wounds and bonds are still unconscious and raw, we
confuse the hag of sovereignty's invitation with the loathsome
pains of childhood and shy away from all the horrors her
monstrous form represents. We remain frantically stuck in
place, still trying to avert a recurrence of old suffering. Then
our defenses and the sense of shame and self-loathing we

have associated with early suffering close us off from participation in life.

Clinically, however, we see again and again that when we can accept what appears as shame filled and repugnant rather than giving in to impulsive instinctive revulsion, we are on the way towards moving from our frozen state to discovering a new perspective to support our individuation. With each acceptance of that which first appears repulsive, we find ourselves daring to become more fully ourselves.[22] Courage grows. Within a group of kindred souls and with a therapist to serve as fosterage, addicts may thus be awakened out of paralysis and into the initiatory process. They may become lovers of Maeve in ways that heal them and the inadequate cultural biases and bifurcations that once drove them out and froze them in liminal and scapegoat status. Then they may claim the strength, intimacy, vision, and regality provided by initiatory rebirths under the higher power, whom here we call Meave.

The simple first step of witnessing and accepting such paradoxical material—without trying to change or caretake or control it, without trying to defend or fight against it—is inevitably both frightening and fascinating. Such an open attitude may be learned from others who have already developed a capacity to see the matrix behind and through the specific, seeming aberrations. This restores kinship. It is part of the fosterage. When we find that our peers and our therapist can empathize with and mirror our struggles, we find our courage to see and accept loathsome reality in life and in ourselves. Fostered by their open acceptance, we can begin to integrate what we have only seen as negative and hateful.

The therapist's modeling of such self-acceptance implies acceptance of her own gifts and limitations as well as those of the recovering addict. This allows fraudulent idealization, destructive envy, sadistic-masochistic splitting, and even tendencies to dissociate to be held inclusively and empathically. Even when the therapist must resist the lures to intervene or gratify with advice (when it would rob the client of discovering inner authority) and yet also stand against destructive acting out, she may empathically find a balance to stand with rather than over or against the client. Then the therapist can companion the client's beleaguered ego in discovering what the consequences of acting out would be, what possible alternative strategies might exist, and what the contemplated behavior is expressing regarding the Self's real goals and requirements. Inevitably the therapeutic process is supported by the initiating goddess or Self, which provides glimpses through the images of dreams or active imaginations of another perspective where positive and negative are aspects of one whole. Such empathic fosterage is thus open to trans-egoic guidance represented by the druid who fostered Niall in the story. In such care the client's panoply of reactions and sometimes questionable behaviors can be sorted to find their meanings.

In a version of the loathsome hag story from India, we are told the value of such a metaperspective, which can grant equanimity. The story tells us how Kali chose her consort by appearing in her ugliest form before Brahma, Vishnu, and Shiva to test them.

Shedding her golden dress, she took the form of an old hag. She was naked, her hair gleamed brightly, she had a lolling tongue and four arms. Her emaciated body was smeared with sweat and glistened like black fire. She was adorned with a garland of heads, was of fearsome appearance, and shrieked horribly. She blazed like millions of fiery stars and had the half moon as her crown.

Only Siva remained composed at this confrontation, so Kali chose him as her consort.

Inevitably such spiritual equanimity is itself the gift of the initiating goddess who presents herself to us as the loathsome and fascinating horror. Developing a capacity to reverence the terrible goddess as reality and maintain some degree of composure is a task that even the gods found difficult to achieve. It requires long practice and some degree of trust, for it can only develop with conscious exposure to fear of the raw depths and repeated survival through such fear. A companion therapist, sponsor, and/or group who has already navigated some of the stresses involved is invaluable for support and clarification. The capacity for such equanimity can also be strengthened by the practice of meditation, as we can see in the story from the figure of Shiva, the Hindu god of both meditative practices and the cosmic dance. The ritual repetitiveness of both therapy and meditation provide the discipline of repeated encounters with the painful thoughts and emotions gripping us. In both disciplines we are gradually helped to develop a witnessing and non-judgmental attitude that enables a relation to the stresses of inner and outer reality without being inundated by them and tempted to flee back into old defenses. Both psychotherapy and meditation foster the evenly hovering observation of psychic processes that develops a form of self-acceptance.

While some individuals combine psychotherapy with Sufi, Sidda yoga, Vipassana, Zen, Christian, and other contemplative practices, others are drawn to the physical meditations of Tai Chi, Hatha Yoga, tennis, swimming, running, etc. All of these meditative methods can provide practical methods of strengthening the capacity to calmly acknowledge and release whatever thoughts and emotions rise into awareness—including addictive cravings. Unfortunately, however, any of these forms of meditation can also become addictive if they become compulsive and their accomplishment becomes the measure of our well-being. Then although we are not so endangered as we are in less positive addictions, we may still lack the sovereign flexibility to keep creative pace with the goddess and Self's ever changing requirements and learn to accept reality without judgmentalism, with what Buddhism calls a "clear mind."

Such a clear mind is essential to permit the embrace of the hag, for it enables seeing beyond the culturally supported dualisms that make her temporary state so revolting. Jung must have come from such clarity regarding his own personal experience of reality when he quoted the Roman slave Terence who wrote,

I count nothing human alien to me.[23]

This cognitive acceptance is the remarkable first step. But it is not the last. Acceptance does not mean to act out or condone the harmful acting out of the vast potential of emotions that are part of human reality. Rather it means to witness them all as part of our animal, human, and godlike natures with as much spacious humor, humility, and equanimity as possible. From this perspective we can learn to see without bias and still remain responsible for the discipline and consequences of our actions.

To *act* from such a true knowledge of reality, we also need more. We need, like the initiated king and those working on the eleventh step of AA, to claim our intuitive "knowledge of [divine] will . . . and the power to carry that out." Life inevitably brings profound quandaries and stress. While they are not necessarily our fault, they may be our responsibility. Sometimes we can rule over our old habits of fear and guilty overresponsibility to learn how to accept such loathsome encounters. Sometimes we must oppose their injurious acting out with all the courage we can muster and always search for "the wisdom to know the difference." AA has aptly enshrined this crucial dilemma in an appropriately central context in the Serenity Prayer:

God grant me the serenity to accept
the things I cannot change,
courage to change the things I can,
and the wisdom to know the difference.

I can think of no more difficult and important a goal for recovery and all of living.

Clinical Examples

When paradigmatic cultural change is in process as it is today, the vision of the exile is extremely precious. It is perhaps even essential in order to create new standards that can inform perception, cognition, and ethics in a new age. But the transition to such a new perspective requires, as the loathsome damsel told Niall, a capacity to suffer through the chaos and backlash battles from the now threatened old standard bearers. In fear and power-driven fundamentalism, the old rulers lash out. Thus the beginning of any cultural shift is fraught with chaos, which forces the new ruling dominant to become conscious of alienation, humility, entitlement, and courage.

These capacities are required on an individual level as well as on a cultural one. For example, a young man with multiple addictions was working in therapy to gain and integrate a coherent sense of himself. He alternated between images of himself as grandiose or worthless; he raged or he abdicated sycophantically. In a dream he met the loathsome damsel as a symbol of loathsome dependency:

I see a hideous woman, big-lipped, slobbery, vampire-like, evil. She's needy, greedy, sucking. Agh. I try to get away from her.

In the dream the dreamer tried to repudiate the loathsome damsel—the horribly devalued, shameful neediness and hunger for affection that are part of life. In identification with the values of his family, he feared these qualities as if they were an evil vampire. But in life he could not escape them. Thus he projected dependency and found himself involved with draining men and women partners. In his early personal experience his narcissistic mother had, as he put it, "sucked off" of him, and he had both loved and hated her suffocating need for him. In order to be the holding parent for her neediness, he had been forced to develop so precociously that he had virtually no childhood. His own repressed dependency needs began to appear in therapy, but they felt loathsome and frighteningly infantile. Still connected to the archaic self, they also had a compelling numinosity. The dreamer feared these needs would devour him as he felt his mother's attentions and demands had done. Indeed, they threatened his identification with the delusional intellectual omnipotence with which he controlled his mother complex and that still functioned as his defender persona-ego. Mixed with his experience of the suffocating death mother, his own needy hunger was sucking for nourishment. Rather than run away, he needed to find the courage to embrace his dependency in order for him to discover and sustain his full psychological territory, a matrix that could hold both sides of his splitting. Only then could he find integrated and appropriate regal power and authority.

Another recovering male alcoholic had switched his addiction to sex. He pursued fascinating troubled and needy women with whom he could fuse in sexual bliss. Soon after he had achieved a sexual liaison, he discovered that each one began to shapeshift in his consciousness into a domineering terror. She then reminded him of his experience of his mother, and his projection in turn induced a maternal possessive domination in his partner. Afraid to leave the relationship and to suffer the woman's hurt and rage and his own abandonment again, he took up with another woman and let the first change fully in his mind into a demanding tyrant. "I go through life," he began to realize, "from one woman to the next like I used to go from one drink to the next." Through role playing in therapy he began to learn the battle skills of the warrior Maeve to stand up to the tyrannical women whom he felt populated the world. In doing so he found he had to face his fear of a loathsome monster, a Medusa that paralyzed him, in order to reclaim some of the power and authority that had been projected onto women like his mother. In the week after he had confronted both a coworker and his female therapist he dreamt:

I am back in my childhood house. I hear a noise and realize it is a
killer monster. There is a door slowly opening. That's where she is. I
am terrified. But instead of fleeing, I rip open the door, and grab the
monster and start to strangle her. It's my mother. I wake up, as
terrified of my murderousness as I had been of the monster.

In sessions he began to face the loathsome and murderous rage and tyranny that he projected onto women as well as his fear of abandonment if he choked the terrible mother. It took him many months to begin to embrace these emotions as acceptable power and need that were authentic aspects of his own identity.

Therapists are also repeatedly confronted with a need to expand their consciousness. This serves as an important source of continuing growth for the healer whose wholeness is also never complete. In therapy I experienced the loathsome hag in relation to a client whom I found to be hateful. A cruelly mothered woman who had became a workaholic and food addict was possessed by a sadistic superego. She was emotionally abusing her own child to relieve her stress because she felt herself to be such an inadequate mother and "to beat some decent behavior and ambition into" the little girl. I was revolted and for some time found myself silently enraged. Blaming her as her own mother had done rather than feeling empathic with her suffering, I fell into identifying with the projection of the rejective mother that she was inducing in me. I was almost unable to bear working with the client. In order to continue our analytic work, I had to confront the loathsome reality of a malevolent and demanding force that was larger than her personal life, that is an aspect of reality itself—the cruel, child-hating, and devouring transpersonal itself. I needed to embrace my own relation to that vast destructiveness, to experience how it had hurt me and how it also operated through me, to see if it might even contain some neutral and valuable energy that I still needed to integrate. Only through such work on myself could I embrace the work with my client to help her to begin to separate from possession by the malevolent force and much later to struggle toward more conscious integration of aspects of the power into her relationships.[24] At first I did not want to acknowledge such loathsomeness. I had to struggle to see that by hating my client rather than finding a place in myself from which to empathize and companion her through the destructiveness, I was also caught in the transpersonal, loathsome contempt that fueled her abuse. I struggled with the help of a trusted colleague to realize how I participated in malevolence against another who could not yet help herself.[25] Finally I dreamt I was "given a cup full of foul body fluids to drink." It was a terrible communion. I think now it must have been one of Maeve's many cups of sovereignty. For as I worked on my own abuse complex in response to my client's analysis, I could begin to rule with some consciousness over my own fear of the annihilating, dark powers without fleeing into ideals and righteous feelings—a pattern that was once as familiar and blindly habitual as any other addiction.[26]

In our relationships to other people, the embrace and incorporation of the qualities of the loathsome hag can bring a greater degree of acceptance and recognition of our mutual humanity. We are not then tempted to see ourselves as false kings who can feel arrogantly righteous. But such sacrifice of judgmentalism requires an empathic feeling capacity for the other and oneself that is based on recognition of the power and reality of the multivalent transpersonal, which exists beyond human categories of good and evil, beautiful and ugly.[27] Thus, such empathy is quite separate from collective superego ideals that split reality into good and bad while they urge us to be kind to or pity the bad. It results from an embrace of the goddess of life's reality—Maeve, as she is, in all her fear and fascination, horror and bounty. When this form of compassion operates within the psyche, a hidden beauty can shine or a handicap can be seen as a gift. When it operates within relationships, what is felt as loathsome in the self and in the other may be transformed as it is companioned and mutually embraced.

When, however, a parent or partner sees us as the loathsome hag and cannot therefore relate to us, we may feel the profound abandonment that may turn into shame and self-loathing. We are then threatened with abandoning our own sovereignty, sometimes even wishing to abandon life itself. One woman in recovery reported disappointment with her lover. When she expressed her passionate intensity to him, he saw it only as "bitchy and ugly." This is what she wrote:

*When G sees my naked force, he is petrified and does not feel its
beauty, but freezes— as if I am as gruesome as the Gorgon. He
cannot accept his fear and still hold his ground or me. So I feel
abandoned and have to struggle not to abandon myself and my
feelings and feel suicidal, or to turn even more gruesome and get
defensively savage. At least now I know, from a Self place, that the
intensity is valid. But its power is not acceptable to G. It's as if he
wants security more than relationship. . . . Then I am left either to
turn soft and pliant and seduce him back into relationship or to tell
him to leave, and know my strength and beauty anyway, but alone.
. . . I know it is his boy's terror of his mother. But I so much want
him braver and as strong as me—to be with.*

When such necessary acceptance is not present in
childhood's intimate relationships, there is the difficult
struggle to find it elsewhere. This hunger can fuel the love
addict's search. Since, however, the addictive seeker for the
accepting beloved has been imprinted with the initial image
of a rejecting partner, the searcher grabs for acceptance in the
wrong sources, as this woman continued to do. The images of
the archetypal patterns of mother/child and Self have been
deeply skewed by their imperfect personal constellation. The
experience of bonding was conjoined with those of rejection
and alienation. In therapy this desperate dissonance can be
worked with as the analyst receives the transference of both
sides of the archetypal image and serves as the constant other
with whom a sense of integration can be created. Then the
Self, as a wholeness pattern encompassing the terrible
experience of split opposites, can be mediated. Its images,
often first projected onto the therapist and the process of
therapy itself, can ultimately be known as a constant source
within one's psychic depths and also in all kinds of life-
enhancing relationships.

The loathsome damsel as an archetype always
holds more than personal shadow. She is the guardian of the
wellspring of life, the goddess who tests us to see if our ego
consciousness is in close enough relation to our Self to be
capable of accepting and metabolizing the reality we see
when we are given those expansive and intoxicating waters.[28]
Maeve in all her multiplicity and power manifests like
Jahweh to Job, as a terrifying epiphany of the reality of life's

fullness with which we must ever and again relate. In her m
we hear that men were deprived of "two-thirds of their strer
when they encountered her.

One workaholic man's dream provided him witl
frightening and awesome sense of the loathsome damsel eve
it provided the fulcrum for change in his life patterns. He dr

*I go into the cellar and find the ugliest person I have ever seen—like a
monster from outer space. She asks me to drink her urine, and for some
reason I do. I am flooded with ecstasy, light. I wake horrified.*

The dreamer associated the cellar to the one in the house in
which he grew up—a dark, musty storage area far from the
family veneer of cheery sociability, the covering denial of the
alcohol problems. Urine he associated to beer, his own binge
drink of choice. About the concept ugly he said,

*My creative, quirky individuality was ugly to the church and my holy,
alcoholic mother with all her [facades of] goody two shoes and
everything-is-fine . . . . Until I went under in college, that originality
came out with my peers. It's what got me the editorship of the literary
journal, but my parents thought that was ridiculous, no way to make
money. And if I wasn't going to be rich at least I should calm down and
go into the church. So I resigned [from the journal] and began working
furiously and then binge drinking.*

The monster was like the horrific queen in a science fiction
Like a giant insect she devoured ruthlessly and produced
offspring. She represented a chthonic life power that terrifie
him. From one perspective she was the force that once ensla
his parents to addiction and that made him succumb to their
authority when he betrayed his calling as a writer. Here rath
than enslaving him, however, she invites him to partake of
intimate communion with her in order to claim the joy and
consciousness of his own sovereignty. And it is not beer he i
drink but the tabooed flow of creative Self expression pourir
from the still loathsome muse.

The archetype of the hideous damsel often appe
modern dreams with such numinosity to mark crucial
confrontations with creative powers once lost in the shadow

Often enough the therapist must help the dreamer to find equanimity and to reverence her. A woman I did not know, whom I later realized might be "addicted to perfection,"[29] called me late one night to tell me a dream. I said I did not know her and could not help with her dream. She persisted. I said it was not my custom to work on dreams with strangers or on the phone and asked if she wanted a consultation. Without answering, she nonetheless began intently to tell me her dream:

There is a terrible goddess in a cave. She is bloody and menstruating, with an awful face. She takes a child who runs in towards her, crying, "Mommy, Mommy," and pops the child into her mouth. I rage, "How dare you take this child. It's mine." She says to me, "Then you have to give up everything, be eaten alive." I say, "All right then." She holds me up to her eyes which suck me in like two black holes. They take all except my soul. Then she puts me down and I find that the throne revolves. It turns and I see a beautiful, transformed goddess, giving birth to a new child. I am given it to care for and take it back upstairs with me. I felt wonderful, energized for days.

Then without pause she said her male analyst didn't "get" the dream. She knew it held more than his interpretation—that she was "meeting all her discarded self, dark and angry, and she needed to get into that, not be so pristine; then she could be messy and creative." Her tone was light, but she was possessed by that terrible outflowing dark goddess energy in her demand that I listen. I felt the implacable power of the numinosity and the compulsion in the dream and her tone. But there was also an inappropriateness in the situation that I needed to address to humanize that transpersonal power. I referred her to her analyst, saying she had a lot to discuss with him. And I asked her if she was aware that she was taking time I had not chosen to give her, impressively and ruthless claiming what she wanted. She said, "Oh dear, I thought you wouldn't answer the phone." "Well," I said, "I did and told you I couldn't help you, and you didn't stop yourself; you just took over." Ruefully she agreed. I paused and then continued, "That was very impressive, and I suppose I could congratulate you. You enacted that bloody, devouring, powerful goddess." She laughingly agreed, and I went on.

"You are acting like that fierce goddess, but are you aware that your tone is light and laughing, far from the tough demandingness that you are *doing*?" She was silent for a moment and then said, "Something will happen if I don't laugh." I told her there was indeed a lot to take back to her analyst. And we hung up. Though she did not give her name, she gave me an example of the process of claiming sovereignty.[30] She was in an early, relatively unconscious stage in the process, where action and image are intermingled, where loathsome hag and ego are in identity and need a mirror and some kind of kiss to reflect, separate, and join them more appropriately.

Exploring Shadow

We can work with the image of the loathsome damsel in many ways outside of therapy as well as in it. We can wonder at different times in our lives what feels intolerable or loathsome. We can ask ourselves to sense viscerally its revoltingness for that is the clue to its verity. With a gesture or grimace or sound we can bodily express the revulsion. We can describe it in an artistic form in all its ugliness and power. We can ask ourselves when that revolting thing was done *to* us and find what memories it may stir. Then if we can put the rank revulsion aside, we can try to feel the quality that seemed revolting as it is in itself. We may be able to feel the quality under our learned revulsion as the expression of a powerful neutral energy. We can wonder further what it would mean to us personally to embrace that quality and to relate to it as a human energy available to us, as part of our own capacity to serve life. We can ask ourselves how that would feel, what it would contribute to our repertoire of available emotions, thoughts, and energies if we embraced that quality. We might find in it a strength and awareness to claim and expand our own sovereignty as we worked to integrate it into our personal lives and relationships.

Chapter 10

Maeve as Divine Appetite

The root is not the drinking, *but the* desire *to drink.*

—Mark Twain, *Following the Equator*

Compulsion is the great mystery of human life. It is the thwarting of our conscious will and of our reason by an inflammable element within us, appearing now as a consuming fire and now as life-giving warmth.

—C. G. Jung, *CW 14*

What is behind all this desirousness? A thirsting for the eternal.

—C. G. Jung, *CW 14*

Dostoevsky wrote to his wife of his own addiction: "I am not just an unscrupulous creature—I am a man devoured by the passion for gambling." He lived possessed by his own lust to win. Even as he was repeatedly losing the money he begged, he sought to "try [to] catch up," or to "hav[e] a last try" to win more. His compulsion brought him nausea and despair, self-hatred and humiliation. It caused him repeatedly to break promises that he was through with gambling.[1] Having once again lost the rescue money his pregnant, penniless, and ever-supportive wife always sent him, he finally confided to her that though he was "devoured by the passion," he knew it granted only an illusion of sustenance. He wrote, "the mirage has been dispersed once and for all and I feel I have been released from this delusion."[2] Indeed with this confession and the accompanying remorse and other emotions, he was suddenly able to recover from his addictive compulsion. He never gambled again.

What is this overwhelming passion at the source of addiction? "Brain-reward circuits"[3] stimulated by habit-forming outer (chemical) and/or inner (hormonal) substances may be a physical means through which the impulse expresses itself. But addiction cannot be reduced to its neural function alone. Addictive behaviors are driven by compulsions that operate even when, like Dostoevsky's, they are pain filled and destructive of life. They operate even after the compulsive behaviors and attachments to mind-altering substances no longer create pleasurable highs. They can grip and twist us like dry heaves in spite of will and health and even sanity. On the other hand addictive behaviors can go into remission. The brain-reward feedback circuit, which calls for inevitable, repeated restimulation, cannot account for Dostoevsky's spontaneous recovery, nor even for the effects of long-term recovery programs.

The overwhelming passion lies deeper and wider than mere brain chemistry. Freud wrote that Dostoevsky's gambling was a repetitive, immature, masturbatory compulsion with opportunities for self-punishment. He asserted that the gambler even enjoyed abasing himself in floods of contrition before his young wife after losing money, much as he might have when expecting punishment from a feared father for indulging in autoerotic satisfaction.[4] This explanation reduces addiction to Oedipal and sado-masochistic dynamics. Freud's view of libido does not take into account the aims of our drives beyond those of infantile pleasure seeking and death itself. Jung, however, pointed to the "inflammable element within us" as also having another source and goal. While it has one root in the infantile shadow propelling us to seek the basic gratifications and human relatedness on which we depend, the other root lies in "mystery." By this Jung meant that one of the propelling forces lies beyond and ahead of consciousness in the spiritual dimension. Jung noted that what he called the spiritual instinct is as gripping and purposive as the drives ensuring physical survival.[5] It underlies the human quest for meaning and the passion that drives us towards wholeness. It motivates us to become what we are meant to be.[6] And, as Jung recognized, it is a potent force in addiction.[7]

Dostoevsky himself had written five years before he was able to forego his own craving for gambling that the desperate hero of his novel *The Gambler* "expected so much of roulette."[8] Not only would it gain him the comforts of wealth and the means to gain his love object, but also, for him, "Roulette is the only solution and salvation."[9] Dostoevsky thus intuited that gambling connects his hero to meaning and the salvific powers that he desperately seeks, albeit as the writer himself recognized later, in delusional form. Anticipating Jung, Dostoevsky expresses his awareness of the lust fueling addiction as the pursuit not only of material and erotic/relational values but also transcendent ones. We have seen how some contemporary addicts also call their crack "god" because it "transforms despair into heaven."[10]

Recognizing that the compulsion underlying addiction arises out of basic life energy coursing into physiological, relational, and spiritual drives, we can remember that in Irish myth the goddess Maeve herself symbolizes the principle of dynamic activity that lies at the base of all of these. She and her sister figures (among them the heraldically displayed females called Sheela-na-gigs that we have discussed among Maeve's portraits) manifest in image form the polymorphous, basic energy of divine appetite coursing through all our passionate hungers and quests. Commanding and claiming her many lovers with her insatiable erotic hungers, Maeve represents the libido that creates our capacity for passionate participation in life. She motivates our grasping to incorporate what species and individual development requires for us, the reaching toward whatever would support growth and the equally important aversion against what might destroy integrity. Supporting oral, assertive and/or aggresssive, and genital hungers, she ensures that we survive. Supporting spiritual hungers, she enforces on those who are ready for them the inebriating expansive deaths and transformations of initiations through which we develop.

Maeve is both the compelling force of divine entitlement and the archetypal appetite necessary to support its fulfillment. She arouses the fierce thirsts that poets and prophets the world over have used as metaphors for all our emotional and spiritual cravings. Exhibiting her thighs and enormous genitalia and/or her cup of inebriating, sacred mead, she is also an image of the font that can assuage our inflamed longings, the mystery of the abysmal encompassing source. While this source is often imaged as the containing mother from whom we have emerged and whom we seek and return to in her many incarnations when we are needy and stressed, it can as well be the adult's beloved partner and the visionary's muse or godhead. In blissful immersion in this source, we may open ecstatically to dimensions beyond ordinary consciousness of time, space, and person.

Maeve's fiery appetite may thus lead us to burn beyond our previous limits as we pursue our desires—as the phallic arrows of the Greek god Eros compelled his victims. Thus she motivated many warriors in *The Tain* to fight to their death for a place in her own or her daughter's bed. But Maeve's appetite in us is also more incorporative. Just as her pleasure requires a line of "one man waiting in the shadow of the next," so the intensely active receptivity of the feminine Self vessel requires us to take in all kinds of experience and to suffer within us the fires of passions that enliven and nourish us. Striving for the satisfaction of such embracing desire even when it may threaten to overwhelm us, the hunger for life leads us to taste and learn through assimilation, to experience the many possibilities that tempt our appetites. Inevitably we may learn to curtail the fillings that leave us untransformed and disappointedly empty or poisoned. But through all of these encounters, we may come to discover what we like and, indeed, what and who we are.

The ancient Chinese book of wisdom, the *I Ching*, asks us to notice what a person seeks for nourishment in order to assess his or her personality.[11] Maeve's craving is such that she "needed thirty men or go with [the god] Fergus once." Archetypal appetite is ferocious, anonymous, and quantitative unless it meets the divine partner and receives fitting satisfaction. This suggests that Maeve can represent the raw craving that has no prejudices and few discriminations in its search for ultimate satisfaction. We find such impersonal appetite most obviously expressed in the cries of a hungry infant, who may suckle ravenously from any available breast even when its stomach must later eject the milk that did not match its particular body's requirements. (A similar clamor is a concomitant of the sexual drive as it rushes through adolescence.) The force of the drive ensures survival before there can be consciousness of individual requirements and the effectiveness to find and claim them. Thus we experience need on an archetypal level before we have an ego to desire and support the intentionality required to fulfill our desires.

We know that when infant needs are met well enough and frustrated within bearable limits by a caretaker representing the bountiful transpersonal source, the child learns both to trust and to wait. She or he can learn to develop the innate capacities for discrimination that are already observable in newborns. When such needs are not optimally met, the craving for indiscriminate quantity that can be the incarnated substitute for spiritual quality becomes a primary factor in addictions. Then concrete quantitative need satisfaction is confused with or polarized against an ideal of bliss: thirty men equal (or are opposed by) Maeve's one divine lover Fergus.[12] Little psychological and spiritual clarity is available to distinguish quantity from quality or to perceive spiritual qualities incarnated in a single experience. We seek more rather than more deeply. We seek excitement and novelty as if they were substitutes for quality. We become greed possessed and increasingly indiscriminate.

In our society we find our addictive troubles amplified as businesses actively compete with one another for expanded, quantitative markets to promote consumption. Our appetites are piqued by advertising that suggests quantity and current fashion could fill the vacuum in our body-Self and assuage all the needs that waken in us through our bodies. We are tempted to believe we will become magically attractive, intellectually deep, materially rich, and spiritually fulfilled if we use a particular product or follow a particular prescription. An example of such perversion on the theme of indiscriminate appetite is reflected in the advertisement of a construction company that displayed the picture of a woman in a bathing suit on its newly erected brick wall with the coarse caption, "We lay anything!"

We start with raw need, but we can transform our relationship to the wild energy. When we find and trust our access to an archetypal source (in whatever forms and figures it is incarnated), we may be freed to forego starved gobbling. Then greed's propulsive, quantitative sweep in us can pause, and we can begin to sense fully and savor what currently satisfies the divine appetite in us. The grip of the archetypal drive on us changes from rampant greed to desire, enabling us to learn to discriminate aesthetic and spiritual qualities. From this transpersonal perspective as the hunger feels truly and well-enough met, we can feel secure enough to trust the joys of temporary fullness and reflect on bearable frustrations. Then Maeve's hungers can serve to stoke curiosity and refined feeling judgments. Greed can become appetite, need can soften into appreciation and create strategies to obtain legitimate satisfaction. Maeve's hungers within the matrix of plenty can thus fuel the acquisition and development of deeply individual tastes. These come about through the inevitable reality that once filled we can rest, but we are soon empty again, feeling hunger and longing, forced to suffer and manifest the ever recurring pangs of desire. Thus though appetite remains fueled by primary drives, the tastes that seek to slake it can change and develop. We can be led to forego what once satisfied in order to seek and claim anew, hence to expand and deepen throughout life, ever moving towards the wholeness that beckons and evades our grasp.

On the other hand, when we are not fostered bountifully enough, when the matrix has been fragmented and we cannot find an adequate-enough source, then Maeve represents the force of rampant appetite, the craving that can never get enough, that knows only lack and the hunger for more and more to fill the endless maw. She inflicts the addictions that bind us in compulsive repetitions of our raw neediness. These focus and partially express their force and yet forbid their differentiation and development. They spin us in wild eddies separated from the currents of developing life.

Maeve's Wild Pigs

The aristocratic Celts, with their rampant intensities and love for sensuous beauty, struggled with the problem of raw need and its discriminations and development. We have seen one tale in which only Maeve and her consort were able to count and disperse the wild pigs that burst out of the cave of Cruachan to ravage the fields so fiercely that the land was blighted for seven years.

What might this mean psychologically? The wild pigs here represent our compulsively rampant appetites. Counting them involves a process of conscious ordering. When we count, we recognize the similar thing or event as it occurs over and over. We are no longer blinded by the force of the mass but can mentally break it up into distinct events. Each one is then given a number through the abstracting power of human thought. This simple ordering allows the real incoherence of what grips us unconsciously to effect us differently. It allows a new relationship to emerge through comprehension. In the myth Maeve provides the ordering system, for only an archetypal form principle can begin to sense and sort the omnivorous drives that are also aspects of

Maeve herself. We see here how the Celts intuited the deep
balance within nature, recognizing that both drive and
number, both energy and discrimination are part of one
whole. They saw that an archetypal rational order coexists
with and can begin to clarify what was a blind compulsive
field. Rather than seeking to repress the drive, the Celts
celebrated a way to mediate and humanize its force. Maeve in
human form orders Maeve's porcine rampage.

In therapy we might follow Maeve to encourage
clients to use numbers and a calendar to help them become
conscious of how often and when the grip of archetypal affect
or addictive behavior seizes. Weight Watchers passes out
sheets to record all second helpings eaten. Smoke Enders
starts by counting the number of cigarettes smoked each day.
Such discriminations begin to clear the space for a conscious
observing function. We also number to prioritize and
determine an order among clamoring needs or emotions that
all seem equally tumultuous at first. When this is done with a
descriptive perspective rather than with the judgmentalism of
the anti-libidinous superego, a conscious core of the
personality can begin to coalesce and relate to the various
drives by seeing how they find their balanced places within
the overall experience of need. The development of such
consciousness also enables some limitations of drive energies
and allows for appropriate dosages of satisfaction that are
related to an individual sense of wholeness. Eventually these
reveal the pattern of necessary desires seeking balanced play
within the personality and establish the basis of a system of
priorities that represent the values that Maeve or the highest
Self gives for each of us.

In human form the goddess-queen assesses the
quantity of her pigs. Through numbering, she discriminates
and thus gains some power over the ravenous foragers that
pour directly and unmediated from the caves of the
underworld. Counting itself, however, is never enough. After
making a count of the swine, Maeve is threatened by one that
jumps over her chariot. Its leap over her head suggests the

inevitable backlash of primitive appetite that evades rational controls. It represents raw compulsivity attempting to reassert its dominion over human order. Just as we are often called to demonstrate that we can manifest the Self's perspective—one that is beyond rational order—even Maeve in the story is not yet finished dealing with the problem of her plunderers. This time she grabs the representative of archaic oral greed in her hand and holds it. In the grip that is a distinctive mark of humans, between the opposites of fingers and thumb, she seizes the one-pointed onrushing maw. Held fast, its hind leg and skin come off in her hand, and with them she gains power over the whole herd. Only then do they disappear, never more to devour the crops of Maeve's people.[13]

The pig is dismembered and gives up one of the legs on which primary greed stood and ran amok.[14] It also gives up its skin to her. We know that in many fairy tales when a person claims the skin of an enchanted animal, that animal must remain humanized. Here Maeve in human form takes ownership of the original porcine container of the drive. Its thick, hairy skin can now be transformed into whatever containers best express the goddess' requirements for the human transformation of oral greed into desire.

The Myth of the Goddess' Sack

In a Welsh myth about the goddess Rhiannon and her wondrous bag, we find some of the issues of this trans-formation masterfully laid out.[15] Renowned for her beauty and the exquisite magic of her singing birds, Rhiannon is similar to Maeve, a mare goddess and a deity of the earth and tribal sovereignty. In a wonderful story she chooses the chieftain Pwyll as her consort and invites him to celebrate their marriage at the feast she goes to grow and then prepare for table. At year's end seated beside his sovereignty-bestowing goddess and desiring to be known as a good and generous king, Pwyll finds himself confronted by a man he does not recognize. The man asks for a boon but does not define it. With regal but premature and too casual generosity, Pwyll offers his wedding guest anything as if he were himself the source of bounty that the goddess is. Unknown to Pwyll, the man is Rhiannon's previously rejected suitor. Sneaking to gain his bride without her consent, he now boldly chooses her person and her marriage banquet. Honor bound to comply with the request, Pwyll finds his arrogance has spoiled his own destiny. The goddess intercedes to proclaim her requirements and to rescue her chosen consort. She asserts that the feast is hers alone to give, and she refuses. To avoid shaming her beloved further, however, she agrees to his rival's claim of marriage but insists on postponing the rites for another year. Secretly she tells Pwyll to come to the next wedding feast as a beggar, and she gives him her magical bag, telling him to request only enough food to fill it.

When Rhiannon's chosen consort comes to his rival's marriage banquet, his disguise manifests his own need and his now conscious dependency. The identity of beggar thus creates a balancing opposition to his previously inflated arrogance and fraudulent generosity. Carrying Rhiannon's sack and obeying her advice, he begs for just enough food to fill the bag. Pwyll's usurping rival, thinking it a little thing to feed a beggar with such a little sack, grants the request. He does not know he is meeting a just redress for his own trickery. He does not know that the sack represents the bountiful goddess at his side in her deathly depriving form, the form that mirrors his own rapaciousness. He orders portions of the marriage feast to be piled into the bag. But the bag is an all-engulfing maw. It consumes everything that is put into it. It will devour the whole feast; the guests will go unsatisfied. No king can claim to rule in Celtdom when there is not enough food since lack of plenty suggests the goddess of the land holds him in disfavor.

At Rhiannon's urging the eager claimant finally gets up to stamp on the food and end the bag's devouring. Putting both feet into the sack, he is lost "over his head in the bag." As he is consumed, Pwyll calls out his hidden helpers to pummel the bag and destroy him. Rhiannon having thus disposed of the unfavored suitor, claims her currently chosen lover, and her feast and story and her sovereign process continue.

This magical bag represents the goddess' powers of fertility and famine, bounty and deathly destruction. The primal womb that might pour forth for the chosen king is, for the greedy usurper, as empty and ravenously devouring as the wild pigs of Cruachan or an emaciated Sheela-na-gig. Like a reversed cornucopia or grasping vagina,[16] it consumes all, threatening to bring about the famine that the Celts felt resulted from thwarting any destined, transcendent process.[17] Like barren soil or a black hole, like the blighting ravages of nature and addiction, the little sack mirrors the usurper's greed. Because he has overstepped his authority in claiming Maeve, he is forced to submit to the earth goddess. Her sack becomes his tomb as she orders her chosen Pwyll to have his men crush the usurper in what the story describes as the beginning of the cruel sport of beating a badger in a bag.

The Motif of the Bag in Modern Addiction

In modern dreams the power of the devouring vessel may appear in images of substance abusers, rapacious beggars, starving beasts, "a mass of quicksand," or "a wastebasket into which everything on the desk keeps falling." These images are harbingers of still unconscious problems with need satisfaction. They suggest the desperate omnivorousness of archetypal appetite when there is extreme destitution. We can sometimes see comparable wild compensatory greed unleashed in society during rampages or wars following natural or political disasters. Feelings or fears of extreme scarcity evoke such ravenous need. Miserable poverty invites it. Inevitably it arises in an individual's life when the appropriate unfolding of developmental needs has been unmet or distorted. When in infancy we are deprived of experiences of constant-enough bounty and the empathic attention that is necessary to mirror and enjoy our infantile needs and style of expressing them, our desirousness feels destitute and despairing. We remain fixated with seeing ourselves from an internalized perspective that cannot appreciate and support our own desirousness. The vital motivating force of desire cannot be developed and refined in us.

Instead we remain stuck with rageful raw neediness and its requirements for concrete fulfillment. In areas of traumatic deprivation we cannot even relax enough to soothe ourselves with images of adequate-enough satisfaction and thus develop a symbolic relation to desire. Although we may learn to conceal our neediness even from ourselves, the thwarted archetypal passions remain in the unconscious and may seduce us to soothe them with behaviors and substances that only lead us further into unassuageable need. Ultimately they must erupt, like the supernatural wild pigs from their cave, as furious cravings that are as primitive as they were in infancy. Their force is made greater by panics—projected from early experience of loss into the endless future—that the uninhibited cravings can never be met or will again alienate or even destroy the giver, leaving us only with more deprivation and terrible shame, abandonment, and desperate attempts to hide or self-limit. Usually the images express the client's still unconscious experiences of parental complexes and the furious starvation left from unmet needs. But they may also represent the autonomous, devouring energies that operate through the pre-ego to spoil bonds to whatever might begin to be nourishing because the present potential stimulates repetition of the painful feelings of despairing loss and helpless rage. Thus in the beginning of therapy such images often convey the quality of spoiling envy that can destroy the therapeutic process, taking displaced revenge on its more bountiful constancy for the losses experienced in early life.

The devouring fear-ringed desire that manifests in these images seizes like spasms of hunger. Jung spoke of this in terms that well describe the destructive power of Maeve's wild pigs and Rhiannon's sack. It is, he says,

a hunger which just wants to eat and assimilate everything. It is that which always wants more and more . . . . It is like the abyss of death; the mouth never shuts; there is only the demand for more. It is a kind of driven passion of eating and eating, and it generally results from an early childhood experience where the child was starved and deprived of love or some other vital need on the psychological and physical level. . . . [T]here is no end to it. It is a divine/demonic quality. [18]

Perhaps not all individuals who suffer this kind of voracious need become addicts, but many of us have pockets of such "divine/demonic" hungers connected to addictive elements in us or as part of a compulsively repetitive complex that manifests in life even as it both expresses and eats at our life energy. Addiction itself is a specific pathology of desire. We can think of it as a complex, the core of which is archetypal need ringed with particular defenses that deny, distract, partially calm, and even focus the divine appetite. It may claim some small parts of our psychic geographies or vast expanses. It expresses itself through "a kind of driven passion" arising out of the deprivation that leaves a voracious black hole in the psyche. The drive to fill this hole is archetypal. It is like the herd of wild devouring swine. Addiction is, however, both the habitual manifestation of primitive need, expressing primal impoverishment through its compulsive attachments, and a defense against the pain of the raw craving. Although it arises out of deprivation, the addiction still honors, momentarily assuages, and even focuses the hunger behind it serving as a distorted and too often destructive form of reverence for appetite itself. As a woman in recovery put it:

I have been terrified of the energy in wanting. It overpowers me, and I feel ashamed of being that full of greed . . . . [On the other hand] from here [in recovery], I can see I tried to press the range of my whole life's needs into one addiction.

Another said:

> *[I am always] craving more because nothing has ever been enough.*
> *. . . That familiar, desperate hunger has been home. . . . Anyone [as]*
> *hungry would have to grab something. I went for drugs. Now it's*
> *food or crises or men, sometimes work . . . . Underneath all the*
> *deprivation is a depressed, hungry baby, so grabby it scares people.*
> *They think I'll devour them. It scares me. . . . I feel like starvation,*
> *like a fierce animal that will burrow until it gets something or*
> *dies. . . . [Because] I've always chosen disappointing, short-term*
> *fillers, drugs or men [who are] very intense, who then drop me, I*
> *could always blame them for my problems and stay deprived. Until*
> *now I never had to face that the appetite itself was the problem. And*
> *mine to take care of in better ways than it ever has been.*[19]

When desire has not been adequately met and mediated within human relationship, it remains ravenous and impersonal in areas of the psyche that we medicate with addictions. Without an experience of good-enough satisfaction from a relatively constant source, desire remains on the magical level of consciousness, connected to illusory ideals of perfection. It wishes for magical, immediate satisfaction from a perfectly matched source that might prevent the pains of frustration that are equated with those of absolute deprivation. Existing in an environment of neglect and scarcity, its aims must be hidden, snatched, or connected to "appropriate" concrete surrogates that mask its deeper reality. Our culture provides access to alcohol and drugs, caffeine, sweet and starchy foods, nicotine, sex, over-driven work, and a host of other pain relievers and stimulants to temporarily deflect desire and stuff the holes of longing. An individualized relationship to archetypal desirousness can easily be diverted.

We know also that conscious relationship to driving need cannot adequately develop when there has been no positive mirror of worthiness from childhood to grant the cup of entitlement in which to receive. Consciousness cannot develop in areas of life where there is no experience of generosity or soothing support to enable us to tolerate the inevitable frustrations that occur when we are temporarily separated from the source of adequate bounty. Without such help we cannot discover and create the security to sense, support, focus, limit, and defend needs. We cannot count our Cruachan pigs, nor can we grab one to humanize its power. We are left instead with abject craving and the frenzy—"get more crack [or booze, adrenaline, sex, or whatever is the drug of choice]—fast."

When the drive to satisfy needs has been spoiled by the circumstances of early care, it also cannot develop. Instead the force of desire becomes split from its purpose. The spoiling fuels the archetypal emotions of despair that there was, is, and will never be enough, of shame that raw need persists and cannot be managed or controlled, of rage that both neediness and deprivation must haunt all relationships, and of fear that the consuming power of the craving will destroy us and others whom we cannot truly love as separate beings but only "fall into need for." These emotions create a fear of the drive towards need satisfaction and often of the unconscious itself. Their heat also enflames primary neediness. Their hormone-stimulated drives may mix with the primitive desire to confuse its aims and prevent receptivity, or the emotions may serve as displacements for the need itself and become habitual and even addictive.

In addictions, as we have seen repeatedly, the craving's intensity alternates with equally intense experience of separation and deprivation. The violent pulsations of enthralling desire and abandonment cleave the integrated cycle of desire in which both satisfaction and returning hunger are made manageable. Instead the two sides fall apart into opposites, and each part of the whole seems over-whelmingly global. Like the force in Tristan and Iseult's cup, the addictive passion tied to such intense experience can sweep us off our feet. It can lead to compulsive seeking of another drink, person, behavior, or chemical substance because that other holds the concretized projection of a physiologic, psychic, and spiritual content that we crave all the more fiercely because we feel so unbearably separated from it.

Because the individual's relation to desire cannot develop in the areas of traumatic deprivation, it often remains linked to the kinds of satisfactions that might actually or metaphorically assuage the needs of infancy. Thus while the person prone to addiction is still possessed by transpersonal energies and appetites, the focus of desire remains limited to concrete specifics: a particular substance or endocrine-altering pattern that can grant the sensations of blissful satiation and security that were too early and radically disrupted (or even the relative bliss of the alleviation of pain and deprivation depression). Repeatedly seeking to control and reclaim such experiences through the search for parts of people or concrete substances and behaviors, the individual cannot gain access to a perspective that permits symbolic realization, for within such a passionately intense focus there is little psychological space or energy to develop an array of actual and symbolic satisfactions. Thus the addict, although possessed by desire, does not really know how to relate to desirousness. There is no energy to learn to count pigs. Desire remains devouring and monstrous, an unlimited appetite.

My passions are not insulated, only squashed, so they go off "splat"—electrocuting people and myself . . . . Neediness shocks me, quite literally.

While there may be some attempt to hold such fearful voraciousness in check with arbitrary rules, the individual possessed in its grip can find no sense of self-regulation attuned to desirousness itself within the demands of time and situation.

I forget about want and don't want. That No side of wanting. I learned to take all and anything, or I'd get nothing. So I grab, even steal when the mood is on me . . . [fearing] there's never enough.

I avoid the deep, depressed suicidal place of deprivation, but I need desires to be in technicolor. They have to be intense and total, so overwhelming I'd kill myself, so strong they'll make me frantic and let me finally go totally passive . . . . I don't even notice faint wishes. I don't know how to find them. I can't just sit and wonder or reflect or go inside myself. That's too empty, too isolated.

On the other hand, need itself feels shame-ridden and abusive or endangering to the self and the other. As one recovering alcoholic put it:

I want to kill off wanting . . . . I know I'm a glutton, but I live on crumbs, make do with nothing [because] I fear retaliation. As if from God . . . . Probably originally from my [alcoholic] father because he never had much . . . [maybe even] hated me for having to give me the attention he never had.

In therapy, as in the rest of his life, this man expected envy from me rather than empathic pleasure in his enjoyment. He did his best to hide his deep neediness and, as he wished his father had done, he cared for it in others on whom it was projected. Only gradually he realized that he nonetheless managed to "stay deprived and resentful." This awareness helped him to begin to take his simmering resentments as clues to where his own needs lay.

A woman confessed her neediness to be "so bad, so disgusting" she defined it as selfishness, casting it out of her own identity and into the unconscious shadow. This gave her an illusion of righteousness and self-control. Finally, however, she revealed that all her life she had gone "in secret to the binge mother." Thus she had evaded the intense anguish of emptiness and been able to maintain a delusion that her deprivation was manageable and her own fault rather than a lack in her early environment. As she revealed with pride and unconscious self-spite:

When I was [an honor student] in high school, my mother used to ask me what I wanted. [It felt] as if it was a reward for making her proud. I was offended . . . . [I didn't want her] to think I had wants or desires or what was really true: a desperate need for sex. I masturbated a lot . . . . All that was hidden, and I hated myself. I was also unapproachable because I was fat as a pig with stuffing myself. Mother supported eating. I think food and pressure to do well in school was all she had to give us . . . . Finally I switched to drinking and smoking and got thin and lots of sex, too.

Since need must be effectively repressed to be safe from persecutory intrusiveness and envy, and/or "killed off" to be good in light of the caretaker's incapacity to give, the addict manages the still archaic libido by focusing it fervently into the addiction. Like Maeve with her line of impersonal lovers, the active addict manifests a split-off undiscriminated oral-genital lust that seeks its immediate gratification with a sense that almost anyone or anything with the right soothing, enlivening chemistry will do. On this primal level the unsatisfied and omnivorous appetite requires satisfactions only from adequately functioning body parts (breasts or genitalia) or surrogates for such part objects. The whole individual is relatively replaceable, as we tend to think is true in nature[20] and see in Maeve's compulsive lusts. Thus also experience of whole persons and the context of situations play little part in satisfaction, and the whole individual is usually not even held in consciousness, as we can see in the example below of a recovering alcoholic who followed a woman's red-stockinged legs. Neither the craved nor the craver exist fully in themselves; they are merely the font of an appetite to claim need and the broken basin to hold its very temporary satisfaction. Such primitive appetite[21] seizes those who participate in its terrors and ecstasies to compel their participation in unexpected and often extremely inappropriate partnerships. These may feel potentially freeing to the adult, since the onrush of appetite disrupts habit and convention. But such wild enmesments are fragile over time and cannot long survive a diminishment of the libidinous rush that brought them into being unless the passion is refueled by fear of loss or can develop into a destructive partnership of alternately enthralling merger and contemptuous repudiation. Such relationships embroil sex and relationship addicts, those "who love too much," just as they embroil addicts who love and hate the drugs or other substitutes for the missing relationship to the Self, which only temporarily fill their pervasive sense of existential emptiness.

Maeve's bold offer of her thighs can thus be experienced as the raw compulsion of nature without regard for limits, discriminations, or persons. Quantity overrides the discrimination of quality. Later courtly lovers could stand separate from their passions to savor them and to reflect in disciplined longing without immediate gratification. In the medieval Welsh myth we saw that Pwyll and his rival were each forced to wait for one year before they might receive gratification. But on the primal level of Maeve's all-commanding passion, there is little time or psychological space for reflection.[22] Maeve "never had one man without another waiting [for her favors] in his shadow."[23] Her pigs would not stop anywhere to be counted until she counted them herself. In the areas of addiction there is thus rarely any conscious experience of desire. Instead addicts suffer eruptive compulsion and/or passive resentful submission to a social standard that is often taken for individual desire. Personal need feels illegitimate at best and more often, a hateful or weak deficiency that is shameful. This shame may operate in relation to internalized parental and collective ideals—unless the addict feels outside of any relational bonds and order. The shame may also, however, operate in relation to the individual's center of authority and conscience (the Self in Jungian terms), for the internal flow of desirousness, which is one manifestation of life and the Self, goes unheeded.

In such an antilibidinous psychological environment, need cannot mature. One woman in early recovery complained enviously:

My wanting is an orphan, one part of me no parent ever noticed. It's not legitimate and I don't know anything about filling it . . . . I even feel ashamed with you [in therapy] because you obviously know how to find your wants and set your limits. I just feel shame and despair . . . . I want you to notice my needs without [my] telling you, but I hate you [for that] because then I feel so vulnerable . . . . I also hate you if you don't notice and satisfy them.

She went on to explain,

If anyone meets my needs, I melt into a baby and disappear as me. Once that happened when I went to the doctor with a terrible fever, and he was kind. All I could do was cry. It was terrible.

Another, turning the destructive envy back against herself in shame and despair, put it:

*I have nothing except empty and unfillable wanting, and that makes
me feel like [I am] a beggar, a bag lady, a total nothing. It's part of
me no one ever took care of, so I did my duty instead. Now I don't
know how to find and fill my needs . . . and I feel shame beside you
because you can. Shame and despair. . . and yes, anger.*

On the other hand, Maeve's offer of momentary
intense gratification is not easy to refuse because it touches
the borders where polymorphous erotic and aggressive
energies meet. Both frightening and fascinating in their
combustion, such energies may be distorted into a
destructive envy of the bounty of those outer others and
parts of the self that seem to thrive or may be twisted into
the violence that sustains the addiction itself. The aggression
may also turn into a power that fuels addiction. It may
operate against the recovering individual as the aggression
against Self that causes a slip and return to the primary
addiction. But it may also operate as an addiction to power
over others. We know that individuals of both genders who
are still in unconscious identity with the goddess as
archetypal desirousness may manage to bludgeon, seduce,
and cajole their way through life. When successful, their
bond with archaic impulses is never challenged. Instead
their identification supports cravings to merge and the
omnipotence that needs endlessly to conquer, but the
bully/seducers themselves remain without real
sovereignty and unable to develop a responsible empathic
ego.

Alcohol and drug addicts, no less than sex addicts,
are remarkable for their capacity to use and elicit another's
unconscious desirousness in such maneuvers. Their own
erotic and aggressive cravings may remain polymorphous,
and their charm and pathos can induce profound reciprocity
in those they entrap because such primal need and power
seek and arouse their own enthralling, symbiotic level in the
other. The archaic intensities stir up resonating emotional
depths in those related to the addict as underlings and codependents. They engender grand impersonal passions,
seemingly blissful fusions, and devotedly caring behavior in
partnerships based on compulsive patterns that replay

variations on the themes of power, abandonment, and need. Sometimes the addict will blame and bully the partner into compliance. Sometimes the partner will tempt the recovering addict into relapse. Sometimes in the shared fusion either or both will use self-pity, self-disparagement, and self-blame to evade responsible request or confrontation and engage in collusive and delusional caretaking. Often these attacks on the self are the result of reversed and covert angry challenges to the partner for exhibiting lack of patience with whatever current crisis is meant to seduce their continued enmeshment. While the need for a collusive partner is based in real fears and lack of objectivity and adaptive skills, these maneuvers also serve to control the other and to avoid the hard work of development necessary for a partnership of equals.

Acknowledging Need

If we return to the myth of Rhiannon, we find that it contains a pattern to help us begin to deal with the raw compulsive neediness that underlies addiction. In the myth, Rhainnon's bag is a manifestation of the goddess of life and death in process, and she decrees that destructive appetite will not be endless. It can be rebalanced and she shows us how. First, she insists that Pwyll become aware of his needs. He must count and catch them as Maeve did the pigs. Then only are they amenable to transformation. Second, Pwyll must experience loss and the real limitations his inflation has covered from his own awareness. The goddess makes him suffer a year's separation from his beloved, and then he must openly manifest the poverty that balances his arrogant generosity by wearing the identity of a beggar. Carrying the bag representing his own emptiness, he is sentenced to ask humbly from the very rival who shamed him and took his bride. Like first-steppers in AA, he is forced to recognize that he is no longer able to manage his fate. He cannot hide his own need for partnership with divine bounty.

Acknowledging such impoverishment is a major step for anyone gripped by an addiction since the addiction itself obviates the problems of divine appetite by providing a compelled and narrow focus for its play. There are humorous folk tales reminding us that when the drunkard is given three wishes by a supernatural donor, he immediately chooses a cup that will never be empty of drink. For his second and third wishes, without noticing his foolishness, he chooses another such cup and still another. Unlike the heroes of Irish myth who speak their three distinct wishes according to the demands of their unfolding destiny,[24] addicts are caught in the bonds of the monomania lashing them to rote repetition of their craving.

An alcoholic man expressed his inability to break free of his repetition compulsion:

I don't even know how to consult a place where I might know [what I really want]. Where could it be? Inside me somewhere? But I feel completely thick, without a space for finding and feeling in.

As we have seen, recovering addicts, having been bound by their desire for a fix or by some learned focus on arbitrary outer authority, have been cut off from interiority. They have little experience of embodied consciousness. Their devotion to intoxicants has maintained the fusion of mind and body in the primitive enmeshment of compulsion. But it has also separated social, persona consciousness (and their rebellioness against it) from the body sensations that could provide a clue to real needs and limits. Thus having no sense of inner articulation in addictive areas of life, these individuals can only experience desire as a compulsive onrush preventing awareness into felt emptiness or thick opacity. Through actual body work and through analytic focus on where and how sensations and desires arise in the body, consciousness can open to the subtleties of articulated interior bodily and cognitive space.

It is vitally important for the therapist to spend the slow time in therapy to ask how things taste and smell and feel, to learn about individual perceptions. Then it is also necessary to ask about specific individual preferences: what feels good to one's body and what doesn't feel good; what feels good in this place at this time with this person in this situation. Inevitably an essential focus must be on learning to become conscious of different levels of need. This eventuates in making priorities and staying loyal to them, so the deepest needs of the whole person are not lost to the next moment's craving or blocked by the superego's ideals or by old patterns of spoiling envy and fear of envy. Lived with, desire then becomes a tentative urge to play. It stimulates curiosity, an eagerness to explore and to know, a refined perceptivity, and a capacity to feel the heart's deepest yes and no. This capacity to discriminate sensitively and evaluate according to the individual Self's standards is what Jung described as the feeling function. It becomes a means to relate to the interiorly based aesthetic and spiritual authority that is the basis of the sense of one's unique individual selfhood.

Not only have many recovering addicts experienced their bodily preferences neglected in childhood, but often they have experienced even their capacity to desire undermined by fantasies or experience of parental attack. One woman in recovery had been told her infant greed had forced her mother to abandon breast feeding, and she had come to feel that her need inevitably destroys the intimacy she craved. As she put it, identifying with the destructive need itself, "I learned that being what I needed to be or having what I need is bad to others, so I must be hateful." She could not stay sober and consciously "killed her needs," rationalizing their suppression with a magic, timeless thought. She said:

There is always a law of deprivation. It is as old as my life experience. It comes up every time desire arises. It says I was deprived, so I should be deprived, not nurtured . . . . My desires are chilled and killed [now by some part of me] and all die unexpressed—even to myself.

This woman had grown up in a working-class home with a sick mother. She still expected and created spoiling deprivation, and she was profoundly needy. Her unconscious, unexpressed demandingness felt like a vampire to others in her therapy group, and they tended to withdraw from her, recreating the atmosphere of deprivation she feared. When she drank before sessions, however, she was able to be more open in her requests for attention and less unconsciously devouring. I came to see her alcoholism and overeating as a means to numb her spoiling superego as well as quell her voraciousness because the addictions partially filled her inner void. Drink also served her as the opiates that have rendered sacrificial victims unconscious throughout the history of human sacrifice so they could more easily accept their fate.[25] Until this client could bear to accept the profound suffering that the corpses of all her unmet archaic desires expressed, she could not stop drinking. Instead she raged paranoically, seemingly vengefully, to quell the wild and fear-ringed hopes that the possibility of gratification might bring her. She projected and reversed her own hatred and anger, attributing them to others to rationalize what she felt was their witholding. She often behaved as the man in the joke who needs to borrow a shovel and goes to his neighbor, thinking as he walks across the field, "probably he won't have one, probably he will resent being asked, probably he thinks everyone should have his own tools, probably he remembers when he wanted a saw and I was using mine."Caught in these negative ruminations as he arrives at the door and finally sees his neighbor's face, the needy borrower explodes, "Keep your bloody shovel, and go to hell, too."

As most individuals caught by addiction, this client lived in her own hell. From its fiery abyss she craved total gratification but was afraid of what she called "the soft mother" who might lure her, like the gingerbread witch, only to another death. The witch carried the projection of her own devouring orality, for she was terrified to experience infantile demandingness. It was split off from consciousness, and she managed raw polymorphous need by focusing it into her addiction. After nearly five years of therapy, she dreamt:

*I am in a luxury hotel—there's everything you would want
there—great food, comfortable rooms with fireplaces and lots of
light, sauna, maid service, hairdresser, shops—the kind of place
that's like a fairyland. I go there two times a week (an allusion to
the frequency of therapy sessions). In the lobby I see a stark life-size
sculpture with a fierce looking mask. I notice that the mask is only a
helmet covering the head of a figure who has been asleep, and I
decide to remove the mask and wake her. I do. Underneath is a
woman, very large. For some reason I sit in her lap. It's sweet, but
as I sit I realize she's soft, like maybe with decay. I am afraid I will
sink and suffocate.*

Musing on the dream image, she began to
understand what her automatic and angry expectation of
deprivation had protected her from waking up into
consciousness. As we explored the dream images, she thought
the hotel was a place of temporary care and potential
gratification feels. "But" she said, "it's too good to be true," an
ideal and seemingly unreal "fairyland for the rich." It's not yet
her own personal space, rather "a place everyone stops over if
they can pay for it." In discussing the setting she recalled visits
to her "independent and generous aunt" who lived in a hotel
because "she liked to be cared for." But she also realized that
she would not like that arrangement herself. She felt anger at
the thought of having to share accommodations and to pay
for the hotel stay. This led to a discussion of her envy of the
therapist's other clients and of the "rich" therapist herself,
who could live in, or might own, such a "perfect place to
stay"—one that she could only visit three times a week. She
then cut off the discussion of her longing with an abrupt
dismissal remembering how "everyone who once seemed
ideal" had disappointed her sooner or later, "even that aunt."
She no longer even claimed her relationship; the generous
woman was distanced as a "that." Angrily she went on with
clichés and globalization to make her contempt more
vehement: "Anything like the comforts of home and
happiness forever and ever is short lived. Why bother [with
it] anyway!" Being at that moment on the magical level of
consciousness, she wanted everything or nothing—to last
forever or else they were worthless. Nonetheless, in this hotel
she discovers a fierce image—like her own defender's bravado
and the feisty attempts she had explained previously "to keep
intimacy at bay, to fight through therapy and everything . . .

hiding hurts and feelings I think you or my mother wouldn't like. I'm playing good-girl for you, all to get a few crumbs." Since this was what she was doing as she discussed the dream, it made the revelation of her defensive behavior all the more poignant.

In the next session she was able to muse further on the dream, noting that the dream ego unmasks the fierce figure. Bravely she wakes up what has been unconscious in her psyche behind her fierce cover. Tentatively she opens to her need for a "soft caretaker, real attention." But the initially pleasurable discovery of a maternal figure suddenly feels loathsome and endangering, for she fears she will suffocate, sinking into the softness that she does not equate with living flesh but only with death and the decay of life needs that lie under the bravado of the hard mask. She discovers the potential of positive nurturance, but her need feels engulfing, suffocating, and she quickly denies the value of her find, reframing it defensively as the more personally familiar death forces against which she has habitually needed to fight. The dream thus brought to awareness the necessity of an approach that could steer between the opposites of her delusional ideal and expected deprivation, between her aggressive asceticism and what she called her "fear of melt down."

The dreamer had repeatedly felt threatened with being sent away for adoption "because I was too much." She remembered the pained look on her mother's face and staccato questions thrown when she had once wanted a party for her birthday: "Who do you think you are [to ask for that]?" "What makes you want THAT?" She learned shame and its silence. Over a period of months in therapy she mused on what had happened to her relation to desirousness.

I learned not to want because Mother was sick, and we were poor. I stopped asking for anything . . . . I made do, staying within the possible, and I got rid of my own wanting because I knew I'd never get . . . . Then somehow I forgot how to want or even how to love, and I see that everything turned to ashes . . . . I feel so sad that I have abandoned my own life . . . . I bound myself with iron controls

and alcohol to avoid feeling all I've given up . . . . No mother, no life,
nothing but the love of drink and food I don't even taste—only the
ashes, as far from the fire as I could get . . . . How could I ever
reopen something so dead? It would come roaring out of the tomb
like a vengeance, unless it's too dead to ever move again. And that
would be worse . . . . So either I die under the onslaught, or it'll be
dead . . . . This work is the pits, isn't it?[26]

Another woman in recovery from alcohol and sex addictions was a successful executive and workaholic when she entered analysis. She described her need for therapy as "uncertainty about the next career step," but it soon became clear that there were deeper issues that were calling her to it. Identified with her persona of valued competence, she managed her underlying feelings and desires by ignoring them "because there is no time for that indulgence, and anyway, I'm too exhausted." At first she was overjoyed to feel flickers of emotion that she associated to "an infant part" of her, one that needed to bask in the glow of a mother's regard and learn to experience the needs that had been bound up by her focus on high achievement. But she had little tolerance for suffering. She longed to be perfectly cared for, which meant to her feeling none of the loneliness and deprivation that had been hidden by her addictions. Thus she soon resisted therapy with the habitual defenses of a lifetime and was angered by the therapist's empathy. "It's too painful; I hate you for making me feel so much," she said for months as she began to relinquish the "plastic skin of work that keeps me from feeling."

As her anesthesia was sometimes dispersed, she began to acknowledge that she expected perfect attunement from the therapist to magically undo her sense of deprivation. The neediness was secret, but she expected the therapist would intuit its aims and supply what she needed. While she wanted the kind of devoted caring a mother might give to a very young infant, her image of a healing environment was soon presented in her dreams as a resort where she would lie on the beach with a rich and devoted lover, to whom she associated a man addicted to cocaine. In spite of this fantasy of comfort, she expected only to unearth again the original depriving parental complex. For months these alternating expectations induced subtle negativity in the analyst's countertransference, which took the form of an inability to take seriously the client's capacity to do analytic work. As the analyst, I had to use the inductions of the countertransference to discover the client's complex emotional reality. Then I had to metabolize her dismissive affect in order to experience the variety of defensive spoiling attacks on relational intimacy her defender complex performed. Many of these were aimed at interpretive statements that mirrored her polarized and mixed- affect states as well as at potential linkings between parts of her psyche. Over time the client began to see herself and how she had functioned. As she once explained, "I always get a fix—now by rushing back to the office and working without a break to exhaustion until I can't feel anything." Work in therapy was very slow and painful for her, but her workaholism was able to serve her positively for a time when it became attached to the work of therapy. Nonetheless, she also fled the therapy for two long breaks when the relationship suddenly became too close for her. She came back each time with reports about how much insight she had accomplished on her own. As all of this was slowly analyzed and assimilated, she settled into a benignly dependent transference that became clamorous, but she initially tried to manage this by clamoring on the phone and skipping sessions.

Others in recovery having no experience of a validated feeling-level standpoint have learned to sidestep the process of focusing desirousness with endless rationalizations about the validity of desirousness. This diverts them from the gap in their experience even as they try to justify themselves. Often having been taught that they could have their needs met only as a reward for the accomplishment of some task, they automatically dwell on their inadequacy and imperfection. This acts to reverse the energy fueling desire and ambition into an attack on themselves. With a pseudo Christian-supported addiction to guilt for lacking perfection, they can thus dismiss the problems of finding and supporting their own needs and desires. "Because I don't deserve anything unless I am perfect," one woman in recovery put it, "I only know how to do with less and less, but not how to find, let alone hold onto, my wants."

The Gap between Craving and Authority

In addiction because the principle of sovereignty is split between limitless drive energy and intensely limiting order, there is an unbridgeable gap between compulsive visceral cravings and a rigid superego authority. This must be addressed in recovery. Because this authority cannot adequately grant meaning or govern, the recovering addict is torn between alternatives from both within and without. Moods may feel they must be obeyed. Thus, too, superstitions, oracles, psychics, and gurus of all kinds (from drug tsars and characters on TV, to rock musicians, religious spokespeople, and even sponsors, self-help books, and therapists) may serve as parent or superego substitutes. Such fonts of wisdom may be consulted frequently because they are easier for a fragmented and weak consciousness to hear and follow than those messages of the Self that usually only reveal themselves as we struggle with the conflicting imperatives of inner and outer life.

The ancient Celts themselves placed great stock in prophecy. The Irish saint Columba complained about his people's confidence in the augury of old women, sneezes, and the flight of birds. The capacity to address meaning patterns in synchronous and seemingly chaotic events is ultimately of great value, opening consciousness to the underlying spiritual order. When, however, the search for meaning is debased to a scrambling for gurus, signs, and magic-level superstitions, it merely subverts personal development and impedes individual access to the authority of conscience or a Higher Power.

Because Self authority is still projected, those dependent on addictions often must operate socially in the dutiful pursuit of what they have been told they should want. They tend merely to accommodate to what others do or to hate themselves for failure. Having no access to flexible interior authority in relation to their own desirousness, they cannot gain awareness of the internal flow of desirousness and priorities. One woman in early recovery from alcohol and food addictions, reflecting on her own relation to desire, felt this gap as personal ignorance. "I am," she said,

ignorant even of what I might want, and Unknowing is terrible. I feel stupid, worthless. But I don't know about wanting for myself, so I settle for some big Should that can take care of things—like I should stop drinking or go for a walk now, or eat, or stop eating. Not because I want to. I'm so stupid I don't even know how to want . . . I have never even formed an idea of wanting in my mind—of wanting that was for me.

Another said:

I have no idea of what I want or need because I have no sense of a Me that I would have to consult for this information. In my world there is no desire from a center. [In relations] with other people I go by what should I do? so I am appropriate and don't get into trouble. I expect other people to relate to me the same way, to think what's the right or proper thing or amount for me. We all live by standards, and I learn them and expect them. Without them I feel alone; I feel lost . . . . I've never known what I want. I don't think about it . . . . But I can always put my needing into food or sex. That's always clear and safe and comforting. Except then somewhere along the way I hate myself for being so fat and needy.

As long as the client idealizes such outer standards, the therapist can only wait and work patiently to help reveal the inner processes that support individual authority. Mirroring conflicts without taking sides, discussing choices, querying body reactions to preferences and aversions, and even supporting the client's need for outer support may all initially be necessaray. Slowly the client may become aware that the therapist will not adopt a polarized position but trusts an interior knowing. Working with dreams is of enormous value in this process of shifting allegiance within, for dreams can readily be seen to come from such an interior source. Since dreams can provide accurate views of current reality, and since dream series seem guided from an inner knowledge of event patterns, the client may gradually grow to seek and trust the inner voice of the Self.

Disobedience, Resentment, and Attentiveness

One woman who had felt initially that she was "entirely ignorant of what [she] might need" began to realize that she had three reactions whenever she was asked what she wanted. One was painful ignorance. A second was compulsive appeasement she hoped would endear her to another person and gain some satisfactory intimacy. A third was automatic resentment and rebellion against any presumed authority that demanded obedience. This rebellion had made her feel justified in venting her shadow desirousness to steal what she wanted and to binge. Now no longer addicted to food and alcohol, she could begin to make her rebellion conscious. "Like a two year old, I say 'No!' to everything," she discovered. "I just enjoy refusing; so offer me something so I can reject you." Playing the role of the rejecter with full pleasure brought her right of refusal to consciousness.[27] Risking conscious disobedience to parental complexes and collective ideals and even expectations of behavior that she projected from her mother complex onto the therapist, she began to set the limits against extrinsic authority that cleared an inner space in which to find her own desires. From within a new experience of bounty, she learned to discard what she did not want. "Narrowing down the field," she could find what she desired. "But saying 'No' is easier." As she then expressed it:

Disobedience frees me to be in a centered place so I can begin to listen to myself. I have to disobey the authority that was automatic until now, that cramped my life and even withered my knowledge of what I need—let alone desire. I have to disobey to clear my own space where I can honor my Self's authority . . . . I hate this feeling of standing even against you, but my defiance has brought me such a strong spirit that I know I will never again be a wimp and pushed

away from my life's larger necessity. This is power for life, Self power
for my own individuality. And I won't collapse even if you don't
support me. Because you taught me to support myself. And now
you'll have to see that I am.

This woman had decided over the summer break
from therapy to leave her "dull job" and take up her first
love, music composition. Since she was unconsciously angry
at the therapist for abandoning her during the holiday, she
regressed from a capacity recently acquired in the therapeutic
relationship to hold the opposites. She reverted to her earlier
polarization between the needs of the body and the soul.
Thus while she chose what she most wanted, she also acted
in rebellion against her overly concretistic mother and in
defiance of the therapeutic perspective. She acted
precipitously without thinking through her need for practical
financial support. As if "bingeing," she regressively filled
herself with creative illusions that still lacked relation to her
reality needs and limitations. Thus the defensive omnipotence
of her defender had cleverly co-opted her rebelliousness into
its old system. With further therapeutic work and with a new
part-time job, she learned that she could have both her music
and the practical means to support it.

Sometimes rather than rebelling, the individual
prone to addiction seeks to remain "safe" as child/courtier to
an outer authority or internalized imperative and "bargains"
to try to win or earn his or her needs indirectly from another.
One recovering alcoholic caught in such indirect desire served
her second husband's needs. She was remarkably intuitive in
discovering them, and she felt some gratifyingly virtuous
satisfaction. But there was a hidden bargain. She served in
order to be rewarded eventually by his willingness to take on
the role of the empathically attuned caretaker that she was
modeling for him. It was a role her mother had never
adequately filled. Because her magical bargain did not work,
she served his needs with increasing resentment. She began
to indulge in secret, rebellious, impersonal affairs.
Disappointed that her husband would not resolve her life
issues magically and take care of her by granting her either

fusion or absolute autonomy from her overly responsible wife role, she was caught in a dilemma. She needed permission to separate and become self-ruling. She was trying to repeat and heal a developmental stage that had not been worked out in early childhood when she had neither been able to bond with nor to separate appropriately from her neglectful mother. Before marriage this woman had unconsciously expressed her need and her rage, directed against herself in alcoholic binges. After abstinence she binged on food, but she felt no sense of bodily appetite. Rather food calmed anxiety and resentment. Marriage had seemed a reward for losing weight, being virtuous before the collective superego ideal. But marriage had not fulfilled the illusion of symbiotic magic care that she had projected into it. Without some kind of surrogate maternal empowerment, however, she could not claim her own sovereignty and build the inner capacities to serve her needs directly. Indeed, she was not accustomed to making her personal needs conscious even to herself. As she said, "If I don't overaccommodate to try to get someone to know my needs for me, I don't know how to be needy and still be me." In therapy she began to probe her resentments and take their loathsome truths seriously. Then she found that her very complaints led her to symbolic awareness of what the Self in her needed. For a long period she struggled to separate appeasement and personal need satisfaction with the help of her resentments, which often showed her when she had accommodated too much. She learned to ask herself when she was appeasing out of habitual fear of abandonment and desire for the power of manipulation and when she wanted to "risk expressing my Self's needs" and struggling for authentic partnership.

When clients learn that they can simply say "I need to . . ." and "I want to . . ." or "I don't like or want that . . ." and feel heard, they often feel awestruck. Then they can also begin in the safe-enough spaces of their lives to claim the authority of inner and felt need. As basic needs and preferences are heard and met in life, these recovering addicts can realize that true desire is the appetite of the Self. Its force opens within us in peristaltic waves as if the inner body were awakening after long and traumatic anesthesia. As one recovering food and work addict said,

The muscles are weak so I don't know what I want. But [there's an]
it [that] seems to want in me. Not the old drugs, but lots of things
that flicker across my mind so fast I can hardly catch them. They
don't feel strong—just shadows—but if I pay attention they grow in
substance and smell and color. Yesterday I just wanted to lie in the
grass. It felt crazy, but I asked my pendulum and it said yes, so I let
myself. And then I remembered my friend's mother, who worked in
her garden and I remembered the smells and colors and the feel of
crumbly earth.

This client had discovered that she was able to gain access to her Self needs as they manifest through her body to rotate a small weight held on a string. Introduced to this means of dowsing by a friend, she found that it was a reliable conduit to real needs that her consciousness could not yet admit. Unlike an external magic authority or guru, her own muscle tension, which made the weight swing, attuned her ego to the Self in the body. Using her dowsing method to find out what that deeper authority wanted to have her accept or refuse, she found that in this instance a "crazy" desire was validated by her body tension as it swung the pendulum.

Further validation came from her unconscious. She reported a dream of that night:

I lie in a field. There is food coming out of my vagina that my
husband eats. It's not like oral sex, which I hate, but more like
something ordinary and good.

The dream imaged her as if she were the earth goddess or a Sheela-na-gig. It radically revisioned her revulsion against oral sex and her own feminine body and shadow. After describing again to the therapist how her relation to her genitals and feminine being had been traumatized so that she considered her "lower parts disgusting and a place of smells," she also realized that the dream tells her symbolically that those devalued parts could nourish. To her husband she associated "eager curiosity, like a boy." When asked what was disgusting to her, she said "stinking greediness . . . and being bossy." Symbolically the place of smells also refers to the root (*muladhara*) chakra in Kundalini yoga, to earth, and the survival drives that support life. Psychologically we could say then that her basic source-ground in the "stinking greediness," which had once fueled her addiction, and in the bossiness she rejected represented the shadow qualities of appetite and authority that could nourish her eager curiosity. By allowing her curiosity to fulfill its desire to lie in the grass, she had taken a step towards heeding her deeper Self and the self-nourishment that might expand and make her life as fertile as the garden of her friend's mother.

The Transformation of Need

Inevitably even after sobriety, the problematic aspects of desirousness remain. An alcoholic sober for over ten years came into analysis, unconsciously honoring the goddess through his addictive womanizing. Not realizing he was now addicted to what he called "sexual bliss-out," he was entangled in many affairs and had sired two illegitimate children for whose support he felt keenly responsible since he identified with them as orphans. He was torn between his various women and his estranged wife on whom he projected his severe superego. Combating the repressive authority he projected onto her, he could justify his affairs as rebellion against "Victorian prudishness" and in the service of "manly independence." But he was not independent. He still bounced along between acted-out passion and fear-driven loss. One evening he found himself stalking an unknown woman's red-stockinged legs for twenty-four city blocks. For him it was not the person but the stockings that represented independence, beauty, strength, and intimacy. His neediness for non-personal intimacy was, thus, regressively fetishishtic.[28] But he had realized in his walk that he wanted to meet the woman and that he was afraid. His neediness for a whole person who would not seduce and tyrannize him because she had her

own center, her own strong red legs, and her own availability
to intimacy was prospective. Desire was pulling him towards
qualities he could not yet find in his own consciousness—
qualities that might enable his own independence, beauty,
strength, and openness to relationship. His passion for the
unknown red-stockinged anima figure was a powerful and
mixed call combining regressive and progressive elements. We
can see that his compulsion was self-destructive and lured
him at least for two-dozen city blocks. We can also see it as a
still unconscious call to expanded awareness or initiation.
Generally we say such behavior is regressive if taken
fetishistically and concretistically, and initiatory if taken
symbolically. Here, as in every addiction, there are sacred
potentials hidden under the concretistic compulsion.

Fortunately, the recovered alcoholic who was still
addicted to the enthralling friendship of Maeve's thighs did
not accost the woman whose legs he followed and fall once
again into a compulsive superficial involvement—all the
while convinced the woman was seducing him. After his hike
he recognized what was happening to him, finally able to
witness and disidentify from the compulsion and to use his
will to refuse the blind call of Maeve. He turned around and
went home. The next morning he brought the experience
into analysis. His abstinence enabled him to begin to work on
the gripping desire as a powerful transpersonal call towards
the perception and development of the qualities in himself,
which until then he could only experience in projection.
Because he had the inner space to hold and suffer his
compulsion consciously, he was ready to begin to take it both
personally and symbolically.

This example leads us back to the myth, for it
remarkably points up the additional tasks connected with
Rhiannon's bag. In the story the chosen consort has been
forced to face his inflation and to accept his neediness.
Carrying conscious relation to need in his disguise as a beggar,
he now learns more about the goddess' power. Holding the
vessel that Rhiannon gave him, an image of her representing

his own emptiness, he is finally able to attend and serve her humbly. Using the same sack, the goddess then deals with the greedy usurper who has not noticed the presumption of his claiming the goddess of sovereignty without her leave. That usurper is in identity with ambition, possessed by it, and as unconscious as any addict of its grip. He cannot disentangle from its hold on him to separate and try to relate to it. Thus he is fated to be swallowed up in the maw that now mirrors his own greedy state.[29] Indeed the claimant gets his union with Rhiannon, but like the kings Maeve bound and killed, he is lost; encompassed in her sack. He meets her as death.

Neither of these ancient Celtic chiefs could have had the kind of capacities for individual consciousness available to the modern ego. Nonetheless the myth lays out the next steps necessary for transforming the grip of compulsive cravings in us. Even though the story itself does not unfold far enough for the dawning of the twenty-first century, it points to the issues that we now must address to stop the blind devouring sack. These can be applied to recovery.

The clue lies in Rhiannon's rite of ending. In the tale she proclaims:

*A true possessor of land and territories and dominions shall arise
and tread down with both his feet the food inside and say,
"Sufficient has been put herein!"*[30]

The ritual of the bag requires that the one undertaking to limit its power of consumption be in true possession of dominions, lands over which he has the sovereign rule. We can immediately see that the tricky usurper has no true possession of authority for his claim has not been graced by the sovereignty goddess of the land. Instead of suffering his rejection and loss as Pwyll has had to do to learn what is required of him, he arrogates possession of the goddess herself without her blessing. His omnipotent behavior is as fraudulent as that of the kings who took Maeve's lands without the rite of sacred marriage. Lacking conscious relation to her higher power and a sense of mutuality or cocreation with its fullness and emptiness, he remains in identity with the emptiness that compels him. Gripped by voraciousness, he cannot sustain the balanced human footing that the goddess requires of the true sovereign. Thus he is devoured by the part of her pattern that possessd him—the endless greed that leads to famine and a wasteland.[31]

There is some clue to societal addictions to power and greed in this tale as well. From our own historical perspective we can also see this usurper as a precursor of the dominative industrializing Western ego that has arrogated divine powers to greedily ravage Earth's resources without concern for balance and restitution. We must hope that we will not all be swallowed into the gullet of the nature goddess by our arrogation of powers that seek to dominate nature for the supposed benefit of our greedy egos and without regard for her processes.

Rhiannon states that the ruler truly in possession of authority and control over dominions can set a limit to the material supplies disappearing into the sack. Pwyll is about to become the true possessor of the goddess' lands. What would it mean for him to set an effective limitation on the devouring sack and on addiction? How is he different from the usurper? We are told that earlier in the myth before his meeting with the goddess, Pwyll had been confronted by the otherworld horned god in the form of a regal huntsman. We know therefore that Pwyll, like Niall and others deemed worthy to be Celtic kings, had been initiated into the rites and disciplines of the horned god, the goddess' consort.[32] Pwyll's story tells us that one day in the woods he had separated from his companions while following the cry of a pack of hounds. The wondrous, shining, white, red-eared dogs pursued and brought down a stag, and Pwyll precipitously drove them off and baited his own dogs on the quarry to claim it. The owner of the otherworld hounds rode up to chide him for his "ignorance and discourtesy" for overstepping the bounds of civilized conduct. Not vengeance but dishonor was to be his punishment. Confronted, Pwyll lost his ignorance. He then asked to redeem his impulsive dishonoring discourtesy by making reparations. The wronged otherworld king agreed and laid out a just exchange. While he ruled in Pwyll's stead and in his shape, Pwyll would take on his form and live in the otherworld kingdom—a liminal, initiatory state—in order to be able, at year's end, to fight and survive a ritual combat. It is a special combat for his future adversary has the capacity to heal himself if struck more than one blow. Pwyll is warned that he must be so focused he can deliver a single mortal blow. Then he must desist from yielding to entreaties from the shadow king, entreaties that might appeal to his fear, generosity, pity, even the wrong kind of courtesy, to wield more than one.

Thus begins a year-long stint in the otherworld kingdom that culminates in a battle in which Pwyll must show he has learned the disciplined restraint of the young masculine ego that he so sorely lacked in the hunt. Living in the guise of the otherworld king for a year before the fight—in literal identity with the god—Pwyll also sleeps in the same bed with the huntsman god's beautiful wife. Taking his responsibility to the king and the ideals of the culture seriously, he turns away from the queen, each night restraining himself from acting out erotic impulses. At year's end he has learned the kingship tasks set by the god of the stag. He has been tested for his capacity to disidentify from the passionate lusts with which he had once been in identity and that might have taken him over again. Initiated into the self-restraint required of a king, he receives the friendship and gifts of the otherworld lord. He has a solid-enough relation to the culture's ideals of masculinity to embody these principles. Thus prepared, Pwyll is ready to encounter Rhainnon, the goddess of sovereignty, and to undertake her initiation.[33]

Now chosen by Rhiannon, the favored consort also knows her bounty and the grace that has granted him his share of it. He has weathered the delay of gratification to which Rhiannon consigns him to atone for his ignorant and excessive generosity in offering his rival anything he wanted. Through consciously suffering the frustration of entitlement and the experience of need in relation to the masculine Self figure and the goddess, he knows his human limitations. He is no longer even inflated with the generosity and power of the ideal king. But neither is he identified with need. He carries his need consciously as Rhiannon bade him. Perhaps he can even feel it as her need through him. Surviving all of these ordeals, he has acquired a keen sense of dependency on the powers that are greater than himself. He has now a sense of his own value, entitlement, and authority through his developed capacity for abstinence and through a beneficent relationship to the source.

Pwyll has been willing twice to endure the frustrations of his inflations. He has consciously suffered both greed and the arrogance of power and bounty. Because he has a more conscious relationship to both sides of the problem, he will not easily fall into identity with either. He can thus hold the sack in its divine ambivalence without identifying with either aspect. He has got both of his feet in an adequate balance to carry the bountiful and devouring vessel of wholeness. Psychologically this implies that he has experience of a spacious inner geography of "lands and territories and dominions" to hold more than one part of the problem at a time. Because he has interiorized the issues through suffering the energies and their consequences in his own life experience, his perspective is wide and deep enough to be able to tolerate the ever shifting energies of the life process in order to find the just and fruitful balances required to rule over the whole.

Through such learning he has thus participated in modifying the compulsive drive that once possessed his psyche. Jung calls this process of modification a "psychization" of libido. It means assimilating the raw instinct to "a pre-existent psychic pattern" that creates a new structure "resulting from the interaction of the instinct and the psychic situation of the moment."[34] This cocreation by transpersonal and personal factors enables the transformation of drive energy and its humanization. It is similar to Queen Maeve's holding the wild pig in her human hand and claiming its skin to make the drive accessible to human consciousness. If Pwyll—or any of us in his footsteps—now limits desire's initial aim, it may still feel painful for any standing against the drive requires the sacrifice of delicious primal impulsivity. Nonetheless, although transferred from their initial concrete requirements, the energies will still be able to flow, now within an ample-enough human consciousness in partnership with the goddess-Self. Carrying the sack as a conscious burden, as Pwyll does, we can hold and suffer the drive. We can be the psychological terrain through which it courses. We can struggle to relate consciously to the problems it brings us in order to transform the divine energy's initial aims and our relation to them. We can learn that while divinely provided appetite insists on fulfillment, it will accept that fulfillment on other than a concrete, material level. Then although it may feel like another diminishment or even another separation from the goddess of our desire, the true possessor can effectively set a limit by participating in changing the drive's aim. While the energies can still flow bringing bounty and loss in celebration of the life process, they will now flow within psyche's dominions.

Following the chosen chief through entitlement, limitation, and sacrifice, we may thus bring about the perceptual transformation that enables us to return from the static hold of addiction into the life process. As we have seen, those prone to addiction have not had an opportunity to learn such conscious discrimination in the areas of their compulsion. They have had no access to the abundance in which to discover it. They are too single-mindedly focused on one undifferentiated state, unable to bear working through the conflicts that foster discrimination. And they have had no adequate experience of a satisfying personal or transpersonal source—except in the addiction itself—to permit interiorizing a sense of the entitlement needed for sacrifice and psychization. Nonetheless, after acknowledging need itself, addicts face this second level of the problem. They must experience transformation of the drive and their own development in relation to its force as they move towards healing.

Limitation

Unless we can claim our sense of inner value and entitlement, we will remain stuck in an attempt to fill divinely sanctioned appetite with those concrete, material, and immediate supplies that are the original focus of the drive. These will never be enough. We will suffer psychological and spiritual starvation if we remain on that level alone. Quantity cannot sufficiently substitute for quality. On the other hand concrete need satisfaction (analogous reductively to what we associate to presymbolic, infantile gratification) is depicted as the inevitable and sufficient prelude to a capacity for regal entitlement and the possession of the sovereign, responsible power that is born through limitation. The unfolding of the myth suggests that it is crucial in childrearing and in therapy not to stand against raw need itself by shaming it as bad or infantile, even if we hope that such suppression will blunt the suffering of existence and encourage development of a surrogate filled with pride and the virtues of ascetic self-deprivation. Unless the need itself can mature as consciousness learns to relate to it and discovers and even plays with alternative satisfactions, such proud virtue serves denial. It also suppports a distorted perception of reality as well as a hidden shame. We cannot then admit inevitable imbalances of the drive and work humanly to atone for them to grow more spaciously towards the rule of our true inner dominions. Since need itself cannot be stopped because it is fueled by divine appetite, the issue is rather of internalizing the entitlement that concrete and emotional bounty brings without defensively indulging it, mixing it with power, and/or impulsively acting it out.

In therapy the client's development depends in part on the analyst's capacity to accept and empathize with raw archetypal need and desire even when they are hidden by hostile defenses, even when they seek to enmesh the therapist or clamor greedily for control and reciprocal response. Then from the perspective of the trusted gratification of empathy, the client in recovery may learn to limit effectively the already less desperate appetite. Since the limitation requires discrimination and discovery of what currently satisfies the transpersonal container, the ritual of the sack fosters the process of libidinous transformation. It provides clues to the different stages of the process that develop divinely monstrous greed into the appropriate appetites that sustain creative human life.

The goddess will gorge endlessly on one level. Appetite for concrete sustenance will not stop as long as life persists. Nonetheless "a true possessor of land and territories"—a legitimate ruler—can stopper the hunger, fill her hole. Just as Maeve's appetite for lovers can be sated by Fergus' giant penis, so the mortal chief identified with Fergus' role as chosen consort can for a time sate primal desire.[35] When from the perspective of authority supported by a sense of life's plentiful feast he is willing to put his foot down and say "enough," he changes the level of the process and can provide a temporary limit.

From such a regal perspective and consciously acknowledged entitlement, we too can limit concrete satisfaction of neediness. This is why timing and empathy are so crucial in frustrating the idealizations and cravings of severely deprived analysands and addicts in recovery. Until a sufficient basis of constancy and the emotional and spiritual support of their valid neediness has been secured, individuals prone to addiction cannot experience their sovereign entitlement to survive and thrive. Without awareness of such an interior, psychological territory, they cannot begin to disidentify from concrete satisfactions. Thus until they have some sense of feeling themselves in possession of their painful experiences of their own land and territories, recovering addicts may need the nearly constant care available at an inpatient detoxification treatment facility, two or three Twelve-step program meetings a day, and/or daily therapy sessions and phone access to the therapist between them. With such plentiful help, they may begin to learn to trust in the relational constancy that validates their experience and initiates a sense of their own value to others. With a growing sense of entitlement to bountiful-enough attention (including noncollusive discipline or tough love), they may internalize the discrimination and care and begin to learn to endure frustrations without collapse. Then in further treatment, they may internalize the capacity for inhibition and abstinence and begin to mourn all the sufferings of previous addictive beggary and famine.

If abstinence is forced sooner, as is taught in various methods of treatment as well as in various religions, the real danger of mutation may ensue. The addiction may switch to another substance or behavior or relapse into the original pattern when an opportunity presents itself. For the problem is not worked through. It is simply evaded by trying to put it away with an authority that the addict does not yet even hold. Thus the addict in recovery may again distort or lose adequate consciousness of the urge towards need satisfaction itself and of a capacity to develop it organically into mature desirousness.

The story tells us that such a regal perspective alone can calm the clutching fear of a fast at the feast, a fear that is analogous to our fear that there is never going to be as much as we assumed we needed to halt and redress the endless repetition of traumatic deprivations. From a sense of relative plenty and with companioned capacity for disciplined discrimination of desire, we may be able to hold our impulsive need by affirming it fully and finding its true aim and source. Then we may be better able to endure the frustrations that our transpersonal cravings inevitably bring us as they meet the limits of what is available on the concrete levels where fulfillment was initially sought. Such development involves a search for and willingness to receive from bountiful alternative sources—both practical and symbolic—whatever provides the special fullness from which we can claim our regality. Seen most poignantly in infancy, the ruthless archaic desire to devour the other in order to live requires a maternal source figure who will survive and stay present, accepting the necessity to be so fiercely treated not only without retaliating but also savoring the satisfaction of contributing to the craving child's eventual autonomy. Otherwise the infant's frustration and pain form into images of horror that mingle with primary need and sustain a necessity to avoid what feels toxic even while desperately craving the bounty imprinted archetypally within it.

Sacrifice

From such fullness we may acquire the capacity to sacrifice. At this point of development forbearance is not masochistic self-denial. It arises instead out of the development of a sense of valued and entitled interiority that permits working within one's own psychological and symbolic capacities to process the problems of gratification. Then we can temporarily let go of our attachment to immediate and material satisfactions to accept a limit of concrete supplies. Suffering the frustration of achieving the drive's concrete aims, we can still hold the drive energy itself in consciousness. The drive's purpose may find conscious expression in images expressing emotion. Then the psyche becomes a conduit for the drive's energy. Thus we both sacrifice in the sense of forfeit and are made sacred (the root of the word sacrifice is *sacrum facere*—to make sacred) as we are freed from the endless and static cycle of devouring to which any addiction consigns us.

A woman well along in recovery from drug and food addiction realized that she had bought and started to gobble up a box of cookies in a moment of relapse. She caught herself and stopped. Rather than plunging into old patterns of self-castigation, she was able to place the partially devoured box on her private altar to the earth mother, a powerful figure she had first met in a dream. Using her spiritual devotion to fortify her resolve to forego eating the addictive chocolate, she began to see the larger and symbolic dimensions of her current neediness. She realized she was not physically hungry. Taking the issue within, she sacrificed the concrete aspect of the compulsion to move the issue to a different level. She reflected on her craving. Disidentifying from the grip of the drive that seemed to have a material aim, she felt into a deeper neediness. Using the compulsive attack the way the our ancestors used sacrificial offerings—as a messsenger between realms—she was able to render up what felt like a personal craving to the transpersonal source of the craving. Identifying the underlying hunger lurking within her psyche, she was able to stay consciously present to witness and address it. The capacity for sacrifice shifted focus and provided energy to the Self as it also built ego consciousness. No longer automatically servile in the grip of the craving, she sat *with* it and found her body rocking gently. The image of a boat rocking in a safe harbor came to her. She called it "a message from the other side." She felt into the image and remembered a night she had spent with dear friends on their boat. She realized her hunger for cookies was calling her to find a similar emotional comfort. Then she recognized that she was indeed anxious and needed support to deal with a stress that had shaken her sense of security even though she had dismissed it with her habitual stoicism. She brought the image and her underlying need to therapy where she decided also to seek comfort from a friend. Through the process, she revalidated her desire for self-care and her connection to the Self, realizing as she said, "that you and friends care about me, and I feel now like I am worth something . . . . I could say I feel like I am a daughter of the earth." In this instance she was able to give the remainder of the cookies away.

As we can see in this example, recovering addicts and individuals prone to addiction will have a particular relation to transpersonal appetite. Their hungers tend to remain archaic and intense. Since these individuals were particularly sensitive to the inevitable frustrations of early life, they have had the results of their experiences deeply imprinted in their basic psychological structures. While nothing can completely heal or assuage these imprints, they provide the fault lines that create the particular ways that symptoms continue to bring us consciousness. The fault lines provide the sibylline cracks through which archetypal drive energies and their images can pour into consciousness to fuel the creative quests of divine appetite through life. Repeatedly the archetypal drives may require the discovery of a capacity for sacrifice of immediate and compelling material gratifications before the larger relational and spiritual dimension. Repeatedly raw drive energy must achieve psychization and passionate affect find its release in image. The potential for such sacrifice comes from work to achieve a committed balance—a standpoint of both feet—one in the here-and-now and one in the symbolic dimension. It can only rise from some awareness of the whole process and from a willingness to accept the pains of reality that curtail some parts of ourselves to find balance by letting other parts grow.

Psychologically we may come to know that Rhiannon's bag is present when the feast begins to turn to fast—when all that we have put into something to develop it begins to go to naught or negativity and leaves us feeling futile, hopeless, meaningless in a wasteland of depression. This is analogous to hitting bottom for the alcoholic, but it happens throughout life and is not necessarily a sign that we are at fault. Its meaning, the story tells us, is to help us find the deeper security and motivation to move on, to sacrifice our old needs and perspectives, sometimes even the principles by which we have operated (our old ruling king, who is currently out of favor with the goddess of life's process).[36] With such a spiritual perspective we can turn over the outgrown system of habits, defenses, ideals, and attitudes— whatever has sustained us as we came to the feast and is now no longer valid. These we sacrifice in order to attune ourselves better to the current demands of the sacred life process, in order for our desires to become more congruent with our destinies. We may then begin to accept, even to love, our fates. Such a perspective requires a religious attitude, a humility before the spirit that guides us. It also requires access to the depths through which this guidance speaks.

Need in the Therapeutic Field

Inevitably the therapist must survive the long initial period of what Joyce McDougal calls "an angry demand for vengeance and the expectation of total reparation" while waiting "for the birth of a true desire in the other."[37] The therapist may notice the client's needs to spoil and secret thefts of anything from interpretations to extra tissues in ways that can feel like subtly triumphant self-care. The therapist may feel the client's envious attacks on therapy and the person of the therapist as an idealized and inevitably disappointing, even a hated source, or may experience the client's attacks on desirousness itself as self-indulgent, fake, weak, and delusional or escapist. The therapist may hear threats and discover acted-out regressions of overindulgence in the old addictive source as a flight from new feelings of dependent connection and the acknowledgment of need. After months and sometimes years, as clients begin to expect the constancy of the therapy and the therapeutic attention, their defenses may become more obvious as manifestations of tentative trust as well as further tests of the therapeutic relationship. Then some clients may defend against the awakening relational need and especially its feared initial surges, which feel so out of control, with compulsive practicality, joking, concretism, jock bravado, and subtle or rage-filled demandingness that almost seeks to provoke refusal. In the refusal to be "a parasite" or "a fool idiot who can be seduced" into what they assume will eventually have to be only another deprivation, clients defend against the dangerous, potentially devouring enmeshment that will make the seemingly inevitable loss all the greater. Sometimes fears of the analyst's death during periods of separation are linked to the deep belief that ultimate loss is unavoidable. This restimulates the familiar anxiety about loss and grants deprivation a power to outway any hope that dependency needs can be satisfied. Gerard Manley Hopkins' line "All life death doth end"[38] is the credo of the despairing devotees of the goddess of the terrible pigs.

During the early phases of therapy, those prone to addiction often image their needs from the perspective of the shaming collective superego. The figures they imagine or dream are loathsome: ugly, bad, disgusting infants; greedy gnomes; killers; "pac-man people who will trash your office and take everything they want." As the raw need turns into desirousness, the images become less threatening. One man then dreamt of a "boorish giant, who eats sloppily but with gusto." Another dreamt of "a starving baby." With further work the rejected desire becomes still more available to the possibility of a conscious acceptance. One woman in recovery discovered the image of "an awfully fat woman, but she does care for her body. She has lovely hair and loves to scuba dive and brings back photos of the creatures in the waters," images she could see were related to emotions that were now ready to become conscious.

As the denied, archaic, impersonal appetite eventually flows into the transference, it manifests initially as intense omnipotent demandingness for the desired object/therapist and as fear and hate for the bountiful but witholding one, who has control through session frequency, phone access, etc., and/or who gives perhaps more to other clients. The emotions of craving and hate are split so far apart in consciousness that they are rarely felt together as reactions to the same person. When the need for a nurturer and the destructive vengeance against a witholder can both be seen in relation to the therapist and the process of therapy, a transformation of the bifurcated drive can occur. Therapy itself can be seen as problematic and inconstant.

At such a point a client brought a dream of "a killer who steals more and more food." First feeling endangered by the killer's theft and projecting the image into the transference, the dreamer said that the therapist was "probably stealing my thoughts and words to feel good about yourself." When this fear was felt through in the present and then dealt with in relation to a family pattern of narcissism and thieving, the therapist asked why the killer might have to steal food. Then the client realized that the dream killer was "a homeless bag person" and had to steal because no one would ever give him enough—"just like I have always felt all my life." The therapist noted that theft seemed to be the only way to get what was needed, and that she, too, was included among the thieves and/or the global deprivers whom the analysand's thief envied. After feeling this affirmed, the dreamer finally dared in the next session to express her voracious need for the unconditional acceptance and care that she had not known in infancy:

*I want you to love me completely and never leave me and never be
upset by anything about me—not even if I binge again, not even if I
am so greedy that I eat you up and kill you.*

Because she had not known the bounty of the indestructible transpersonal maternal source mediated for her in any good-enough personal relationships, this woman's demand for it was still raw and mixed with fear of primitive aggression. But she could now feel both her need and her murderous revenge together. Both emotions gripped her with insatiable cravings for satisfaction, and she felt, in a cognitive reversal, that they were as destructive as her addictions had been. Over time the desire to take and the desire to destroy needed to be accepted, humanized, and eventually discriminated and developed in the therapy. The therapist became the primary transferential Self object that could be craved and destroyed without disappearing. Thus the greedy baby part of the analysand could eventually disidentify from its terrorizing and exhilarating symbiotic grip onto the death goddess and sacrifice its negative grandiosity to be born into a relationship as an ordinary, though desperately hungry, mortal child.

Before this birth, therapy itself tends to become addictive, as we have seen in other contexts. It seems to grant an illusion of satisfaction, and only the spaces between sessions become identified with deprivation to be fled from into "another session fix." The therapist becomes the great authority and ideal model "to be sucked up three times a week," as one recovering addict put it. The addictive and split qualities of the transference buffer the client's inner suffering, which is a concomitant of developing consciousness. If both the addiction and polarizations can be contained within the analytic field and if the therapist works empathically to companion the opposing fragments, the analytic process may serve to prepare the matrix for the birth of the client's authentic ego.

When dreams suggest the client is ready to begin working on the projections that have been carried by the therapist, the subtle bingeing on the rewards of defensive idealization and therapeutic attention and the equally subtle bingeing on vengeful rage can slowly be made conscious. Then there is often an unsettling shame to be dealt with. The raising of awareness can make the client fear that the therapist has now become a depriving critic. When both sides of this polarization are accepted and suffered, both desire and frustration can begin to enter the sessions and find expression. As true desire finally was born in her, one client finally expressed her painful multivalent emotionality:

I'm wanting to look at you, but I am afraid to really see your breasts. . . . I will feel my neediness and emptiness and wish [that] I had been your baby . . . . I will have to hate your children if you have any . . . and [I will] feel incredibly sad . . . . I might have to look all the time or not look at all.

The confusion provides a new space with all its unlived potentialities. The sadness is analogous to the conscious acceptance of orphanhood and beggardom. It can only exist when the client has felt the true self child has been born in the therapy and chosen for bounty. Just as Pwyll was chosen by the goddess and came to sit at the table of her feast, so the client can come to feel the deep acceptance of primal need through the archetypal matrix that stands behind the enduring presence of the therapist in his or her life. Then the grip of the leprous Maeve and her addictive and fragmenting defenses loosens, and the true self can be delivered to the process of having and losing that is fundamental to Maeve. Only now can there be grief for the mortal child's losses and abuses and for the separation from bounty that has made the black void in the client and created such demanding need. Working with the grief is a never-ending process that may ultimately yield to the wonder of accepting one's fate. Such *amor fati* permits the waters of life to flow into the wasteland and softens the fragments that were part of the heroic defense system to become the moist earth of a redeemed inner landscape. In this world the authentic individual and Maeve's desires within it may grow.

Maeve's desire is ultimately a transcendent force like the Socratic Eros. It is the passion that sustains the quest for goodness and beauty in life as manifestations of the eternal immanent spirit. Split off and unconscious, the drive too often expresses the needs of the Self through compulsive, destructive, or collective disguises. The wild passion of Maeve's desirousness may then bind us to the delusional gratifications of addictive substances and primitively fused relationships. In the process of recovery each person prone to addiction needs to discover the deep needs that support individuation and relationship and learn how to develop the psychological ego muscle to hold them with balance and constancy.

The issue of desirousness remains a critical one throughout life. The temptation to revert to an addictive solution never leaves completely, but we can gain some awareness of the kinds of addictions we pursue. Ultimately the strength of focused intention grows into the desire to become and to express one's authentic identity consciously, sometimes even by binding the occasionally raging appetites into the positive cravings that sustain health. Together passion and assertion fuel an ambition to pursue the Self's goals.

Honored with personal attention and attunement to the body-Self's requirements in balance with our relationships to outer and inner figures, Maeve as libido makes us seekers and ultimately supports our yearning for the eternal. Thus the divine discontent in us turns into the lifelong quest to discover the next step in our process of becoming what we are meant to be. The appetite that discontent engenders is thus very closely related to the instinct for individuation.

The transformation of libido seems to proceed according to archetypal patterns. Even when our capacities to process it are blocked, we can discover that the life energy itself is not. It may erupt or drag us into depressions. It may compel the addictive patterns in which we may try to live in denial of need or with basic drive energy safely caught into habitual delusions and behaviors to reduce suffering. We are then secret beggars, desperately hungering after the satisfactions projected into our addiction. When we can find a relationship in which the promise of bounty can revive and sustain our hopes for nourishment and care, we can begin to reach out and learn to receive and to give. The archetypal developmental process that had been stunted can sometimes, *dea concedente*, be restimulated to enable the energy's expression in the full and varied channels that are necessary for physical, emotional, and spiritual life. We move then from hunger for the addictive substances and behaviors that hold and hide our neediness to desire for life's bounty and actualized security and relationships. We move to hunger for participation with others and our own interiority, struggling to claim the spacious yet humble dominion that arises out of the conscious process of relationship to the individual Self. We learn that the Self speaks to us through our desires as well as through conscience, dreams and visions, thoughts, and life events.

As the great Sufi sage and poet Rumi wrote:

New organs of perception come into being as a result of necessity [need]; therefore . . . increase your necessity that you may acquire new organs of perception.[39]

Following the path of hunger, we thus may learn to seek and serve the archetypal source of the appetite itself. Such transformative developmental potential is inherent in the structure of the force field of divine appetite as we live its myth onwards.

Chapter 11

Maeve as Mediating Vessel

Ecstatic experiences can open us to aspects of consciousness
that we call extra-ordinary. These may be archaic and
regressive states connected to infancy with its archetypal
emotions and magical thinking. They may be unknown and
positive aspects of our personal shadow, or rejected and
loathsome elements in our current functioning that shake our
sense of identity. When we perceive, experience, metabolize,
and relate with conscience to such material, however
unsettling it may be, we can enlarge our sense of identity.
In altered states, we can also reclaim aspects of ourselves that
could not fully incarnate. Experiencing them, we may
become more self-accepting and spacious. The extra-ordinary
to which we open may also include visions of our own
transcendence, connecting us to trans-egoic states and
capacities for mystical attunement with the Self and, through
the matrix underlying life and death, with all that exists.
Exstasis can move us in many directions, bringing potentials to
extend consciousness in all of them.

Individuals recovering from active addictions
know the defensive uses of altered consciousness. They have
drunk the *medb* in its various brews as mother's milk for its
capacity to grant soothing relaxation and emotional
stimulation. They have used it to feel empowered and
distracted from unthinkable anxieties. They have sought its
visions to provide escape from the anguish of traumatic

relationships. They, like Madge's man Red James, have known the temporary joys of transport to states beyond distress—to "far-far."

Like Red James, those in recovery have learned that whatever they may have thought, they were not the hag's master. While they may have eagerly and naively caroused and even ridden away with her, they were like the kings of another story who would not acknowledge her sovereignty. As did those usurpers, they too found themselves her lovers unto death, enthralled by the *medb's* awesome sweet horror and dragged into unconsciousness. Claiming *exstasis* to fill up or escape personal emptiness, they were swept away from productive life and bound into service to leprous Maeve. Thwarted by a force greater than any addict's bravado could muster, they eventually had to acknowledge the dangers in succumbing to the sovereignity of that numinous power.

In recovering from addictions, however, clients eventually come to see that the quest for Maeve is not over. Having originally sought Maeve's brew in mind-altering behaviors and substances, the literal spirit in a bottle, they often find they have acquired a thirst for altered consciousness and the transcendence it conveys. Thus, while adults in recovery may use therapy to work through their relationship to the ego functions Maeve represents and develop beyond the defensive requirements for the *medb*, they do not lose their desire for ecstatic and transpersonal expanded consciousness. Without it, life feels dull, stale, flat, and unprofitable.

One man stated his personal sense of the issue:

I have to have access to the wild, passionate, unformed energy. I can't keep it locked into addictions that numb reality and swell me secretly any more. I need to let it flow to mold and refine it. But how can I refine it without losing the power of the raw that fuels my life and that I now want in my art?

While his questions are central to creative life, they are acute in the recovery of individuals prone to addiction.

This client, like many individuals whose original psychological structures were weak and fragmented, had maintained access to powerful primal emotions in recovery and after years of therapy. Because he was integrated enough to stand as a somewhat disidentified witness from their onrush, he was no longer terrified of their potency. Nor was he comfortable with the isolating grandiosity and shame that had infused him when he was passive before the currents that lifted and swung him between opposite perceptions and emotions. Yet he knew the value of such intensity. Now he faced the challenges of discovering structures that could mediate it into his own expanding creativity.

To bland out such exhilarating vehemence is a loss I would never survive. . . . I know my painting [ability] disappeared when I began to hold my passionate nature in a cage—the "right" cage to get married, get ahead, be appropriate. . . . I was weird even before that, or I wouldn't have become a teenage alcoholic. I know now I used drink as a veil, a covert way to get things started so I didn't have to face fear. But when I decided I had to have a normal life, I began living capped with the bingeing to let off pressure. That destroyed my art and me . . . . I know that isn't an option now. Only I have to face into the raw fear. I can't find the rush I used then to get beyond it and to find everything streaming onto a canvas. And I can't live with the old, compressed [sense of] normal. . . . It's complicated to have to discover something beyond anything I've ever known.

Indeed it is complicated and difficult for individuals to find their own creative relationship to the ecstatic, expanded consciousness that is necessary for life. Maeve's rapture destructures familiar pragmatic and socialized sensibilities. The Celts, like most traditional cultures, had special initiatory channels to convey its effects meaningfully. Without them, we often find ourselves propelled out of our depths into turmoil and the emotions that are the concomitants of such disorder—fear, helplessness, shame, alienation, and despair. When we cannot be carried safely and creatively through the induced destructuring to integrate its potential for transformed and expanded consciousness, we are likely to cringe away from development in terror of electrocution by the raw and open circuit or seize upon old defenses and old polarizations to buffer the influx of the new. Without a reliable psychological/spiritual container to hold us, we automatically cling to accustomed expectations and defenses, even when they are the result of traumatic experiences long past. Without them we face directly into anxiety, and its onslaught resonates with old fears of annihilation.

We need to ask ourselves how we can discover or create structures that can mediate into life the forces that destructure consciousness. How are we to approach the archetypal energies and images that clamor against our sensitivities and force us to leap beyond our illusions of security? How can we bear or even midwife what is beyond our capacities to encompass and still pressing to be born? We need to wonder how we can even witness the processes of its slow incarnation patiently enough to "wait without hope" and realize that our pre-existent hopes "would be hope for the wrong thing."[1] We need to question how we can endure the chaos of those transformative processes when we cannot know what the unknown will be or what it will require of us. How can we even receive the new as it enters our lives? How, when it has emerged in all its fresh clamor, can we work with it creatively to shape the raw energy into the forms that enhance individual and cultural life?

There are never simple answers to such questions. They invite us, however, into the process of searching. To begin, we can look at some of the approaches that individuals in recovery are finding. We will touch on some issues regarding the structure and containment of states of altered and ecstatic consciousness that emerged in their therapy—issues of individuality, ritual, and therapy as ritual, of relations to Earth, community, the arts, and to the body and balanced consciousness itself.

Considering these different channels for trans-personal energy brings us around again to ponder the images of Maeve. We have seen that as Queen, she is the figure who pours the *medb*, mediating her own potent flowing mead into our cups and consciousness. Thus, not only does she represent the spirit that transforms us, she is also the force that shapes its containment and guides its direction. In weaving together, yet again, images from Maeve's mythology with some of the discoveries of individuals in their clinical work, we may expand our awareness of the kinds of vessels that the feminine principle uses to transport the rich brew that can transport us.

The Female Mediatrix

In many cultures it is the task of the matrix or feminine principle to embody the structuring form through which sacred energy or libido can incarnate. Mary, the compassionate mother of Jesus, serves this function for Catholics. Indeed she is the intermediary between the father god and his humanly incarnated son. She is also the intercessor between suffering and sinful humankind and the judging deity. Behind her, and still manifest in the middle ages in the sculptures of the revered Black Madonnas, lies the ancient image of the earth goddess as the sacred vessel that receives, forms, contains, and pours forth.

Older than pottery itself,[2] this image of the feminine is based on the "fundamental symbolic equation of the feminine," an equivalence of woman, body, vessel, and world.[3] We have seen that in the imaginal system of the ancient Irish, a well-spring, river source, hill, or cave-like structure in the landscape body of the earth goddess are vessels analogous to the goddess' vulva and belly, the queen's breasts, and the ritual cup for blood, red mead, and claret.[4] From these the goddess dispenses her divine energies and fluids to her devotees in healing, nourishing, and initiatory ceremonies similar to those honoring ancient goddesses the world over. We have seen that the original communion drunk from the body of the earth goddess or queen, or from the cup she gave, contained sacred waters, animal or human body fluids, or herbal psychoactive brews identified with her. Thus at the deepest stratum of Celtic culture, the vessel mediating intoxicating expansiveness is as much an aspect or gift of the goddess as is the inebriating substance itself.

Throughout Celtic myth we find a divine female figure representing and/or holding the vessel of bounty and initiation.[5] In the Irish tale called "The Wooing of Etain," we are even told that the true queen of the land could be discovered through her "special talent" in pouring out the drink.[6] The king could recognize his sovereignty-bestowing queen because she has the Celtic goddess' gift. Such skillful serving of the wine symbolizes the attuned fit that creatively modulates transpersonal appetite and ecstatic consciousness into daily life. It is analogous to the ways a lover attunes to the beloved. It is analogous to the ways a mother perceives, holds, and metabolizes her infant's extreme, potentially disintegrating emotions, and returns them empathically in dosage and forms that fit the particular child. This special talent in pouring enables their productive assimilation. In Maeve's myths the ruling female principle, the goddess-queen, offers herself to hold and pour forth the powers of the *medb* with appropriate, measured, even artful grace. Like the mother, her ritual task is to facilitate and form the flowing source of the vital, transcendent spirit into individual and communal life through the vessel of herself.

As we have discovered, the theme of the mediating vessel is evident throughout Maeve's material. There are cups from which to drink, ritual vats and embraces in which to contain and assuage fiery energy, cauldrons and goblets providing initiatory libations, and the breasts and vulva of the queen herself granting communion. Maeve thus conveys both ecstatic mystery and its containment within a primal unity.[7] In her image the ancient Celts acknowledged that both the sacred vessels that channel it and the ecstasy that destroys form originate from the same archetypal source.[8] We have already seen that Maeve's ordering and grip match and balance the rampaging, destructive force of her wild pigs. Here both structuring containment and inebriating contents fit and balance one another in the primal order of the matrix.[9] Only such a vessel is adequate to channel transcendent force for human use.[10] What can this mean for us?

The Feminine Aspect of the Self as the
Source of the Mediating Vessel of Individuality

In Celtic myth Maeve herself, as the archetypal matrix of tribal life, provides the chalices that contain and serve the expansive ecstasy of her *medb*. As do the maidens of the Grail stories and the queenly pourers at the feast table, she serves each guest at the banquet of life. We have seen her providing the goblet and libations of sovereignty to those chosen for kingship. She also grants to the individual heroes the cups that distinguish them from one another.

In one story the three greatest warriors of Ulster, each ambitious to be called champion of his tribe, go to the court of Maeve and one consort Ailill to seek judgment.[11] Recognized by Maeve, who cools their initial ardor in vats of cold water, the heroes are welcomed. To settle their rivalry, the men are then given an ordeal designed to test their courage in the face of instinctual fury, a capacity crucial in a champion. While the men eat, three terrible cats are released into the hall from Oweynagat, the Cave of the Cats. It is the same cave from which the swine emerged to ravage the province until Maeve asserted her dominion over them. In this tale Maeve's dominion over otherworldly beasts is immediately clear. They are hers to send forth to test the heroes. When the terrible cats arrive, two of the Ulstermen leave their food and flee to the rafters where they remain all night. Only Cuchullain

did not budge when the beasts approached him; when one beast stretched its neck out to eat, Cuchullain dealt it a blow on the head, but his sword glided off as if the creature were made of stone. The cat settled itself, then, and Cuchullain neither ate nor slept until morning. At dawn the cats left, and the heroes were found where they spent the night.[12]

Now Ailill is too afraid of the rage of the losers to render judgment even though the outcome of the challenge is evident. The men, who hid in the rafters, protest that the ordeal is unfair, "for it is not beasts that we fight but men." The storyteller recounts that "the problem brought to [Ailill] was so perplexing that for three days and three nights he neither ate nor slept." Finally Maeve calling him "a weakling," insists, "if you are a judge, then judge." Since he still refuses, protesting the difficulty of the task and his wretchedness, Maeve claims her clear sovereignty and asserts the differences between the men. Taking her own counsel, she decides to award them three "sure token[s] . . . whereby the Champion's Portion may be assigned to one of them." Not wanting to collude with patrifocal competitiveness nor "to intensify the strife" in her own court, however, she serves a special cup full of undiluted wine to each one separately. To Loegaire she gives her wine in a goblet of bronze with a bird chased in white gold on its bottom. To Connal Cernach she gives one of white gold with a golden bird. To Cuchulainn she offers herself and her praise, acknowledging the superiority of his youth and beauty, courage and valor, fame and renown. She then hands him "a cup of red gold, having a bird chased on the bottom of it in precious dragon stone, the size of his two eyes." Each of the heroes has received his unique cup from the goddess queen, yet Maeve gives them more tasks to prove their skills and strength. The two losers hear the mockery at their further failures as applause while Cuchullain cannot accept the shouts of praise as anything but scorn driving him to accomplish more astonishing feats. As if she recognizes the insatiable need of the heroes for more ordeals through which to gain fame, Maeve sends them to be tested again by her foster parents in combat with specters and an invincible horse and rider. Each time Cuchullain succeeds, but the other two do not apprehend the reality that would challenge their passionate identification with the champion's role. Finally the three return home. When at the king's table they lift on high their tokens of merit, each of them thinks he has been awarded the cup of highest honor. Then finally they see, "not alike are the tokens we brought off with us," and Cuchulainn rightfully claims the Champion's Portion.[13]

Maeve as cup giver here represents the original form-bestowing aspect of the divinity or of the Self. Competition for the one highest honor prevented the heroes from seeing that her bountiful gifts were not withheld from any of them; rather they were given to each according to his merits. We could take the cups as descriptive judgments of reality, for even in this story of rivalry, she provides each one who asks for it with a uniquely styled form. It matches and mirrors the individuality of the recipient's style of expressing life energy— of being and performing in the world. The vessels in which Maeve served the champion's drink vary in structure, material, size, and decoration.

We know that a unique style pervades all the behavior and expressions of an individual. Recognizable even in infancy, it is a destined given or a gift of life. We can usually appreciate this uniqueness as it finds expression in body, gesture, rhythm, voice, handwriting, fingerprints, dress, etc. In a developing personality—one that is on the way to becoming all she or he is meant to be—such a mode of being can be as readily perceived and defined as an individual artist's style. In less developed personalities it is perceivable to an empathic observer who may be able to mirror some of its form to the individual. To describe it, we use metaphors that suggest structure, qualities, lacunae, and even forms of consciousness. In literature and psychological studies, we point to an individual's psychic shape and material, psychic substance, modes of containment and expression. We speak of psychic size. We use adjectives and images to convey the quality of spirit that the person can drink in and bring forth. Such descriptions are analogous to the different cups by which Maeve conveyed her judgments to the three heroes of Ulster.

The story of Maeve's gifts of cups suggests that the vessels originate from subtly attuned, empathic mirroring of individuality that is a gift of the archetypal feminine. The story also suggests that the gift comes to individuals who demonstrate the heroic capacity to risk responding to the challenges presented to them rather than seeking to avoid struggle as an active addict does. The gift is given to those with the courage to show up and try to encounter each unpredictable and unknown peril that life provides. Even if we cling to the rafters sometimes and protest the difficulties with loud plaints, we do not remain in the fear-beaten track of addiction.

One alcohol- and then food-addicted client who was terrified early in therapy of becoming psychotic like his father discovered the beginnings of his heroic capacity to risk one small step. He reported:

I can't die in the ocean anymore, and that's a loss and also a relief. But I can scoop up enough of the great sea in my own cup to feel its water flowing into my one little painting. . . . [Then I can] smell its grand pungency. And with all that and some sense of good limits, I can guard my own work time, so I **can** *paint.*

He was beginning to sense his capacity to maintain the boundaries he needed to protect him from the overpowering flow of transpersonal emotionality, the illusory ideals that once had flooded his capacity to act, and his own craving for human bonding that had left him no privacy. Beginning the struggle to feel effective, he was able to claim his hero's cup. With it he could contain and channel the inspiration that he felt into authentic self-expression.

The transcendent judge of our capacity for authentic feelings and uniqueness is like Maeve. It often speaks to us in dreams where we are shown symbolic and metaphoric views of our being and actions by the Guiding Self. Sometimes we are even given image vessels similar to Maeve's cups. They mirror our particularity in symbolic forms that can help us to assimilate our objective reality. In one example a woman was made to confront the value of her own style of being:

I go to the center of town and find a room where there is an art exhibit. One pedestal holds a large, clay goblet, quite primitive but with vibrant colors. The label says it was made by me. I have no idea when I made it. How did they get it?

The dreamer had been working on her damaged exhibitionism. Not only had she been shamed, but she had been frequently compared to an aunt who was considered "dirty and loud." Addicted to success but falling too often into what she considered failure, she had, like the aunt, married an alcoholic and begun drinking in her early twenties. Her alcoholism merely confirmed her doom to herself. Now sober for twenty years and in therapy, she is urged by the dream to reevaluate the parental devaluation (and her own introjected self-loathing) by taking a look at her own Self-given, worthy, and unique style. She was initially unhappy to see her goblet as "primitive" and had to work with the concept. It had been spoiled by her clan that saw it as "dirty and loud." Thus she had to embrace its seeming loathsomeness and reevaluate it in more objective terms. She discovered it could mean "prime like primitive art, which is vital and intense and unabashed, worthy to be on exhibit."

Another woman's dream images a variant of the theme of receiving her individual cup. It came to her when she was deeply troubled by her felt incapacity to do the work in her graduate program and was reacting with the habitual, narcissistic competitive defensiveness that described her addictions to work and control. She was possessed by the adrenaline rage of intoxicating warrior energy—very similar to an heroic, bristling Celt—and concerned only about her cup of championship. She dreamt:

All the students are gathered in an anteroom. We go slowly into a lower hall where there is a central table with many different kinds of glasses and a vat of some kind of drink. A woman is in charge. She serves the drink. It's like a New Year's Eve party. As we file past and receive our cups, I notice that we each have been given the same stuff, but it's differently colored and shaped by each glass. I feel this is a mystery of some kind that affirms something that I have needed to know—that there is enough and each of us can have our own special style—no competition is necessary.

Her dream gave her a fuller vision of the particularity of her own individual style—a unique style with which to partake of the pattern of wholeness that we are here calling Maeve but which at other times has also been called the grail, the pleromatic source, the infinite. The dreamer was reassured she did not now have to scramble to claim her desires in an environment of extreme scarcity nor adapt to the demands of the giver as she had done in childhood. That there was enough for everyone and that her style would be honored rather than demeaned felt profoundly numinous to her.

The dream also affirms that in the modern world many individuals have the task of building their own styles of resilient creative individual consciousness to partake of and express the vastness of the source. Although we come to discover our creative resources in many ways, each of them can help us to channel, metabolize, and creatively pour forth in symbolic form the direct and ecstatic experiences of transpersonal libido. These experiences inevitably lead beyond old forms towards the discovery and creation of new ones. And as in the dream, they enable us to share in the communion with all others at the gathering.

Emptiness

The Tao Te Ching tells us that the value of a vessel lies in "the space within"—its emptiness.[14] Such empty, receptive space is often represented as a cave, belly, womb, mouth, maw, or tomb. The Chinese connect it with *Yin* and distinguish it from the active, grasping, hot principle, *Yang*. The poem's metaphors suggest an attitude of open-handed acceptance with which to approach the inevitable emotional turbulence of life. They also draw us to contemplate the empty categories or innate, archetypal patterns that structure existence. These form potentials lie vacant and expectant, waiting to be filled. When they are brought into relation with what will adequately manifest them, they are perceived and actualized or released into conscious experience.

Emptiness also has other connotations in an overly rational order that fails to perceive the paradoxical wholeness behind polarities. Generally the striving, heroic, patriarchal ego, by cutting off from the values of its matrix, feels identified with dynamic, boundaried substance and assailed by emptiness, which feels weirdly other. The ego tries to control its fear through actions in the outer world and through domination of the feminine, which is identified with the void and with matter and the slow processes through which it is shaped or incarnated. On the other hand, in clients with little positive experience of holding, the potential spaciousness may feel terrifyingly vast. Then it can stir fear of an endless void. An image of such terror frequently presented by clients appeared in the dreams of a recovering marijuana addict. He dreamt of being in interplanetary space not attached to any space ship of supplies, in an emptiness where he would fall forever.

Inevitably the emptiness is formed and mediated by the matrix in its material aspects. Matrix, matter, mother, Earth, and body shape our unknowable beginnings and endings. Feared and thus devalued by the patriarchy, the matter that receives form is subject to domination, misuse, rape, and all the attitudes and actions that bespeak distancing, disrespect, and violation. For a woman living within patriarchal values, the body around her inner spaces may thus be experienced as bad or too much, fat or dirty, matter that is out of place.[15] Then the woman cannot feel integrated and "Many-shaped," the title of the beautiful damsel whom Niall recognized when he embraced the loathsome hag and thereby gained the power to embody the kingship. Instead, so negatively valenced, the body/Self may not be perceived as spacious and flexible enough to permit reverence for its interiority, physical changes, and rhythmic processes. With such a devalued vessel of incarnation, women and men may have difficulty welcoming each new physical, aesthetic, and/or spiritual potential that is seeking to enter through receptive emptiness to find its gestation and birth. Unable to feel valued and many shaped or many faceted, a person may then be unable to mediate between the forms that the receptive principle embodies materially, instinctively, and culturally and the particularity of the flowing processes underlying growth and seeking to incarnate through those forms. Then the individual child or particular creative project cannot manifest both its own uniqueness and its adequate accommodation to the cultural vessel through which its uniqueness is to be poured.[16]

Ritual Vessels

We have seen that among the Celts the structures represented by Maeve's cup were often the sacred, collective, and initiatory rituals of the goddess. These mediated the euphoric expansion of her sacred and intense polarized emotions to warriors, merged relatedness in their community to tribespeople, artistic inspiration and visionary spirit to druids and bards, and overarching regal identity to kings. The rites function to affect the deep psychosomatic structures in which psychological and physical life rests. They were created to mediate archetypal energy patterns into culture. For the ancient Irish there was no divergence of aim between the supernatural and natural. Like many pre-Western societies, they experienced all of life still secure in the supernatural-natural continuum. A created goblet or gold-plated skull-cup of the sacred ancestor and/or animal was analogous to the vulva and body of the queen as goddess of the all-containing land. Equivalent in form and function, the created forms could thus safely convey the coequal water, blood, or wine libation.

Merely by contemplating the mystery of these symbolic equivalencies, we may today partake of a deeply Celtic mode of apperception, for in that contemplation we are invited, as surely as if we were following the lines on a megalith at Knowth or Newgrange or an intricate Celtic interlacing design, to open our minds to the underlying and overlapping patterns of energies. The coiling forms within and between figures and letters in medieval Celtic art show us that the illuminator continued to celebrate the force that runs through myriad forms and to suggest the aesthetically coherent and wondrous interplay of the barely contained and the containing. The restless energy, which the eye experiences as it traces the lines, is secured by the larger abstract and more static shapes. These, however, suddenly reveal a face, then shift to abstract patterns of coiling lines that rest the eye until they, in turn, become the forms that suggest some imaginary monster. As we struggle to comprehend the shapes, our minds race through memories of animals we have known. Since nothing natural fits the imaginary creatures that confront us, we are suspended between worlds and forced to apprehend their interpenetration. In the combination of abstract lines that build into surprising revelations of shape shifting quasi-natural forms, we thus experience the Celtic sense of a deep and intimate connection between the transpersonal energy seeking incarnation and the temporary structures shaped by its flow.

In art as in ritual, the Celts found a way to express the meld. We can see throughout the field of Celtic studies that their consciousness dwelt in the unity both before and beyond what we have bifurcated as culture and nature, natural and supernatural, secular and sacred, ego and Self. We have seen that individual identity was not separated out, as we have learned to do, from the matrix of nature and tribe and the continuum of life and death. Living in such a vast continuum so open to the forces of the other world and to the realm of the archetypes, containment during life transitions and in other periods of stress was essential. Thus participation in communal rituals was mandatory for individual and community well-being, and exclusion from ritual by the tribal druid was as dire a threat as being sent beyond the ninth wave in a coracle with no oars—the punishment for murder.

We too have our rituals of church, family and communal relationships, and psychotherapy. These mediate the forces of life energy and desire when we most need access to their powers and when we are also most vulnerable to their potential for disruption—during periods of personal and social transformation.

Whenever there is a sense of a living spirit, ecstatic relationship to it may be expressed and contained in rituals: rituals involving food, prayer, music, poetry, art, and dance. While these are often connected to heterodox forms of worship in Western culture, some rituals are traditional ones. For centuries the Christian Mass has served passionate celebrants to commemorate the living spirit conveyed through the incarnation of a crucified and resurrected deity.[17] The communal wine in the Sabbath and Seder cups allows the traditional Jewish family to celebrate joyfully together the blessings of the patriarchal god, who is the creator of bread and the fruit of the vine. Dance and drink are enjoyed at weddings, and sex is mandatory for every orthodox, ritually clean couple on the Sabbath. Many of our contemporaries also have other daily and weekly rites of gratitude and realignment with the higher powers when we can open our consciousness to thank them for our food or join others in communion and celebration.

While some still find personal meaning in traditional models, others are seeking to recycle the older exoteric vessels as they discover their passion for essential teachings. Increasingly contemporary Jewish and Christian communities are seeking forms to pour more participatory, embodied religious intensity into worship and daily activities. The celebrants at a large temple in New York sing and dance their praise of the Sabbath. The monks of a Vermont priory commune with round dance and song, following the non-canonical evidence that Jesus once led a mystical dance for his elect followers.[18] Another contemporary Christian group celebrates with rock music and all-night dancing, forbidding at its gatherings the usual modern routes to such passionate *participation mystique*: drugs, alcohol, and violence. Others use chanting, charismatic preachers, and pentecostal frenzy.

Some Western seekers explore traditions outside the ones in which they were raised. The dervish dancing and *zikrs* of Rumi's modern Sufi followers, the meditative koan study, passionate chanting and visualizations of Buddhist and Hindu converts, and the vision quests, peyote sharing, shamanic workshops, and sweat lodge ceremonies of those hungry for the spirit revered by indigenous peoples are all manifestations of such questing.

Others, like the painter seeking to discover something beyond anything he had known, may feel so exiled and/or alienated from convention that they cannot return to established methods of containing ecstasy. They cannot pour the new wine into old bottles. For them the traditional structures that mediate archetypal energy into daily life feel spoiled, insufficient, or meaningless and hypocritical.[19] Thus many contemporary individuals are creating their own rituals according to a sense of emotional need and a willingness to explore and expand the traditional rite's potential for mediating experiences of transcendence into personally satisfying forms. The results may be variations on collectively sanctioned themes, as in individualized wedding or memorial ceremonies. They may be new rituals called into being by the hitherto unsanctified excitements and travails accompanying a boy's first shave or a girl's first menstrual flow, by adoption, miscarriage, abortion, divorce, or menopause. They may be ceremonies individually discovered and created in therapy or with family and close friends to mediate the intense passions of any life stress—i.e. from taking an exam, achieving sobriety, nursing a sick or aged loved one, dealing with grief and aloneness. Inevitably these ceremonies express individual styles of functioning melded within containing archetypal structures that have held and mediated human relationships with the vast forces of nature and divinity from time immemorial. Thus they express combinations of personal and transpersonal factors.

Since the ritual forms are created and discovered from the archetypal stratum of energies and emotions that engender stress, they can express, dose, and channel those energies and emotions. The patterns established by time and place, by participants, dress, movement, sound, color, expression, taste, etc., have a felt sense of being similar to, or isomorphic with, the flow that seeks mediation into life. This congruence of force and form provides us with a sense that the contemporary created vessels, through which we feel the energies of the larger matrix pouring, are adequate. Held in the ritual's effective form, the participants can experience a relaxation of bodily held anxiety. Coming full circle, the individual's experience of an underlying spacious psychological and spiritual coherence permits, in turn, a deepened awareness of all existence attuned within the larger matrix and its meanings.

We have seen that many individuals in the recovery process create their own forms of ritual containment. A repeated river song bore a woman through the anxiety that might have sent her back to addictive comforts. Her private altar contained the tempting cookies on which another woman began to binge, reminding her of her newly conscious devotion to the symbolic meanings of the sweet grains in her life. These rites served as transitional forms between the archetypal energies and meaning patterns and the temporarily turbulent individual psyche. Thus they could take over and expand the function that the literal addiction had once played.

Other addicts in recovery found such specific forms of spiritual practice as akido, labyrinth-walking, meditation, journal writing, and dream work to provide channels for divine energy. One man attended workshops for singers and athletes on attunement with the trans-egoic flow of energy. Although he found the work profoundly meaningful, he discovered that he was unable to discipline himself to do the exercises without the presence of others. Thus he also had to claim his need for a ritual community in which to sustain his practice.

The particular forms of ritual are less important than the fact that some form of spiritual practice may be essential for all of us, and especially for individuals prone to addiction. Jung's advice to the founders of Alcoholics Anonymous pointed out that the particular creed was irrelevant. Native Americans may join the peyote church; others may take up dream work or running or meditation. The attitude that reveres the source of life energy and desire in a disciplined, constant, and formalized ritual context is what is significant.

As part of such an attitude, many recovering individuals are called to take part in healing others. AA supports such work in its last step. Such work means keeping acutely conscious of the need for connection to a Higher Power and also keeping acutely mindful of the need to work with toxicity, still awed in proper fear of what is always beyond us, yet clear about the need to serve soberly and with conscience. Many in recovery from the woundings once salved by addictive dependencies thus feel called to undertake training to become counselors or therapists.

Therapy as a Mediating Ritual Vessel

In addiction the individual container of consciousness has no adequate means to channel emotional intensity. There is no safe way to hold ecstatic energies and perceptions except by separating the opposites and/or seeking immediate and concrete relief from the struggle. Without a relatively coherent vessel of consciousness, there is thus no way to learn to endure frustration, no way to achieve balance and synthesis. A large part of therapy, as we have discussed, is concerned with discovering and creating the psychological and spiritual structures to withstand and disidentify from Maeve's inconstant and intense ebbs and flows.

At first the rituals of the therapeutic frame and the therapist's attention provide a holding environment and model a secure yet open embrace for the sufferings of shame, deprivation, despair, fear, and fragmentation that any individual prone to addiction may feel. As the client is helped repeatedly to hold together the suffering and the desire to abate such pains, she can learn a different way of relating to the inconstancy within the archetypal pattern—to Maeve herself. Then the recovering addict does not have to lurch wildly for immediate security but can begin to endure the tension of ambivalence. With experience of a larger holding vessel that encompasses both need and deprivation, she or he can begin to stand separate from the grip of craving and the terror of abandonment. Over time the qualities of openly acceptant and secure holding by the therapist's attitude and by the therapy itself may be internalized as the basis of the recovered addict's ego consciousness and identity.

All of our addictions provide us with the numbing required to cover, evade, and deny the pains of a death of hope that so many today have experienced when we are too fragile to face or deal with those pains consciously. Our addictions help us to blot these losses from memory even as they somewhat physiologically and psychologically substitute for the soothing and enlivening supports that replace what we never adequately had. In the long agonies of healing, we must open that constantly feared pain and survive it in the present within a therapeutic human relationship—one that is similar enough to the inconstant one of infancy to evoke its compelling, seducing/rejecting structure, yet dissimilar enough to support new development. As this new relationship becomes the focus of intense dependency, it carries—as we have discussed—all the dangers of compulsive acting out and enslavement that addiction connotes. The therapeutic relationship must be thus similar enough in its own structure to allow the blocked and distorted passions of the child-ego for the parent-Self to return to consciousness. But it must also constellate the archetypal ego-Self relationship as a more embracing, humanly sturdy, and transpersonally supported vessel. It must by reason of the therapist's symbolic and clinical understanding and the ritual forms of therapy itself enable the potency of the maternal/child archetype to be released to flow forth and support the individual's maturation.

At first this inevitably aggravates the distorted patterns of the complex, making the dissociated suffering available to consciousness. In therapy, for example, silence can feel like an empty vessel, a blank space that can eviscerate the client, "like the devouring space around a Giacometti sculpture," like a depressed mother's stare. Then the client, like our culture, may seek to fill the void with illusory fillers—a focus on superficial talk, acting out, or compulsive emotionality. Or he or she may numb out into oblivion and silence. Gradually through its reenactments in the therapeutic relationship, the client and therapist may gain a sense of the shape of the original defensive vessel created between the once malleable child and its experiences of early trauma and care.

Adequately deep healing cannot occur without working through in a new kind of relationship the misconstellations growing out of disturbed primary bonds. When the therapeutic vessel is substantial enough and grounded in the therapist's own relation to her individual Self and to the potencies of the symbolic and transpersonal patterns behind the disease, it can usually withstand the recovering addict's despair and hate. As these stark emotions are companioned into consciousness, they can provide access to the rich panoply of emotionality that results from the inevitable sufferings (and joys) of bonded, constant-enough human relationship. The hate, anger, and love expressed safely within the therapeutic relationship can permit separation and individuality with a sense of self-esteem and trust in an effective capacity to focus on the creation of a unique life that meets one's deepest needs. Thus the client may discover how to attune with his or her particular needs as well as to the more flexible shapes through which more of his or her potential can be born. Internalized, the forms that fit may become part of the client's life, partially replacing the original malformations. Such a companioned process permits the ego once bound by *medb*'s toxicity to find conscious connection to the overarching, healing symbol, Maeve.

Because the contemporary culture in which psychotherapy exists is already more attuned to the matrix and the many-shaped, flexible, holding functions of the maternal archetype, therapy can function as a vital institution to mediate back into culture what the patriarchal age co-opted and tried to control.[20]

The Therapist's Vessel

The therapist herself also requires access to an encompassing vessel. The frames of the analytic hour, the structures of the theories through which we perceive and interpret client material, the images that enter our minds to symbolize emotional and energic patterns are all containers for the therapist's consciousness during the turbulence of deep analytic work. In order to be able to remain open, especially when client material exacerbates one of our own complexes, the therapist needs to feel held within the many shapes created by concentric or interlaced physical, psychological, cultural, and religious matrices as these stir our imaginations during the analytic hour. Not only do they orient us to the deeper currents, they can also stabilize the anxiety that is a concomitant of a complex reaction. Thus during the onslaught of an envy attack from a borderline addict, I found I needed to image myself under an ancient oak tree to maintain access to my own rootedness and capacity to survive as well as to the potentiality to offer her calm shelter in which to begin to process her emotions. Working with another client, a rageaholic whose outbursts made me defensive, I was given a vessel in a dream. In the dream a priestly woman placed a sturdy bronze firepot like an old Chinese *ting* on the corner of my office desk, a spot where in daily life I often set a vase of flowers. She instructed me that it was to be used as an hibachi, an open indoor stove that could safely hold the flames. I realized then that I had to deal with my own anger and begin to cook and assimilate the still too raw complex from which it emanated. At other junctures in therapy, other images and/or theoretical concepts arise to give meaning to turbulent countertransferential emotions and thus help contain potential toxic infusions into the interrelational field from the therapist's own psychology.

Just as the individual woman who serves as a vessel of adequate incarnation for her infant and child needs to be able to be sensitively attuned, so the individual care-taker mediating the archetypal energies to the client who requires a holding environment needs to work to remain open and flexible. Thus the vessels supporting the therapist's ability to embody the image of necessary constancy through transformation, as well as those vessels of meaning through which we companion clients to become conscious of themselves and to relate to others and their wider cultural matrix, must be supple and adaptable as well as firm. Out of all of them we may find our ways of welcoming and supporting individual life and its potentials for development.

Earth as Vessel

We have seen in Maeve's portrait that the land and its features, inhabitants, and products, as well as the seasonal and transformative processes of nature, were all aspects of the goddess. Within this sacred space-time matrix, the tribes dwelling on the land found the physical, emotional, and spiritual embrace to enable their meaningful survival and establish the order in which to arrange tribal activities. In spite of the temporary suffering brought about by too much cold or heat, too many storms, diseases or insects, too little rain or too much flooding, the people of the land related to the physical/spiritual geography and its processes as to an encompassing matrix that held them and could be magically influenced to support their life. In tune with cosmic processes perceived as part of a larger balanced cycle, the folk endured the temporary upheavals that seem so callous toward the individual. As in the mathematics of turbulence, the temporary events found their meaning and pattern within the larger, deeper view. This was perceived both sensately through experience and intuitively through visions and conveyed to the tribe as part of its vast oral traditional lore. Thus daily events and even nature's inconstant seasons were themselves held within the larger-scale perspectives manifest through event patterns in earth and sky. These were read and trusted as parts of the tribal divinity.

The earth aspect of Maeve's vessel is sometimes found in recovering addicts as a craving for a concrete home or piece of land or a passionate concern for the preservation of natural resources. While ecological issues are important in many fields and are even part of some therapies that seek to restore the balance between the isolated individual and the larger context of our life in nature, they often become essential for those in recovery. For example, one client came to feel an ineluctable pull to acquire land outside of the city, which she came to identify with her own empty anonymity and drivenness. When she had worked through enough of her shame and despair to feel the self-acceptance to claim it, she concretized her need for a homestead. Her relationship to the acreage she acquired was ecstatic. It enabled energy to flow into her to stimulate her learning about gardening and house construction. After building a cabin, she began to study the properties of local herbs and ways to relate to plant energy.

The marijuana addict who imaged himself in an free floating space suit became temporarily obsessed with buying a cemetery plot where he could lie in death near an uncle he had admired. He initially equated his place on earth with the cold tomb granted by the death goddess. "At least," he said, "it would be peaceful," unlike the fearful turbulence in which he had spent his childhood with an hysterical mother and an intermittently raging, alcoholic father and his youth on the killing fields of Vietnam. Later in the therapy he remembered a childhood visit to the farm of his maternal ancestors. It was the first positive memory he had recalled, and it sparked a new behavior. He began driving into the country on weekends. Later he became intent upon finding a piece of farmland for himself. The quest came to function as a psychological beacon, orienting him symbolically to a sense of belonging on Earth, and in the living landscape of an increasingly secure inner geography. When stressed by authorities at his work, he found he could imagine himself on his own farm. The reveries might have led him out of life, but he did not use them for addictive escape but rather for the temporary solace necessary to enable him to return to meet the challenges he increasingly felt he could handle. Planning his own farm made him feel more securely grounded and substantive in nature's containing space-time field. Never becoming a farmer, he eventually became the father of a daughter, attending his wife at the birth and sharing a sense of the miraculous fertility that brought forth the child and the numinousity of every stage of the little girl's development. Then realizing he might be overly attentive to her, he worked in therapy on what he was projecting into the well-loved child and began also to nurture those qualities in himself.

Communal Vessels

Another client's need for containment arose in her early years when her sick mother could not care for her. She discovered then the wider kinship of her aunts and grandmother as her first fosterage. She remembered more poignantly than the death of her mother the depression she experienced when she was taken away from these women. Years later, in recovery from alcoholism, she explained the profound tribal allegiance she felt towards her spiritual community and the pain of exile she felt again, this time when she recognized that her psyche had outgrown its embrace:[21]

We went into the convent together and spent hours on our knees and in the mission together. We knew the transcendent together and could tell with a glance at each other that we knew and shared the experiences. We met with our souls open, and we had a container built from our own longing and pain and joy, holding all that we experienced. We served the spirit and our vows to it. And I will treasure the memory of that companionship in the spirit as my Company of the Holy Grail . . . . Now the church has become too tight and small. My closest friends, who were brilliant and passionate, were always too emotional. Our caring and passion were too big for the dogma. . . . The others got physically and psychologically ill. To survive I know I have to leave the Order a different way. But it is like contemplating exile—a loss beyond loss.

After years of devoted analytic work and a new capacity to weather dependency in an individual relationship, this woman found herself able to hold the grief of separation from her communal fosterage. Slowly she was able to build other bonds where her deep need for spiritual kinship could be validated without curtailing her individuality.

The sense of belonging within a communal kin group with shared values, rituals, roles, and stories is deep in all traditional societies. One of the functions of the druidic *fili* was to serve as historians and pedigree experts to recount the genealogies of their listeners and bond the clan together. Like the early Hebrews with whom the medieval scribes identified the old Irish, primary identity was in the clan descended from deified figures and historical and/or mythic ancestors. A keen sense of the "deity by whom my people swear" focused and supported the Celtic tribal organism within which each member exists. Such a sense of belonging to a group spirit is one we all know, for individual life begins with dependence on community. Before any sense of individual subject or "I" develops fully, we know ourselves as the object or "me" of others' regard. That "me" is embedded within the bond to mother and kin and must be so to survive. We gain our initial identities for good or ill within such intimate and interdependent relationships. Later in life, even after we have more sense of individual personhood, we often identify ourselves according to our membership and roles in various communal groups and feel bereft and insignificant if we are alienated from the group soul.

The Celts institutionalized years of fosterage with a chieftain's family for the young sons and daughters of the warrior class. This practice insured the children's protection and education. Importantly it also assured their clan loyalty. Irish hero tales inevitably lay out the web of relationships created with foster parents and siblings. Other tales remind us of apprenticeship fosterage and the close knit bonds among teacher and pupil. Still others tell of the *fianna*, privileged clan-like groups of initiated warriors who lived together under their chiefs in the forests sharing homoerotic bonds and serving as a kind of protective militia for the region. We read also of the Company of the Wondrous Head, the Round Table, and the Knights of the Grail, describing intimate companionships that sought and served the spirit together. All such social and religious communities function as vessels to buffer, dose, shape, and give meaning to the flow of powerful drive energies and ecstasies that otherwise might overwhelm an individual. In exchange for loyalty, the cultural group offers protection and the security of established patterns of relationship to the transpersonal. Our churches and even our fervent kinship, political, vocational, and social groups began from such communities.

Often individuals prone to addiction experience the need for such clan embrace as both overwhelmingly strong and also fearful due to early experiences of alienation, inferiority, and shame. Then in their defensive bravado, they may pretend they can survive in isolation. Here Twelve-step work asserts an important balance, for it does not enshrine the grandiose hero but serves actively to combat such narcissistic defenses. Thus it provides a necessary communal stage often missing in the lives of addicts, one that can help them begin to trust themselves to more intense personal relationships. When the person dependent on addiction can accept that identity, he or she is automatically melded into a group of spiritual kin that asks only for the sharing of their common name and the addict's showing up in the struggle against a common enemy. Possessed and endangered by various forms of the *medb*, the members hear and support one another: "one drunk talking to another." Humbly they serve their own sobriety and—in the words of the Celtic affirmation—the "god [their] people swear by" through the group bond. Since this provides a new sense of valued identity, the addict often feels rescued from the death mother of addiction, reborn and sustained through community. Some addicts remain in identity with their Twelve-step group, continuing to feel themselves an alcoholic or addict, as fully merged in sacred and safe anonymity into the clan as are Celtic kinspeople.[22] Others eventually find this collective identity inadequate for their individuation, but I have not yet found an initiate into Twelve-step work who did not feel gratitude for the process it began and the sense that return to the group was always possible if such a home was again needed anywhere on Earth.

The Arts as Mediating Vessels

Among the Celts it was said that no demon could enter the house as long as a story was being told. They knew the value of art to hold and convey powerful emotions and to hold at bay powerful, destructuring chaos. They knew that in the creation of an image, ritual object, or performance, what might run amok as madness can be contained and channeled into artistic expression. In the process of forming this expression, thoughts and passions are shaped through the media of sounds, colors, tastes, gestures, scents, plastic forms, and words to find their place both within the particular performance and within a larger cultural tradition. This enables the thoughts and passions to take up their separate life and allows the creators of the works expressing them to stand as witnesses, somewhat disidentified from the impulses that engendered them. Such aesthetic form is vastly different from the grand, symbiotic—and potentially psychotic— merges with affect or a maternal figure that the addict craves. It is limited and separate, with functions that are situationally apt. It is both humanly created and also attuned with the archetypal energic contents that it is to convey. In this sense the created and discovered forms of all of the arts are vessels. They serve to integrate perceptions, thoughts, and emotions, even ecstatic, creative frenzy, within limited form.

Such enduring artistic compositions (as well as the structures of science, mathematics, and religious and social ritual) have an inherent order or inner coherence that finds resonance with the aesthetic and spiritual expectations of their audience. Even when the images give shape and definition to what is frightening, not yet apprehended, or prophetic, they can channel the influx of transcendent or unconscious forces clamoring for expression. Therapy that enhances the creative multileveled telling or painting or dancing of the client's story decants the emotional flow over and over until it has found its own context and objectivity and its spacious many shapedness. Rather than seeking to be rid of their symptoms, individuals find that their emotions, defenses, and even symptoms are transmuted into the order of shared meaning. Thus the demons, caught in the web of art, are kept from overrunning the house. In art forms their essence is rendered and used as a source of further creativity. For those prone to addiction it is probably never possible to live without the mediating assistance that an art form provides.[23]

Recovering addicts will inevitably need a creative outlet to safely express and mediate the fluid and intense transpersonal energies that have swept through them. Their need to find a skillful means to pour out the *medb* in their lives is imperative. As recovery progresses, an initial compulsion to pursue the object of addiction may shift into a compulsion to serve the process of creation.[24] A recovering alcoholic moving along the gradient from unconscious frenzy to disciplined artistic fervor explained:

I don't yet trust my own style of framing passion except when I'm painting. Then I am totally seized and productive while the force of the creative process finds its own form . . . . I still go crazy if someone interrupts me before the frenzy is spent, and sometimes I end up totally exhausted. . . . I may not be as violent as my father, and myself in my [previous] binges, but this ground sometimes still feels volcanic.

The painter was struggling to assess his ambivalent role in the creative process, feeling himself both the grand framer of passion and the passive instrument through which creative frenzy found its own form. Rather than alternating between the polarities of manic power and passivity or exhausted despondency as he had done most of his life, he was beginning to articulate a wider position that might enable his consciousness to flow between the opposites. "There must be something between all-out Icarus and the dark ocean," he mused. Reflecting further on the consequences of the creative seizure that gave intensity and meaning to his life, he began to see a need to balance his passionate service to his muse and his need to disidentify from the exciting/aggressive volcanic furor that threatens human relationships. As his ambivalence grew more tolerable and flexible, he was able to extend his sense of creativity to include both "my painting and a few beloved people."

Another artist had used alcohol to drown a persecutory superego that filled her with fear of shame and prevented access to imagination. She was convinced that sobriety and therapy would ruin her creativity, but she also knew that her survival depended on them. Without the support of her spirits in the bottle, she felt sure she could not be creative. After an initial hiatus during which she did not paint but wrote copiously in a journal and in letters to her therapist, she began to draw the emotions aroused in therapy. Her images expressed the miserable loneliness, neediness, and rage that had lain under her defenses. Although the drawings were "too ugly to show anyone except you," she felt their authenticity. Over seven years of therapy she struggled to find her own center and authority. The struggle made her conscious of her passionate responses to the oppositions between ego and unconscious, form and flow, and human craft and transcendent source. Wrestling with these tensions, she gained confidence to show the new material in the world.

As did these painters, each individual may discover and create within the vessels of the arts, sciences, and religions new forms into which the transcendent archetypal energies can flow. The creations assist personal survival for they image and mirror back integrative structures furthering growth and the transformation of personality. They may also serve the larger culture to create new forms for the ever new wine.

The Body-Self as Mediating Vessel

Addicts, even in recovery, have little sensed experience of body. They tend to treat their bodies as visually distant objects, identifying consciousness with the eyes that saw their child-self abusively and/or judgmentally, if they saw it at all. Dissociated, most addicts confess they have "left [their] body in childhood," because the attention given them was felt to be emotionally and/or physically negative. They therefore tend to remain unaware of internal states of hunger, fatigue, emotional stress, etc. When asked to tune into the feel of tight clothing or to experience their breath or the weight of their limbs, recovering addicts usually feel blank, helplessly awkward, and frightened. They have often maintained control through dissociation—anesthesia and disavowal of bodily needs—or through focusing on fragmented parts of themselves. Sometimes they may be acutely aware of genital arousal but not of hunger, or the reverse. They are often unable to experience parts of their body kinesthetically, especially the orifices or centers of assertive power when these have been the focus of early problematic attention. When asked to draw a person, their figures may be distorted, fragmented, and/or weak. They lack the sense of an integrated whole body that can safely experience, contain, and effect reality. They also lack the sense of security in body processes and of coherent interior body space.

Learning to trust bodily perceptions again is a crucial step in the healing of addiction (as it is for much early pathology). Such perceptions can provide an initial source of interior authority that helps the individual to separate from abusive and "crazy-making" introjects and to coalesce as a valid individual. Tuning in to bodily clues instead of making an automatic rush for the addictive substance or activity permits the recovering client to ask consciously what would satisfy the body's real need at the moment. Then need may transform into desire, as we have seen. One man discovered that instead of a drink, he really wanted some confident energy for his writing. A woman saw that her yearning for chocolate hid her deeper desire to express the anger she felt about her partner's neglect.

Body work is probably essential for all analysands trying to stay sober. In a safe-enough therapeutic space, it may slowly bring them back inside, into the body home they lost in childhood when they had to dissociate from any sense of sensitivity and cohesive integrity.

One man's dream images the importance of body work in his recovery:

In Czechoslovakia, I see people safely and happily floating in the river. We are on the way to the town hall where there is to be a meeting of the new, democratic government.

He explained that his body therapist was Czech, and he was particularly thrilled with the recent revolutionary events there, which had brought an artist to the presidency. He said that he had never learned to swim because he always sank "like a stone." In the dream his fear of the water's grip on the undifferentiated stoney mass of his body was undergoing a revolution. He could see in the dream image that parts of himself already had the capacity to float securely in the water of life, and he is on his way to meet the new creative central administration of his psyche—a new potential for attunement with transpersonal process. In his Feldenkreis body therapy, the revolution was occurring through his learning to feel his body's structural subtleties and breath. As he said:

I have never known such freedom. I have always been scared and holding on to drink or food or women. I could never trust my body to the river, because I didn't know my body except as disgusting, and I didn't know anything could hold—or would be willing to hold—me for more than one night. Now I am learning to feel into it and to breathe deeply and to be aware of breathing. I tune into breath when I feel panic. With all that air in me I can't sink.

The body work paralleled and supported his analytic work. When he had this dream, he was also learning that he could find support for his creative impulses if he relaxed his vigilant fear and trusted the ideas they brought him as much as he could trust his body to breathe constantly. His habit had been to abandon his own priorities when stressed and revert to a punitive superego system of duty that excluded support for his Self's passionate desires, one of which was his obsession with drawing. Then he "sank like a stone" into the unconscious where frightening impulses and blasting shame made him cringe further back into the body memory of his tense tiny pre-ego. He was beginning to sense the flickers of autonomous inner process and focused desire that could sustain him, just as his muscles and bone structures and breath could sustain his body—if he gave himself time enough to attune to them in their rich variety.

As both the initiating drink and the cup containing it, Maeve represents flowing transformative potential and its containment. This is a profoundly embodied and emotional image. In Maeve's stories both her body and crafted cup mediate and contain the energy of the drink. They give particular shape to the liquid flow. This image and the rituals of Maeve's drink point to the necessity of experiencing psychological dynamics not only in mind but also in a sense of the fluidity of body processes.

In archetypal feminine experience, energy and form fit together on a body level. We may lose touch with body, as those prone to addictions often have, but the body both participates in and expresses archetypal dynamics and mirrors individual wholeness. The body-Self, when carefully and conscientiously heeded, can provide essential guidance throughout life. We can learn to trust our bodies not only to move, eat, rest, and provide clues that we need such self-care but even to attune us to our own psychological/somatic depths and to others in the energy fields in which we find ourselves. Through somatic sensitivities we can thus open to awareness of the guiding Self as it teaches and directs us. Dowsers and body workers and many visionaries rely on this basic body-Self-cosmos alignment.

In the image of the goddess, spirit and form are not split apart.[25] Maeve's incarnation is not through a descent of spirit into matter. Her incarnation is imminent, already present, and is celebrated in our experience of body and affect being coequal and integrated with spirit. It represents the preexistent unity of matter and spirit that Jung called psychoidal. We know this conjoined state in childhood and in states of magic and ecstatic consciousness. Such knowledge makes experience of spirit vivid in us and makes matter feel full of energy and polymorphous, intimately flowing with spirit. Analogously we know that both consciousness and its forms change together. Such *gnosis* makes living on Earth a process that is never fixed but always in change—like the reproductive cycle and our body rhythms. New inputs bring chaos as they threaten and destroy old gestalts, old structures. New energies and awareness bring the discovery and creation of new structures to accommodate them.

The body and its senses provide a primary and life-long sense of identity. Through them we gain early awareness of ourselves and others. When we can open to experience their subtle messages, we come to realize that, like a good mother, the body itself has held us, constantly present through sickness and health, through shame and ecstasy, alone and in relationships with others. It accompanies us throughout life. Even as it is ever changing and sometimes a source of torment and inevitable break down, we can learn to rely on its companionship. We can even try to read its messages, knowing that the history of our life is enfolded in it, and we may learn to understand the crucial chapters that were written before we had words.

Maeve represents the mystery of the body as it is now and already sacred. This numinous body is casket and grail and flowing process. In modern psychology this image of Maeve as drink and cup, flow and body, restores an original pattern of wholeness to consciousness. This image blesses the body as carrier of the energies and experiences of the Self; thus it blesses the core of human experience. For a woman and for the receptive in a man, the assimilation of the drink in its cup of sovereignty implies the assimilation of the consciousness of cosmic processes residing in the body and in nature.

This experience of the body as an aspect of the Self underlies a special sense of identity. The body itself is permeable and powerful, subject to penetration and elimination, to insemination from outer and inner others as well as to illness, healing, and willed activity. It is subject to inevitable and radical physical and spiritual changes and initiations from infancy through old age. It is subject to solar,

lunar, gestating, birthing, bonding, and separating rhythms
that convey emotional experiences of participation in cosmic
cycles. These cosmic cycles are personally felt as embodied
rhythms in flow—rhythms of breathing, metabolizing, sensing
emotionally, and reproducing. We can perhaps best describe
the energies with triadic clusters of gerunds that emerge from
and express the flowing source of energy just as Maeve's
three mill-wheel-turning rivers emerge from her abundant
vulva. We may express the three-in-one cycles with terms
such as

taking in, holding, and letting out;
assimilating, metabolizing, and expressing (excreting);
creating, sustaining, and destroying;
merging, interrelating, and separating;
needing, enduring/suffering frustration, and providing.

Such a female sense of identity and consciousness
requires living with emotional and embodied processes. Over
some of these a person can have little or no control. Some
that transgress body and emotional boundaries bring
experiences of permeability, fragility, suffering, ecstasy, and/or
participatory strength. All of these experiences may be
numinous as sources of joy and pain. All of them embed our
conscious identity with the body-Self in changing
relationships to inner and outer events. Thus hormonal and
energy variations in all our biorhythmic cycles, even if they
make us feel awkward, moody, or regressed, represent
important transitions that bring awareness. We come then to
know ourselves as an open and flowing system that is always
paradoxically both itself and its own becoming in relation to
its whole flowing context. This is a vastly different sense of
body vessel from that of the heroic, dominative ego, which
knows itself in activity and opposition and strives to maintain
closure against "other."

The body can also provide a panoply of options
that open the individual to transpersonal experiences. Dance,
subtle movement, breath work, various kinds of sensory
awareness and touch are all paths to explore. The many
avenues that sexuality itself extends have long been honored

in the Tantric traditions of India, and these are the subject of much open contemporary exploration. Knowing that there can be such embodied, ritual containment is inevitably reassuring to addicts in recovery. The rituals support the psychization of drive energies that once found release only in addictive behaviors.

Balanced Consciousness

We have considered some of the many-shaped vessels through which individuals prone to addictions and the ancient Irish claimed access to the flowing matrix of life energy and ecstatic awareness. Because these focus us on forms that are isomorphic with the many shapes of the flow, I feel that they may provide relevant archetypal models for us in our own search for new vessels for the ever new wine. Unlike the patriarchal tendency to overvalue vessels of individuality that are seemingly separate from the matrix, we can see that all the containers of our individuality are aspects and gifts of that matrix and remain part of it, emerging and receding into awareness, as consciousness itself flows to find different perspectives on itself throughout life.

We never lose our need for primary and communal vessels, our interdependent connections with all other forms of life. We cannot have individual integrity without acknowledging that reality. We cannot be sufficiently aware of individuality without acknowledging its budding forth through dependence on others. Yet we cannot know this interdependence fully until we have found some separate viewpoint from which to sense and see the vastness running through even our separation. In this paradoxical singularity that is intimate with all, we mirror Maeve herself.

Maeve received and honored each courageous individual with a particular and artfully crafted cup. Often we theorize that the structures of such individual consciousness are dependent on *yang* and heroic qualities. But increasingly we have found that a one-sidedly separative, polarizing consciousness that too rigidly discriminates self and other and too forcefully abstracts from emotional, contextual embeddedness cannot pass through the transformations Maeve requires of us.[26] The rituals of Maeve as cup giver suggest that we need, instead, a vessel from the goddess that mirrors our particularity in itself, with its own shapes and meanings and sometimes terrible beauty. Such individual consciousness, able to relate to Maeve as hero, nourisher, druid-magus, and ruler embodies capacities to mediate the expansive flow of libido in its many forms through time and change. It is relatively immune to the bifurcating judgmentalism of Judeo-Christian culture that separates us from our own completeness and its congruence with our body-Self.

The ultimate vessel is thus a new kind of consciousness based on a capacity to be able to attune to the inconstant matrix and serve it with the panoply of forms and capacities that are inherent in consciousness itself.[27] For consciousness is not simple. Different parts of our brain perceive and process differently, bringing us a variety of modes of perceiving and knowing.[28] We need to know ourselves well enough to perceive the many shapes of consciousness itself and to use them adaptively. Such an "aperspectival" overview of the spectrum of consciousness available to us gives us the flexibility to attune to a wide spectrum of experiences.[29] It enables us to make our own balances in a world of many cultures and perspectives that is now larger than any local tribe and is itself in continual turmoil. We need such a broad overview also to find and create our balance within the inner world of emotionally driven complexes, the parts of us over which we need a Self perspective to rule.

A recovering client beginning to grasp this said:

The shift is forming in me from my fear-driven way to some [ability for] embracing the moments that make up the present and flow through time. From past on to now and maybe beyond. . . . I begin to get a sense that I will be sufficient unto this moment, or even the next one, even if it takes learning. That [consciousness] lets me relax

*into something that feels larger than me without losing [a sense of]
my own integrity.*

While there are many ways to formulate this
paradox that we call consciousness, I like to think of it the
way modern physicists think about light. We know light as
both waves and as particles. Similarly, consciousness is like a
wave, at one with the currents of life energy and participating
intimately in the web of interdependent awareness that
makes up the matrix of all earth forms. I have called this
matrix consciousness. Jung, following Levy-Bruhl, called this
perception of connection *participation mystique*. Erich
Neumann used the terms lunar or matriarchal consciousness.
Others, overvaluing a separative consciousness they consider
the norm, name it merely an altered state. Within this mode
we can attune with others because we perceive and
understand that we are all interdependent aspects of the
larger continuum in which our senses enable us to feel with
the shifting life forms and awarenesses around and within us.

We know that consciousness is also like a particle,
separative enough to witness its own experience, to see the
limits and edges of each perception and relationship. Even in
meditation, we can be aware of the observing, though
intimately knowing, mind. Through this separative modality
that is sometimes named secondary process, rational, or solar,
we can know the boundaries between the different
manifestations of the one energy and experience that there
are many discrete, sometimes even conflicting aspects of inner
and outer reality. We can discriminate that consciousness
itself is the expression of "several independent simultaneously
processing sources of awareness recording perceptions."[30]

With consciousness of both flow and form, we
mirror Maeve and can live with the necessary inconstancy of
life that brings us experiences of timeless, ecstatic, imaginal
union and experiences of this present here and now.
Recognition of the equilibrium and discriminations within
consciousness as well as between unconsciousness and
consciousness comes at various points in analytic work with

individuals in recovery. It reassures them that they have not
sacrificed their need for transcendence in their quest for living
soberly, nor will they be flooded and endangered with
abandoning sobriety. One example comes from a session with
a recovering alcoholic who was previously prone to acting out
aggressively. He had just realized he had acted responsibly
and in accord with a dream message during the preceding
week without struggling to know right from wrong in his
usual obsessive way. He tried to find words for his new
awareness:

*I am discovering that there is an aliveness left when all the thinking
that I thought created my identity leaves, when I have no sense of
boundaries and effort in the old way . . . . It's as if there's some new
access [to an expanded perspective] that's not by drinking where I
can sense things and values and be moved from something so far
underneath that it's a different kind of clarity. And it's easy and
strangely joyful.*

In Jungian terms he was discovering his access to Self
processes that include both wave- and particle-like qualities
within a constantly shifting balance. His previous experience
of participatory flow had led to binges and sometimes serious
compensatory violence. He held cognitions in rigidly
separative categories. Through sobriety he had enough self-
awareness to know the horror of his outbursts and the futility
of his obsessions. He was beginning to be able to attune with
the Self processes that could guide him when he allowed
himself to trust in their preverbal, preconceptual currents and
to witness and relate verbally to their multisensory input and
feeling values.

The alive consciousness that can participate in
both the spontaneous perceptual recognition of the underlying matrix and the capacity to abstract and form meaningful
expressions of such matrix experience represents the balance
for which we struggle. Such creative, individual human
consciousness becomes a channel through which the energies
and ecstasies of life can be held and poured forth by each of
us in a valued style of being and doing that can relate
securely and intimately to our own depths and to those

around us. Relaxed into "something that feels larger," such consciousness provides particularized and flexible form to witness and sometimes help to mediate into our culture the ecstatic visions of the vast matrix that is beyond form. This kind of balanced consciousness is able to feel moved by the cosmic principles and patterns that underly and support all formation and transformation, to perceive the patterns underlying the random-seeming flow of events and relationships, and to feel the wonder of their significance.[31]

Then, rather than leaping away from life's inevitable pains into the arms of our addictions in this age of addictions, we can instead consciously open ourselves to healing attunement with the matrix of energy and awareness. Building an ego sensitive to its own many shapes and permeable to the ground of being, we can also open to experiences of ecstatic aliveness and vision that relativize the old order and its outworn controls to expand ourselves and find attunement with the process of transformation, the path that is both one of individuation and intimate communion with others and the earth herself.

Moving closer to embodying the potential of such balanced ecstatic and limited consciousness, we may be able with Yeats, in the poem quoted on page 30, to hear the music of Maeve with her water-born women, Maeve

the Queen of all the invisible host, [who]
. . . sleeps high up on wintry Knocknarea
in an old cairn of stones . . .
[and calls her] water-born women . . .
up on the land [to] dance in the moon.

Then as we dream on the myth to enter the age of the Aquarian water pourer, we may recognize that we have already met her in our ecstasies and addictions. We may greet her as Maeve in another yet familiar guise and courageously seek our individual places within the vast interweaving patterns of her dance.

Endnotes

Introduction Notes

1 Jeffrey Gantz. *Early Irish Myths and Sagas*. New York: Penguin, 1981, pp. 37-59.

2 Frank Delaney. *The Celts*. Boston: Little Brown, 1986, p. 59.

3 Cf. John Rhys. [1901] *Celtic Folklore: Welsh and Manx*. London: Wildwood House, 1980. pp. 308-309.

4 Sylvia Brinton Perera. "Ritual integration of aggression in psychotherapy," in *The Borderline Personality in Analysis*. N. Schwartz-Salant and M. Stein, eds. Wilmette, IL: Chiron, 1988. pp. 233-266.

5 Perera. "War, madness and the Morrigan, a Celtic goddess of life and death," in *Mad Parts of Sane People in Analysis*. M. Stein, ed. Wilmette, IL: Chiron, 1993. pp. 155-193.

6 The forms in the old family valentine were an important stimulus for an article in which I drew analogies between the processes of dream appreciation and Celtic spirals and interlaces. See my 1990, "Dream design: Some operations underlying clinical dream interpretation," in *Dreams in Analysis*. N. Schwartz-Salant and M. Stein, eds. Wilmette, IL: Chiron. pp. 39-79.

7 It is unlikely that I would communicate my perceptions to the client. The use and timing of amplification are dependent on my clinical judgment in each specific situation. See Edward C. Whitmont and Sylvia Brinton Perera. *Dreams, A Portal to the Source: A Clinical Guide for Therapists*. London: Routledge, 1989, pp. 109-110.

8 See James Gleick. *Chaos: A New Science*. New York: Viking, 1987.

9 As one astute critic recently noted of the Celtic myths, the monastic scribes recorded "modes of thought and presentation with likely enough pagan oral roots [that] were fitted by assimilation to biblical and other ecclesiastical norms for a role in the emergent syncretistic literary *senchus* [historical lore] firmly under the Church's control." See Kim McCone, *Pagan Past and Christian Present in Early Irish Literature*. Maynooth: An Sagaart, 1990, p. 237.

10 There are many studies by Jungian writers on this subject. See, for example, Donald Sandner. *Navaho Symbols of Healing*. New York: Harcourt Brace and Jovanovich; Edward C. Whitmont, 1970; and *The Alchemy of Healing: Psyche and Soma*. Berkeley: North Atlantic Books, 1993.

11 Numbers 21: 6-9.

12 The Leicesstershire Community Alcohol Services program run by Douglas Cameron, M.D., is one such center.

Chapter 1 Notes

1 Pagan myths were reinterpreted and combined with ecclesiastical models in the *scriptoria* to suit early medieval monastic culture. See, for example, McCone, pp. 154-157. McCone carefully deliniates the pagan and Christian layers in the interpretation of Maeve as a figure symbolizing sovereignty. He deals mainly with literary evidence. For more on the corpus of pagan archaeological remains as well as the folk traditions, place names, and rites in which the pagan tradition persisted relatively unalloyed, see Anne Ross' studies: *Pagan Celtic Britain: Studies in Iconography and Tradition*. London: Routledge & Kegan Paul, 1967; and *The Pagan*

Celts. New York: Barnes and Noble, 1986. See also Ralph Whitlock, *In Search of Lost Gods: A Guide to British Folklore.* Oxford: Phaidon, 1979.

2 Donald Winnicott puts this on a personal level: "The patient needs to reach back through the transference trauma to the state of affairs that obtained before the original trauma." See "The Psychotherapy of Character Disorders," in *In One's Bones: The Clinical Genius of Winnicott.* Dodi Goldman, ed. Northvale, NJ: Aronson, 1993, p. 87.

3 Yeats tells us that "[T]he gods of pagan Ireland . . . who when no longer worshipped and fed with offerings, dwindled away in the popular imagination, and are now only a few spans high." See Introduction, *Fairy and Folk Tales of Ireland.* W. B. Yeats, ed. New York: Macmillan, 1973, p. 11.

4 Then Lugh or Mannanan and his female attendant became purveyors of the cup of the king's truth and sovereignty.

5 Maeve as sovereignty was subsequently changed into an allegory of the beautiful bride mediating between human life and the sinless Christian otherworld. See McCone, p. 157.

6 T. F. O'Rahilly describes her representation in *The Tain (Tain Bo Cuailnge)* and related Ulster tales as "no longer a goddess but a masterful human woman, with the inevitable result that her character has sadly degenerated, so much so that she is no better than a strong-willed virago with unconcealed leanings towards a mutiplicity of husbands and paramours." Cited in McCone, p. 148.

7 In one medieval tale Maeve and her consort Ailill crucify two men, perhaps suggesting an analogy between these pagan rulers and Pontius Pilate. See McCone, p. 151.

8 1892. "The Countess Cathleen." In W. B Yeats. *The Collected Plays of W. B. Yeats.* New York: Macmillan, 1934, pp. 11-12.

9 "The Witches' Excursion." Told by Patrick Kennedy. In Yeats, 1973, pp. 152-154.

10 See Donnachadh O' Corrain and Fedelma Maguire. *Gaelic Personal Names.* Dublin: Academy, 1981, p. 135.

11 Jung says, "The gods have become diseases." "We are still as much possessed by autonomous psychic contents as if they were Olympians. Today they are called phobias, obsessions, and so forth: in a word, neurotic syptoms." 1929. *CW 13.* §54. James Hillman and his followers have written movingly of the Greek archetypes behind much modern pathology. See, for example, Hillman. *Re-Visioning Psychology.* New York: Harper & Row, 1975.

12 A similar process happened to the ancient Horned God. He became identified with Robin Goodfellow and Herne the Hunter, as well as Saint Corneille and Satan.

13 Ross, 1967, p. 360.

14 Marie-Louise Sjoestedt. *Gods and Heroes of the Celts.* Miles Dillon, tr. Berkeley, CA: Turtle Island Foundation, 1982, p. 50. Anne Ross calls Maeve the "complete Celtic personification of the mother-warrior deity." 1967, p. 224.

15 Thomas H. Odgen. *The Primitive Edge of Experience.* Northvale, NJ: Jason Aronson, 1989, p. 53. Italics added.

16 As newborns, we may not be initially able to visually perceive this unity. Nonetheless, sound, smell, and kinesthetic clues attune the infant into the whole body and emotional context of the mother and support the early bonding process. I sometimes wonder if writers more focused on visual figures and a pantheon of deities are more visual or have not consciusly experienced or retrieved the early body levels of more participatory awareness.

17 The unitary image provides an analogue of the Self, a term Jung used throughout his works to describe both a hypothetical entity that symbolizes individual completeness—including conscious and unconscious aspects of the psyche—and the processes supporting individuation.

18 Brian Goodwin provides a recent overview of developments in this field. See *How the Leopard Changed Its Spots: The Evolution of Complexity*. New York: Scribner, 1994.

19 Michael Talbot. *The Holographic Universe*. New York: HarperCollins, 1991.

20 For further discussion of some of these issues from a Jungian perspective, see J. W. T. Redfearn, *My Self, My Many Selves*. London: Academic Press, 1985; and Andrew Samuels, *The Plural Psyche: Personality, Morality and the Father*. London and New York: Routledge, 1989, p. 19. Thomas Ogden views them from a post-Freudian vantage. See *Subjects of Analysis*. Northvale, NJ: Jason Aronson,1994.

21 Julius Caesar tried erroneously to identify Celtic deities with the Roman pantheon, finding a Mars, Mercury, Apollo, Jupiter, and Minerva where there was no similar division of attributes and functions among the Gallic divinities. *De Bello Gallico*, vi 17. 20.

22 The renaming story arose in a medieval written text about the same time that the Christian literati were writing about the goddess as a foolish, virago queen. The story may have resulted from a scribe's confusion of *sechtmaine* meaning "of the seven days of the week" with *secht Maine* meaning seven men named Maine. The story alleges that Maeve gave the same name to all of her sons in order to fulfill a druid's prophecy that one of such a name should kill her enemy Conchobhar mac Nessa. See Daith O hOgain, *Myth, Legend and Romance: Encyclopedia of the Irish Folk Tradition*. London: Ryan, 1990, pp. 285-286. Even if the story of her sons is "a literary fabrication" to subsume her divine powers and make her susceptible to druidic advice and word magic, it still serves to show that the goddess represents energies that easily overrun discriminatory consciousness.

23 And yet she also forces us to make and face our human differences as she did the three champions of Ulster. She gave each one separately the cup of victory with its accolades, but she secretly marked the cups to reveal her judgment of intrinsic distinctions. See chapter 11.

24 Winnicott gave us the term "the environment-mother." See 1963, "On Communication," in *The Maturational Processes and the Facilitating Environment: Studies in the Theory of Emotional Development*. New York: International Universities Press, 1965, p. 181. Christopher Bollas amplifies the concept clinically. See *The Shadow of the Object: Psychoanalysis of the Unthought Known*. London: Free Association, 1987. Joyce McDougall writes, "To the infant, its mother and itself make up one whole person. Mother is not yet a distinct object for her nursling, but at the same time she is something much vaster than simply another human being. She is a total environment, a 'mother universe,' and the infant is but a small part of this emmense and exciting unit." *Theaters of the Body: A Psychoanalytic Approach to Psychosomatic Illness*. New York: W. W. Norton, 1989, pp. 32-33.

25 Like the Hindu *shakti*, she represents primal and encompassing power.

26 These rivers are sometimes said to have been the product of her divine urination and *Fual Medba is* identified with "Medb's Urine." See Ross, 1967 p. 224. I think the connection to menstruation is more likely.

27 Thomas Kinsella, tr. and ed. *The Tain* (*Tain Bo Cuailnge*). London: Oxford University Press, 1970, p. 250. A similar "cunt" is the spring source of the Kennet River near

Avebury. See Michael Dames. *The Silbury Treasure: The Great Goddess Rediscovered*. London: Thames & Hudson, 1976, pp. 106-112.

28 To mock the goddess they reverse the motif of the pure waters of Christian paradise, which allegorized the five senses.

29 See Giorgio de Santillana and Hertha von Dechend, *Hamlet's Mill: An Essay on Myth and the Frame of Time*. Boston: Gambit, 1969.

30 The triplication of many deities in Celtic and Hindu lore is well known. It expresses wholeness and potency as well as the process-oriented qualities of the divinity. Such threeness became associated with the Christian god and with the triadic nature of society and truth in later Celtic lore. Then strength, wealth, and wisdom were the three human functions expressed by warrior, peasant, and craftspeople/druid/poets. The king must possess all three. Christian writers saw truth as needing to be compatible with nature, scripture, and informed conscience. See McCone, chapter 4.

31 Fowls were buried at the meeting of three waters in connection to another Great Goddess of the Celts, Brigid. See Sjoestedt. 38. Sacrificial human remains have also been found in bogs and ancient Celtic holy wells and the pits near them. Skeletons and skulls of children and adult males and females, as well as animal heads and bones, at these ritual sites attest to the ancient sacrifices of all forms of life to the deities of the flowing and healing waters. See Janet and Colin Bord, *Sacred Waters: Holy Wells and Water Lore in Britain and Ireland*. London: Granada, 1985, pp. 123-125; Whitlock, p. 172.

32 See Ross, 1967, chapter 2.

33 See Pamela Berger, *The Goddess Obscured: Transformation of the Grain Protectress from Goddess to Saint*. Boston: Beacon, 1985, chapter 2.

34 A group of carvings stand on White Island in lower Lough Erne. They are dated before A.D. 900. One with short cloak, sitting cross-legged with a displayed vulva, seems to be a smiling Sheela-na-gig. The one that originally stood next to her is holding what may be a casket. See photo in Michael Dames, *Mythic Ireland*. London: Thames & Hudson, 1992, p. 183.

35 In the older form the one who spies upon the goddess betrays a mystery and meets with punishing disaster. Later tales relieve the spy of responsibility for managing erotic passion by laying blame on the female body for its capacity to arouse desire. They also make worship of the goddess into shamefull voyeurism. Participation in the cult worship of the goddess and her sacred waters is thus seen very differently in patrifocal renditions of the story. In the Maeve version the son of an Ulster warrior chief spies on the bathing goddess in order to violently desecrate her. See also material on Lady Godiva in Barbara C. Walker. *The Woman's Encyclopedia of Myths and Secrets*. San Francisco: HarperSanFrancisco: 1983, pp. 347-348.

36 T. W. Rolleston. *Myths and Legends of the Celtic Race*, London: George G. Harrap, 1911, p. 245. O hOgain gives us several versions of these tales in English. He says of them, "[T]he writers were obviously dealing with a jumble of names and were arranging them in narrative order by use of whatever motifs suggested themselves." See O hOgain, p. 295. From a psychological perspective we can take the various arrangements that suggested themselves to indicate varying points of view regarding the ancient goddess through the millennia. Together they reveal the many facets of her portrait available to consciousness.

37 The most famous of these today are the Paps of Anu in Co. Kerry. I am grateful to

Frank and Siobhan Lewis, of Muckross, Co. Kerry, for describing to me this old custom and its continuation.

38 Jack Roberts, *The Sacred Mythological Centres of Ireland*. Ireland: Bandia, 1996, p. 32. Here the ancient deities of Ireland were said to have been buried until a queen of the *Tuatha De Danaan* persuaded her partner to adopt the eastern *Brug na Boinne* as the royal tomb.

39 Jean Markale, *Celtic Civilization*. London: Gordon Cremonesi, 1976, p. 65.

40 We know that this persisted into the twentieth century in isolated Celtic areas. A recent study of the inhabitants of St. Kilda tells us that until they were forced to leave their island, they "never regarded themselves as individuals. Each and every one was a component of a community" held together by a daily meeting in which they reached a consensus about activities. All property was held in common; the catch of the day was piled together and divided by the households on the island. This equality of distribution prevented competition. There was no outstripping of a neighbor or personal advantage. The communal system, while it stifled initiative, ensured the keeping of other ancient customs. Thus the islanders maintained the old Celtic respect for the clan chief for protection, justice, and prosperity and in return gave their lives for the chief's cause. They still honored the chief with ancient rites of hospitality and the willing gift of left-over produce. In other ways too, they used methods we know were part of Stone Age life: they lit bonfires on the hilltops to get attention from nearby Hebridian communities and maintained the old customs of telling time by the motion of the sun from one hill or rock to another or by the tides. See Tom Steel, *The Life and Death of St. Kilda*. Glasgow: Fontana, 1975.

41 Sjoestedt, p. 50. *Bile* refers to a sacred tree.

42 Ross, 1967, p. 35.

43 The tree is androgenous, like the deity. Some recent commentators consider that the Maypole is a phallic symbol. However, while the form is erect and masculine, the sustaining life force within it, like the *shakti* power in India, is considered feminine. This conjunction is shown in India by sculptures of the goddess in the *lingam* and also by the fact that the pigmented markings in the *lingam* stones from the Narada River are identified with the goddess.

44 Dylan Thomas, *The Collected Poems of Dylan Thomas, 1934-1952*. New York: New Directions, 1952, p. 10.

45 Animals on the shoulders are a typical sign of the bird-mother goddesses in Gaul also. Maeve is said to have had a squirrel and a bird on her shoulders. Ross, 1967. 223. Marija Gimbutas sees the bird goddesses among the most ancient deities of Old Europe. See her [1974] *The Goddesses and Gods of Old Europe, 6500-3500 BC: Myths and Cult Images*. New and updated ed. Berkeley: University of California Press, 1982.

46 Sjoestedt, p. 50. That the wolf was the first domesticated animal also suggests the antiquity of a cult centered on Maeve.

47 Ross, 1967, p. 317.

48 Sjoestedt, p. 50. She is like the northern Irish goddess Macha in this trait. The ponies of the western counties are similar to those depicted in Lascaux. They may have been present in Ireland before the islands broke off from the continent, thus antedating the arrival of the aristocratic, warrior invaders into Ireland who came with larger war horses. Maeve bridges all eras, however, from the earliest hunting

cultures through stone, bronze, and iron ages, and on to the modern era, as we have seen in the folktale of Madge.

49 Sjoestedt, p. 50.

50 Ross, 1967, p. 223; and O hOgain, pp. 195-197. The coronation stone of Ireland was called "the penis of Fergus." At Tara, site of the high kings' *raths*, this megalith named the *Lia Fail* stood once pointing to the sky on top of the neolithic mound temple now called the "Mound of Hostages." Like the later *lingam* in *yoni* sculptures of India, this conjunction of symbolic forms represents the balance of male and female energies. In myth, when a true king stood on it, the *Lia Fail* screamed to affirm his right to rule. Its scream has been called "the ultimate ejaculation." See Charles Roy, *The Road Wet, The Wind Close: Celtic Ireland*. Dublin: Gill and MacMillan, 1986, p. 80. As the lingam itself, Fergus represents the masculine potency sufficient to balance the goddess' power. I think the mythic connections between Fergus and Maeve as well as the placement of his stone "penis" on the goddess' mound suggest that Fergus represented the initiating divinity behind kingship rites. Fergus' table was said to be so bountiful that it could feed a multitude for seven days, a sure mark of his favor with the goddess of the land. Maeve's "going with Fergus" may thus hint at kingship rituals. As the consort of the deer goddess of the woodland Flidais, Fergus was probably a stag deity in pre-Celtic Ireland. In the Welsh Mabinogion story of Pwyll, such a horned god appears in the guise of an otherworldly huntsman of stags. It is he who initially initiates the king-to-be.

51 In relation to rituals practiced in Vodou, an African religion brought by slaves to Haiti and the United States, Karen Brown discusses the motif of being ridden by the deity. See her 1991. *Mama Lola: A Vodou Priestess in Brooklyn*. Berkeley: University of California Press. By contrast Madge's man, being initiated into her coven, rode the broomstick and then sat on a stallion to partake of her mind-altering libation. He had taken her broomstick and was thus in her place, riding the horse. For material on broomsticks in the Old Religion, see Walker, pp. 119-121.

52 Jung calls this larger whole the Self—"a psychic totality and at the same time a center, neither of which coincides with the ego, but includes it, just as the larger circle encloses a smaller one." See Jung, 1940/50. *CW 9i*. §248. He also writes, "This 'letting go' [of the ego position is] the *sine qua non* of all forms of higher spiritual development, whether we call it meditation, contemplation, or spiritual exercise." Jung, 1934/1950. *CW 9i*. §562.

53 See Edward Edinger's discussion of the ego-Self axis in his *Ego and Archetype: Individuation and the Religious Function of the Psyche*. New York: Putnam, 1972, chapter 1. A modern writer who has studied shamanic traditions tells us, "Life without ecstasy is not true life and not worth living. Without ecstasy the soul becomes shriveled and perverted, the mind becomes corrupt and the body suffers pain. Ecstatic union with nature is necessary for normal health. It is necessary for survival." Eliot Cowan. *Plant Spirit Medicine*. Newberg, OR: Swan Raven, 1995, p. 29.

54 In Judaism, for example, the mystic pathways connected with the Kaballah were until very recently open only to older orthodox men. The trance cults celebrating the unity of body and spirit and using music and dance have existed in or alongside orthodox Western religions, but they have been peripheral and often associated with descendants of Celts, Africans, and Native Americans.

55 Perera, "Earth Mother Body Self: Therapeutic Process as Return and

Re-emergence," in *Restoring the Temple: A Celebration of Feminine Spirit*, Audio Tape #1. Chicago: C.G. Jung Institute of Chicago, 1996.

56 John Donne. "Holy Sonnets, xi," in *John Donne: A Selection of His Poetry*. John Hayward, ed. London: Penguin, 1950, p. 172.

57 The Gospel of Matthew. 18:20.

58 See Perera, 1988, pp. 233-266. Edinger discusses the cyclic inflationary and deflationary relationship of ego and Self that he describes as the ego-Self axis. See 1972, chapter 1.

59 Prosinias Mac Cana, 1957. "Aspects of the Theme of King and Goddess in Irish Literature," in *Etudes Celtiques* 7:88.

60 Jean Markale. [1972] *Women of the Celts*. A. Mygind, C. Hauch, P. Henry, trs. London: Gordon Cremonesi, 1975, p. 165.

61 See McCone, chapters 5 and 6.

62 From "The Wooing of Etain," in Gantz, p. 49.

63 Translated by Myles Dillon. Quoted in Ross, 1986, p. 90.

64 From "The Destruction of Da Derga's Hostel," in Gantz, p. 67. I have changed Gantz's translation of the word *imbas*.

65 The goddess similar to Maeve in South Ireland was called the *Cailleach* or Hag of Beare. Seven kings received their sovereignty through their sacred marriages to her, and she was renewed and grew old with each of them. See "The Lament of the Old Woman of Beare," in Kuno Meyer, *Selections from Ancient Irish Poetry*. London: Constable, 1959, pp. 90-93.

66 Maeve sent into battle many bridegrooms promised to her daughter, Findavair/Guinivere in *The Tain*. Each went to his death against the champion Cuchullain. Similarly in a Welsh tale called "The Lady of the Fountain," the heroine's maid urges her lady to take the champion who slew her previous husband: "take as husband a man who would be as good as, or better than he. . . . [for] Had he not been doughtier than he, he would not have taken his life." Gwyn and Thomas Jones. [1906] 1949. *The Mabinogion*. London: Everymans. 168-169.

67 "[S]he is *tyrannical*, in the ancient sense of the word." Markale says the word's meaning is related to *tur* (to give) and connotes the "tyrant queen of societies with gynocentric leanings [that] must have had the task of *giving* life, food, drink, prosperity, happiness, and also naturally, death, since we begin to die as soon as we are born." Markale. [1972] 1975, p. 241.

68 Her consort Ailill was content to let her erotic relationship with Fergus alone, explaining that it was necessary for her to act that way for the success of the expedition. Markale. [1972] 1975, p. 165. In *The Tain*, a tale of the emerging patriarchy written down by a Christian scribe, the goddess was belittled to lusty harlot and harridan.

69 Kinsella, p. 53.

70 The name Cruachan is derived from that of the goddess said to be Maeve's mother, *Crochen Croderg*, a personification of the setting sun. She was said to be a maid of the sun goddess, dropped out of the sun's apron as she passed over the western lands towards the sea and its magical otherworld islands. See Roberts, p. 32. Another story tells us that Etain, the solar goddess, and her consort Midir gave the *sid* dwelling under Cruachan (entered through the cave of Oweynagat) to *Crochen Croderg* and then left for their home in the East. See Dames, 1992, pp. 237-239. The opening of this sacred cave is alligned with the mid-summer sunset. The

goddess' name itself conveys a multisensory experience of the process of sunset. *Croch* means saffron; *Crochen* means drinking cup. *Croderg* is red, the color of blood. The various meanings suggest the cup of inebriating substance that was part of the ancient kingship rites that took place at Cruachan. Vividly they also invoke the encompassing waters stretching below Maeve's cairn on Knocknarea sometimes made red as a birthing womb by the setting sun. This cairn is visible from many sites in the region and seems to allign with the midsummer setting sun, balancing the great cave mound in the east at Newgrange, which alligns with the midwinter sunrise. In all of these clues, we may intuit some hint of the reverence with which the ancient Irish honored the vast scope of the ancient goddess.

71 After Conchobhar mac Ness came Tinne mac Connrach, Eochaidh Dala, and Ailill mac Mata.

72 Meyer's translation, quoted in Ross, 1967, p. 223.

73 *Esnada Tige Buchet.* Cited in McCone, p. 159.

74 Alwyn and Brynly Rees, *Celtic Heritage: Ancient Tradition in Ireland and Wales.* London: Thames & Hudson, 1961, p. 75.

75 This grouping of nine generations from a single ancestor represents a typical clan in the geneological tables of ancient Ireland.

76 O hOgain, p. 293.

77 Kinsella, p. 171.

78 Brendan O Hehir, A Christian revision of "Eachtra Airt Meic Cuind Ocus Torchmarc Delbchaine Ingine Morgain," in *Celtic Folklore and Christianity: Studies in Memory of William W. Heist.* Patrick K. Ford, ed. Los Angeles: University of California Press, 1983, p. 168.

79 This is poignantly demonstrated in the story of Etain. See Introduction.

80 Yeats' 1902 play "Cathleen ni Houlihan," in Yeats, 1934. 57.

81 Meyer quoted Ross, 1967, p. 223.

82 The storytellers "never played with or analysed [these figures] in the romantic fashion. There is beauty enough in the brief descriptions and rapid touches of the old poets, but it is never that cultivated beauty induced by the cool examination of a sentiment under different lights and in shifting moods . . . [rather they sought to portray a] vision so clearly seen, so surely and swiftly rendered [of] instant emotions." Robin Flower, *The Irish Tradition.* Oxford: Clarendon, 1947, pp. 138-139. There is no remnant of an old Celtic love goddess like Aphrodite or even Inanna. The literature tells us of abundant beauty, lustful passion, and loss, not eroticism, romance, or coy flirtation. Early Irish women and men may not have had to resort to such indirect and reflective expressions of sexual desire since there was no dogma inhibiting its natural assertion. The closest we have to more modern love poetry is in the songs of grief in which heroines like Dierdre mourn their beloveds. Here the fulfillment of instant emotion is inhibited by the chasm of death. On the other hand the lack of romantic sentiment in the writing may also have resulted from the increasingly inhibited, even misogynous, perspective of the medieval churchmen who wrote down the tales. Their portrayal of women expresses their own sexual inhibition. Sjoestedt tells us pointedly that "To wonder that we do not find a goddess [re]presenting [an equivalent of Venus or Aphrodite] to the exclusion of all others is to judge Celtic mythology by foreign standards, and so to condemn oneself to a misconstruction of its intimate system." Sjoestedt, p. 51.

83 Even Cuchullain has to bed his trainer's daughter before he can gain access to the woman warrior herself. Kinsella, p. 30.

84 Nonetheless rather than seeing the goddess in her earlier immortal and sovereign position, medieval monks stressed the downfall of her powers and described her as a tragic "ewe between two rams," who has no recourse but suicide, and her beloved, no fate but death at the hands of the old king. See, for example, "The Exile of the Sons of Uishliu," in Gantz, p. 267.

85 Often the peculiar lack of overt eroticism in the literature alongside sensuous physical descriptions and references to heroes enraptured by women of the *sidh* and the otherworld Isles of Women suggests censorship. Disguised reference in tales like that of Meilyr and the bawdiness of games, songs, and dances protested by churchmen remind us that Irish culture did not lack passionately ecstatic and erotic energies. The expression of the erotic as an aspect of spirituality and fertility symbolism may have been as widespread as it was in the cults of the goddess worldwide and as it remains today in India. Under the influence of medieval Christianity, however, the scribes coarsely mock Maeve as a lustful virago, or they belittle Dierdre to a pathetic "ewe between two rams." Rather than representing the revered female for whom her consorts battle, Dierdre is passed like a chattel between them and portrayed as a grief-struck, suicidal pawn of their power to overturn the goddess' ancient sovereignty. See Gantz, p. 267.

86 Friel's play "Dancing at Lughnasa" is about this survival. See *Dancing at Lugnasa*. London: Samuel French, 1990. For the definitive study of this festival, see Maire Mac Neill, *The Festival of Lughnasa: A Study of the Survival of the Celtic Festival of the Beginning of the Harvest*. Dublin: Oxford University, 1962.

87 A churchman was quoted in the early 1990s in *The New York Times* asserting that the Catholic Church is not against lust, only it insists that lust must remain within marriage.

88 There are two examples in the tale called "Cuchullain, His Training in Arms" in *The Tain*. See Kinsella, pp. 31, 33.

89 See Jorgen Anderson, *The Witch on the Wall*. London: Allen & Unwin, 1977. See also Eamonn P. Kelly, *Sheela-na-gigs: Origins and functions*. Dublin: Country House/The National Museum of Ireland, 1996.

90 Douglas Fraser. "The Heraldic Woman: A Study in Diffusion," in *The Many Faces of Primitive Art: A Critical Anthology*. Douglas Fraser, ed. Englewood Cliffs, NJ: Prentice-Hall, 1966, pp. 36-99. The birth-giving posture is depicted in a sculpture of 21,000 B.C. in France. A birth-giving goddess presides over the bulls heads in the goddess shrine at Catal Huyuk (dated seventh millenium B.C.). Similar figures, which Gimbutas calls frog goddesses, are from Akilon, a site in Old Europe. See Gimbutas [1974] 1982, pp. 176-177.

91 For some of the background of this obscure name, see Walker, pp. 931-932.

92 Martin Brennan, *The Boyne Valley Vision*. Portlaoise, Ireland: Dolmen, 1980, 21ff.

93 English monastic prayer from ca. 1100, quoted in Michael Dames, *The Avebury Cycle*. London: Thames & Hudson, 1977, p. 96.

94 Fraser, pp. 36-99.

95 Placing the Sheelas on church walls may have been one way the Norman church sought to bring the custom of visiting the sacred natural sites within its own purview. Such pilgrimage around the body of the earth goddess ensured fertility of land and herds. Touching the womb, belly, or cunt of the sheela is analogous to

the modern custom of throwing rice at the bride. Evidence of such rubbing of the belly and vulva is manifest on some of the relief sculptures themselves. See Andersen, p. 31.

96 One was so treated until 1935. See Dames, 1976, p. 94.

97 See Heinrich Zimmer, 1938. "The Indian World Mother," in *The Mystic Vision: Papers from the Eranos Yearbooks*. Princeton, NJ: Princeton University Press: 1970, pp. 89-91.

98 The same motif, reduced to a simple hole of rebirth, appears in the *gallan*-like gravestone of a Christian monk in the churchyard of St. Malachedar, Co. Kerry. The stone also bears a runic inscription of the monk's name.

99 Many of the Irish examples of the displayed female figure are on the castles of the conquering invaders. While the Normans may have used the figure as an apotropaic guardian on their keeps, they may have also have secularized Maeve by evoking her mainly as the emblem of sovereignty (*flaithius*), flaunting their newly empowered rule over the tribal lands of Ireland by claiming the goddess. In the ancient traditions of kingship a sacred marriage ritual or *hierosgamos* with the goddess of the land solemnized inauguration. There are references to the fact that actual possession of the queen, as the embodiment of sovereignty, was considered a necessity to legitimate rule even when the old chief was overthrown or killed. This connection has not to my knowledge been explored, and I am not cognisant enough of the placement of the various figures to be able now to do more than hypothesize. I am grateful to Dr. Patrick Wallace, Director of the National Art Museum in Dublin, for calling my attention to the large proportion of Irish sheelas positioned not on church architecture as in Britian and Gaul but on the walls of Norman castles. See also Anderse, *The Witch on the Wall*.

100 The word is related to "mead." Its Welsh cognate, *meddw*, means "drunk." Sjoestedt, p. 75. Ross translates the name as "Drunk Woman."

101 In a Welsh triad we learn that a bee is one of the children of a goddess called Henwen [Ancient Sow]. Along with a single grain of barley (the source of the bread, porridge, fodder, straw, and the malt used in ale), this figure gives her people the substances they need in order to participate in the rituals of her sacred inebriation. While there does not seem to be any known connection between Henwen's Irish counterpart and honey or bees, Maeve's name itself tells us that she is related to honey in its fermented form. See Rachel Bromwich, *Trioedd Ynys Prydein: The Welsh Triads*. Cardiff: University of Wales: 1961, TYP No. 26. See also discussion in Rhys, pp. 503-508. As queen bee, deity of honey and the hive, the goddess represents the center of fertility in a swarm of consorts, an apt analogue of the undying goddess served by many kings.

102 Rees and Rees, p. 76.

103 In other traditions these blood rivers of life that flow from the belly or vulva of the goddess are called the "Four Rivers of Paradise," the Styx, or the red carpet. See Walker, pp. 635-645.

104 It has been equated with the "claret wine" (claret means "perception" or "enlightenment" and is a synonym for blood) offered from the Fairy Queen's lap to Thomas Rhymer as "communion with female life-essence . . . menstrual blood." Walker, p. 994.

105 Rees and Rees, p. 75.

106 Such embodied sexual imagery survived in heretical Gnostic celebrations of the Christian Last Supper as the actual ingestion of male sperm and female

secretions, including menstrual blood. Markale mentions this as a Phibionite practice in the third century A.D. He tells us further that the name of the Indian goddess Satyavati means both "truth" and "stinking fish." He explains this appelation by the fact that vaginal fluid and decomposing fish both contain the chemical trimetyalamine. The original cup of sovereignty, which enabled discrimination of truth was, by implication, the vagina. Taboos against oral sex and the tasting of menstrual fluid remain strong in modern times. Rather than being rituals to honor and participate in the female partner's sacred sexuality, such actions came to hold only negative numinosity. They are still considered pornographic (from the Greek work for sacred prostitute) and unlawful in some parts of the United States. See Markale [1972] 1975, pp. 171ff.

107 Walker, p. 635. So too Maeve may have withheld her flow for battle power and released its "gush" at the end of the war.

108 Walker, p. 636. There are also extensive rituals of menstrual blood in India. See A. Mookerjee, *Kali: The Feminine Force*. Rochester, VT: Destiny, 1988, pp. 30-35. See also Zimmer, pp. 89-91.

109 Similarly Indra by drinking soma straight from the goddess Lakshmi became king of the gods and identified with the goddess—"the Mount of Paradise with its four rivers, 'many-hued' . . . rich in cattle and fruiting vegetation. The Goddess' blood became his wisdom." Walker. 637.

110 Richard Cavandish, *Prehistoric England*. New York: British Heritage, 1983, p. 10.

111 Markale, 1976, p. 86.

112 Quoted in Markale, 1976, p. 309.

113 Ross, 1986, p. 72.

114 Joan Eckstein, personal communication.

115 Anne Ross, "Material Culture, Myth and Folk Memory," in *The Celtic Consciousness*. Robert O'Driscoll, ed. New York: George Braziller, 1982, p. 207.

116 See E. R. Laurie and T. White, 1997. "Speckled Snake, Brother of Birch: Amanita Muscaria Motifs in Celtic Legends," in *Shaman's Drum*, No. 44: 52-65. See also Weston La Barre, "Hallucinogens and the Shamanic Origins of Religion," in *Flesh of the Gods: The Ritual Use of Hallucinogens*. Peter T. Furst, ed. New York: Praeger, 1972, pp. 261-278.

117 "Recent ethological and laboratory studies . . . and analyses of social and biological history, suggest that the pursuit of intoxication with [fermented fruit and] drugs is a primary motivational force in the behavior of organisms." Ronald K. Siegel. *Intoxication: Life in Pursuit of Artificial Paradise*. New York: E. P. Dutton, 1989, pp.10-16.

118 Diodorus Sicilus, quoted by J. Markale, 1976. *Celtic Civilisation*. London: Gordon and Cremonesi, p. 57.

119 Livy, quoted by Markale, 1976, p. 57.

120 O'Grady, Desmond, *The Gododdin: A Version by Desmond O'Grady, Ink Paintings by Louis Le Brocquy*. Dublin: Dolmen Editions, 1977, p. 27.

121 The difference is similar to that which Victor Turner makes when he distinguishes liminal and liminoid states. See *From Ritual to Theater: The Human Seriousness of Play*. New York: PAJ Publications, 1982.

122 Throughout what follows I will use the capitalized word Maeve to indicate the goddess and *medb* to refer to the intoxicant. Both words are however pronounced and spelled the same in Gaelic.

123 "The Adventures of Art, Son of Conn" and "The courtship of Delbchaem,

Daughter of Morgan," in *Ancient Irish Tales*. T. P. Cross and C. H. Slover, eds. New York: Henry Holt, 1936, p. 499.

124 See Mary Gormley, 1989. *Tulsk Parish in Historic Maigh Ai: Aspects of Its History and Folklore*. Roscommon: Roscommon Historical and Archaeological Society. 12.

125 There are *ogham* runes on a stone on the roof of the inner grotto at Oweynagat. One set on the lintel of the passageway reads *Vraicci Maqi Medvvi*, identifying the place as the cave of Fraech son of Maeve. If the stone was taken from a nearby grave, as its 1864 discoverer Samuel Ferguson thought, what is the significance of the buried man being called a son of Maeve? This name in several texts has led scholars to wonder about the identity of the mythic Fraech. Garrett Olmsted discusses the names that link various mythic characters to a single deity called Fraech, the dying and resurrected son, nephew, and partner of the goddess Boann-Maeve-Aife. In one story the wounded Fraech is carried into the Cave of Cruachan and returns the next day healed. In another the dead Fraech is carried into what is probably the same cave, now called *Sid Fraich*, by a group of women. This leads us to wonder if this cave in Roscommon served the same purposes as other temple mounds across Ireland where the dead were placed for resurrection. Was the cave bearing Fraech's name a site of death and rebirth rites where those entering had to themselves become identified with Fraech as a reborn initiate? See Garrett Olmsted,1992, "The Earliest.Narrative Version of *The Tain*: Seventh-century Poetic References to *Tain Bo Cuailnge*," in *Emania: Bulletin of the Navan Research Group*. No. 10. 11-16.

Local folklore tells us there is a tunnel linking the cave of Oweynagat to other legendary caves at Keshcorran twenty miles north in the Bricklieve Mountains of Sligo. This suggests an underworld mythic geography joining centers of power and/or centers where the underworld powers emerge into the world of humans or take humans into their domain. It gives us an awesome sense of the exchanges of energy between human and transhuman powers, connections that our ancestors felt to be so palpable they could image them under and through the forms of the landscape.

Not surprisingly Oweynagat was renamed in Christian times—like many other pagan cult centers—The Hell's Mouth of Ireland. Today visitors are warned more secularly. They are told not to venture inside, for badgers have taken over the cave for their den.

126 "The breast contains the beast of death," Gimbutas tells us. *The Language of the Goddess*, San Francisco: HarperSanFrancisco, 1989, pp. 187-189, 195. Melanie Klein has reintroduced this idea into psychology with the polarization of modern rational consciousness that bifurcates the opposites. She thus hypothesizes that the infant experiences a separate good and bad breast, one a source of nourishment and one a source of frustration also containing the infant's rage and envy of the plentiful source.

127 Gimbutas, 1989, p. 158.

128 Yeats writes of a red-haired jolly youth who "sleeps away all Time" in a drunken sleep inside "the pleasant nook" of "the Hell Mouth at Cruachan" or Oweynagat. Feeling as blessed as a rabbit in his safe hole, he resents being awakened and explains that he is waiting for Judgment Day when "there be nothing but God left." See "The Hour Before Dawn," in Yeats, *The Collected Poems of W. B. Yeats*. New York: Macmillan, 1955, pp. 114-117.

129. See the episode of his encounter with the Morrigan. Kinsella, pp. 132-133, 135-137.

Chapter 2 Notes

1 For these divisions I am indebted to the work of Georges Dumezil, who found three functions in Indo-European and Vedic culture: those supporting material abundance, those supporting war, and those supporting law and religion. I have separated the druidic/poetic/shamanic and kingly functions because there is strong evidence from the *medb* initiations—as well as in the literature—that they had different rites and purposes in Celtic society. Rees and Rees follow Dumezil rather too far in their otherwise excellent introductory volume. For a discussion of the limits of Dumezil's theory, see McCone. 58-59.

2 Letter to Mr. W. January 30, 1961. In C. G. Jung, *Letters: 1951-61,* vol. 2. Gerhard Adler, ed. in collaboration with Aniela Jaffe. R. F. C. Hull, tr. Princeton: Princeton University Press, 1953-74, pp. 623-625.

3 Dated about 550 B.C., excavated by Dr. Jorg Biel in 1978. See Ruth and Vincent Megaw, *Celtic Art From Its Beginnings to the Book of Kells.* London. Thames & Hudson, 1989, p. 42.

4 Delaney, pp. 21-22.

5 Kinsella, p. 6.

6 Kinsella, p. 25.

7 A. O. H. Jarman, "The Heroic View of Life in Early Welsh Verse," in *The Celtic Consciousness.* Robert O'Driscoll, ed. New York: George Braziller, 1982, p. 165.

8 Death was not considered a final end by the Celts. They adopted the beliefs of the earlier tribes honoring the goddess of nature as presiding over the cycle of birth, death, and regeneration. Roman writers hint that they were such intrepid and foolhardy fighters by Roman standards because they believed in some kind of rebirth. Stories of the reanimation of dead warriors and the restoration of body parts by druid healers, of heroes living eternally in the *sidh* mounds, and of men's debts paid in the otherworld all suggest various kinds of limitless existence. We know also that their sense of individuality was still embedded in the tribe, thus individual survival was important only in relation to the well-being of the group and its values. Ulster warriors were praised as fearless before death, described as boasting of their mortal wounds, and they revered and were said to continue to offer food to the heads of their worthiest decapitated rivals. Certainly they believed they would live on in the heroic renown of their poets. In their desire for fame, they were thus hotheadedly passionate and even able to suicide for the perceived good of the family or tribe, much as *kamakazi* pilots and terrorists do in the modern world.

9 In Celtic times the earth goddess was honored during peacetime, but raids and wars required that libido be shifted towards the energies imaged as the male gods or the death and warrior goddesses. Thus, as we will see in chapter 9, the king kept his feet in the lap of the goddess unless he was away securing the boundaries of the kingdom or at war. Heroic fame among peers for performance unto death to honor the war chief became more important to the warrior aristocracy than the sense of existential security acquired through relationship to the all-embracing maternal sourceground.

Today we have separated the values of performance and being much farther. As much Western culture extolled the dominative heroic ideal, it lost consciousness of the need for relationship to the matrix, and we are only beginning to reclaim our sense of its value. Psychologically we know that when the mother (and the earth goddess) are demeaned, the values connected to the feminine will not be honored and therefore affirmed in society and in each child's development. There will not be an adequate sense of validated primary existence, per se. Thus our age is struggling to bring back what the Celtic period was struggling to repress in its development of heroic individuality. For us, self-worth has become overly dependent on performance and the renown earned by heroic accomplishment. Winnicott discusses the psychological ramifications of this poignantly. See 1971. *Playing and Reality*. New York: Basic Books.

10 Such sacrifice was deemed essential to build libido for the masculine and father god with the sacrifice of mortal paternity. See Rene Girard, 1977. *Violence and the Sacred*. Patrick Gregory, tr. Baltimore: Johns Hopkins University Press.

11 O'Grady, p. 49.

12 O'Grady, p. 63.

13 Jarman, p. 166.

14 O'Grady, p. 48.

15 Quoted by Jean Markale. *Merlin: Priest of Nature*. Rochester, VT: Inner Traditions International, 1995, p. 53.

16 Similarly Viking warriors ate fly agaric to produce the ecstatic recklessness that earned them the name beserkers. See Seigel, p. 66. In ancient Persia, warriors took hashish to get high and then followed their leader's orders to go forth to kill. The killers were called *hashshashin* (hashish eaters), from which comes our word assassin (Whitney Asher, private communication).

17 Kinsella, p. 131.

18 Erich Neumann, referring to the magical power of pulque in Mexican cults, describes the use of intoxicants to instill liveliness and to bridge the warrior into easy death. He calls it "a means employed by the war goddess to make men braver in battle, but it was also the symbol of the deadly power of the Feminine itself, in which intoxication and death are mysteriously interwoven." Neumann, *The Great Mother: An Analysis of the Archetype*. New York: Pantheon Books, 1955, p. 301.

19 Thus it could create a greater sense of the single warrior's grandiose capacity to act effectively and without fear. Such a primitive sense of effective capacity supports the early heroic ego while the individual is still embedded in group dynamics and dependent on both ideal leader and consciousness-altering substance for direction and motivation.

20 From this perspective *The Tain* can be seen as one warrior's heroic stand against the powers of the goddess. Because Cuchullain is an outsider and, like his father god Lugh, a representative of new cultural dominants, he does not succumb to the collective debilitation that was the curse of the old agricultural goddess on the men of the tribe of Ulster. Not included in Macha's malediction, he can thus stand against Maeve and her massed armies. Repeatedly he combats Maeve's heroes one by one—providing us with an image of the heroic, disciplined will necessary to counteract the aroused enmity of otherworld or unconscious forces as well as an image of the continual effort needed to combat the ever seductive lure of the *medb*.

21 Irish bishops objected to the "lewd songs [and] brutal tricks" that took place at "unchristian wakes where the corpse is present, and where games, dances, singing and drinking are carried on." Repeatedly the churchmen "forbade rough games at wakes and recommended the recitations of prayers and the reading of spiritual books instead." Sean O Suilleabhain, *Irish Wake Amusements*. Dublin: The Mercier Press, 1967pp. . 38-75, 153-154.

22 These were undoubtedly remnants of ancient fertility magic.

23 O Suilleabhain, pp. 149-150.

24 In Irish mythical history Bres was satirized and had to withdraw as king because he was stingy. See Cross and Slover. 33. In Christian medieval law when Sundays were sacred, one obligation of the Irish king was to provide banquets where the people could "drink ale on Sundays, for there is no regular sovereign (*flaith techta*) who does not promise ale (*laith*) every Sunday." See Georges Dumezil. [1971] *The Destiny of a King*. Alf Hilttebeitel, tr. Chicago: University of Chicago Press, 1973, p. 93.

25 See McCone, pp. 124.

26 Brian Friel has brought this fact poignantly to modern audiences in "Dancing at Lughnasa."

27 New York Irish protested the media picture of their celebration of St. Patrick's day as a drunken orgy. See *The New York Times*, March 16 and 17, 1990. We know that an ancient spring ritual underlies the modern saint's day and its orgy. Evidence comes from many sources in the British Isles. In Co. Kerry the modern debased version of the midsummer harvest and trade assembly, called Puck Fair, climaxes with the crowning of a goat by a young virgin. Goat and maiden represent the horned god consort of the ancient goddess and the eternally young goddess herself. Other rites celebrate the May King and Queen whose nuptuals occured at Garland Day or Beltane. See Whitlock, pp. 140-142.

28 "It has generated conditions that can only be described by such global and imprecise terms as *esctasy* or *madness*. Some feel closer to everything in their environment. Still others look for a rainbow, an Emerald City, a wizard's powers. But for all of us the experience is a rite of passage that takes us into a state of *toxicity*, hence the word *intoxication*." Siegel, p. 12.

29 William James quoted in Arianna Stassinopoulos and Roloff Beny, *The Gods of the Greeks*. New York: Abrams, 1983, p. 109. The *medb*—as well as gold adornments— was given to bards, *filids*, and *vates* by their chiefs in payment for service. The drink was equivalent to and supported druidic service, just as the mead feast was equivalent to and supported the warriors' service.

30 Jung writing of qualities associated with the mother archetype. 1938/1954. *CW 9i*. §158.

31 See Felicitas D. Goodman, *Ecstasy, Ritual, and Alternate Reality: Religion in a Pluralistic World*. Bloomington: Indiana University Press, 1988. Gerald of Wales describes the 12th-century Welsh poets (*awenydd*) taken over by awen (inspiration). See *The Journey through Wales: The Description of Wales*. Lewis Thorpe, tr. Harmondsworth: Penguin, 1978. See also the discussion of *imbas forosnai* in Patrick K. Ford, *The Poetry of Llywarch Hen: Introduction, Text, and Translation*. Berkeley: University of California Press, 1974, pp. 58-62.

32 We know that hemp and opium were widely grown in ancient Britain, perhaps for their hallucinogenic properties as well as for cloth and food. E. R. Laurie and T. White suggest there is evidence that hallucinogenic mushrooms were also part of Celtic cult practice. See 52-65. In medieval Irish legends we hear that druids ritually ingested the broth and meat of a sacred, white bull to fortell the future king in a dream (*tarbfeis*). Cross and Slover, p. 97. The druids also used red pig meat and salt to provide prophetic dreams. See Rhys, pp. 317-320.

33 William Beattie, ed. *Border Ballads*. London: Penguin, 1952, pp. 223-226.

34 *The Mabinogi and Other Medieval Welsh Tales*, tr. and ed. by Patrick K. Ford. Berkeley: University of California Press, 1977, pp. 159-187. Magus and druid were equated in ancient and medieval texts. See Markale, 1995, p. 142.

35 Markale, 1995, p. 47, describing Taliesin's contemporary and colleague Merlin.

36 Lady Charlotte Guest. *The Mabinogion from the Welsh of the Llyrf Coch o Hergest.* London: Bernard Quartch, 1877, p. 482.

37 Ford, 1977, pp. 172-173.

38 This description is of Flann Mainistrech of Monasterboice Abbey. McCone, p. 140.

39 Siegel, p. 81.

40 Jung in a letter to Mr. Bill Wilson. See 1953-74. vol 2. pp. 623-25.

41 Yeats comments in his preface to Lady Gregory, *Cuchulllain of Muirthhemne: The Story of the Men of the Red Branch of Ulster Arranged and Put into English.* Gerrards Cross: Colin Smythe, 1902, p. 14.

42 Descriptions of actual voyages by early Irish sea farers all the way to America may have influenced some of the accounts. Biblical descriptions of Paradise have also left their mark on these poems. In turn these Irish *imramma* (stories of voyages) have influenced later European journey literature, perhaps even Dante's *Divina Commedia*.

43 Markale, 1995, pp. 108-111.

44 Meyer, "The Isles of the Happy," pp. 3-6.

45 Myles Dillon, *Early Irish Literature.* Chicago: University of Chicago Press, 1948, p. 118.

46 "The Hosting of the Sidhe," in Yeats, 1955, p. 53.

47 Meyer, p. 6.

48 Yeats preface to Lady Gregory, 1902, p. 13.

49 Goodman discusses religious trance and the necessity of a ritual, communal context when using psychedelics. "In a specific religious context, once you 'get there,' you always know what to expect and why you are there. In other words, there is always a reason why you are going, and there is a guide to show you around your society's alternate reality into which the drug provided an extrance." "During religious ritual, the drug acts as the stimulus that induces the trance, acting on the nervous system much like a drum signal or a certain dance step. Religious communities that use drugs to this end teach their members how to switch from the intoxication to the religious trance." See Goodman, pp. 35-43.

50 Eleanor Knott. [1957] *Irish Classical Poetry: Filiocht Na Sgol.* Kildare: Leinster Leader, 1966, p. 17.

51 The altering of consciousness was imaged as a leap to another plane in both Indian and Celtic lore. Thus the leaping salmon was a fish of wisdom. The Peaked Red One, an archaic, shamanic, cult figure whom Finn encountered sitting in a tree with his animals, was distinguished "by the powers of his leaping." See Ross, 1967, p. 337. Various saints of Christian Ireland were said to have had similar powers to leap. Saints Suibne Gelt and Molling each took three leaping steps to another dimension. See Rees and Rees, pp. 77-78.

52 This state was presumed in India to be brought about through the action of soma, and Indravishnu was praised "in the intoxication of soma you took vast strides." Rees and Rees, p. 79. In Persia haoma was used. Egyptians of the third millenium BC partook of "the liquor of Maat" to "wash their inward parts" and to convey consciousness of life after death as well as truthfulness. Walker, 1983, p. 562.

53 Pleromatic here implies the transcendent fullness of the uncreated. In Kabbalah it is *Ein Soph* or Infinite Nothingness. Similar to the Buddhist sense of emptiness that is full, this Absolute Reality is perceived by enlightenend consciousness. Cf. The

Sufi poet Kabir's line "[T]he wheel of ecstatic love turns around in the sky." Robert Bly, *The Kabir Book*. Boston: Beacon Press, 1977, p. 59.

54 Such conscious experience of union with divine reality allows the mystic to perceive the one beyond categories of existence and non-existence, "beyond limitations of 'I' and 'other'. . . then each perceives that he contains the entire universe within himself—that he *is* the entire universe. Full consiousness of this more than godlike state is, as accomplished mystics have discovered, accompanied by a bliss that is inconceivable." John Blofeld, *The Tantric Mysticism of Tibet: A Practical Guide*. New York: E. P. Dutton, 1970, p. 53.

55 Andrew Harvey, *Love's Fire: Recreations of Rumi*. Ithaca, NY: Meeramma Press, 1988, p. 76. The image of drink as a source of such experience occurs frequently in Sufi literature. The soul among Sufis must dare to get drunk on spirit. Kabir writes: "In the sky temple . . . decorated with the moon and many jewels . . . . The man who has drunk that liquid wanders around like someone insane." Bly, p. 14.

56 Although I use the term visionary, I do not mean to imply that such trans-egoic knowledge is perceived merely through the eyes. Such overextension of the optical term has led to a false reliance on and expectation of needing to have visual images of the transcendent. Body sensations, scents, auditory experience, and intuitions that seem to arrive without any sensed basis are all means by which we attune with what is beyond ego functioning, hence transcendent. Jung coined the term transcendent function to point towards a psychological capacity to discover and create a Self-based perspective bridging between seemingly opposed positions. It also expresses itself through images that can be heard, seen, danced, etc.

57 Fred Hanna, 1992. "Reframing Spirituality: AA, the 12 Steps and the Mental Health Counselor," in *Journal of Mental Health Counseling*. 14:2. 173.

58 Blofeld's description of the effects of a mystical experience on his sense of identity points to the same consciousness: "There was awareness of undifferentiated unity embracing perfect identification of subject and object; logic was transcended and I beheld a whirling mass of brilliant colors and forms which, being several, differed from one another and yet were *altogether the same* at the moment of being different! The concept of 'I' had ceased to be; I was at once the audience, the actors and the play! Secondly I recognized the unutterable bliss I was experiencing as the *only* real state of being, all others amounting to no more than passing dreams. Thirdly came awareness of all that is implied by the Buddhist doctrine of 'dharmas'. . . namely the doctrine that all objects of perception are devoid of own-being, mere transitory combinations of an infininite number of impulses. I experienced the rising of each impulse and the thrill of culmination with which it ceased to be, waves mounting and dissolving in a sea of bliss." Blofeld, p. 33.

59 An alternate translation is "gives Fire to the Head." See Jean Markale, 1976, p. 126.

60 From "The Book of Leinster," in John Koch, ed. *The Celtic Heroic Age: Literary Sources for Ancient Celtic Europe and Early Ireland and Wales*. Malden, MA: Celtic Studies, 1995, p. 259. See also Rees and Rees, p. 98.

61 Jung, 1935. *CW 18*. §218.

62 R. Gordon Wasson, "The Divine Mushroom of Immortality," in *Flesh of the Gods: The Ritual Use of Hallucinogens*. Peter T. Furst, ed. New York, Praeger, 1972, p. 198.

63 La Barre, pp. 261-278. For discussion of some of the psychological and physiological variables in religious trance, see also Goodman, especially chapter 4. She discusses some differences between secular and religious trances induced by drugs.

64 Goodman, p. 41. This function is similar to what AA teaches its members to do when they switch from taking in literal drink to participating in experiences of their relation to a Higher Power—a power some members call, "God-Consciousness." See *Alcoholics Anonymous: The Story of How Many Thousands of Men and Women Have Recovered from Alcoholism*. 3rd ed. New York: AA World Services, 1976, p. 570.

65 The Medieval Welsh tale of Branwen in *The Mabinogion* contains the remnants of a pre-Christian mystery connected with the very ancient cult of the severed head and sacred waters. The prime implement of this cult was a sometimes gold-covered skull cup from which the waters of a sacred well were drunk for healing or inspiration. There is much evidence throughout the British Isles that this cult was significant for the Celts, just as it has been in India and Tibet. See Ross, 1967, chapter II.

66 Wasson, pp. 201-213. Wasson convincingly argues that soma is a potion derived from the fly agaric mushroom. Used by shamans in many cultures, it flourishes under the birch tree that he believes was the original tree of life and shamanic *axis mundi*. There is ample evidence that the birch fungus allowed "divine possession, poetic frenzy, supernatural inspiration"—all forms of visionary flight between worlds. While we have no evidence of the growth of these agaric mushrooms in ancient Ireland, Laurie and White suggest that they may have been imported.

67 Jeremiah 23:9.

68 Forughi Bastami. "Midnight Sun," in P. L. Wilson and N. Pourjavady, eds. *The Drunken Universe: An Anthology of Persian Sufi Poetry*. Grand Rapids, MI: Phanes Press, 1987, pp. 53-54.

69 *Kharabat* is a Persian word meaning "the state of being ruined" and "tavern," thus by analogy it connotes both a Sufi meeting place and a person who has become intoxicated with divine love.

70 Rumi, translated by Harvey, p. 85.

71 Blofeld, pp. 33-34 footnotes.

72 Blofeld, pp. 33.

73 Erich Neumann, 1961. "Mystical Man," in *Spring* 12: 9-49.

74 Neumann, 1961, p. 20.

75 Milton Erickson's hypnosis work influences the practitioners of many schools of psychotherapy today. Selver, Feldenkreis, Alexander, Reik, Lowen, and other body-centered therapists have shown us how to effect psychic changes through focus on bodywork. The traditions of Yoga and the oriental martial arts have a similar purpose.

76 Goodman describes her research on the psysiological concommitants of trance states. See Goodman, p. 39. See also E. C. Whitmont, 1993.

77 Guest, p. 482.

78. Similarly the Dagda, chief of the gods of the Irish Tuatha de Danaan, had to undergo the rite of gluttony before he could mate with the Morrigan in "The Second Battle of Mag Tuired." See Cross and Slover, p. 39.

79 Michael Paull, private communication.

80 Gerald of Wales, a Norman cleric of Wesh descent, visited Ireland in 1185 as a secretary to Prince John. His *Topography of Ireland* was completed in 1187. This translation is quoted in Roy, pp. 66-67.

81 There are parallels in India, the Near East, and the Aegean. See McCone, pp. 117-

118. He discusses the larger issues of sacred kingship and ritual marriage between kings and the goddess of sovereignty called *Medwi* after the mead drink involved in the ceremony. See also chapter 5.

82 The order of the Ulster ritual is the opposite of that in myth where the cup is taken before the "lying together." I wonder if the ceremony expresses an older version of the pattern. It is similar to the horse sacrifice of India where the queen mates with a stallion that is then sacrificed.

83 The Gaulish royal name *Epo-maduos* contains the words *epo* [horse] and mead. See J. Puhvel, "Aspects of Equine Functionality," in *Myth and Law Among the Indo-Europeans.* J. Puhvel, ed. Berkeley: University of California Press, 1976, pp. 164-167.

84 For discussion of the psychological issues involved in the choice between poison and healing draught, killing and curing, see chapter 5.

85 Medea's rejuvenating cauldron destroyed the old king. Medea comes from the land of the Hyperboreans, northern tribes equated with the Celts. Robert Graves. *The Greek Myths.* New York: George Braziller, 1957, pp. 251-253. Her use of magic potions in relation to kingship suggests that she has strong affinities to Maeve. There may be closer connections between Maeve and Medea that I have evidence for now.

86 Akin to Tibetan past-life memory tests that determine the reincarnation of a *tulku* or master, the druid sanctioned choice of object test may express another link between Irish and Eastern cultures. There were also special magic ordeals, called the Tara tests, that confirmed the rightful ruler. Administered by druids to the high king, these were analogous to those that the smith gave to Niall and his brothers preliminary to the *feis* with the goddess queen in the tale, "The Adventures of the Sons of Eochaid Mugmedon." Cross and Slover, pp. 508-513.

87 An interesting parallel on the animal kingdom is described by Ronald Siegel. Experimental research suggests that the king rats in each colony are able to resist dependency on alcohol. In the laboratory rat colonies of researcher Gaylord Ellison, the dominant male feeds first, takes the best burrow, and dominates the others but "is an extreme nonconsumer of alcohol." The high consumers were less socially active, less dominant, perhaps more easily stressed. Siegel. 116. We can perhaps wonder if the qualities supporting the capacity for regality circumvent excessive need for addictive substances even in rats.

88 Liam Breatnack cites a passage in the *Bretha Nemed* describing the "true ruler [as] a cauldron that cooks together every raw thing." Quoted in McCone, p. 174. In this the ruler takes on the vessel functions of the goddess herself. The Dagda, chief of the Tuatha De Danaan, was known to possess a ladle so large it could hold a mating couple. He also had a wondrous club, one end of which could kill nine with one blow and the other restore nine to life. These two implements represent the chief's functions to rule over and contain the opposites.

89 Edward Edinger describes this as a *circulatio* process between ego and Self. See Edinger, 1972, chapter 1.

90 Emily Dickinson, *Final Harvest: Emily Dickinson's Poems.* Selected by Thomas H. Johnson. Boston: Little Brown, ca. 1861, p. 33. Many analytic clients have similar intoxicating problems with positive experiences; hence they must be dosed carefully in therapy. See Perera. *The Scapegoat Complex: Towards a Mythology of Shadow and Guilt.* Toronto: Inner City, 1986, p. 72.

91 Jung writes: "The [S]elf, in its efforts at self-realization, reaches out beyond the ego personality an all sides; because of its all-encompassing nature it is brighter and darker than the ego, and accordingly confronts it with problems which it would like to avoid. . . . From this we can see the numinous power of the [S]elf. . . . For this reason *the experience of the [S]elf is always a defeat for the ego.*" 1955-56. *CW 14.* §778.

Chapter 3 Notes

1 Part of the prophecies attributed to Merlin in Geoffrey of Monmouth's *History of the Kings of Britain.* Quoted in Markale, 1995, p. 172.

2 Phaedrus quoted in E. R. Dodds, *The Greeks and the Irrational.* Berkeley: University of California Press, 1964. Socrates distinguished several types of mania. That of merely human origin was not deemed creative.

3 More obscure Greek divinities like Medea, Circe, Aphrodite-Urania, and Hecatebelong to an earlier stratum, as archaic as that of the Celtic/Vedic goddesses. While Dionysus represented the ecstatic for the later Greeks, he represented the opposite of Apollo in the Greek patriarchy and—like Pan and the horned god of the Celts—Satan in Christianity. In the Hebrew tradition King David was chided for dancing before the ark. Saul was damned for consulting the prophetess of Endor. Christ, although he offered his blood as wine, cannot invite full-bodied and spiritual ecstasy within the traditional Christian Church since body and feminine were lumped together and eschewed. The sacramental wine of the mass is tasted symbolically to inebriate the soul in communion with the godhead. It is not meant to inebriate the body. Indeed within the Christian churches, intoxication is more often induced by ascetic and righteous behaviors. The metaphysical poets, some 16th-century Italian Mannerist art, and Bernini in his sculpture of St. Teresa provide exceptions, portraying the ecstasies of the erotic as part of religious devotion. Passionate pentecostal Christian groups have flourished mostly locally and outside the main traditions. Within Judaism the esoteric (and male-oriented) traditions of Kaballah and the Hassidism have introduced an ecstatic connection to the divine expressed through prayerful movement and music.

4 Charles Grob and Willis Harman, 1995. "Making Sense of the Psychedelic Issue," in *Noetics Sciences Review.* Autumn. 9:5-9, 37-41.

5 Marija Gimbutas, 1989, p. 318.

6 Peg Streep speaking of the process of hybridization among the Greeks, *Sanctuaries of the Goddess: The Sacred Landscapes and Objects.* Boston: Little Brown, 1994, p. 167.

7 McDougall, p. 35.

8 A partial shift to support homage to the feminine occured in the 12th-century courts of courtly love and Marian cults. It is beautifully manifest in the musical works of Hildegard of Bingen, especially in her "Canticles for Mary."

9 Thus keening for the dead continued and was even recorded in this century for Folkway Records, but it was practiced only out of earshot of the local priest.

10 Abusive drinking among Irish-Americans has been directly related to religious repression and called "a reaction to psycho-sexual and authoritarian tensions imposed by Catholicism." See M. O'Carroll, *The Relationship of Religion and Ethnicity to Drinking Behavior: A Study of North American Immigrants in the United States.* Berkeley: University of California School of Public Health, 1979.

11 Brian Friel brilliantly conveys some of this process in his plays "Dancing at Lugnassa" and "Translations."

12 Wolfgang G. Jelik sees this as a cause of alcoholism among Native Americans. See his "Traditional Medicine Relevant to Psychiatry," in *Treatment of Mental Disorders*. N. Sartorius *et al.*, eds. Geneva: World Health Organization, 1993, pp. 341-390. See also Dwight B. Heath, "A Decade of Development in the Anthropological Study of Alcohol Use, 1970-1980," in *Constructive Drinking: Perspectives on Drink from Anthropology*. Mary Douglas, ed. Cambridge: Cambridge University Press, 1987, pp. 35-40.

13 Victor Turner's distinctions between liminal and liminoid rites can be applied to the Celtic and modern uses of alcohol. See *From Ritual to Theater: The Human Seriousness of Play*. New York: PAJ Publications, 1982, pp. 53ff.

14 Heath, pp. 21-23, 34.

15 Frank McCourt poignantly describes the ceremony of the first pint of stout bought by his father to celebrate a 16-year-old youth's birthday, his coming of age among the men in the pub. See his *Angela's Ashes*. New York, Scribner, 1996. See also Richard Stivers, *A Hair of the Dog: Irish Drinking and American Stereotype*. University Park: Pennsylvania State University Press, 1976.

16 Jay C. Wade, 1994. "Substance Abuse: Implications for Counseling African American Men," in *Journal of Mental Health Counseling*. 16:4. 415-433.

17 Gerald of Wales, pp. 116-117.

18 The witch of Endor fills a similar role in the Bible, and there are millions since who have been persecuted because their healing and extrasensory gifts have been attributed not to deity but to demon. More recently we have often blithely tended to equate mystics with psychotics. Jung himself, while stressing "you need not be insane to hear [the] voice . . . of the inner friend of the soul" that he calls the Self, has warned against regressive encounters wherein "the unconscious has swallowed up ego-consciousness." See 1940/1950. *CW, 9i.* §236; and 1939. *CW 9i.* §520. This kind of possession or identification with unconscious archetypal factors does not lead to transformation. Jung calls it hysterical and the mark of "abnormal people—ecstatics, somnambulists, sensitives." 1905. *CW 18.* §700.

19 Jung writes: "The creative mystic was ever a cross for the Church, but it is to him that we owe what is best in humanity." 1955-56. *CW 14.* §531.

20 Some modern psychologists persist in derogating all ecstatic passion as only "grandiosity" or "inflations with affect." They may be such when the material they bring overwhelms the ego or when it functions as part of a defensive escape from painful emotions, but they may also be transformative if honored and served with appropriate consciousness and respect. Then, Jung, commenting on Mircea Eliade's work on shamanism, tells us, they are comparable to a shaman's ecstatic journeys, since "by means of [such] posession [by his familiar or guardian spirits] he acquires his 'mystical organs,' which consitute his true and complete spiritual personality." See 1945/54. *CW 13.* §462. Such "'letting go' [of the ego is] the sine qua non of all forms of higher spiritual development, whether we call it meditation, contemplation, or spiritual exercises." See 1934/50. *CW 9i.* §562.

21 Morris Berman. *Coming to Our Senses: Body and Spirit in the Hidden History of the West*. New York: Simon and Schuster, 1989, p. 35.

22 Steven Fox. Jan, 19, 1990. "Archetypal Drug Addiction," in *The Bulletin of the Analytical Psychology Club of New York*. Fox sees the soaring inflation of the drug as an analogue to Icarus' flight towards the sun that precipitated his death.

23 Kinsella, p. 129.

24 In a variant of this story, Macha, the Ulster counterpart of Maeve, bound the

usurpers and forced them to become her slaves. She made them serve her to build the ramparts of her sacred precincts. Sjoestedt. 42.

25 This is similar to the law of Ereshkigal that made Dumuzi a balance for Inanna. See Perera. *Descent to the Goddess: A Way of Initiation for Women.* Toronto: Inner City, 1981, pp. 81-89.

26 Jean Gebser's term for the capacity to move appropriately between archaic, magic, mythological, and intellectual modes of cognition. See Gebser. [1949 and 1953] *The Ever-Present Origin.* Noel Barstad and Algis Mickunas, trs. Athens: Ohio University Press, 1985, pp. 97-102.

27 See Perera, "Archetypal Self-Spite in a Tale of the Arising Patriarchy," in *To Speak or Be Silent: The Paradox of Disobedience in the Lives of Women.* Lena Ross, ed. Willmette IL, Chiron Publications, 1993, pp. 160-165. The recent archaeological excavations at Navan Fort in Ulster affirm that the mound is the conscious creation of Celtic tribes taking over the site at Emain Macha. The story of Macha's race and self-sacrifice while giving birth to twins suggests the motive for the contemporary erection of the mound as the burial place of the mare goddess. Created from old worn stones under a structure that was raised to be sacrificed, the mound of the first century B.C. replicated the outer form of third- and fourth-millenium passage grave temples like Newgrange and the Mound of the Hostages at Tara. This conscious recreation of the ancient goddess' temple suggests that the energy of the nature deity of the area was being ritually transformed to support the purposes of the new rulers. The powers of the bountiful mare goddess were thus sacrificed—just as Macha was in the story—to enable her figure to become more congruent with the structures and values of the new culture.

28 That the scribes used this disease to describe the goddess may be because of its presence in the Bible as a symbol of uncleanness and ritual separation, henceevidence of god's punishment. It is the disease with which Jahweh punished Moses' sister and made her an outcast for daring to move ahead of her brother. Marcia Dobson has kindly informed me that the word leprosy in the classical world derives from *leukos*, white, and connotes fragmentation. She cites Pausanius and Apollodorus who tell us that Proitides suffered it. Private communication.

    In Greek myth we are told that Dionysus' maenads tore apart animals in their ecstatic sacrifices to their god. King Pentheus, who sought to ban the rites of Dionysus, was himself dismembered by the god's devotees, including his own mother. His refusal to honor the religious rituals mediating the experience of ecstasy led to the king's fragmentation and death just as such repudiation does in the Maeve story.

29 This matrix is analogous to what Neumann calls "the Great Round." Erich Neumann, 1955, chapter 12.

30 Already in Celtic poetry the heroes sing sadly of their waning powers:
    When my warrior spirit no longer drives me,
    My days are short now, and my house is in ruins
    The wind pierces me. . . .
        I am no longer loved by the young woman.
Llywarch Hen. Poems 10 and 11. In *The Red Book of Hergest,* quoted in Markale, 1995, p. 194. See also the nostalgic "Colloquy of Old Men," in Cross and Slover, pp. 457-468.

31 Wilfred Sheed writes movingly of this slow slide into drug dependency. He writes of a similar slide into alcoholism: "Alcohol is the classic best friend turned worst

enemy for the denizens of the frozen north." *In Love with Daylight: A Memoir of Recovery.* New York: Simon and Schuster, 1995, p. 183.

32 Paul Antze. "Symbolic Action in Alcoholics Anonymous," in *Constructive Drinking: Perspectives on Drink from Anthropology.* Mary Douglas, ed. Cambridge: Cambridge University Press, 1987, p. 156.

33 Although the American Medical Association labeled addiction a disease in 1956 and a disability in 1980, many addicts on the street today have reclaimed the devilish name for themselves. To them it connotes a more active commitment to drug culture than does junkie.

34 For help in working with dreams from a Jungian perspective see, for example, Whitmont and Perera and the many references cited therein.

35 This range of drug use comes from Shafer's Commission report. See R. R. Shafer, *First and Second Reports of the National Commission on Marijuana and Drug Abuse.* Washington, DC. U. S. Government Printing Office, 1972-73, pp. 95-97.

36 G. Spruell, quoted in Karen Colapietro Seybold and Paul R. Salmone, 1994. "Understanding Workaholism: A Review of Causes and Counseling Approaches," in *Journal of Counseling and Development.* 73: 4.

37 Increasingly many people heed the meaning of the statement attributed to Jesus in the Apocrypha and frequently quoted by Jung: "If you know what you are doing, you are blessed; but if you do not know what you are doing, then you are cursed and a breaker of the Law." Quoted in S. Hoeller, *Jung and the Lost Gospels: Insisght into the Dead Sea Scrolls and the Nag Hammadi Library.* Wheaton, IL: Theosophical Publishing House, 1989.

38 See Anne Ross and Don Robins, *The Life and Death of a Druid Prince: The Story of Lindow Man, an Archaeological Sensation.* New York: Summit Books, 1989, pp. 117-124.

39 See Linda Schierse Leonard. *Witness to the Fire: Creativity and the Veil of Addiction.* Boston: Shambhala, 1989, p. 4.

40 In 1991 an estimated 20 percent of the child abuse cases receiving medical attention in New York city were due to drug or alcohol problems. Twenty-five percent of New York city drivers in fatal accidents had cocaine in their blood. Address by Dr. Kleber to medical students graduating from New York Medical College.

41 This term means "woman of the *sidh*" (pronounced shee), the otherworld under the Earth. Banshees were said to shriek to foretell death in folklore. Originally they were the goddesses of life, death, and regeneration that were repressed by Christianity.

42 Mary Doyle Curran [1948] *The Parrish and the Hill.* New York: The Feminist Press at The City University of New York, 1986. See also McCourt's portrait of his father in his autobiography.

43 Reported by Toni Atmore, Assistant Superindentent of the Hampden County Pre-Release Center for Ludlow, MA. See Thomas W. Marino, "Addiction and Incarceration Are Common Partners in Crime," in *Counseling Today.* January. 6, 1995.

44 Andrew Greeley. *Ecstasy: A Way of Knowing.* New York: Prentice-Hall, 1974, pp. 56-72.

45 See, for example, Henry Krystal, and Herbert Raskin, *Drug Dependence.* Detroit: Wayne State University, 1970; and Gary G. Forrest, *Alcoholism, Narcissism and Psychopathology.* Springfield, IL: Charles C. Thomas, 1983.

46 Douglas W. Detrick correlates varieties of drugs used with specific kinds of

developmental deficits. Detrick, "Alterego Phenomena and Alterego Transferences," in *Progress in Self Psychology*, vol 1. Arnold Goldberg, ed. New York: The Guilford Press, 1985, p. 249.

47 McCourt. 75.

48 Kohut in his early work discusses addiction in terms of severe disturbances of the idealizing developmental line. The mother, "because of her defective empathy with the child's needs (or for other reasons), did not appropriately fulfill the functions (as stimulus barrier; as an optimal provider of needed stimuli; as a supplier of tension releiving gratification, etc., which the mature psychic apparatus would later be able to perform (or initiate) predominantly on its own. Traumatic disappointments suffered during these archaic stages of development of the idealized selfobject deprive the child of gradual internalization of early experiences of being optimally soothed, or being aided in going to sleep." Kohut, *The Analysis of the Self*. New York: International Universities Press, 1971, p. 46.

49 Michael Balint, *The Basic Fault: Therapeutic Aspects of Regression*. London: Tavistock Publications, 1968, p. 56.

50 Heinz Kohut states the problem in his 1977 *The Restoration of the Self*. New York: International Universities Press:

> [F]rom the beginning, the child asserts his need for a food-giving selfobject—however dimly recognized the selfobject might be. (In more behavioristic terms we might say that the child needs empathically modulated food-giving, not food.) If this need remains unfulfilled (to a traumatic degree) then the broader psychological configuration—the joyful experience of being a whole, appropriately responded-to self—disintegrates and the child retreats to a fragment of the larger experiential unit, i.e., to a pleasure-seeking oral stimulation (to the erogenic zone) or, expressed clinically, to depressive eating. It is this fragment of psychological experience that becomes the crystallization point for the later addiction. . . . It is the increasing awareness of the depressive-disintegrative reaction to the unempathic selfobject milieu—not an increasing awareness of the drive (and an, in essence, educational emphasis on the mastery of the drive)— that becomes the basis from which a renewed movement toward psychological health can proceed. (p. 74.)

Kohut goes on:

> To summarize in more general terms, the establishment of drive fixations and of the correlated activities of the ego occurs in consequence of the feebleness of the self. The unresponded-to self has not been able to transform its archaic grandiosity and its archaic wish to merge with an omnipotnent selfobject into reliable self-esteem, realistic ambitions, attainable ideals. The abonormalities of the drives and of the ego are the symptomatic consequences of this central defect in the self. (p. 81.)

51 See discussion of Harlow's work in John Bowlby. *Attachment and Loss: Attachment*. vol 1. New York: Basic Books, 1969, pp. 213-216.

52 I am varying Donald Winnicott's wonderful formulation to include the archetypal dimension here since that is what opens in the psychic void created by the absence of a good-enough personal caretaker-child relationship to mediate the positive archetypal factors required for thriving. See also Jung's discussion of the interrelationship of archetypal and personal maternal figures that he calls the dual mother. In *CW 5*. §464-612.

53 I am indebted to J. C. Ryan for this quote from one of her clients.

54 Sometimes this negative constellation was carried by actual caretakers who mishandled or abused the needs of the developing infant. Sometimes it was carried genetically or through the prenatal environment of the womb itself in which the fetus was exposed to the effects of maternal binges with alchohol or toxic amounts of stressful hormones. Sometimes the negative matrix reflected a painful environment or physical impairment from which the caretaker could not shield the infant.

55 Balint, p. 56.

56 Jung, 1953-74. vol. 2. 622.

57 Interview on Morning Edition. *National Public Radio*. November 7, 1989.

58 Philippe Bourgois, "Just Another Night on Crack Street," in *New York Times Magazine*, November 12, 1989, p. 94.

59 Thomas Wolfe, *Look Homeward Angel: A Story of a Buried Life*. New York: Scribner, 1929, pp. 411-412.

60 The backlashes of religious and ethnic fundamentalism in many countries only confirm this fact as the vehemence of the Counter-Reformation only confirmed the force of the Reformation in Europe.

61 David A. Stewart, *Thirst for Freedom*. Center City, MN: Hazeldon Press, 1960, p. 55.

62 See B. R. McElderry, *Thomas Wolfe*. New Haven: Yale University Press, 1964, p. 127.

63 Dillon, pp. 102-107.

64 Jones and Jones, pp. 39-40.

65 Neumann, 1961, p. 44.

66 Sigmund Freud. [1930] *Civilization and its Discontents*. Garden City, NY: Doubleday. 1958.

67 That the individual Self is first incarnated through the mother in the patriarchy that demeans women creates a difficult double-bind that is foisted on each child. The pattern forces the heroic ego to repudiate its matrix in order to rule over its separated destiny. This predisposes the patriarchal ego to become alienated from its source and overly focused on issues of performance and control. As a result, the pangs of alienation cry out for reunion. Such alienation can motivate a conscious, individual search, but it can also be a powerful incentive to pursue addictive illusions and delusional fusions.

68 The alternation is a perverted form of the archetypal drama of the Year King consorts of the goddess. See Perera, 1986b. Much of the psychology of the modern codependent personality also falls into this pattern of failed and bifurcated sovereignty.

69 Other Jungian writers see this double authority as a divergence between the paths of Dionysus and Apollo. See Jan Bauer, *Alcoholism and Women: The Background and the Psychology*. Toronto: Inner City, 1982; and Marion Woodman, *Addiction to Perfection: The Still Unravished Bride*. Toronto: Inner City, 1982. The Greeks did not, however, have an ethical superego that blasts judgmentally and shames. This malevolent form of collective authority is a product of a perverted Judeo-Christian tradition in the West. It underlies the potential for the false sovereignty that often results when we enthrone an animus or collective authority and ruthlessly pursue its imperatives. Sovereignty and self-rule over our lives and bodies from a Self perspective must be distinguished from adherence to an ego ideal based on this societal superego. Such differentiation in our personal lives is required whenever we face transitions and must wrestle with the difficulties of Self rule.

70 See E. C. Whitmont. *The Symbolic Quest: Basic Concepts of Analytical Psychology.* revised
    ed. Princeton: Princeton University Press, [1969] 1991, pp. 316-320.
71 Mark Twain, *Following the Equator.* Hartford: American Publishing Co., 1897, p. 29.
    I am indebted to Suzi Naiburg for calling my attention to this work.
72 It is interesting to consider the story of the Garden of Eden from this perspective.
    Eating of the fruit of the tree of life—to provide awareness of ecstatic connection
    to the whole—was permitted in paradise. The fruit of the tree of the knowledge of
    good and evil created a new polarized consciousness that broke up the original
    sense of oneness with all. Such knowledge was forbidden in paradise, but it
    created the consciousness of opposites necessary for extraparadisical life. After
    expelling Adam and Eve, the patriarchal god kept the potential for original
    oneness for himself—i.e. unconscious. It was lost to humans except during certain
    rituals. Drunkenness was a regression from Jahweh's regulations for behavior, and
    its ecstasy was equated in the Old Testament with matrifocal, earlier religions.
    Noah's intoxication was considered shameful and to be denied or looked away
    from. While mild inebriation was made part of the rituals of the Jewish Sabbath
    and Seder and carefully dosed in communal settings, at Purim, the reclaimed
    festival of the goddesss Ishtar/Esther, the celebrants are ritually to drink so much
    they cannot tell the difference between the villain Haman and the righteous
    Mordecai. Under the aegis of the goddess, they are to lose consciousness of the
    opposites. Sexual forms of embodied ecstasy were also sanctified in "The Song of
    Soloman," a collection of ancient canticles to the Hebrew goddess, and celebrated
    weekly by married couples as the visitations of the Shekhina to their required
    Friday night lovemaking. Not only not shamed nor prohibited, ecstatic behavior
    was thus ritually prescribed and held. This may account for a lower incidence
    among Jews of addictive behaviors until the modern erosion of the old rites.

Chapter 4 Notes

1 I am coalescing here my reading in anthropology, archaeology, and mythology
    with the accounts of individuals who have lived with tribal people still in touch
    with aspects of their ancestral mentation and willing to share it with these
    students. Even though there is probably no one who has not been affected by
    contemporary civilization, there are pointers in the accounts to a mind-set that
    we have generally lost. I realize that we can never really fathom the subtleties
    and depths of a life perspective so foreign to Western rational consciousness, but I
    want to suggest its outlines. After this book was in press, I discovered the
    wonderful volume by David Abram in which he discusses many differences
    between the worldviews of peoples living within the oral and written traditions.
    Like the ancient Celts, the tribes he studies have a keen awareness of their
    sensory participation in their natural environment. See Abram *The Spell of the
    Sensuous: Perception and Language in a More-Than-Human World.* New York: Vintage,
    1996.
2 David Bohm. *Wholeness and the Implicate Order.* London: Routledge & Kegan Paul,
    1987.
3 See for example J. E. Lovelock, *Gaia.* Oxford: Oxford University Press, 1979;
    Michael Talbot, *The Holographic Universe.* New York: HarperCollins, 1991; and
    Whitmont, 1993.
4 Nigel Pennick. *The Ancient Secret of Geomancy: Man in Harmony with the Earth.*
    London: Thames & Hudson, 1979.

5 Jung, 1947-54. *CW 8*. §503.

6 The old Celtic solar deities were female as they were in many cultures.

7 In the Cuchullain myths it is significant that the one brother-at-arms Cuchullain most loved and suffered separation from is the man who was his foster-brother when he lived with the initiating warrior goddess Scathach. Homoerotic love was apparently commonplace among the *fianna* (war bands). While this same-sex bonding may support masculine identity against the mother in an early patriarchal culture, it may also tell us that the values of attachment and dependency still found legitimate expression within the heroic brotherhood.

Among my male homophobic clients, envy and fear of dependency seem to be as strong as the insecure gender identity expressed in their contemptuous repudiation of what unconsciously attracts them. Thus the women they tend to choose do not threaten their need for domination.

8 Clients in identity with the heroic ethos are often shocked to realize that dependency and dependent attachments are acceptable after childhood. Their inhibition makes the dependent transference all the more powerful (and often initially erotic) when it does flower.

9 Cf. for example, the figures of Mother Holle in Grimms' *Fairy Tales* and Baba Yaga in the Russian story of Vasilissa.

10 Jung made us aware that defensive energies arise out of the Self, not the ego, and he taught us to respect the client's defenses. Neumann has written on the relevance of the terrible mother as adversary for the development of the heroic ego. But her ugliness in the insistence upon her own prerogatives has not been sufficiently recognized. The assertion of such fragmenting potential is not to say, as Leopold Stein does, that there are defenses of the Self prior to the ego that serve to defend against unthinkable infantile anxieties. These may be better thought of as refusals of the Self to incarnate when that involves participation in the agony of abusive or traumatic relationships. Just as seeds refuse to germinate in dry soil, so the Self resists its germination, the development that represents the deintegration from its original wholeness into an individual personality. This resistence seems to arise from the Self's sovereignty rather than from a sense of Its being cornered. When later in a therapeutic relationship a more adequately receiving environment may be achieved, the potentials of the Self hitherto unreleased from the matrix may incarnate into life. Donald Kalshed, who argues from Stein's perspective, has discussed some of the issues as they relate to clinical practice in a paper on the fairy tale Rapunzel, and in his book, *The Inner World of Trauma: Archetypal Defenses of the Personal Spirit*. New York: Routledge, 1996.

11 Winnicott, 1971. 85. "After being—doing and being done to. But first, being."

12 Jung speaks of one aspect of the unborn potential in us as the inferior function, the fourth, "which remains under the spell of the unconscious . . . [and] acts as a painfully disturbing factor." See his 1951 *CW 9ii*. §430-431. This part inevitably connects us to what is unconscious and trans-egoic. Hene it forms a bridge to the greater personality he calls the Self.

13 Cf. A. Guggenbuehl-Craig. *Power in the Helping Professions*. New York: Spring, 1971.

14 Jung was the first to point to the intersubjective field as the inevitable arena in which interaction with the unconscious as well as conscious aspects of both analyst and analysand took place. See his 1929 paper, "Problems in Modern Psychotherapy," in *CW 16*. §71-75. Cf. also his 1946, "The Psychology of the Transference," in *CW 16*. §221-222. Here we find Jung's famous diagram of a

pattern of the interrelated conscious and unconscious field that applies to "counter-crossing transference relationships."

15 In bulimia the two impulses alternate. Bingeing alternates with killing off the greedy binger by purging. This maintains a terrible bifurcation between—in Kleinian terms—the ideal breast that would satisfy any, albeit hidden, greed and the bad witholding one that forbids and destroys satisfaction. Internally the bifurcation is felt as a battle between impulsivity and control (Fairbairn's libidinous and anti-libidinous conflict) that maintains the only kind of balance possible without any sense of matrix for the opposites. Such awareness of an encompassing matrix comes about through experience of what Winnicott called a good-enough holding environment and what Jungians call the positive archetypal maternal aspect of the Self.

16 All the perversions of the sacred use of the *medb* are characteristic of borderline personalitites or of borderline sectors in the personality. They, in fact, define the clinical, diagnostic category of borderline. Gerald Adler sees lack of constancy as the primary factor in such pathology. See his *The Borderlne Personality and Its Treatment*. Northvale, NJ: Jason Aronson, 1985.

17 This alternation is similar to that experienced by Buddhist meditation practitioners between what they call absolute and relative reality.

18 See Edinger, 1972, chapter 1.

19 Hillesum explains "what is deepest inside me . . . for convenience I call God." *An Interupted Life: The diaries of Etty Hillesum, 1941-43.* New York: Washington Square Press, 1983, p. xi. This inner capacity for authority and guidance is close to what Jungians would call Self.

Part II Notes

1   Jung, 1936. *CW 12.* §328. Jung amplifies this in his letter to AA cofounder Bill W. "Unless the alcoholic could become the subject of a spiritual or religious experience—in short, a genuine conversion, the addiction was hopeless." See Jung, 1953-74. *Letters.* vol. 2. 623.

Chapter 5 Notes

1   "Drug Control Strategy," in *The Psychiatric Times*. October 1990, pp. 35-38.

2   Bill W.'s letter to Jung dated January 23, 1961, speaks of the value of therapy for those in recovery. See "The Bill W.—C. G. Jung Letters," in *The Grapevine.* Appendix 3. 126.

3   For an important account of other aspects of the process of witnessing in psychoanalysis, see Dori Laub, "Bearing Witness or the Vicissitudes of Listening," and "An Event Without a Witness: Truth, Testimony and Survival," in Shoshana Felman and Dori Laub. *Testimony: Crises of Witnessing in Literature, Psychoanalysis, and History.* New York: Routledge, Chapman and Hall, 1992, pp. 57-92.

4   Edward Edinger's phrase in a class lecture on Jung's *CW 14*, 1974.

5   For discussion of the homeopathic process, see E. C. Whitmont, 1993; and also his 1995, "Alchemy, Homeopathy, and the Treatment of Borderline States," in *Zurich 1995: Open Questions in Analytical Psychology. Proceedings of the 13th International Congress for Analytical Psychology.* Mary Ann Mattoon, ed. Einsiedeln: Daimon, 1997.

Chapter 6 Notes

1   Kinsella, p. 208. Known from the oral tradition of the first century BC with written versions from the seventh centuries and later.

2   It is not surprising that tales of the famous Cuchullain lived on to balance Irish humiliation during their eight hundred years of domination by the English. In McCourt's autobiography, they were felt to be a personal gift to the young Frank from his ineffectively raging alcoholic father.

3   Kinsella, pp. 53-54.

4   Jean Markale, [1972] 1975, pp. 37, 165.

5   Kinsella, pp. 53-55.

6   Kinsella, p. 153.

7   This relativization of ego into its various contexts is clearly expressed in Celtic languages by the grammatical construction itself. "Love, or anger, is at me to him" is the Gaelic manner of saying, "I love, or am angry with, him." See Elmar Ternes, "The Grammatical Structure of the Celtic Languages," in *The Celtic Consciousness*. Robert O'Driscoll, ed. New York: George Braziller, 1982, pp. 69-78. Our closest analogy lies in our expression of the encompassment of individual consciousness when we say we are "in love" or "in a rage" and possessed by emotions or compulsions that carry us beyond ourselves.

8   Kinsella, p. 72.

9   Kinsella, p. 175.

10 Kinsella, p. 199.

11 Kinsella, pp 197-205.

12 Kinsella, p. 247.

13 Kinsella, p. 251. This perverted reminder of Maeve's role as a mare goddess is a curious reversal of the reality that Irish horse breeders must have known: the herd and even the stallion is always led by an alpha mare.

14 The more archaic earth, life, and death goddesses in Irish myth, like the Morrigan, for example, were not warriors; they worked directly on the emotions by magic. See Sjoestedt, pp. 44-51; and Perera, 1993, pp. 155-193.

15 From the *Fochann Loingsi Fergusa*, cited in Garrett, p. 11.

16 Kinsella, pp. 29-31.

17 See Cross and Slover, pp. 361-363; and Jones and Jones, 198-199. In these figures the force of focused emotionality that underlies the effectiveness of magic is joined with trained physical skill to provide power from both levels.

18 Markale, [1972] 1975, p. 253.

19 See Markale, [1972] 1975, p. 38.

20 The spectrum of unconscious permutations of the power drive are spelled out further in Perera, 1986b.

21 The warrior attitude is similar to the one that his teacher Don Juan taught to Carlos in the Castaneda books.

22 Sometimes such aversion in modern addicts is helped medically by antidotes such as Antabuse or antidepressants and tranquilizers. These are, however, most effective when the recovering addict is motivated to become abstinent.

23 Jung, 1953-74. *Letters*. vol 2. 625.

24 Because some addiction counselors and addicts cannot subscribe to the idea of a deity, this term is often problematic. Then the Higher Power can more readily be equated with the Self, Jung's term for the felt center of authority, guidance,

integrity, order, and meaning in each individual. Its processes are often first perceived when a client becomes aware that a dream series provides ongoing creative balance and commentary to the events of daily life and has the seemingly timed and intentional purpose of focusing consciousness on the most important issues that currently need to be addressed.

25 Markale, [1972] 1975, p. 241.

26 Like the Orphic Gnostic sect that worshipped Dionysus, god of wine, through a wine feast at initiation and afterwards abstained from such communion with their god, the AA community reverences the wine, which is the basis of their shared focus, by forever abstaining from it.

Chapter 7 Notes

1 The Finn cycle of legends tells us that on boar-shaped Ben Bulben, beautiful Diarmuid, a consort of the solar goddess Grainne and his foster brother (in the form of a boar) killed each other.

2 Dated from the sixth millenium, this group of dolmens and passage graves lies along a line of monuments stretching across Ireland from the Boyne River Valley through Loughcrew and Carrowkeel. See Michael O'Kelly, 1989. *Early Ireland: An Introduction to Irish Prehistory*. Cambridge: Cambridge University Press. 106-109.

3 Peter Harbison, *Guide to National Monuments in the Repulic of Ireland*. Dublin: Gill and Macmillan, 1970, p. 217.

4 Similarly, a team from University College, Galway, is surveying the sites but has no intention of probing them until noninvasive techniques are developed. Michael Paull, private communication.

5 For discussion of the Avebury site see Dames, 1976; and 1977, *The Avebury Cycle*. London: Thames & Hudson.

6 Maire Mac Neill does not mention Knocknarea as the focus of a particular pattern, or saint's festival, at least on Lughnasa. Rather Ballysadare Bay near the well at Tullaghan was where the folk assembled in recent times until a fateful Lammas Sunday in late July in 1826 when the Catholic clergy's prohibitions of the pagan festival were echoed in a terrible storm, "when lightning flashed forth again and again with constantly increasing force and brilliance, and peal after peal of deepening thunder echoed and rolled between Slieve Gamh and Knocknarea, seeming to shake the very earth and to rattle the very bones of the Firbolg king and the Tuatha de Danaan princes under the cairns" and a panic seized the crowds that fled and never reinstated the festival. See Mac Neill, p. 116.

7 O hOgain, p. 285.

8 Bromwich, p. 188.

9 Finnabair, the name of Maeve's daughter, corresponds to the Welsh *Gwenhwyfar*, meaning white and spirit, phantom, or fairy. See Bromwich, p. 380. King Arthur's wife Guinevere is one of three goddesses, originally a triple goddess, of the same name. We can assume with Markale that this figure is a generic title of queenship when the queen represented the goddess. Since daughters of the queen inherited her kingdom and qualities, as daughters of the goddess were said to be incarnations of her, we can further assume that this description is an aspect of the goddess-mother-daughter-queenship incarnation pattern.

10 Chevalier a la Charrette. In Chretien's *Perceval le Gallois* quoted in Markale, 1975, p. 164.

11 See Berger.

12 Harold Searles, *The Non-Human Environment in Normal Development and in Schizophrenia*. New York: International Universities Press, 1960.

13 Jung, 1911-12/1952. *CW 5*. §508.

14 Bollas identifies the "analytic space as an invitation to regress in the care of a transformative object," 1987, p. 29. Michael Fordham reminds us that "the energy previously directed into the symptom is now transferred to the person of the therapist." See 1957, "Notes on the Transference," in *Techmique in Jungian Analysis*. M. Fordham, *et al.*, eds. London: Heinemann, 1974, p. 120. Nonetheless analysts of all schools are warned to distinguish between benign, transformative, therapeutic regression, and the "destructively parasitic demand" for exciting overinvolvement and the potential for "addiction to an artificial intensity of experience" that can turn it into a malignant and fixating experience. See, for example, Peter Lomas.*The Limits of Interpretation*. Northvale, NJ: Aronson, 1987, p. 87.

15 This self-envious mechanism has led other writers to name the dyad of defender and infant the superego and the object-loving self (Bion) or the anti-libidinal ego and the libidinal ego (Fairbairn). Like Klein's bad and good breasts, this dyadic pattern leaves out the addictive defense as well as the matrix, which is the essential ground of the opposites. This encompasing, or Self, matrix is present from the beginning and the various parts of the personality deintegrate (Fordham's term) from it.

   In Maeve's patterns we can see the relationship to the archetypal matrix may be structured to function defensively and addictively, as an escape enabling obliteration of consciousness and/or regressive fusion with Self, or progressively as the maternal ground supporting development, relational capacities, and expanded consiousness.

   In therapy with the many clients who have not experienced adequate early constancy and holding, a conscious relationship to the matrix may not occur until the individual is able to tolerate an abiding yet ambivalently sustaining and frustrating relationship to the analyst. Held within such a humanized matrix, the client may be able to coalesce and separate from identity with the archetypal matrix in order to witness and bear the tension of the opposites intrapsychically. This process is an aspect of the psychization about which Jung writes. See chapter 10.

16 Renegade is a term Esther Harding used to describe the lotus-eating sailors who forsook Odysseus' journey. It represents for her the inertial, entropic elements in the psyche that resist development. See *Psychic Energy: Its Source and Goal*. Washington, DC: Pantheon, 1947, pp. 54-56.

17 Edward C. Whitmont, 1964. "Group Therapy and Analytical Psychology," in *The Journal of Analytical Psychology* 9:1. pp. 1-22.

18 See Jerome Levin, 1987. *Treatment of Alchoholism and Other Addictions*. Northvale, NJ: Jason Aronson.

19 Wilfred Bion's concept of attacks on linking often provides a very useful therapeutic model for the therapist. See Bion: *Second Thoughts: Selected Papers on Psycho-Analysis*. New York: Jason Aronson, 1967, pp. 93-109.

20 For discussion of some of these issues see, Perera, 1986a, pp. 59-85.

21 See Whitmont and Perera, chapter 12.

22 Saint Anne is a Christian incarnation of Anu/Danu, the great earth and river goddess of the Celts. The name is found in many landscape features from the river

Danube to The Paps of Anu in Co. Kerry. She was the mother of the gods. In Breton Christianity, Saint Anne became the midwife of the Virgin Mary.

23 "Bricriu's Feast," in Gantz, p. 237. This is a shortened version of a similar ritual to cool Cuchullain's beserk warrior possession from *The Tain*. I have written about this issue in more detail in 1988. Much of this discussion is borrowed from that chapter published in *The Borderline Personality in Analysis*.

24 "The boyhood deeds of Cu Chulaind," in Gantz, p. 146.

25 In Eriksonian or Neurolinguistic programming terms, we would say that the client's habitual perceptual frame was broken, and he fell into mild trance wherein he was open to the possibility that new learning could take place.

26 If, however, the rupture results from unethical and/or unconscious acting out of power or dependency in the countertransference, these complexed reactions indicate that the therapist has not worked sufficiently on her or his own relationship to Maeve to have discovered and created the transpersonal vessels required for doing therapeutic work with this particular client. The presumed healer will need to seek help in full awareness that working with individuals prone to addiction provides the severe tests that bring out the analyst's own inevitable flaws and stimulate further psychological development.

27 Letter dated January 23, 1961. "The Bill W.—C.G. Jung Letters," in *The Grapevine*. Appendix 3. 126.

Chapter 8 Notes

1 In myth it later became the underground dwelling (*sidh*) of Boann's partner, the Good God [*Dagda*], who allowed their son Angus to claim it.

2 Brennan, pp. 31-32.

3 Brennan, pp. 47ff.

4 Brennan, p. 60.

5 Knott, p. 17.

6 Liam De Paor, "The Art of the Celtic Peoples," in *The Celtic Consciousness*. Robert O'Driscoll, ed. New York: George Braziller, 1982, pp. 126-127. The comment in his article refers specifically to *The Book of Kells*, but it serves as a generalization about one perspective on Celtic consciousness.

7 See the illustrations in Gleick, 1987.

8 Dames, 1992, pp. 181-183.

9 Robert Graves, *The White Goddess: A Historical Grammar of Poetic Myth*. New York: Vintage, 1958, p. 439.

10 Ross, 1967, p. 110. In Celtic lore the severed heads of fallen warriors were also smoothed with oil and their hair combed to honor the magical potency felt inherent in them.

11 Harold Bayley, *The Lost Language of Symbolism*. vol. 2. London: Williams and Norgate, 1912, pp. 179-180.

12 Marie-Louise von Franz. *The Interpretation of Fairytales*, New York: Spring, 1970, chapter VII, pp. 50-51.

13 This story occurs as one of placename tales to explain the origin of the name of Lough Erne. It first showed its "troubled waters" when the maiden and her companions fled to the plain where the lake now lies. See Dames, 1992, pp. 181-182. In Irish creation myths many rivers and lakes are said to be the result of a goddess' passage or flight.

14 Dames, 1992, pp. 181-182. The name *Olca* means "he who wrongs a saint." *Ai* means "poetic inspiration." We can see the giant as a pagan god. He psychologically represents an outpouring of impulsivity or enthusiasm that cannot be integrated into the structures supporting the Christian virtues.

15 These modes are prevented from developing by both the culture that refuses credence to ecstatic trance experience and by the individual's incapacity to mature beyond magic consciousness in the areas of traumatic complexes. Such incapacity is reinforced by the addictive disease itself. Thus these primitive modes themselves cannot serve in the place of "traditional" forms in Celtic and other cultures.

16 Such cognitive manoeuvres seek to manage painful experience in ways that are also typical of borderline states. Because of the distortions, cognitive therapy is a useful form of treatment in dealing with some aspects of addictive behavior when a transference alliance can be formed.

17 See Gertrude Ujhely, 1980. "Thoughts Concerning the *Causa Finalis* of the Cognitive Mode Inherent in Pre-Oedipal Psychopathology." Unpublished diploma thesis. C. G. Jung Institute of New York.

18 Heinz Kohut, 1977, p. 74.

19 "As a child, feeling that his self was crumbling and/or empty, he had tried to obtain reassuring pleasure from a fragment of his body self." Kohut, 1977, p. 76.

20 Erich Neumann, 1988. "Stages of Religious Experience and the Path of Depth Psychology," in *Quadrant* 9:2. 17-18.

21 Berman, p. 35.

22 While this stage of sorting and active negativity tends to make the client feel more "crazy" and beleaguered than the more primitive ones, it usually feels less oppressive to the analyst. The client no longer unconsciously evacuates excruciating emotional material into the analytic field. The madness, neediness, and sadism are now put out more directly into what is felt as a safe-enough therapeutic relationship. Thus the analyst's own psyche is somewhat relieved of its initial requirement to perceive and process the material through projective inductions that stir the primitive depths of her or his own complexes.

23 Bion, pp. 93-109.

24 See "Math, Son of Mathonwy," in Jones and Jones, p. 55. This tale tells the end of the goddess' role as footholder. Through rape and shaming, she is supplanted by males in the patriarchy. We only have historical records of the footholder (*troediawc*) role being held by males. The office had special privileges including that of granting freedom to those condemned by the king's judgments—a mediating function the Church saw in the Virgin Mary. See Markale, [1972] 1975, pp. 131-132.

25 Neumann sees our necessary subjection to the sovereign goddess of process from the perspective of the fearful male ego:

> The male remains inferior to, and at the mercy of, the Feminine that confronts him as a power of destiny. Thus the king was deposed and killed when he was foresaken by the fortunes of war, or when the earth withheld the harvest for which he was responsible. Like all males, he was merely the "bondsman" of the powers, on whose favor he depended. (1955, pp. 303-304.)

26 Philip Booth, *Relations: Selected Poems 1950-1985*. New York: Viking, 1986, p. 4.

27 Music affects the endorphin levels, the autonomic nervous system, and the heartbeat. At Yale University Hospital, surgeons use music to relax patients about

to undergo surgery; at NYU Medical Center Dr. Matthew Lee uses it to reduce pain and to synchronize movements in rehabilitation medicine. In another form of modern music therapy, the therapist uses music that matches the client's emotions. Then gradually, by changing the kind of music played, the therapist shifts the emotional state that the client experiences. Eliot Forest, "Classical Music and the Mind," on *WNYC, National Public Radio.* September 11, 1993.

28 The Gnostics, the Sufis, and Jung, among others, have explored these connections. See Stephen A. Hoeller. See also R. A. Ammann, *Healing and Transformation in Sandplay.* Chicago: Open Court, 1991, pp. 41-42.

29 Jung, 1928. *CW 8.* §63. He also called our attention to the bivalent psychological manifestations of alchemical Sulphur. While both are unassimaled expressions of the Self, one aspect represents shadow behaviors in their sulphurous capacities to inflame and compel. The other holds a potentiality for awe that can support development. See *CW 14.* §134-153.

30 This is similar to Maeve's confronting the warrior with the breasts of her fifty women.

31 He was playing with the title of the Beatles' song about the hallucinogenic drug LSD: "Lucy in the Sky with Diamonds."

32 This represents an aspect of the process of psychezation, in which what was previously acted out can begin to be worked with in the psyche. See chapter 10.

33 See Patrick Ford, 1977. For the beginnings of a psychological discussion of the tale, see Perera, 1996b.

34 In the language of astrology we would call this Neptunian. It represents a propensity for ecstacy, altered consciousness, addiction, and powerful visionary imagination. Negatively it can increase a susceptibility to boundary weakness and lead to experiences of environmental and psychological toxicity. Since the watery Neptune enhances propensities to feel lost in visions, emotions, and over-identification with the other, a sense of personal identity can seem inundated and washed away. The individual can, hence, easily feel shame and inferiority. In the birth charts of those who have a tendency to become addicted, their natal Neptune is often strong in placement or aspects.

Chapter 9 Notes

1 A. K. Coomaraswamy. "On the Loathly Bride," in *Coomeraswamy, Selected Papers: Traditional Art and Symbolism,* vol. 1. Roger Lipsey, ed. Princeton, NJ: Princeton University Press, [1945] 1977, pp. 363-365.

2 The loathly damsel appears in Celtic, Hindu, and Zoroastrian myth. She provides an important theme in Medieval English lore where we know her in the Arthurian and Grail legends as Lady Ragnell, Orgeuleuse, and Kundry and in Chaucer's "Wife of Bath" tale. See Coomeraswamy, pp. 352-370.

3 Cross and Slover, p. 510. There are similar descriptions of the Irish goddess Morrigan as a hag. See Ross, p. 233. Kali is similarly described in Indian texts. See Kinsley, *The Sword and the Flute: Kali and Krsna, Dark Visions of the Terrible and the Sublime in Hindu Mythology.* Berkeley: University of California Press, 1975, p. 81.

4 These two lines from the original do not appear in Cross and Slover. I have added them from the translation in Rees and Rees, p. 75.

5 Niall was King of Ireland ca. A.D. 358. Text translation is from Cross and Slover, pp. 510-512.

6 He had already passed the magical kingship tests set by the tribal smith-shaman. His embrace of the hag reaffirms his primacy over his brothers and ensures his acceptance by the goddess of sovereignty.

7 In patriarchal, Mahayana Buddhist tradition, the ugly female may serve, as does Kundry in the Grail saga, as a confrontative messenger to the questing soul. Naropa's encounter with the "old woman with 37 ugly features" is understood as his vision of the 37 dissatisfactions of samsara, the 37 impure substances of the perishable body of samsara as well as the 37 pathways and kinds of creative potentiality. See Herbert Guenther, *The Life and Teaching of Naropa*. London: Oxford University Press, 1963, pp. 24-25. A kiss itself is a draught of the living waters, like a drink of the sovereignty cup, or soma in Hindu parallels. Kissing is a means of disenchantment. Coomeraswamy describes a scene from the Rig Veda in which Indra drinks soma from the mouth of the loathly Apala, "He verily drank the Soma from her mouth and whoever comprehending this myth, kisses a woman's mouth, that becomes for him a Soma-draught," a drink of the water of life. Apala is earth, the animate furrow, and Indra is Lord of the field who gains the soma and restores Apala. Apala is at first scaly, reptilian and bald. She invites Indra to replant her barren field, "and this below her belly." Coomeraswamy, p. 356.

8 The human partner in the Celtic *feis* had to be unblemished and complete. If he lost an arm, as did Nuadu, king of the Tuatha de Daanan, or suffered a distorted countenance as did Fergus MacLeide, chief of the Ulstermen, then he was considered too imperfect to incarnate the divine role, and he was replaced. Such a need for the unblemished ideal is a requirement of magic-level consciousness since it is so permeable. The demand for perfection is an attempt to assert magic control. The demand is sometimes found in psychotherapy clients when they are fixated in or working through early developmental issues. Then they may be extraordinarily upset by a modification in the person or office of their therapist as if their very grip on reality is being disturbed. They may also subscribe to ideals of perfection for themselves and others as the only pattern capable of surviving the chaotic turbulence of the devouring matrix of unconsciousness and raw emotions in which they are caught.

9 Coomeraswamy, pp. 358-359.

10 When we go to war, such images of the enemy are created to arouse aggressive hatred against them. See Sam Keen, *Faces of the Enemy: Reflections of the Hostile Imagination*. San Francisco: HarperSanFrancisco,1986.

11 An alternative defense involves the incorporation of the needed caretaker's negative qualities into the individual's own identity to maintain an unambivalent image of the other's goodness. Then the person feels swollen with negativity that goes well beyond any personal allotment. When stressed, he or she is unable to allow aggression to find its outer focus and serve legitimate needs. Instead aggression is refluxed or vented backwards with attitudes of self-contempt and behaviors that are self-spiting.

12 Thus we are witnessing eruptions of extraordinary savagery among brethern tribes in the Balkans, Middle East, and Africa. A correspondent reported that when the Belgians valued the height of the Tutsi tribespeople, the shorter Hutu of Ruanda began to value this trait. Enviously they also began to hate and persecute members of the tribe with whom they had previously lived peacefully. One act of

early violence was the widespread cutting off of the Tutsis' legs to bring them down to Hutu size. *The New York Times.* August, 2, 1994.

13 *Alcoholics Anonymous,* pp. 59-60. Italics in original.

14 *Alcoholics Anonymous,* p. 60.

15 W. Wilson, 1944. "Basic Concepts of Alcoholics Anonymous," quoted in Antze, 1987, p. 158.

16 As Eleanor Roosevelt is said to have quipped, "No one can make you feel guilty without your consent."

17 Jung, *The Visions Seminars.* Zurich: Spring Publications, 1976, p. 89.

18 In this medieval myth the older pattern of the unchanging goddess of the land with her many consorts has been shifted to a more patrifocal one. Niall gains his legitimacy as son of the king rather than as son of the goddess and queen. Nonetheless his elevation to kingship depicts a historical fact. The clan of the Ui Neill of Meath supplanted the Ulaid as the dominant power in Ireland in the fourth century AD and even appropriated the place of their central Assembly at Emuin Macha. The people of the goddess of Mide moved into the lands of the goddess of Ulster, Macha. Perhaps the stepmother in the tale represents the rejecting, but ultimately dominated, old queen of Ulster.

19 Jung writes that the alchemists equated the goal of their work with the "orphan" stone or the "widow," implying that the experience and ongoing relationship to the individual Self is born out of losing what one personally depended upon, 1955-56. *CW 14.* §13-14.

20 Fosterage was an institution among the Celtic aristocaracy. Boys and girls were sent to live with other families for five to ten years. The responsibility of their care and training was taken seriously by the foster parents, and strong ties developed to knit the tribe closely with fosterage bonds.

21 See his valuable study on addiction as failed initiation. Luigi Zoya, *Drugs, Addiction and Initiation: The Modern Search for Ritual.* Marc Romano and Robert Mercurio. trs. Santa Monica, CA: Sigo Press, 1989.

22 Philip Zabriskie, 1979. "The Loathly Damsel: The Motif of the Ugly Woman," in *Quadrant* 12:1. 47-63.

23 Jung, 1935. *CW 18.* §91n.

24 Since I am not a family therapist, who is required by law to report child abuse, and since I did not think such intervention would be effective or beneficial at this point to the already self-loathing mother, I insisted that my client contact me every time she felt impelled to lash out at her daughter. We could then arrange to discuss the issues leading to her felt need to erupt. This method almost immediately allowed her to express her overwhelming emotions through alternative and more responsible behavior. It eventually led to some empathic consciousness of her own psychology and the total cessation of her abusive behavior to her child.

25 For a fine discussion of this problem, see Barbara Sullivan Stevens, "The Disliked Patient." It is the final chapter in her *Psychotherapy from the Feminine Principle.* Wilmette, IL: Chiron, 1990.

26 I discuss this example in "A Small but Difficult Step," in *Psychological Perspectives 27,* Fall/Winter, 1993, pp. 160-165.

27 Niall represents a capacity for such empathic perception, as does the Arthurian hero Gawain, who married the loathsome Lady Ragnell and gave her sovereignty.

28 Cf. Joseph Campbell's discussion of the Indian figure of Kirttimukha in his 1972. *Myths to Live By*. New York: Viking, pp. 103-104.

29 A term Marion Woodman has made part of colloquial speech after using it as the title of a book.

30 I have had to quote this material without her permission. It is such a beautiful and anonymous example of an archetypal process that I hope this courageous woman, who used me, will not feel too unduly used in return.

Chapter 10 Notes

1   Andrew R. MacAndrew, "Introduction to Dostoeyvsky," *The Gambler*. New York: W. W. Norton, 1964, p. 7.

2   Dostoevsky's letter to his wife, April 28, 1971. Quoted by Andrew R. MacAndrew, p. 7.

3   Eliot L Gardner. "Studies Reveal Findings in Brain-Reward, Drug Addiction Relationship," in *The Psychiatric Times*, October, 1989, pp. 12-15.

4   Sigmund Freud [1928] "Dostoevsky and Parricide," in *Collected Papers*, vol. 5. James Strachey, ed. New York: Basic Books, 1959, p. 238.

5   Jung, 1928. *CW 8*. §95-108.

6   Jung, 1955-1956. *CW 14*. §152.

7   The spiritual instinct may have been an important force in Dostoevsky's healing. As he became a father, his need to lose everything at the gambling table and his abasement before his pregnant wife, which Freud likens to the pleasures of masochistic abasement before a severe superego-father, may have been transformed. Not only did his wife not serve as a sadistic superego, but she maintained a supportive and loyal relationship to him even as she expressed the painful reality of their situation. Her pregnancy and motherhood were part of this. Thus we may wonder if, when he was forced by circumstances to incarnate the father principle himself for his own children, Dostoevsky may have felt both a new self-esteem and a new relationship to the archetype of order that enabled his sudden and reponsible sobreity. Becoming a parent is often of momentous importance in the lives of individuals in recovery since it forces a revaluation of the old parent-child patterns that maintained the gulf between impulsivity and control in the areas of addiction, and it creates a potent area of self-esteem.

8   Dostoevsky, p. 28.

9   Dostoevsky, p. 33.

10 J. S. Baca's poem "El Gatto."

11 Hexagram 27, The corners of the mouth—providing nourishment. In *The I Ching or Book of Changes*. Richard Wilhelm, tr. Princeton: Princeton University Press, 1950, p. 107.

12 The opposition of fantasy as an addictive alternative to even abundant quantities of concrete maternal supplies is represented by one client addicted to marijuana and television. As a child, he had been unable to ward off what he felt was the "octopus mother" and her omnipresent suffocations experienced through excessive food, extravagant material attentions, and her tendency to agree to everything anyone said. Unable to claim his own style of desire and fearing to be swamped in her tentacles, he early "fled to fantasy and television."

13 Ross, 1967, p. 317.

14 This dismemberment recalls the alchemical motif of the lion whose forepaw is cut

off, signifying the inhibition of rampant drive energy, or as Jung puts it, "the subjugation of concupiscence." 1955-1956. *CW 14.* §512n.

15 Jones and Jones, pp. 9-17

16 In Irish custom (and throughout Europe) the clan chief or king had the right of first intercourse with the brides of his people. While we see this clearly to be an expression of patriarchal power over the female and all the offspring of her body, it also suggests that earlier there was felt to be a powerful, potentially destructive magic in the female that only the chosen king was initially fit to confront. A lesser male might meet the fate of Pwyll's rival and be swallowed in the devouring sack or vagina. The ritual of the first night also represents the chief's domination of the men of the tribe, who must submit to the king's authority and even right of first entry into the bodies of their brides. We can see how difficult this was for the warrior Cuchullain when we read of the tribe's fear of his fury as his newly won Emer was taken to the king's bed. See Kinsella, pp. 38-39.

17 This motif is like that of the famine caused by the Greek earth and mare goddess Demeter in her raging grief at being separated from her beloved daughter by Hades. While there may be some influence from the Greek motifs in Celtic lore, we can often see new dimensions in the Greek tales when we examine them through the lens of the more matrifocal Celtic treatments of similar material.

18 Quoted in Marie-Louise von Franz, *Puer Aeternus.* Santa Monica CA: Sigo, 1981, pp. 252-253.

19 These quotations are taken from sessions over a period of six months.

20 While neonates can already recognize their mother's smell and sounds after a few days, the infant will, readily and of necessity, accept food and care from suitable others until later in the first year when stranger discriminations become compelling.

21 This feature of sexuality we see acted out in our culture during adolescence when the heat of rising hormones can feel nearly unbearable, especially when self-control has not been adequately mediated. This can occur both when there is too lax a control or when control has been constellated in such a severely repressive form that the drive tends to erupt from under the repressions that forbid its outlet.

22 In another tale, Grainne (the goddess whose name signifies both "ugliness" and "the sun") uses her cup to put her unwelcome suitor to sleep and to gain access to her beloved Diarmuid. Then she seizes the youth and lays a fate-bond, or *geis,* on him to be her lover. See Cross and Slover, pp. 373-374. Tristan's passion was equally compelled and fated. Dierdre's famous lament for her beloved is a song of longing, a recollection from the perspective of limitation, that mourns lost sweetness and evokes it to mind and memory. See Kinsella, pp. 16-19.

23 Kinsella, p. 53.

24 See chapter 1.

25 Cf. Patrick Tierney, *The Highest Altar: The Story of Human Sacrifice.* New York: Viking, 1989.

26 These quotations come out of sessions over a period of several months as the issue of desire came up in relation to work and to a partner.

27 Winnicott beautifully understands this need for "an early ruthless object relationship." He writes: "The normal child enjoys a ruthless relation to his mother, mostly showing in play, and he needs his mother because only she can be expected to tolerate his ruthless relation to her even in play, because he really hurts her and wears her out. Without this play with her he can only hide a

ruthless self and give it life in a state of dissociation," in a footnote he sites Lilith as an image of a ruthless figure. See his "Primitive Emotional Development," in *Through Paediatrics to Psycho-analysis*. New York: Basic Books, [1945] 1975, p. 154.

28 All fetishism rests on this magic-level dynamic of a part concretistically standing for the whole. Seen symbolically, the fetish represents a transpersonal focus and value.

29 The motif of the the goddess' sack shows us dramatically what Jung meant when he taught that the unconscious relates to us as we relate to it, for the sack has different meanings for each of the chiefs. To Pwyll it represents the humble neediness with which he was out of touch; to the usurper it represents his identity with unconscious voraciousness.

30 Jones and Jones, p.14.

31 Indeed, later in the myth the motif of the wasteland appears as magical vengeance for the rejected suitor's demise. The land is made barren by a cohort of this rejected chief, who also leads a horde of ravenous mice to destroy the newly ripened grain of Rhiannon's son and next consort.

32 Maeve's consort Fergus is also the husband of the deer goddess. He represents the older stag god in the culture of cattle-herding agriculture. His ancient and archetypal hornedness is symbolized in the megalithic phallic stone at Tara.

33 Jones and Jones, pp. 3-9. Many of the initiatory elements of this part of the tale are echoed in the later literary masterpiece *Sir Gawain and the Green Knight*.

34 Jung, 1937. *CW 8*. §234.

35 The high king has achieved sacred status and tribal authority over his possessions and dominions in the kingship ceremony at Tara. There he has passed the Tara tests and been affirmed by the shriek of the stone of Fal.

36 See chapter 9.

37 McDougall, p. 116.

38 "Carrion comfort," in *Poems and Prose of Gerard Manley Hopkins*.W. H. Gardner, ed. Harmonsdworth: Penguin, 1953, p. 61.

39 Idries Shah, *Tales of the Dervishes*. New York: E. P. Dutton, 1969, p. 197.

Chapter 11 Notes

1 T. S. Eliot, "East Coker," in *Four Quartets*, New York: Harcourt, Brace, 1943, p. 15.

2 Gimbutas, 1989, p. 26.

3 Neumann, 1955, p. 43.

4 Cf. Dames, 1976, pp. 110-114.

5 Later tales placed the principle of sovereignty in the otherworld where the king visited the realm of archetypes to receive his libation and cup from the hand of a maiden who was no longer goddess but a servant of a male deity, Lugh or Mannanan mac Lir. We can see in this shift that the principle of sovereignty underwent cultural change. It was removed from nature and the goddess and subsumed under a male god. With this shift rulership itself changed from being a temporary consort arrangement with the queen-goddess of the land, inevitably involving the consort's sacrifice and replacement when prosperity failed, to an hereditary rule through the male line. Irish tales document the several stages of this shift. The cup itself became the cup of truth.

6 Gantz, pp. 58-60. See the discussion of the story "The Wooing of Etain," in chapter 1. The queen's capacity to incarnate the goddess depended on her ability

to serve the sacred *medb*. Maeve's connection with Etain, an ancient solar goddess, is preserved in the lore. Maeve's mother was a lady-in-waiting to Etain. The goddess accompanying the light god Lugh in his stories may be Etain. Here she functions as the ancient solar server of the cup of life and kingship. In other tales, this was Maeve's function.

7 In Greek myth Apollo stands as the form-giver of Dionysus' dismembering madness. Dionysus' original rituals were the *tragodia* and the dance. Through these he conveys passion and form in a sacred unity, just as does Maeve with her ritual vessels.

8 In the Kaballah the lightening wave of divine energy is mediated by the divine vessels (*sephirot*) of the tree of life. In alchemy, which holds many elements similar to those found in Celtic and Gnostic lore, the vessel is considered the feminine aspect of the philosopher's stone. It is the retort in which the various transformative processes take place. Jung writes of many aspects of this *vas* in his alchemical works.

9 In the Celtic cult of sacred waters the cup used to transfer the healing, fluid source to the communicant is sometimes the skull cup of an ancient tribal hero-shaman. In this later version of the communion, the skull vessel is analogous to the womb. Just as the womb bears the new life, so the skull offers transformation into the new health that comes with attunement with the source. For more on this ritual, see my forthcoming *Mythic Rites in Modern Therapy*.

10 This paradoxical congruence underlies the original, holy communion and the later mysteries of the Grail. The motif became one of the roots of the Grail story, for the maiden who carries the sacred vessel, cloaks the initiate as consort, and serves as queen is the goddess incarnate who mediates both the blessed and wasteland phases of the land. As Mugain in the story of "Cuchullain's Initiation into Arms," and Maeve in "Bricriu's Feast," the Queen serves to mediate the warrior's beserker energies into the tribe by offering her breasts and then enclosing him in her cloak of initiation. Similarly Rapanse in Wolfram's *Parzival* sends the Grail hero and king her cloak and carries the Holy Cup in the Grail procession as Grail Maiden and Grail Queen.

   Not only in legend but also in actual practice, the role of women as pourers of the sacred drink continued. Into the sixth century in Bretony, as part of the early Celtic Christian Church celebration of the mass, women, called *cohospitae*, served the wine of communion while male priests served the wafers. See Ward Rutherford [1978] *The Druids: Magicians of the West*. New York: Sterling, 1990, p. 153.

11 "Bricriu's feast," in Cross and Slover, pp. 254-280, especially 268-271.

12 Gantz, pp. 238-242.

13 Even though this story of Maeve's gifts is a patriarchal tale to determine the champion's place in the warrior hierarchy, we can see in it elements of an older culture in Maeve's wish to avoid strife, in her possession of the libation and serving vessels, and in her generous granting of gifts to each applicant.

14 *Lao Tsu: Tao Te Ching*. Gia-fu Feng and Jane English, trs. New York: Vintage, 1972, p. 11.

15 Often the human female, in identity with the heroic values of the patriarchy and without sufficient sense of the merit and significance of the matrix and her own relationship to it, feels equally afraid of her own inner space and the substance of flesh around that space. Then in defensive identity with matter and the concrete and here-and-now that the heroic age seeks to dominate and possess, she loses

connection to the empty, transcendental otherness that the patriarchy finds so uncontrollable and frightening. On the other hand, the well-enough mothered female, a woman in touch with the bountiful divine goddess in her own mother and herself, has experienced her flesh and her emptiness cherished and blessed. She can then develop relationships between aspects of herself as container and the void in which spacious openness and continent paradoxically coexist. When she knows the inner void—whether physical or psychological and spiritual—as a relatively secure space, she can open to welcome otherness.

16 Even when actual liquid flowing into and from the vessel is easily able to change its form, there can be problems if the vessel is too small, too narrow, or broken. Issues of adequate fit betwen container and contained are far more complicated when the child transiting through the maternal vessel is formed by preexisting archetypal and genetic patterns. Then the mediating maternal consciousness needs capacities for empathic perception and flexibility (a potential for many shapes) in order to receive and fit enough of that child's particular forms and requirements to enable it to have a secure and thriving life. Too often the mother's sense of acceptable forms of adaptation have been congealed by fear and the normative controls and ideals of a culture that derogates the matrix itself. Then it is hard for her to serve as mediatrix between the new life requiring an adequate vessel and the culturally devalued feminine in order to create, mirror, and support a sense of the child's worthy and desirable individual existence. Only many-shaped emotional mirroring can affirm the reality and particularity of the individual child.

While it is also the parental task to mediate cultural values to each child, overly rigid attachment to preexistent categories and ideals can brutally twist and distort the new life into fraudulent and despairing conformity or rampant and furious rebellion. These are as sour as the taste inflicted by old vessels on any new wine.

17 See Jung, 1942/54. *CW 11*. 201-296. See also Edinger, 1972, chapter 9. There is evidence that some clergy become addicted to drinking wine because it is one of the few embodied experiences of ecstacy permitted them when body and mind are split by doctrine and sexuality has been taboo for Roman Catholic clergy since the Synod of Pavia in A.D. 1022.

18 See Max Pulver "Jesus' Round Dance and Crucifixion According to the Acts of St. John," in *The Mysteries: Papers from the Eranos Yearbooks*. New York: Pantheon [1942] 1955, pp.169-193. See also the poem by the German mystic Mechtild of Magdeburg (1212-1277) in which the Lord commands her to "dance as deftly as my elect have danced before." Translated in Hoeller, p. 133.

19 Until very recently in our dominant culture, we rarely sought new and adequate vessels to mediate the powers of Maeve. Around the globe the peoples honoring her energies in ancient earth religions have been lured or ripped away from their own traditional contexts in which there was a continuum of the natural and supernatural honored through ecstatic rites celebrating the flow between them— ripped without concern for the creation of new structures that could adequately maintain those connections to the spiritual source of all life.

Instead in the patrifocal world when there has been an opening towards ecstatic, enlivening, expanding, and potentially transforming powers, there has also been a backlash against them and a hardening of binary, mechanical, and fundamentalist ideals of good and evil. Polarizing too far out of fear of loss of controls, those who espouse fundamentalist standards have often repudiated the ecstatic as regressive, demonically possessing, or merely weird and cultic even as secular and potentially toxic variations of ecstatic behavior are overlooked and/or indulged. Heavy episodic drinking in colleges, for example, has only recently become considered a problem. See Henry Wechsler *et al*, 1994. "Health and Behavioral Consequences of Binge Drinking in College: A National Survey of Students in 140 Campuses," in *The Journal of the American Medical Association*. 272: 21, pp. 1672-1677.

   As long as the patrifocal mainstream distorts or still fears to honor the spiritual necessity of release and transcendence, because these seem to threaten the ideals on which it is based, we will have addicts who are psychopathic and drug traffickers who are rich.

20 It is, however, not an accident that there are backlashes from patriarchal institutions like insurance companies with their current threats to intrude into the analytic vessel and limit the long-term therapy that is usually essential for the treatment of severely damaged clients with inadequately formed and resiliant vessels of incarnation.

21 Such communities originally strengthened the ego. The convents permitted women to live free of the very few and constricting roles accorded them in medieval society. Their talents could flourish within the confines of the Church. Now such communities serve an important function during one phase of development but may weaken the individual ego if containment within them persists after it is outgrown.

22 Identification with clan and church is a potent force among Irish clients with whom I have worked. This is not surprising given Celtic traditions of close communal bonding in community. We have a glimpse into aspects of these traditions through accounts of the natives of the Scots island of St. Kilda. See Steel, pp. 46-47.

23 This fact makes the inadequacy of public support for the arts in education and culture not only impoverishing and disgraceful but also dangerous.

24 Then "creativity itself can become entrapping," repetitive, and/or a source of addictive manic intensity. Susan Kavaler-Adler, *The Compulsion to Create: A Psychoanalytic Study of Women Artists*. New York: Routledge, 1993, p. 20.

25 Out of this matrix, the ego separates and develops. Returning into it, the individual may seek to experience the ecstasies, visions, and magical potentials of the archetypal dimension.

26 Marion Milner writes about the change within post-Freudian psychology to re-evaluate the supposed developmental superiority of secondary process mentation: "Slowly over the years, primary process seems to have changed its meaning, so that now it is seen . . . as part of the integrating function of the ego: that is it serves to join up experiences and assimilate them into the ego, in order to preserve the ego's wholeness. As such it is not something to be grown out of, but, rather, is complementary to secondary process functioning and as necessary as male and female are to each other. It is primary process that enables one to accept paradox and contradiction, something that secondary process does not like at all, being itself bound by logic, which rejects contradiction." Milner. "D.W. Winnicott and the Two-Way Journey," in *Between Reality and Fanasy: Transitional Objects and Phenomena*. Simon A. Grolnick and Leonard Barkin, eds. New York: Jason Aronson, 1978, p. 42.

27 Jean Gebser has defined this as integral consciousness. It enables comprehension of the structures and capacities of all the various levels: archaic, magic, mythological, and rational.

28 Freud and Jung focused on the distinctions between consciousness and unconsciousness. Jung further differentiated consciousness with his typological studies. Recent studies of consciousness force wider expansions and make us aware that "awareness is not unitary but an aggregate of messages from different parts [of the mind]. . . that are developmentally and evolutionarily distinct." "[I]t is actually normal to have several independent simultaneously processing sources of awareness recording perceptions." "[T]he brain works in this manner. . . but as far as anyone knows, humans cannot subjectively experience more than one of these streams of consciousness at a time." Jenny Wade. *Changes of Mind: A Holonomic Theory of the Evolution of Consciousness*. New York: SUNY Press, 1996, pp. 66, 44.

29 Gebser uses the term "aperspectival" to indicate a consciousness that is not bound to a single perspective, one that can appropriately shift its focus even on itself.

30 Jenny Wade, p. 44.

31 It is an awareness not unlike the kind that saw the awesome reality of the winter solstice and, using a vocabulary of dark and light, earth and air, fullness and void, manifests this comprehension in the architecture of Newgrange. So potent is the experience of this temple that many today who emerge from its depths feel reborn, their consciousness transformed.

References

Abrahm, David. 1996. *The Spell of the Sensuous: Perception and Language in a More than Human World*. New York: Vintage.

Adler, Gerald. 1985. *Borderline Psychopatholgy and Its Treatment*. Northvale, NJ: Jason Aronson.

Alcoholics Anonymous: The Story of How Many Thousands of Men and Women Have Recovered from Alcoholism, 3rd ed. 1976. New York: AA World Services.

Ammann, R. A. 1991. *Healing and Transformation in Sandplay*. Chicago: Open Court.

Andersen, Jorgen. 1977. *The Witch on the Wall*. London: Allen & Unwin.

Antze, Paul. 1987. Symbolic action in Alcoholics Anonymous. In *Constructive Drinking: Perspectives on Drink from Anthropology*. Mary Douglas, ed. Cambridge: Cambridge University Press. 149-181.

Artress, Loren. 1995. *Walking a Sacred Path: Rediscovering the Labyrinth as a Spiritual Tool*. New York: Riverhead.

Balint, Michael. 1968. *The Basic Fault: Therapeutic Aspects of Regression*. London: Tavistock Publications.

Bauer, Jan. 1982. *Alcoholism and Women: The Background and the Psychology*. Toronto: Inner City.

Bayley, Harold. 1912. *The Lost Language of Symbolism*. London: Williams and Norgate.

Beattie, William, ed. *Border Ballads*. 1952. London: Penguin Books.

Beck, A. T., et al. 1993. *Cognitive Therapy of Substance Abuse*. New York: Guilford Press.

Berger, Pamela. 1985. *The Goddess Obscured: Transformation of the Grain Protectress from Goddess to Saint*. Boston: Beacon Press.

Berman, Morris. 1989. *Coming to Our Senses: Body and Spirit in the Hidden History of the West*. New York: Simon & Schuster.

Bion, Wilfred R. 1967. *Second Thoughts: Selected Papers on Psycho-Analysis*. Northvale, NJ: Jason Aronson.

Blofeld, John. 1970. *The Tantric Mysticism of Tibet: A Practical Guide*.New York: E. P. Dutton.

Blum, Kenneth with James E. Payne. 1991. *Alcohol and the Addictive Brain: New Hope for Alcoholics from Biogenetic Research*. New York: The Free Press.

Bly, Robert. 1977. *The Kabir Book*. Boston: Beacon Press.

Bohm, David. 1987. *Wholeness and the Implicate Order*. London: Routledge & Kegan Paul.

Bolas, Christopher. 1987. *The Shadow of the Object: Psychoanalysis of the Unthought Known*. London: Free Association Books.

Booth, Philip. 1986. *Relations: Selected Poems 1950-1985*. New York: Viking.

Bord, Janet and Colin. 1985. *Sacred Waters: Holy Wells and Water Lore in Britain and Ireland*. London: Granada.

Bourgois, Philippe. 1989. "Just Another Night on Crack Street," in *The New York Times Magazine*. November 12. 4.

Bowlby, John. 1969. *Attachment and Loss*. New York: Basic Books.

Brennan, Martin. 1980. *The Boyne Valley Vision*. Portlaoise, Ireland: Dolmen Press.

Bromwich, Rachel. 1961. *Trioedd Ynys Prydein: The Welsh Triads*. Cardiff: University of Wales Press.

Brown, Karen. 1991. *Mama Lola: A Vodou Priestess in Brooklyn*. Berkeley: University of California Press.

Campbell, Joseph. 1972. *Myths to Live By*. New York: Viking.

Cary, Sylvia. 1990. *The Alcoholic Man: What You Can Learn from the Heroic Journeys of Recovering Alcoholics*. Los Angeles: Lowell House.

Cavandish, Richard. 1983. *Prehistoric England*. New York: British Heritage Press.

Condren, Mary. 1989. *The Serpent and the Goddess: Women, Religion, and Power in Celtic Ireland*. San Francisco: HarperSanFrancisco.

Coomeraswamy, Ananda Kentish. [1945] 1977. "On the Loathly Bride." In *Coomeraswamy, Selected Papers: Traditional Art and Symbolism*. vol. 1. Roger Lipsey, ed. Princeton: Princeton University Press. 352-370.

Cowan, Eliot. 1995. *Plant Spirit Medicine*. Newberg, OR: Swan Raven.

Cross, T. P. and C. H. Slover, eds. 1936. *Ancient Irish Tales*. New York: Henry Holt.

Curran, Mary Doyle. [1948] 1986. *The Parrish and the Hill*. New York: The Feminist Press at The City University of New York.

Dames, Michael. 1976. *The Silbury Treasure: The Great Goddess Rediscovered*. London: Thames & Hudson.

————— 1977. *The Avebury Cycle*. London: Thames & Hudson.

————— 1992. *Mythic Ireland*. London: Thames & Hudson.

Danielou, Alain. [1979] 1992. *Gods of Love and Ecstasy: The Traditions of Shiva and Dionysus*. Rochester, VT: Inner Traditions.

De Paor, Liam. 1982. "The Art of the Celtic Peoples," in *The Celtic Consciousness*. Robert O'Driscoll, ed. New York: George Braziller. 121-142.

De Santillana, Giorgio and Hertha von Dechend. 1969. *Hamlet's Mill: An Essay on Myth and the Frame of Time*. Boston: Gambit.

Delaney, Frank. 1986. *The Celts*. Boston: Little, Brown.

Detrick, Douglas W. 1985. "Alterego Phenomena and Alterego Transferences," in *Progress in Self Psychology*. vol 1. Arnold Goldberg, ed. New York: Guilford Press. 240-256.

Dickinson, Emily. 1961. *Final Harvest: Emily Dickinson's Poems*. Thomas H. Johnson, ed. Boston: Little Brown.

Dillon, Myles. 1948. *Early Irish Literature*. Chicago: University of Chicago Press.

Dodds, E. R. 1964. *The Greeks and the Irrational*. Berkeley: University of California Press.

Donne, John. 1950. *John Donne: A Selection of His Poetry*. John Hayward, ed. London: Penguin.

Dostoeyvsky, Fodor. 1964. *The Gambler*. New York and London: W. W. Norton.

Douglas, Mary, ed. 1987. *Constructive Drinking: Perspectives on Drink from Anthropology*. Cambridge: Cambridge University Press.

Dumezil, Georges. [1969] 1970. *The Destiny of the Warrior*. Alf Hilttebeitel, tr. Chicago: University of Chicago Press.

_____ [1971] 1973. *The Destiny of a King*. Alf Hilttebeitel, tr. Chicago: University of Chicago Press.

Edinger, Edward. 1972. *Ego and Archetype: Individuation and the Religious Function of the Psyche*. New York: Putnam.

_____ 1996. *The Aion Lectures: Exploring the Self in C.G. Jung's Aion*. Deborah A. Wesley, ed. Toronto: Inner City.

Flower, Robin. 1947. *The Irish Tradition*. Oxford: Clarendon Press.

Ford, Patrick K. 1974. *The Poetry of Llywarch Hen: Introduction, Text, and Translation*. Berkeley: University of California Press.

_____ 1977. *The Mabinogi and Other Welsh Stories*. Berkeley: University of California Press.

Fordham, Michael. 1978. *Jungian Psychotherapy: A Study in Analytical Psychology*. Chichester: John Wiley and Sons.

_____ [1957] 1974. "Notes on the Transference," in *Techmique in Jungian Analysis*. M. Fordham, *et al*, eds. London: Heinemann. 111-151.

_____ [1969] 1970. *Children as Individuals*. New York: Putnam.

Forrest, Gary G. 1983. *Alcoholism, Narcissism and Psychopathology*. Springfield, IL: Charles C. Thomas.

Fox, Steven. 1990. "Archetypal Drug Addiction," in *The Bulletin of the Analytical Psychology Club of New York*. January 19.

Fraser, Douglas. 1966. "The Heraldic Woman: A Study in Diffusion," in *The Many Faces of Primitive Art: A Critical Anthology*. Douglas Fraser, ed. Englewood Cliffs, NJ: Prentice-Hall. 36-99.

Freud, Sigmund. [1928] 1959. "Dostoevsky and Parricide," in *Collected Papers*. vol. 5. James Strachey, ed. New York: Basic Books. 222-242.

_____ [1930] 1958. *Civilization and its Discontents*. Garden City, NY: Doubleday.

Friel, Brian. 1981. *Translations*. London: Faber and Faber.

_____ 1990. *Dancing at Lughnasa*. London: Samuel French.

Furst, Peter T. 1972. "To Find Our Life: Peyote among the Huichol Indians of

Mexico," in *Flesh of the Gods: The Ritual Use of Hallucinogens*. Peter T. Furst, ed. New York: Praeger. 136-184.

Galanter, Marc. 1993. *Network Therapy for Alcohol and Drug Abuse: A New Approach*. New York: Basic Books.

Gantz, Jeffrey. 1981. *Early Irish Myths and Sagas*. New York: Penguin.

Gardner, Eliot L. 1989. "Studies Reveal Findings in Brain-Reward, Drug Addiction Relationship," in *The Psychiatric Times*. October. 12-15.

Gebser, Jean. [1949, 1953] 1985. *The Ever-Present Origin*. Noel Barstad and Algis Mickunas, trs. Athens, OH: Ohio University Press.

Gerald of Wales. 1978. *The Journey through Wales: The Description of Wales*. Lewis Thorpe, tr. Harmondsworth: Penguin.

Gimbutas, Marija. [1974] 1982. *The Goddesses and Gods of Old Europe: 6500-3500 B.C.: Myths and Cult Images*. Berkeley: University of California Press.

———— 1989. *The Language of the Goddess*. San Francisco: HarperSanFrancisco.

Ginzburg, Carlo. [1989] 1991. *Ecstasies: Deciphering the Witches' Sabbath*. Raymond Rosenthal, tr. New York, Random House.

Girard, Rene. 1977. *Violence and the Sacred*. Patrick Gregory, tr. Baltimore: Johns Hopkins University Press.

Glasser, W. 1976. *Positive Addictions*. New York: Harper and Row.

Gleick, James. 1987. *Chaos: A New Science*. New York: Viking.

Goodman, Felicitas D. 1988. *Ecstasy, Ritual, and Alternate Reality: Religion in a Pluralistic World*. Bloomington: Indiana University Press.

Goodwin, Brian. 1994. *How the Leopard Changed Its Spots: The Evolution of Complexity*. New York: Charles Scribner.

Goodwin, D. 1981. *Alcoholism: The Facts*. New York: Oxford University Press.

Gormley, Mary. 1989. *Tulsk Parish in Historic Maigh Ai: Aspects of Its History and Folklore*. Roscommon: Roscommon Historical and Archaeological Society.

Graves, Robert. [1948] 1966. *The White Goddess: A Historical Grammar of Poetic Myth*. New York: Farrar, Straus & Giroux.

———— 1957. *The Greek Myths*. New York: George Braziller.

Greeley, Andrew. 1974. *Ecstasy: A Way of Knowing*. New York: Prentiss-Hall.

Green, Miranda. 1989. *Symbol and Image in Celtic Religious Art*. London: Routledge.

Gregory, Lady. 1902. *Cuchulllain of Muirthhemne: The Story of the Men of the Red Branch of Ulster Arranged and Put into English*. Gerrards Cross: Colin Smythe.

Grob, Charles and Willis Harman. 1995. "Making Sense of the Psychedelic Issue," in *Noetics Sciences Review* 9. 5-9, 37-41.

Groesbeck, J. 1975. "The Archetypal Image of the Wounded Healer," in *The Journal of Analytical Psychology* 20:2. 122-45.

Grof, Christina. 1993. *The Thirst for Wholeness: Attachment, Addiction, and the Spiritual Path*. San Francisco: HarperSanFrancisco.

Guest, Lady Charlotte. 1877. *The Mabinogion from the Welsh of the Llyrf coch o Hergest.* London: Bernard Quartch.

Guenther, Herbert. 1963. *The Life and Teaching of Naropa.* London: Oxford University Press.

Guggenbuehl-Craig, A. 1971. *Power in the Helping Professions.* New York: Spring Publications.

Hanna, Fred J. 1992. "Reframing Spirituality: AA, the 12 Steps and the Mental Health Counselor," in *Journal of Mental Health Counseling* 14:2. 166-179.

Harbison, Peter. 1970. *Guide to National Monuments in the Republic of Ireland.* Dublin: Gill and Macmillan.

Harding, M. Esther. 1947. *Psychic Energy: Its Source and Goal.* Washington, DC: Pantheon.

Harvey, Andrew. 1988. *Love's Fire: Recreations of Rumi.* Ithaca, NY: Meeramma Press.

Heath, Dwight B. 1987. "A Decade of Development in the Anthropological Study of Alcohol Use: 1970-1980," in *Constructive Drinking: Perspectives on Drink from Anthropology.* Mary Douglas, ed. Cambridge: Cambridge University Press. 16-69.

Heggenhougen, H. K. 1997. *Reaching New Highs: Alternative Therapies for Drug Addicts.* Northvale, NJ: Jason Aronson.

Herity, M. and G. Eogan. 1977. *Ireland in Prehistory.* London: Routledge & Kegan Paul.

Hill, John. 1987. "Hero and Goddess: Archetypal Patterns in Irish Myths, Literature and Politics," in *Harvest* 33. 135-151.

Hillesum, Etty. 1983. *An Interupted Life: The Diaries of Etty Hillesom,* 1941-43. New York: Washington Square Press.

Hillman, James. 1975. *Re-Visioning Psychology.* New York: Harper & Row.

Hoeller, Stephan A. 1989. *Jung and the Lost Gospels: Insight into the Dead Sea Scrolls and the Nag Hammadi Library.* Wheaton, IL: Theosophical Publishing House.

Hopkins, Gerard Manley. 1953. *Poems and Prose of Gerard Manley Hopkins.* W. H. Gardner, ed. Harmonsdworth, Middlesex: Penguin.

Jarman, A. O. H. 1982. "The Heroic View of Life in Early Welsh Verse," in *The Celtic Consciousness.* Robert O'Driscoll, ed. New York: George Braziller. 161-168.

Jelik, W. G. 1993. "Traditional Medicine Relevant to Psychiatry," in *Treatment of Mental Disorders.* N. Sartorius *et al,* eds. Geneva: World Health Organization. 341-390.

Jones, Gwyn and Thomas Jones. [1906] 1949. *The Mabinogion.* London: Everyman's.

Jung, C. G. *The Collected Works of C. G. Jung.* Herbert Read, Michael Fordham, and Gerard Adler, eds. William McGuire, executive editor. R. F. C. Hull, tr. Princeton: Bollingen Series XX, Princeton University

Press. Referred to in the footnotes by date and volume number of the Collected Works (*CW*).

———— 1905. "On Spiritualistic Phenomena," in 1976, *The Symbolic Life*. *CW 18*. 293-308.

———— 1911-12/1952. *Symbols of Transformation. CW 5*.

———— 1928. "On Psychic Energy," in 1960, *The Structure and Dynamics of the Psyche. CW 8*. 3-66.

———— 1929. "Problems in Modern Psychotherapy," in 1954, *The Practice of Psychotherapy: General Problems of Psychotherapy. CW 16*. 53-75.

———— 1929. "Commentary on *The Secret of the Golden Flower*," in 1968, *Alchemical Studies. CW 13*. 1-55.

———— 1934/1950. "A Study in the Process of Individuation," in 1959, *The Archetypes and the Collective Unconscious. CW 9i*. 290-352.

———— 1934/1954. "Archetypes of the Collective Unconscious," in 1959. *The Archetypes and the Collective Unconscious. CW 9i*. 3-72.

———— 1935. "The Tavistock Lectures," in 1976. *The Symbolic Life*. *CW 18*. 1-182.

———— 1936. "Individual Dream Symbolism in Relation to Alchemy," in 1944. *Psychology and Alchemy. CW 12*. 39-223.

———— 1937. "Psychological Factors Determining Human Behavior." In 1960. *The Structure and Dynamics of the Psyche. CW 8*. 114-125.

———— 1938/1954. "Psychological Aspects of the Mother Archetype," in 1959. *The Archetypes and the Collective Unconscious. CW 9i*. 73-110.

———— 1939. "Conscious, Unconscious, and Individuation," in *The Archetypes and the Collective Unconscious. CW 9i*. 275-289.

———— 1940/50. "Concerning Rebirth," in 1959. *The Archetypes and the Collective Unconscious. CW 9i*. 121-147.

———— 1942/54. "Transformation Symbolism of the Mass," in 1958. *Psychology and Religion: West and East. CW 11*. 201-296.

———— 1945/1954. "The Philosophical Tree," in 1968. *Alchemical Studies. CW 13*. 251-349.

———— 1946. "The Psychology of the Transference," in 1954. *The Practice of Psychotherapy. CW 16*. 163-323

———— 1947-54. "On the Nature of the Psyche," in 1950. *The Structure and Dynamics of the Psyche. CW 8*. 139-234.

———— 1951. *Aion: Researches into the Phenomenology of the Self. CW 9ii*.

———— 1911-12/1952. *Symbols of Transformation. CW 5*.

———— 1955-56. *Mysterium Coniunctionis: An Inquiry into the Separation and Synthesis of Psychic Opposites in Alchemy. CW 14*.

———— 1958. "A Psychological View of Conscience," in 1964. *Civilization in Transition. CW 10*. 437-455

———— 1953-74. *Letters*: *vol. 1: 1906-1950; vol. 2: 1951-1961*. Gerhard Adler, ed. in collaboration with Aniela Jaffé. R. F. C. Hull, tr. Princeton: Princeton University Press.

———— 1976. *The Visions Seminars*. Zurich: Spring Publications.

Kalshed, Donald. 1996. *The Inner World of Trauma: Archetypal Defenses of the Personal Spirit*. New York: Routledge.

Kasl, Charlotte. 1989. *Women, Sex and Addictions: A Search for Love and Power*. New York, Ticknor and Fields.

Kavaler-Adler, Susan. 1993. *The Compulsion to Create: A Psychoanalytic Study of Women Artists*. New York: Routledge.

Keen, Sam. 1986. *Faces of the Enemy, Reflections of the Hostile Imagination: The Psychology of Enmity*. San Francisco: HarperSanFrancisco.

Kelly, Eamonn P. 1996. *Sheela-na-gigs: Origins and Functions*. Dublin: Country House in association with The National Museum of Ireland.

Kertzner, Robert M. 1987. "Individual Psychotherapy of Cocaine Abuse," in *Cocaine Abuse: New Directions in Treatment and Research*. Henry I. Spitz and Jeffrey S. Rosecan, eds. New York: Brunner Mazell. 138-155.

Kinsella, Thomas, ed. and tr. 1970. *The Tain* (*Tain Bo Cuailnge*). London: Oxford University Press.

Kinsley, David R. 1975. *The Sword and the Flute: Kali and Krsna, Dark Visions of the Terrible and the Sublime in Hindu Mythology*. Berkeley: University of California Press.

Knott, Eleanor. [1957] 1966. *Irish Classical Poetry*. Kildare: Leinster Leader.

Koch, John, ed. in collaboration with John Carey. 1995. *The Celtic Heroic Age: Literary Sources for Ancient Celtic Europe and Early Ireland and Wales*. Malden, MA: Celtic Studies.

Kohut, Heinz. 1971, *The Analysis of the Self*. New York: International Universities Press.

———— 1977. *The Restoration of the Self*. New York: International Universities Press.

Krystal, Henry and Herbert Raskin. 1970. *Drug Dependence*. Detroit: Wayne State University Press.

La Barre, Weston. 1972. "Hallucinogens and the Shamanic Origins of Religion," in *Flesh of the Gods: The Ritual Use of Hallucinogens*. Peter T. Furst, ed. New York: Praeger. 261-278.

Lao Tsu: Tao Te Ching. 1972. Gia-fu Feng and Jane English, trs. New York: Vintage.

Laub, Dori. 1992. "Bearing Witness or the Vicissitudes of Listening, and An Event Without a Witness: Truth, Testimony and Survival," in Shoshana Felman and Dori Laub. *Testimony: Crises of Witnessing in Literature, Psychoanalysis, and History*. New York: Routledge, Chapman and Hall. 57-92.

Laurie, Erynn Rowan and Timothy White. 1997. "Speckled Snake, Brother of Birch: Amanita Muscaria Motifs in Celtic Legends," in *Shaman's Drum* 44. 52-65.

Learning Factors in Substance Abuse. 1988. Washington, DC: The National Institute on Drug Abuse.

Leonard, Linda S. 1989. *Witness to the Fire: Creativity and the Veil of Addiction*. Boston: Shambhala.

Levin, Jerome D. 1987. *Treatment of Alchoholism and other Addictions.* Northvale, NJ: Jason Aronson.

Levin, Jerome D. and Ronna H. Weiss, eds. 1994. *The Dynamics and Treatment of Alcoholism: Essential Papers.* Northvale, NJ: Jason Aronson.

Lomas, Peter. 1987. *The Limits of Interpretation.* Northvale, NJ: Jason Aronson.

Lovelock, J. E. 1979. *Gaia.* Oxford: Oxford University Press.

MacAndrew, Andrew R. 1964. "Introduction," in Fodor Dostoevsky. *The Gambler.* New York: W. W. Norton.

Mac Cana, Proinsias. 1957. "Aspects of the Theme of King and Goddess in Irish Literature," in *Etudes Celtiques* 7. 76-114, 356-413; 8. 59-65.

_____ 1980. "Women in Irish Mythology," in *The Crane Bag* 4:1. 7-11.

Mac Neill, Maire. 1962. *The Festival of Lughnasa: A Study of the Survival of the Celtic Festival of the Beginning of the Harvest.* Dublin: Oxford University Press.

Marino, Thomas W. 1995. "Addiction and Incarceration," in *Counseling Today.* January. 6.

Mallory, J. P. and G. Stockman, eds. 1994. *Ulidia: Proceedings of the First International Conference on the Ulster Cycle of Tales.* Belfast: December Publications.

Markale, Jean. [1972] 1975. *Women of the Celts.* A. Mygind, C. Hauch, P. Henry, trs. London: Gordon and Cremonesi.

_____ 1976. *Celtic Civilization.* Gordon and Cremonesi, trs. London: Gordon and Cremonesi.

_____ 1995. *Merlin: Priest of Nature.* Rochester, VT: Inner Traditions International.

McCone, Kim. 1990. *Pagan Past and Christian Present in Early Irish Literature.* [Monograph 3]. Maynooth: An Sagart.

McCourt, Frank. 1996. *Angela's Ashes.* New York: Scribner.

McDougall, Joyce. 1989. *Theaters of the Body: A Psychoanalytic Approach to Psycho-Somatic Illness.* New York: W. W. Norton.

McElderry, B. R. 1964. *Thomas Wolfe.* New Haven: Yale University Press.

Megaw, Ruth and Vincent. 1989. *Celtic Art from Its Beginnings to the Book of Kells.* London: Thames & Hudson:

Meyer, Kuno. 1959. *Selections from Ancient Irish Poetry.* London: Constable.

Milner, Marion. 1978. D. W. "Winnicott and the Two-Way Journey," in *Between Reality and Fantasy: Transitional Objects and Phenomena.* Simon A. Grolnick and Leonard Barkin, eds. with Werner Muensterberger. Northvale, NJ: Jason Aronson. 37-42.

Mookerjee, A. 1988. *Kali: The Feminine Force.* Rochester, VT: Destiny Books.

Neumann, Erich. 1955. *The Great Mother: An Analysis of the Archetype.* New York: Pantheon.

_____ 1961. "Mystical Man," in *Spring* 12. 9-49.

_____ 1970. *The Origins and History of Consciousness.* Princeton: Princeton University Press.

_____ 1988. "Stages of Religious Experience and the Path of Depth Psychology," in *Quadrant* 9:2. 5-34.

Ni Bhrolchain, Muirreann. 1980. "Women in Early Irish Myths and Sagas," in *The Crane Bag* 4:1. 12-19.

O'Carroll, M. 1979. *The Relationship of Religion and Ethnicity to Drinking Behavior: A Study of North American Immigrants in the United States.* Berkeley: University of California School of Public Health.

O' Corrain, Donnachadh and Fedelma Maguire. 1981. *Gaelic Personal Names.* Dublin: Academy Press.

O'Driscoll, Robert, ed. 1982. *The Celtic Consciousness.* New York: George Braziller.

O'Grady, Desmond. 1977. *The Gododdin: A Version by Desmond O'Grady, Ink Paintings by Louis Le Brocquy.* Dublin: Dolmen Editions.

Ogden, Thomas H. 1989. *The Primitive Edge of Experience.* Northvale, NJ: Jason Aronson.

_____ 1994. *Subjects of Analysis.* Northvale, NJ: Jason Aronson.

O Hehir, Brendan. 1983. "A Christian Revision of Eachtra Airt Meic Cuind Ocus Torchmarc Delbchaine Ingine Morgain," in *Celtic Folklore and Christianity: Studies in Memory of William W. Heist.* Patrick K. Ford, ed. Los Angeles: University of California Press. 159-179.

O hOgain, Daith.1990. *Myth, Legend and Romance: Encyclopedia of the Irish Folk Tradition.* London: Ryan.

O'Kelly, M. J. 1982, *Newgrange.* London: Thames & Hudson.

_____ 1989. *Early Ireland: An Introduction to Irish Prehistory.* Cambridge: Cambridge University Press.

Olmsted, Garrett. 1992. "The Earliest Narrative Version of *The Tain*: Seventh-century Poetic References to *Tain bo Cuailnge*," in *Emania: Bulletin of the Navan Research Group.* 10. 5-17.

O Suilleabhain, Sean. 1967. *Irish Wake Amusements.* Dublin: Mercier Press.

Pennick, Nigel. 1979. *The Ancient Secret of Geomancy: Man in Harmony with the Earth.* London: Thames & Hudson.

Perera, Sylvia Brinton. 1981. *Descent to the Goddess: A Way of Initiation for Women.* Toronto: Inner City.

_____ 1986a. "Ceremonies of the Emerging Ego in Psychotherapy," in *The Body in Analysis.* N. Schwartz-Salant and M. Stein, eds. Wilmette, IL, Chiron. 59-85.

_____ 1986b. *The Scapegoat Complex: Towards a Mythology of Shadow and Guilt.* Toronto: Inner City.

_____ 1988. "Ritual Integration of Aggression in Psychotherapy," in *The Borderline Personality in Analysis.* N. Schwartz-Salant and M. Stein, eds. Wilmette, IL: Chiron. 233-266.

_____ 1990. "Dream Design: Some Operations Underlying Clinical Dream Interpretation," in *Dreams in Analysis.* N. Schwartz-Salant and M. Stein, eds. Wilmette, IL: Chiron. 39-79.

_____ 1992. "A Small But Difficult Step," in *Psychological Perspectives*. 27. 160-165.

_____ 1993a. "War, Madness and the Morrigan: A Celtic Goddess of Life and Death," in *Mad Parts of Sane People in Analysis*. M. Stein, ed. Wilmette, IL: Chiron. 155-193.

_____ 1993b. "Some Archetypal Foundations of Self-Spite in the Welsh Mabinogion," in *To Speak or Be Silent: The Paradox of Disobedience in the Lives of Women*. Lena Ross, ed. Willmette IL: Chiron. 160-176.

_____ 1996a. "Earth Mother Body Self: Therapeutic Process as Return and Re-emergence," in *Restoring the Temple: A Celebration of Feminine Spirit*. [audio tape #1] Chicago: C. G. Jung Institute of Chicago.

_____ 1996b. "Samain and Self: Uncanny Images of Transformation," in *Text of Papers Presented at the 1996 National Conference of Jungian Analysts*. New York.

Piggot, Stuart. 1968. *The Druids*. London: Thames & Hudson.

Puhvel, J. 1976. "Aspects of Equine Functionality," in *Myth and Law Among the Indo-Europeans*. J. Puhvel, ed. Berkeley: University of California Press. 159-172.

Pulver, Max. [1942] 1955. "Jesus' Round Dance and Crucifixion According to the Acts of St. John," in *The Mysteries: Papers from the Eranos Yearbooks*. New York: Pantheon. 169-193.

Purcell, Brendan, 1985. "In Search of Newgrange: Long Night's Journey into Day," in *The Irish Mind: Exploring Intellectual Traditions*. Richard Kearney, ed. Dublin: Wolfhound Press. 39-55.

Rado, S. 1933. "The Psychoanalysis of Pharmacothymia (Drug Addiction)," in *The Psychoanalytic Quarterly* 2. 1-23.

Redfearn, J. W. T. 1985. *My Self, My Many Selves*. London: Academic Press.

Rees, Alwyn and Brynly Rees. 1961. *Celtic Heritage: Ancient Tradition in Ireland and Wales*. London: Thames & Hudson.

Rhys, John. [1901] 1980. *Celtic Folklore: Welsh and Manx*. London: Wildwood House.

Richards, Henry Jay. 1993. *Therapy of the Substance Abuse Syndromes*. Northvale, NJ: Jason Aronson.

Roberts, Jack. 1996. *The Sacred Mythological Centres of Ireland: An Illustrated Guide*. Ireland: Bandia.

Rolleston, R.W. 1911. *Myths and Legends of the Celtic Race*. London: George G. Harrap.

Rosenthal, Elisabeth. 1990. "When a Pregnant Woman Drinks," in *The New York Times Magazine*. February 4.

Ross, Anne. 1967. *Pagan Celtic Britain: Studies in Iconography and Tradition*. London: Routledge and Kegan Paul.

_____ 1982. "Material Culture, Myth and Folk Memory," in *The Celtic Consciousness*. Robert O'Driscoll, ed. New York: George Braziller. 197-216.

_____ 1986. *The Pagan Celts*. New York: Barnes and Noble.

Ross, Anne and Don Robins. 1989. *The Life and Death of a Druid Prince: The Story of Lindow Man, an Archaeological Sensation*. New York: Summit.

Roy, Charles. 1986. *The Road Wet, The Wind Close: Celtic Ireland*. Dublin: Gill and MacMillan.

Rutherford, Ward. [1978] 1990. *The Druids: Magicians of the West*. New York: Sterling.

Salman, Sherry. 1986. "The Horned God: Masculine Dynamics of Power and Soul," in *Quadrant* 7. 7-25.

Salzman, Leon. 1968. *The Obsessive Personality*. Northvale, NJ: Jason Aronson.

Samuels, Andrew. 1989. *The Plural Psyche: Personality, Morality and the Father*. London: Routledge.

Sandner, Donald. 1970. *Navaho Symbols of Healing*. New York: Harcourt Brace and Jovanovich.

Scheper-Hughes, Nancy. 1982. *Saints, Scholars and Schizophrenics: Mental Illness in Rural Ireland*. Berkeley: University of California Press.

Searles, Harold. 1960. *The Non-Human Environment in Normal Development and in Schizophrenia*. New York: International Universities Press.

Seybold, K. C. and P. R. Salmone. 1994. "Understanding Workaholism: A Review of Causes and Counseling Approaches," in *The Journal of Counseling and Development* 73. 4-9.

Shafer, R. 1972-73. "Marijuana: A Signal of Misunderstanding, and Drug Use in America: Problem in Perspective," in *First and Second Reports of the National Commission on Marijuana and Drug Abuse*. Washington DC: U.S. Government Printing Office.

Shah, Idries. 1969. *Tales of the Dervishes*. New York: E. P. Dutton.

Sheed, Wilfred. 1995. *In Love with Daylight: A Memoir of Recovery*. New York: Simon & Schuster.

Siegel, Ronald K. 1989. *Intoxication: Life in Pursuit of Artificial Paradise*. New York: E. P. Dutton.

Sjoestedt, Marie-Louise. 1982. *Gods and Heroes of the Celts*. Miles Dillon, tr. Berkeley, CA: Turtle Island Foundation.

Stassinopoulos, Arianna and Roloff Beny. 1983. *The Gods of Greece*. New York: Abrams.

Steel, Tom. 1975. *The Life and Death of St. Kilda*. Glasgow: Fontana Books.

Stern, Daniel. 1985. *The Interpersonal World of the Infant*. New York: Basic Books.

Stewart, David A. 1960. *Thirst for Freedom*. Center City, MN: Hazeldon Press.

Stivers, Richard. 1976. *A Hair of the Dog: Irish Drinking and American Stereotype*. University Park: Pennsylvania State University Press.

Streep, Peg. 1994. *Sanctuaries of the Goddess: The Sacred Landscapes and Objects*. Boston: Little Brown.

Styron, William. 1990. *Darkness Visible: A Memoir of Madness*. New York: Random House.

Sullivan, Barbara Stevens. 1990. *Psychotherapy from the Feminine Principle.* Wilmette, IL: Chiron.

Szasz, Thomas S. 1973. *Ceremonial Chemistry.* Garden City, NY: Anchor Books.

Talbot, Michael. 1991. *The Holographic Universe.* New York: HarperCollins.

Ternes, Elmar, 1982. The Grammatical Structure of the Celtic Languages. In *The Celtic Consciousness.* Robert O'Driscoll, ed. New York: George Braziller. 69-78.

Thomas, Dylan. 1952. *The Collected Poems of Dylan Thomas, 1934-1952.* New York: New Directions.

Tierney, Patrick. 1989. *The Highest Altar: The Story of Human Sacrifice.* New York: Viking.

Turner Victor. 1982. *From Ritual to Theater: The Human Seriousness of Play.* New York, PAJ Publications.

Twain, Mark. 1897. *Following the Equator.* Hartford, CT: American Publishing.

Ujhely, Gertrude. 1980. "Thoughts Concerning the *Causa Finalis* of the Cognitive Mode Inherent in Pre-Oedipal Psychopathology." Unpublished diploma thesis. C. G. Jung Institute of New York.

von Franz, Marie-Louise. 1981. *Puer Aeternis.* 2nd ed. Sisa Sternbach-Scott, ed. Santa Monica, CA: Sigo Press.

_____ 1970. *The Interpretation of Fairytales.* New York: Spring.

W., Kathleen, ed. n.d. *12 Steps to Freedon: A Recovery Workbook.* Freedom, CA: Crossing Press.

Wade, Jay C. 1994. "Substance Abuse: Implications for Counseling African-American Men," in *Journal of Mental Health Counseling* 16. 4.

Wade, Jenny. 1996. *Changes of Mind: A Holonomic Theory of the Evolution of Consciousness.* New York: State University of New York Press.

Walker, Barbara C. 1983. *The Woman's Encyclopedia of Myths and Secrets.* San Francisco: HarperSanFrancisco.

Wasson, R. Gordon, 1972. "The Divine Mushroom of Immortality and What was the Soma of the Aryans," in *Flesh of the Gods: The Ritual Use of Hallucinogens.* Peter T. Furst, ed. New York: Praeger. 185-200, 201-213.

Westermeyer, J. 1991. "Historical and Social Context of Psychoactive Substance Disorders," in *Clinical Textbook of Addictive Disorders.* R. J. Frances and S. Miller, eds. New York: Guilford Press. 23-40.

Whitlock, Ralph. 1979. *In Search of Lost Gods: A Guide to British Folklore.* Oxford: Phaidon Press.

Whitmont, Edward. C. 1964. "Group Therapy and Analytical Psychology," in *The Journal of Analytical Psychology* 9:1. 1-22.

_____ [1969] 1991. *The Symbolic Quest: Basic Concepts of Analytical Psychology* [revised ed.]. Princeton: Princeton University Press.

_____ 1992. *Return of the Goddess.* New York, Crossroad.

_____ 1993. *The Alchemy of Healing: Psyche and Soma.* Berkeley: North Atlantic Books.

_____ [1995] 1997. "Alchemy, Homeopathy, and the Treatment of Borderline States," in *Zurich 1995, Open Questions in Analytical Psychology: Proceedings of the 13th International Congress for Analytical Psychology*. Einsiedeln: Daimon. 285-299.

Whitmont, Edward C. and Sylvia Brinton Perera. 1989. *Dreams, A Portal to the Source: A Clinical Guide for Therapists*. London: Routledge.

Wilson, P. L. and N. Pourjavady, eds. 1987. *The Drunken Universe: An Anthology of Persian Sufi Poetry*. Grand Rapids, MI: Phanes Press.

Winnicott, D. W. [1945] 1975. "Primitive Emotional Development," in *Through Paediatrics to Psycho-Analysis*. New York: Basic Books. 145-156.

_____ 1965. *The Maturational Processes and the Facilitating Environment: Studies in the Theory of Emotional Development*. New York: International Universities Press.

_____ 1971. *Playing and Reality*. New York: Basic Books.

_____ 1993. "The Psychotherapy of Character Disorders," in *In One's Bones: The Clinical Genius of Winnicott*. Dodi Goldman, ed. Northvale, NJ: Jason Aronson. 81-93.

Wolfe, Thomas. 1929. *Look Homeward Angel: A Story of a Buried Life*. New York: Scribner.

Woodman, Marion. 1982. *Addiction to Perfection: The Still Unravished Bride*. Toronto: Inner City.

Wurmser, Leon. 1978. *The Hidden Dimension: Psychodynamics of Compulsive Drug Use*. Northvale, NJ: Jason Aronson.

Yeats, W. B. 1934. *The Collected Plays of W. B. Yeats*. New York: Macmillan.

_____ 1955. *The Collected Poems of W. B. Yeats*. New York: Macmillan.

Yeats, W. B., ed. 1973. *Fairy and Folk Tales of Ireland*. New York: Macmillan.

Zabriskie, Philip. 1979. "The Loathly Damsel: The Motif of the Ugly Woman," in *Quadrant* 12:1. 47-63.

Zimmer, Heinrich. [1938] 1970. "The Indian World Mother," in *The Mystic Vision: Papers from the Eranos Yearbooks*. Princeton: Princeton University Press. 70-102.

Zoja, Luigi. 1989. *Drugs, Addiction and Initiation: The Modern Search for Ritual*. Marc Romano and Robert Mercurio, trs. Santa Monica, CA: Sigo Press.

Index